RONNIE BIGGS

Odd Man Out: The Last Straw

with Chris Pickard

First published in Great Britain in 2011 by Mpress Ltd.

Parts first published in Great Britain in 1994 by Bloomsbury Publishing.

Picture Sources
Ronald and Michael Biggs' private collection, with thanks to family and friends
Press Association, *Daily Mail:* Cartoon by Mac, Agencia JB/Vidal da Trindade
CBS Records, Brazil (Balão Magico), Virgin Records (Sex Pistols)
Jean-Jacques Limbourg, David Worrow, Christopher Pickard

Cover from 24 October 1969 reproduced by kind permission
of *Private Eye* magazine.

Every reasonable effort has been made to trace copyright holders, but if there are any errors or omissions, Mpress Ltd will be pleased to insert the appropriate acknowledgement in any subsequent edition.

Book and text design by Paul Moulder and Mpress Ltd.
Printed in Great Britain by Mpress Ltd.

ISBN NUMBER (Hardback) 978-0-9570398-2-7

designed and printed by m press LTD.
Unit Four, Ashton Gate, Harold Hill, Romford, RM3 8UF

This, my final book, is dedicated to my family, friends, fans and foes, present and absent. My journey would have been nothing without you. Thanks for the ride.

Contents

CONTENTS

A Final Chapter: Confessions, Apologies and Thanks   7
Let me introduce to you, the one and only... Ronnie Biggs   11

1.   The Great Train Robbery   20
2.   Thursday, 8 August 1963   36
3.   Aftermath and Capture   46
4.   Trials and Tribulations   65
5.   Escape: The Making of a Legend   88
6.   On the Run: London–Bognor–Antwerp-Paris–Sydney   102
7.   The Wizard of Aus: Time Down Under   119
8.   The Pacifics: Melbourne to Rio   146
9.   Mr. Haynes Settles in Rio   157
10. Caught: Slipper Drops The Catch   185
11. Celebrity Status: Life in the Spotlight   204
12. Kidnapped   227
13. A Caribbean Excursion: Barbados and Back   245
14. A Star is Born: Mike Biggs   281
15. An Englishman Abroad: Old Friends Come Calling   294
16. A Long Dark Tunnel: Death & Failing Health   321
17. Time For Home: Saudades For Rio   338
18. Justice for Some: The Prison Years   364
19. Clutching at Straws: In Sickness and Wealth   388
20. Fifty Years On: End of the Line   406

The Life & Times of Ronald Arthur Biggs: A Timeline   425
Ronnie's Frequent Flyer Miles   464

'Aw, Dad. You promised to stay away from trains when you felt better.'

A FINAL CHAPTER: CONFESSIONS, APOLOGIES AND THANKS

'Ronnie is a gambler and this is the final adventure for him. This is the final chapter in his life and it is the right way for it to end'.

Bruce Reynolds, Leader of the Great Train Robbers

My name is Ronald Biggs. Ron or Ronnie, if you prefer. But I guess you already know that! Welcome to what is my final chapter.

The Ronnie Biggs who came back to Britain in May 2001, and who was released from prison on compassionate grounds in August 2009, is a very different man to the one who went on the run from HMP Wandsworth back in July 1965.

Not only are there many, many more miles on the clock, but also there is the damage done to my body and soul by the strokes and other health problems that should have killed me already; and may have already done so by the time you get around to reading this.

I lay no claim to having been a perfect man who has lead a faultless life, and never have, but I am a better man for the experiences of the past 50 years, a period in which I spent over three quarters of my life trying to honestly maintain my family and myself as best I could.

It has been said by those who don't know me – and who have never even met me – that I have no regrets, but that simply isn't true. I have always regretted the hurt I caused by my actions, and especially to my own family and friends.

My wife, Charmian, and our sons, Chris and Farley, I am truly sorry for everything I put you through. It was not fair, and I know that. I love you all very much and never stopped loving you, despite what I may have given you good reason to think.

To my 'Australian' grandchildren, who I have never had the chance to meet, I will always regret that I could not be there for you and play the role of the doting grandfather. Hopefully I would not have been a bad influence, but your grandmother will probably not agree. In later life try not to judge me on what people who have never met me have to say. Please just read this book. This is my story and my life and, by default, part of your lives as well.

To my son Mike, and his wife Veronica, and the apples of my eye, my 'Brazilian' granddaughters, Ingrid and Lilly, I have put you all through unimaginable stress and sorrow since my strokes and return to the UK. I am so very sorry, but without your constant love, presence and support I would not have survived my time in prison, or have had this precious time in which to reflect on life. Thank you for everything.

I also want to make it clear that I, and I am certain everyone involved in the Great Train Robbery, have always regretted that Mr Jack Mills was injured during the robbery and was put under such pressure during and after the trial. I apologise to Mr Mills, his family and to everyone else who was affected in any way by what happened on Thursday, 8 August 1963 and after. But there is nothing I can say or do that will wind the clock back. I have no magical Tardis, as much as I would like one.

As my last chapter beckons the time has come for me to take responsibility for my life. I have already lost one son (or perhaps that should be three), and know you can't replace what is lost, that is why what time I have left as a free man is so very precious. Time I want to use to make my peace, say thanks and show my love to my family and to everyone who supported, encouraged and extended the hand of friendship and forgiveness over these many years. You all know who you are, even if you do wish to remain anonymous for whatever reason.

I don't know how much time I do have left, and that time may have already passed, but it surely won't be enough to thank everyone personally.

My heartfelt thanks and love go out to the people of Brazil for generously putting up with me for all those years. Especially Rosa, a friend first, a housekeeper second. You all taught me so much. Saudades.

The same is true for the people of Australia who have always looked out for me and the family I left behind. The land down under supplied me with many of my happiest moments and memories.

My thanks go out to the staff and my fellow inmates at Norwich and Belmarsh prisons for the kindness and consideration that many of you showed to this frail old man when he returned to Britain. Thank you to the Parole Board, who recommended my early release and fought to have that ruling upheld, and to my legal team and close friends who for years worked so hard and against the odds and persons unknown to win my freedom.

I would also like to thank Mr Jack Straw and the Ministry of Justice for showing me compassion and allowing me to spend what time I have left with my family and friends. Your compassion and understanding, however it was reached, is appreciated more than you can imagine.

Thank you to all the magnificent staff of the Norfolk and Norwich University Hospital for looking after me, and for keeping me alive when the odds did not look so good. Sorry for the disruption my presence might have caused you.

My appreciation and gratitude also go out to my new family, the wonderful staff and residents of Carlton Court Care Home who look after me so well. You have kept me in such good spirits, that I have managed to live a lot longer than even I or the *Death List* ever expected. I do appreciate how lucky I am, even if I don't always show it. I won't embarrass you by mentioning you all by name, but you all know who you are. Please take a bow, and accept my love, friendship and appreciation for all that you do for me. Now can I have the remote back?

Roy, thank you for your friendship, companionship and your help and support since my release. You have been a rock, despite your unwavering support for Spurs.

Chris, thank you for your time spent on the M25 and your patience with the spelling board. I think we may have surpassed ourselves with this book. When do we start the next one?

Although it might seem strange, I also want to give special thanks to the media in Britain and around the world without whom, as you will discover, there would have been no 'Ronnie Biggs'. At times I am simply your creation.

And thanks again to the late, great Paul Seabourne without whom most of what follows would not have been possible or taken place.

As a free man, all I can now ask is that the public and the media judge me fairly and on my life as a whole, not just on one night back in August 1963 and on the stories and myths that surround it and me. I can guarantee that I offer no threat to society, nor do I need to ever be locked away again. I can also guarantee that what you are about to read is my life story. No spin, no dramatisation, simply what actually happened to me during my life as I remember it. I have taken the liberty of changing a few names to protect both the guilty and the innocent. It is the least I could do.

After so many years on the run and looking over my shoulder, I hope to now have the opportunity to gaze upon England's green and pleasant land and make my peace with my homeland. It would be nice if Arsenal could pick up the odd trophy along the way, but beggars can't always be choosers.

So God bless all of you, family, friend or foe. Whatever you do think of me, I do respect your views. That is one of the great joys and benefits of freedom. Enjoy yours, it is far more precious than you can ever imagine.

My name is Ronnie Biggs, but you already knew that! This is my story.

LET ME INTRODUCE TO YOU, THE ONE AND ONLY... RONNIE BIGGS

What is it that fascinates so many of us about Ronald Arthur Biggs and makes him a household name in so many countries around the world?

Is it the man or the myth that makes Ron, Ronnie, Biggsy, call him what you will, a latter-day Robin Hood, the man who is best remembered from a gang of sixteen who held up a mail train in August 1963?

One thing is for sure; the name of Ronald Biggs still stirs the full range of emotions from respect and admiration to outright loathing. Yes, there are still many who believe, over fifty years on, that hanging is too good for the likes of Biggs, and will never let him rest in peace.

Ronald Arthur Biggs was born in London in the borough of Lambeth on 8 August 1929 to Henry Jack Biggs and Lillian Edna Clayton of Dalyell Road, Stockwell, SW9. The youngest of a family of five he had a sister, Iris, and three brothers, Jack, Victor and Terrance, who was to die at an early age. His family was working class, but he does not consider them to have been poor, as he wasn't left wanting for anything.

The family moved to 30 Kimberley Road in 1936, and Biggs was sent to school in Lingham Street, close to what is now Stockwell tube station.

In 1940, as war raged across Europe and the bombs fell on London, Biggs was separated from his family and evacuated to the relative safety of Coombe-in-Teignhead in Devon and later to Delabole in Cornwall. He returned to London at the end of 1942 and was sent to Santley Street School. In May 1943 his mother died from a duodenal ulcer. She was just fifty-three and Biggs just thirteen.

Around this time Biggs, now studying at the Brixton School of Building, discovered that if he was good at one thing it was taking objects of whatever size or value without having to pay for them. This led in February 1945 to his first appearance in court for stealing a pen refill and eraser from a shop display in Littlewoods. He was fifteen.

That same year, in the June and November, he made two further court appearances for petty pilfering, but appeared to be back on the right track when he volunteered for the Royal Air Force in 1947. It was during his short time in the RAF, although he had volunteered for eight years as a regular and four years in the reserves, that Biggs learned how to cook: his father, who had been a professional cook at one time, had already instilled in him an interest which he was never to forget.

The RAF proved to have its temptations for a man with Biggs' talents, although his first run in with his superiors was for going AWOL and not for any of his more light-fingered activities.

But his luck soon ran out and after breaking into a chemist shop he found himself up before the London Sessions in February 1949, an appearance, his first as an adult, which resulted in a six-month prison sentence and a dishonourable discharge from the RAF. He was nineteen and apparently already destined for a life of crime.

Released from Lewes Prison for Young Prisoners in June 1949 he was up before the North London magistrates the following month for taking a car without the owner's permission. He was sent to Wormwood Scrubs and then on to Lewes, where his path crossed for the first time with Bruce Reynolds, the man who would turn out to be the driving force behind the Great Train Robbery and the reason Biggs was there.

Biggs was now firmly off the tracks, and a life of crime, court appearances and imprisonment, including in Dartmoor and Norwich, was to follow over the next fourteen years.

As years go 1963 was a remarkable one by any standards and one that is now seen as a watershed in modern history as people tried to throw off the shackles of a 1930s and war time mentality and start to enjoy and embrace the swinging sixties.

1963 is probably best remembered as the year when John F. Kennedy was assassinated, but it was also the year when Martin Luther King had a dream and the popular Pope John XXIII died to be replaced by the less charismatic Pope Paul VI. 1963 was a year when the US, USSR and Great Britain signed a nuclear test ban treaty; Sir Winston Churchill was given honouree US citizenship by President Kennedy; the Soviet Union put the first women into space; the Pan Am building in New York opened its doors for the first time, while on the west coast Alcatraz closed its doors to prisoners for the very last time. Concorde had been developed to full mock-up size and the BAC-1-11 flew for the very first time. Mary Quant was becoming a household name.

Jim Clark won the Formula One racing championship in 1963 but his great rival, Graham Hill, won the Monaco Grand Prix. Manchester United beat Leicester City in the FA Cup Final, Everton won the league and, at Wembley Stadium, the main soccer international of the year took place in May and pitted England against the 1962 World Champions, Brazil. A one-all draw, it was probably the first time that the thirty-three year old Biggs had come across the Brazilians.

1963 saw the start of Beatlemania as well as being the year their great rivals to be, the Rolling Stones, released their first single. It also saw the death of Edith Piaf but the birth of George Michael, a man who would also come to discover Brazil.

More sinister things were going on behind the scenes, things that were directly to affect the fate of Ronald Biggs when it came to his next day in court.

The British authorities, in the shape and form of the Conservative Party, who had held office since Churchill's return to Downing Street in 1951, were starting to lose its grip on power and all the trappings that go with it. So were the civil servants and other sundry hangers-on who had served the government comfortably over a twelve-year period.

A disastrous by-election in Orpington resulted in the then Prime Minister Harold Macmillan sacking seven Cabinet ministers on 13 July 1962. It reassured nobody. In the autumn of the same year, an Admiralty clerk in the office of the Civil Lord was arrested for spying. The Soviet spy, William John Vassall, was convicted and sent to prison, as were, in a parallel case, two journalists for the allegations they had made in articles regarding the Civil Lord, Tam Galbraith, and Vassall. The case did not endear the government to Fleet Street.

In 1963, the press had a chance to get their revenge after rumours started to circulate that John Profumo, who had been Macmillan's Minister of War since 1960, was having an affair with a nineteen-year-old nightclub hostess, Christine Keeler. To make matters worse Keeler was also seeing the Soviet naval attaché, Eugene Ivanov.

The government might have got away with Profumo's indiscretion if some of Keeler's other lovers had been a little more discreet. Unfortunately, one of them, Johnny Edgecombe, tried to shoot his way into the house of Dr Stephen Ward, a society osteopath who had introduced Profumo to Keeler and who had invited Keeler and her friend, Mandy Rice-Davies, to share his house.

The shooting put Keeler's name back on the front pages and resulted in an anonymous call to George Wigg, the Labour Shadow Spokesman on Defence, who had clashed with Profumo in the Commons over the Vassall affair. The caller told Wigg to forget Vassall and concentrate on Profumo.

While the press kept their distance, thanks to threats from Profumo's lawyers, although there were no super-injunctions in 1963, Wigg used his Parliamentary privilege to raise the matter in the Commons. Profumo was not in the House but issued a statement the following day that denied his involvement or any 'impropriety' with Keeler, although admitting that he had been introduced to her and Ivanov by Ward at Cliveden, then the home of Lord Astor.

Sensing that he was about to be made the fall guy for the entire Profumo affair, Ward wrote to George Wigg, MI5 and the Home Secretary, outlining the true course of events.

On holiday in Venice, Profumo admitted to his wife, the actress Valerie Hobson, that the rumours were true and that he had lied to the Commons. The house of cards came tumbling down and in the June, less than two months before the Great Train Robbery, Profumo resigned leaving an already unpopular government with even more egg on its face. A show trial of sorts was set up to prove Ward was Keeler's pimp and distract attention away from the government. Rather than go to prison, Ward thwarted the government's plans and took an overdose of pills. He was buried in London on 10 August 1963.

Over fifty years later it can be seen that the Great Train Robbery, which took place on 8 August 1963, was one of the final straws that broke the camel and the government's back. After the Profumo débâcle it once again brought into question the very fabric of law and order in Britain, and made a mockery of the government and its institutions. Much to the delight of the general public, a cheeky London gang had audaciously made off with millions of pounds of the government's own money – and from one of its own trains. The government had to face the fact that a gang of train robbers were shown more respect and affection by the general public than they were.

We may never know what went on in the corridors of power during this period, but pressure was put on Scotland Yard to solve the robbery quickly and bring to justice the people that appeared to have mocked the government. Even, as it turned out, if they were innocent.

Thanks to the discovery of Leatherslade Farm, where the gang had hidden before and after the robbery, and a few tip offs, it was not long before the Yard tracked down many of the gang. But it was still long enough for Prime Minister Macmillan to have resigned on the grounds of ill health so that Sir Alec Douglas-Home could take his place and give the Conservatives a fighting chance of hanging on to power at the next election.

Four members of the Great Train Robbery gang known to the police, including its leader, Bruce Reynolds, were still at large, while the trial of those captured only added to the government's embarrassment. The trial culminated on 15 April 1964 with the sentencing of members of the gang, including Biggs, to terms of thirty-years' imprisonment, a far longer sentence than was being given out at the time to murderers or spies. While the powers-that-be may have thought that this would act as a salutary lesson to society as a whole, it backfired and made even bigger popular heroes of the gang. It also sent a message to the criminal fraternity that they should arm themselves, as the use of a firearm would not add one day to their sentence.

Charlie Wilson's escape from Winson Green Prison on 12 August 1964 was another nail in the government's coffin. On 15 October 1964,

Labour won the general election, albeit by a small majority, and Harold Wilson became Prime Minister.

Conventional ways and days had been swept aside for more unconventional times.

Events of the last fifty years have made us all the more cynical and suspicious. At the time, the death of Marilyn Monroe on 5 August 1962 was seen as a straightforward suicide and John F. Kennedy's assassination in Dallas on 22 November 1963 the work of a lone assassin. Today we wonder if Marilyn was not murdered by people directly linked to the President of the United States, and question if the death of that President was not a coup d'état orchestrated by the various interested parties who wanted to see the escalation of the war in Vietnam.

Just as we may never discover what really happened to Marilyn Monroe or John F. Kennedy, we may never know the true extent of the government's involvement in the Great Train Robbery and the trial that followed. Certainly the gang don't know – they were not political animals. But who in the government at the time of the robbery was so outraged and humiliated by Ronald Biggs' flight to freedom that he and others gave their okay and support to have him kidnapped in Rio de Janeiro nearly twenty years later?

Whoever they are or were, they would be the first to call foul if a foreign power tried to kidnap one of its nationals from the streets of London, and did as much when Alexander Litvinenko was poisoned in London in 2006. They, and Margaret Thatcher's government at the time of Biggs' kidnapping in 1981, remained remarkably tight-lipped when Biggs was snatched from Brazil. Although it is known who was involved, nobody has ever been charged or even reprimanded for the Biggs' kidnapping. The worst that has happened so far was that one of the kidnappers, Fred Prime, was barred from entering Barbados when he returned on holiday 27 years later.

If ill health had not intervened, Biggs would surely have seen out his days in Rio de Janeiro. In November 1997 the last legal avenue for the British government to follow in the hope of getting Biggs back to the UK had been blocked. The Brazilian Supreme Court ruling that the statute of limitations had run out on the train robbery as a crime, if that was what was to be used for Biggs' extradition request.

In failing health, and with little prospect of ever earning a living again, Biggs chose to return to the UK in 2001, and you could not say the government had not been warned. When *Odd Man Out* was first published in 1994, Biggs had stated: 'Pretty soon I'll be entering into the last scene of all and, if I'm to become a dribbling nuisance, one of Her Majesty's hostelries might be just the place to spend my twilight years.'

The smart move by the British government might have been to tell Biggs that he was not welcome in Britain and could stay where he was. But Biggs knew that there were still people working the corridors of power who would not rest until he was back behind bars in the UK. Not for one moment did Biggs think that he would not be welcomed back to Britain, and with open arms. He also knew the consequences would be a lengthy prison spell, although even he could not foresee that most of that would be spent in Belmarsh, one of the UK's highest security prisons.

Given his health and the fact that Biggs came back to the UK on his own volition, he was hardly a flight risk or a danger to the great British public. It has been argued that he was left in Belmarsh because of his ill health, but at the time there were many sicker people in the prison system that didn't get such star treatment. More likely it was a final vindictive act by a small group of people who have had too much time in their lives to think and ponder about Ronald Arthur Biggs.

Biggs' release from prison in 2009 was to be equally farcical and is surrounded by more unanswered questions including if there is a vendetta or conspiracy against Biggs by person or persons unknown? Or are the authorities simply that incompetent when it comes to dealing with him? Only they know for sure.

By June 2009 Biggs had ticked all the right boxes, as far as his eligibility for parole was concerned. He had been a model prisoner (except for a certain escape in 1965), and had served the required time to be eligible for parole. He was certainly of no danger to anyone, as he had shown in the manor in which he had conducted his life in both Australia and Brazil.

The Parole Board decided Biggs was fit to be released, and that was its recommendation to the Justice Department. That should have been the end of the story. Biggs' bed was made up in the nursing home and waiting for his arrival, that was until the Justice Secretary, Jack Straw, stepped in to block his release just two days before the agreed date.

As abruptly as his release under parole had been blocked, there was a total about face four weeks later when Biggs found himself released on compassionate grounds. He was a very ill man, but it was still totally unexpected by the people close to him who had less than 24 hours warning.

And yes, Biggs was a very, very ill man. His son had twice been called to Norfolk & Norwich University Hospital, as they feared the end was close, yet each time Biggs fought back from the brink. Decisions had been taken that if he suffered another stroke or heart attack, he would not be resuscitated.

Biggs is a fighter, if he wasn't, he would not have survived this long. As you read Biggs' own story, never forget that there is a very thin line between a hero and a villain; it all depends on which side of the fence you are sitting at the time and what your race, creed, colour or social background may be. Biggs was no saint, but then neither was Robin Hood or Butch Cassidy, or more recently a number of politicians, bankers or protesting students.

Ronald Biggs is a remarkable man. A survivor who time and time again beat the odds that were stacked against him. At the time of the Wild West or in wartime he would have been a hero for his daring escapes and escapades; in peacetime he is still a villain. But let us never forget, Ronald Biggs is not a modern-day folk hero because of what he did in the early hours of the morning of August 8, 1963, but rather for the manner in which he - your basic man in the street - kept himself one step ahead of the government and media posse which chased him around the world since his daring escape from Wandsworth Prison in July 1965.

Those who know Biggs well know a considerate, kind and generous man. A family man, a loving father and grandfather, a man who has accepted with good grace and humour the rough with the smooth, even his ill health, knowing all along that he was destined to be that odd man out.

The final irony for Biggs must surely be that if he had held up a train in his adopted country of Brazil and been sentenced to a thirty-year stretch, the British government and the media would have been outraged and demanded his immediate release and return. They do as much today for convicted drug smugglers as long as they are British and the forces of law and order are Johnny Foreigner.

Biggs never looked for a pardon, as the papers often claimed, only a little forgiveness and understanding. Something that the last fifty years have shown only comes from governments when there is a financial or political interest at stake. Did it take fifty years for Britain to 'forgive' Germany and Japan for the war? Did it take fifty years for the British government to 'forgive' the terrorist atrocities in Northern Ireland and ask them to share power?

If there is a government in the world that can honestly put its collective hand to its heart and say that it has committed lesser crimes than Ronald Biggs over the last fifty years, then it can cast the first stone.

Read on, but as you do, remember that however remarkable the story of Ronald Biggs appears, what you are reading is fact and not fiction. It is also the truth, the whole truth and nothing but the truth as far as Biggs can remember. But as is clear from when we first published Biggs' autobiography in 1994, although there are people who claim they want the truth, there are others that simply can't handle it and must hang on to the myths that suit their version of events and of Biggs.

In case you had any doubts, Ronnie Biggs very much exists: he is not a myth. This is, as he has already said, his story.

Christopher Pickard
Rio de Janeiro, Brazil / London, UK

Chapter One

THE GREAT TRAIN ROBBERY

A Glasgow-to-London mail train was stopped and robbed in Buckinghamshire early today. It happened at Cheddington, near Tring, at about 3 a.m. The driver and fireman were attacked and injured; and two coaches of the train were detached. They contained mail of all kinds, including registered post. A police spokesman said a short time ago that it's believed a large number of men took part and that they got away with a considerable amount. Neither the driver nor fireman was badly hurt. Every senior officer of the Buckinghamshire police force has gone to the scene of the robbery.

Transcript of the first BBC news broadcast at 8 and 9 a.m. on Thursday, 8 August 1963

It was just after 3 a.m. on the morning of Thursday 8 August 1963 when the walkie-talkie came to life. It was Bruce Reynolds: the train had passed through Leighton Buzzard and was now less than a mile away. After a wait of nearly one-and-a-half hours by the side of the main line between Glasgow and London the moment had come – a moment that would come to be known as the Great Train Robbery.

Sixteen of us were scattered about the embankment that night, four of whom were never to be caught.

A good few stories have been told since about the robbery and what happened that night. Stories that have included everything from a German SS connection to a Mr. Big linked to the government of the day. I have even read in the Brazilian press that I shot the driver in the head at point-blank range, and I am still often accused of having coshed the driver, despite not even being on the train at the time.

The true facts, as always, are somewhat different.

The train robbery was the work of two different London gangs who came together for the 'Big One'. I was a member of neither gang, yet after everything I have read and heard since it is often difficult to believe that it was my friendship with one man, Bruce Reynolds, and the work I had done as a legitimate builder for a retired train driver, that brought me to be lying on a grass embankment in Buckinghamshire that August night. I was the odd man out.

My journey to the embankment can probably be traced back to 1949 and my first spell in Lewes Prison at the age of 19 as a YP (Young Prisoner). It was during this first time in Lewes - I went there twice - that I met a young ex-Post Office sorter by the name of Albert Kitson.

Kit, as we called him, was serving an eighteen-month sentence for taking part in the robbery of the Post Office where he had been working. He had made a wax impression of the key to the safe where the cash was held and passed it on to an old pro.

Kit and I used to walk together during exercise periods, and more than once he made reference to 'large sums of money' that were transported by British Rail.

'If a group of really game lads got together,' he said, 'they could pull off the tickle of a lifetime.'

The following year I met Bruce Reynolds in Wormwood Scrubs Prison. I was back inside again with a three-month sentence for 'taking and driving away a motor vehicle without the owner's consent.' From the start it was clear that Bruce was a cut above the other cons. We became good friends over time and discovered a mutual interest in music, literature and breaking the law. I told him what Kit had told me about the large sums of cash being transported by rail. It was a piece of information he was never to forget.

Our paths crossed several times during the ensuing years - in and out of prison - but we never got up to any villainy together prior to the train robbery itself.

It was after a rather longer stretch in Lewes Prison, four years for burglary, that I concluded that it was time to have a go at honest employment and I found work as a carpenter. I had learned the basics of the trade in prison and the work really interested me. When I came out of jail on that occasion I went to live with a pretty tough lady in Merstham, Surrey. Her name was Ivy and she was a very good friend of Bruce's. She was quite fearless and wouldn't shy away from a punch-up if she found herself facing one. But Ivy was a good sort and if you were a friend of Bruce then you were a friend of Ivy's. She had little, if any, time for Old Bill and could always be depended upon to sell a bit of bent gear or to take care of the odd box of gelignite.

Bruce would visit us from time to time, usually arriving in a ritzy sports car of some kind and always impeccably dressed. He was moving up in the world of villainy and was beginning to build a reputation as the 'Prince of Thieves'.

In the late fifties a train was held up on the London-to-Brighton line – about a mile from where I was living at the time. The signals had been tampered with and the train had stopped at a quiet spot close to a bridge which spanned the road from Merstham to Redhill. The thieves got away with precious little, but it was believed to be 'the work of professionals', according to a police report at the time.

In late 1957 I changed jobs leaving a muddy building site in Redhill for the cleaner work of erecting partitions in offices, mostly in and around central London. The job entailed travelling to London by train and it was on one of these journeys that I first saw Charmian Powell, the future Mrs Biggs, then sweet seventeen. We were mutually attracted and in less time than it takes to say 'rabbit' we were making mad, passionate love in hotels, empty train carriages and on the floor of the classrooms of the school where Charmian's father was headmaster. It didn't take Ivy long to discover my 'little piece on the side' and I was promptly given colourful marching orders.

In a romantic moment Charmian and I decided to elope, but like most young lovers we were hard up. Then, with just a little persuasion from me, Charm dipped her hand into the cash-box where she was working and filched £200 (now about £3500). And just before Christmas 1957 off we went `a la Bonnie and Clyde minus the firearms, with my good friend Michael Haynes, a man who was going to play such an important role in my life, at the wheel of a hired Vauxhall Victor. We headed west from London as I had a fancy to see Devon and Cornwall again. I had been evacuated to Coombe-in-Teignhead in Devon at the beginning of the war and later, as the bombing got worse, to Delabole in Cornwall. There was a slate quarry close to Delabole and I remembered how easy it had been to get into a shed where the explosives were stored. What I planned to do with explosives I can't remember, but it was all rather academic, as long before we got to Cornwall the money had run out. So Mike and I decided to try a break-in or two with Charm acting as lookout.

Sadly, one snowy evening after a hair-raising chase through the tortuous roads of Swanage, our luck ran out and we were nicked. A string of charges followed, including my usual: 'taking and driving away a motor vehicle without the owner's consent.'

Charm got her first - and only - taste of porridge in the women's wing of HMP Exeter and was soon up before the governor for smuggling in cash which was strictly against prison regulations. Mike and I fared better. We were sent to HMP Dorchester where, as we were more experienced, our money wasn't found!

On the 1 April 1958 – an April Fools Day Charmian was never to forget - we appeared before the judge at the Dorset Quarter Sessions. A love-story was presented to the court by our learned counsel, but the prosecutor declared us 'a threat'. Our fate was now in the hands of the red-faced judge. The court adjourned. Everything, I was told by my brief, was going to depend on whether his lordship's lunch had been satisfactory or not.

Stifling a burp, the well-fed judge returned to pass sentence. Charmian and Mike were put on two years' probation, while I ended up with two and a half years in prison - not a bad result, considering. With remission I was looking at twenty months so Charmian and Mike would still be on probation when I got out.

And that's the way it turned out. I was sent to Norwich to do my time, but regularly, once a month, Charmian came to visit. We sat holding hands and making plans for our future. We were going to get married and 'settle down'. We exchanged long and passionate letters. I thought my sentence would never end.

At the time I could not have foreseen that I would be returning to Norwich nearly 50 years later for what is hopefully my last spell inside. I was pleased to see in July 2007 that the roof I had helped to build in 1958 was still standing and in good nick. Thanks to 'health & safety' prisoners are never likely to be invited to build the roof over their own heads again!

I was finally released on a cold, foggy morning in mid-December 1959. I had been transferred to Wandsworth Prison in London to finish my time and Charmian was waiting outside the gate to meet me. We made a beeline for our favourite hotel and booked in as Mr and Mrs Biggs. Champagne and a double serving of bacon and eggs were sent to the room.

It was late evening when we emerged and caught the train to Redhill. I had arranged to stay with friends, John and Violet Goldsmith, until I could find a place of my own. It was good to see old friends again and we sat around drinking tea and laughing about old times. Charmian could not stay long as she was anxious not to infringe the terms of her probation. She didn't want 'Old Saddle-Bags' – Miss Sadler, her probation officer – to read her the riot act.

I got a job with the Reigate Borough Council working as a carpenter. Not very well paid, but plenty of tea and sympathy from the housewives. From my wages I managed to rent a small furnished flat on Elm Road where Charm and I spent as much time as possible together. We were more keen than ever to get married but Charmian's father, far less fond of me since having to fork out the £200 his daughter had pilfered as well as her legal fees, was dead against the idea of our union. In the end we decided to force the old man's hand. We would get Charm pregnant and present our case as fait accompli.

The wedding took place at the Reigate Registry Office on 20 February 1960. For us it was the Wedding Of the Year.

I changed my job shortly afterwards and started working for an elderly Redhill building contractor by the name of Sid Budgeon. Sid allowed me to get in as much overtime as possible as soon there would be a third Biggs to feed.

Nicholas Grant was born on 23 July 1960 at Redhill County Hospital. The proud and happy parents could be seen wheeling His Nibs through the streets of Redhill in an enormous plum-coloured baby carriage. The pram had cost an arm and a leg but 'Mother' had insisted that it had to be the very best.

I was happy with the way things were going. I was being offered so much work that I decided it was time to set up in business for myself, hiring help whenever necessary. We also moved into larger premises at 37 Alpine Road.

When Nicky was nearly one year old, our close friends Ron and Janet Searle invited Charm and I to spend a week with them in a caravan in Hastings. Although I couldn't really afford to take the time off I finally allowed myself to be persuaded to go. Janet was most enthusiastic about fortune telling and things of that nature, things that I considered at the time to be nothing more than mumbo jumbo.

We drove to Hastings in the Searles' car and for much of the time Janet was raving on about her pet subject, trying to persuade us all to have our fortunes told.

The second day in Hastings Charmian did go and see a fortune-teller on the pier. A certain 'Professor Cullen' was her seer. When she rejoined us some twenty minutes later she was visibly shaken. The professor had told her things that she thought only she and her mother knew.

'It really was remarkable,' she said.

Janet looked triumphant.

'You see,' she gloated. 'Now it's your turn, Ron.' I declined her invitation, insisting that it was still all hocus-pocus. The next morning, however, when everyone was asleep I went into town and found myself a fortune-teller. Ten shillings she charged for her services. Half a quid! It was daylight robbery, I thought.

The fortune-teller was a frail-looking old lady of seventy odd. She invited me to put my hands on her crystal ball and told me straight away that in later years I would suffer with 'kidney problems'. This, it turned out, had nothing to do with fortune telling – she deduced it from my sweating palms. She then went on to tell me that I was a self-employed carpenter and that when I had worked for other people I had always had 'foreman trouble'. She said that I was on holiday in Hastings but could ill-afford to take the time off because of pressing work commitments. I was with a wife - nine to ten years younger than myself - and had an only son who was just one year old. She saw me forming a partnership with a man who worked with 'bricks and mortar' (at that time I knew of no bricklayer that I would take on as a partner).

Until that point everything she had said had been totally correct. How, I wanted to know, out of all the trades and professions that exist could she know that I was a carpenter - and a self-employed one at that? Her credibility took a tumble, however, when she told me that I would 'travel extensively around the world and that I would have a child with a woman with long, black hair.' Now, I thought, we were really in the realms of gypsy flim-flam. But I was impressed. She told me I would never be rich but I would always be a good 'breadwinner'. Then, as I was leaving, she called me back.

'I have some advice for you,' she offered. 'If you want anything out of this life be sure you pay for it.'

A year passed and one day over lunch Charm told me that she had run into an old school chum, Janet, who had moved into the neighbourhood with her husband, Ray Stripp. They would be coming along on Saturday evening for drinks. Ray was a bricklayer and Charm had told her friend that I might be able to fix him up with some weekend work. As history shows we became partners, splitting the expenses and profits down the middle. We went from strength to strength taking on more workers until we had a gang of ten. On paper we were making a substantial profit, but some of our clients were slow to pay and there were times when I found it difficult to meet my half of the payroll.

Christopher Dean, our second son, was born on 24 March 1963. A little beauty - and the image of his dad. Christopher brought with him additional expenses and one weekend in June I found myself particularly strapped for cash. I decided to phone my old pal Bruce Reynolds and see if he could lend me £500 - that would be about £8500 today - to tide me over until better times.

'Normally, as you know, I would be only too happy to help you out,' Bruce said when I called him. 'But at this exact moment all my dough is tied up in a piece of business, something that I would like to talk to you about, only not over the phone.'

We made an arrangement for him to visit us at the weekend. He arrived at 37 Alpine Road in Redhill with his wife Frances and his baby son, by coincidence also called Nicholas. While the girls were in the garden cooing over the kids, Bruce said that he was in a position to put me into his 'piece of business', details of which he could not give me right then. I thanked him for the offer but pointed out that I was now working for a living and was very happy with married life. I also wasn't keen to put my liberty at risk.

'I'm pleased to hear it,' Bruce said, 'but if you want to make one I can guarantee you a minimum of forty grand for your whack.'

'Jesus!' I replied. 'Can I have some time to think it over?'

'You can, but there's one condition. If you want to take part you will have to come up with someone who knows how to drive a diesel train.'

As luck or fate would have it, I was working for an elderly train-driver. I was renewing the front windows of his house in Redhill.

I found it hard to sleep that night. Forty grand was a lot of money to even dream about. It was enough money to buy four new four-bedroomed houses in the best part of Reigate. I phoned Bruce early the next morning and put my name on the list.

'I'm in,' I said. I gave him the train-driver's address and told Bruce that I would be working there for at least another week.

A few days later Bruce drove down from London with his brother-in-law, John Daly. They wanted to get a close look at the old man. The train driver - let's call him simply Peter, although I believe he has to be dead by now - saw Bruce and John pull up in Bruce's sporty Lotus. We went off to a nearby pub to discuss a plan of action.

My first priority was to see if the old boy would join the gang. All he would have to do was to drive a diesel train for a mile or so for a straight £40,000 (nearly £665,000 at today's rates). When I returned to the house Peter was watering his garden - his pride and joy.

'What would you do for £40,000?' I asked casually.

'£40,000?' he repeated. 'Blimey, I'd do just about anything for that kind of money although I wouldn't hurt or kill anyone for it. Why are you asking?'

'Would you rob a bank?'

'Yes I would,' he affirmed after a moments thought. ' Are you serious?'

'Suppose I was to offer you £40,000 for your share, would you join me in a robbery?'

'I would. If you want me to help you with anything like that I'd be in like a shot.'

'But what if you were to get caught?'

'I'd keep my mouth shut, if that's what you mean, and if I got time I would tread it out. But what is this all about? Are you really thinking of robbing a bank, Ron?'

'I can't tell you anything yet. But if I ask you to join me, you will?'

Peter put his hand out and we shook on it. His interest in his roses had wilted somewhat. He kept asking questions - most of which I honestly could not answer - and he wanted to know if it had anything to do with the people he had recently seen in the white Lotus.

The first time I met the whole gang was in Roy James' flat in Nell Gwynn House in Chelsea. I have to say they looked a pretty formidable bunch. With a few exceptions they were all big men and even though they were well dressed the majority still had the distinctive look of villains.

The basic plan for the robbery had already been well established when I entered the scene. Jimmy White was the 'quartermaster' responsible for the provision of army uniforms and overalls to be used in the raid. Charlie Wilson was chosen to stock the hideout with food and drink. Roy James and the man I will call Mr One, a member of the gang who would never be caught, would take care of transport. And so forth.

Bruce formally introduced me to the gang and I was invited to tell the assembly what I could about the train driver. They asked questions about him. What kind of trains was he working on? How well would he hold up if he got nicked? No stone was left unturned.

Most decisions taken by the gang were made on a show of hands and a vote was called for as to whether the old man should be brought in or not. All hands were raised with the exception of one, Roy James. The gang listened intently as Roy argued that the old man had no experience in the world of villainy.

'It's all very well for the old chap to say that he would keep his mouth shut,' Roy went on, 'but he had never been trampled on by a fifteen stone copper.'

It was a strong argument and I knew from experience how ugly Old Bill could get during an 'interrogation'. But where would we stand, countered one of the gang, if the actual train-driver refused to cooperate? We had to have a back up driver, it was that simple. On a second show of hands yours truly and the old man were voted in.

Now that I had been formally accepted, Bruce filled me in on the details of the plan and when the robbery would take place. I would have to take Peter to Euston Station and let him see the kind of train that he would be expected to handle.

'He's got to be sure that he knows how to drive this particular train,' Bruce emphasized.

A couple of days later Peter and I went to Euston Station. I bought a platform ticket and sat on a bench at the far end of the platform close to the sleek diesel engine of a train preparing to leave. I hid behind a copy of the Daily Mirror. After a minute or two Peter came along dressed in his railwayman's blue dungarees, an oily rag hanging from his jacket pocket. He gave the driver of the train a cheery greeting.

'What-ho, mate. I'm going on one of these big buggers next week - I wonder if you'd like to give me a few tips?'

'Sure,' replied the driver, clearly only too happy to help one of his colleagues, 'hop up.' Twenty minutes later I 'bumped into' Peter in a café near the station. He was confident and clearly enjoying the part.

'It's a piece of cake,' he said. 'There is almost no difference to the engines I am working on in Redhill.'

It was all arranged. Bruce would meet Peter and me at Victoria Station at 8 a.m. on Tuesday 6 August. So that we could get away from our homes for what might be as much as two weeks I concocted a story that I had been contracted for a tree felling job 'somewhere in Wiltshire'. Peter was 'invited' to go with me as a cook and applied for two weeks' leave of absence from his job. Charmian was disappointed that I was going to be away from home for my thirty-fourth birthday, which fell on 8 August, but I convinced her with the argument that I was going to be well paid for my labours and that we could celebrate in style upon my return.

Monday 5 August was a bank holiday. I had promised to take Charmian and the children to Brighton for the day. Early that morning my partner, Ray, appeared at the house with a £50 cheque for some work we had done in a nearby house. He was to give me half the value of the cheque but only had £15 in cash. Before he arrived I had been studying the form and looking over the many runners and riders scheduled for the races that day. Ray lived above the Inkpen, a betting shop, and on the spur of the moment I decided to make a bet with the £10 he owed me. I wrote down the bet on a piece of paper. It was to be a £5 each-way double. Dameon and Rococco. Two horses at different meetings. Ray thought I was mad to be gambling such an amount (about £170 at today's values), especially on two horses that appeared on paper to have little or no chance. I said nothing to Charm, either, as she had no faith whatsoever in my gambling 'hunches'.

We travelled to Brighton by train and had what appeared to be a happy family day. The fact that I was going off on 'the business' the following day was very much on my mind and I wanted to enjoy ourselves to the full. It just could be our last day together as a family for quite a long time. I tried to push these negative thoughts from my mind - I should be coming back from my trip with forty grand!

I took Nicky for a ride in a speedboat, followed by ice-cream, toffee-apples and the inevitable flop in a deck-chair on the pier.

There was horseracing in Brighton that afternoon and after looking over the runners and riders in the midday newspaper my 'special selection' was the favourite in the last race with Ron Hutchinson up. I tried to get Charm interested in a ten quid 'investment' but we settled for a fiver. I went off to place the bet. After a dinner of fish and chips I bought the late evening paper to see if the nag had obliged; it had, and there was eight pounds to collect.

Standing in line at the betting-shop to collect my winnings, I found myself looking at the day's racing results, which were chalked up on a number of blackboards. The name Rococco caught my eye. It was one of the horses I had asked Ray to bet on and it had won at odds of 10 to 1. Then I saw Dameon, a 9 to 1 winner.

If Ray had placed the bet I had won over £600, but would get £500, or about, £8,500 at today's values, which was the bookmaker's limit on any one bet. I said nothing about it to Charm, but when we got home I urgently telephoned Ray to check that he had in fact placed the bet. He said he had and asked if I had won anything. I told him, and loud enough so that Charm could hear me in the kitchen, that I had indeed won and £500 to boot. I asked him to go over to the bookmaker in the morning and pick up my winnings. My partner was dumbfounded.

'You jammy bastard,' he said.

My devoted spouse was not in the least bit dumbfounded, but was considerably less convinced.

'That will be the day when you win £500 on a bet. I know you and your little games. Don't think you can fool me.'

I rose early the next morning: I had a train to catch! A light breakfast, hugs and kisses and a final reminder not to forget to write when I got there. 'And behave yourself,' were Charmian's parting words.

At Redhill station I was glad and relieved to see that Peter was among the early morning travellers to London. We had previously agreed not to travel together. At least not as a pair.

During most of the journey to Victoria I was deep in thought. I had set out to borrow £500 and I had won exactly that amount. I remembered what the old fortune teller had said: 'If you want anything out of this life, be sure you pay for it.' But the die was cast and there was no turning back. In truth, I knew I didn't want to.

Bruce was waiting for us in a café in Wilton Road, next to Victoria Station. He was with his brother-in-law, John Daly, and two other members of the gang that I had met at the gathering in Roy James' flat. They were Jimmy White, the quartermaster, and the biggest man in the group, the man who coshed the train driver; he was one of the four men never to be caught, and I'll call him Mr Three.

After a cheese sandwich and a cup of tea we climbed into a green army Land-Rover which was parked nearby. Soon we were on the open road and heading for Bucks. The weather was still good and the day seemed full of promise. We were generally light-hearted, laughing and joking as we went along. Peter was sitting next to me in the back of the Land Rover and appeared quite relaxed.

'Nice vehicles, these Land Rovers,' he said at one point. 'Who do they belong to?'

Jimmy White, who was driving, responded: 'Don't know, Dad. We nicked it the night before last in the Strand.'

'Nicked it?' exclaimed the old man, losing his smile. 'Christ! You can get pinched for that kind of thing!' We all cracked up and Peter joined in, happy to be the cause of our merriment and the centre of attention.

It was mid morning by the time we arrived at our destination, Leatherslade Farm, a small farm located 300 yards off the B4011, the Thame Road, close to the villages of Brill and Oakley in Buckinghamshire. The nearest towns of note were Bicester and Thame. We were the first part of the gang to arrive; the rest would be arriving at staggered intervals. We explored the two-story farmhouse and the various outbuildings. Precious little had been left behind by the former tenants. A rusty generator seized the attention of Jimmy White who immediately set about trying to get it to work. Mr Three and I volunteered to fix a lunch of steak, chips and runner beans. Old Peter, for his part, found a deck chair and relaxed in the sun, puffing away at his pipe and blending in with the pastoral surroundings. He might as well have been in his own back yard.

During the afternoon, the second group arrived in an Austin army truck. Among the group were Tommy Wisbey, Jim Hussey, Bob Welch, Buster Edwards, Mr. One and Mr Two, two other members of the gang who were lucky enough never to be caught or even suspected. On the way to the farm the group had stopped off at a nearby town to buy further provisions. Bobby Welch, who liked a drink or two, bought a number of pipkins of ale, an act that subsequently led to his arrest and conviction. The pipkin of ale, with his fingerprints, is today a prize exhibit at Scotland Yard's own private Crime Museum.

Roy James and Charlie Wilson arrived soon after in a second Land Rover, bringing yet more supplies. John Daly had thoughtfully brought cards and games to while away the time and I was one of the first to start a game of Monopoly along with John, Tommy Wisbey, Charlie and Roy. Soon enough the game turned into an unruly riot with much shouting and laughter. Charlie was the runaway winner.

Peter - 'Dad' to the gang' - was happy to be the tea boy, quite taken with the friendliness shown by one and all.

It was just after dark when Roger Cordrey arrived at the farm carrying a large suitcase. He was popular with the gang and received a vociferous welcome. By now there were fifteen of us at Leatherslade Farm - only Gordon Goody was missing.

At the time, Gordon was at the home of solicitor's managing clerk, Brian Field and his German wife Karin, in Pangbourne, close to Reading. An hour's drive from the farm. He was waiting for a phone call from a certain Post Office worker in Carlisle. Described as the 'Ulsterman' in the media and in various books about the robbery, this person was in league with the gang and the call that Goody was waiting for would tell him when the extra big load of registered cash had been despatched. Who the 'Ulsterman' is - or was - I cannot say, but when the loot was eventually split up into shares, the Ulsterman got his full whack.

Leonard 'Nipper' Read, who at the time of the robbery was an officer in Scotland Yard's Murder Squad, wrote in his autobiography *Nipper - The Man Who Nicked The Krays* that: *'an Irishman was responsible for planning robberies and then selling them on to the perpetrators... I am sure from all the information I had that he (the Irishman) drew up the plan for the Great Train Robbery, but it was Bruce Reynolds who honed, polished and fine-tuned it.'*

We were not certain what day the big load would be sent to London after the bank holiday weekend, so we had arrived at the farm on Tuesday (6 August) just in case we had to 'go to work' in the early hours of Wednesday morning.

Goody arrived at Leatherslade Farm just before 11 p.m. making something of a dramatic entrance, swigging from a bottle of Johnny Walker. 'You can all relax,' he announced as he caught us trying on our army uniforms. 'There's nothing doing tonight.' Groans greeted this piece of news. We had been raring to go.

Few of us felt like sleep that night. We sat around in the kitchen, chatting, playing cards and drinking warm beer. It was late when we finally stretched out our blankets and sleeping bags in the various rooms of the farm.

Dawn broke with the promise of another warm and sunny day. I got up and made breakfast for the early risers - eggs and bacon, of course. Rural sounds were coming through the kitchen window, a mixture of livestock and the mechanical sounds common to farms.

It had been decided on the previous day that we would show as little movement as possible. For that reason we were 'confined to barracks' and only allowed out to make use of the privy situated some thirty yards from the house.

During the morning that plan changed after a visitor turned up and knocked on the front door. Everyone slipped silently out of view and Bruce went to take care of the caller. It turned out to be a Mr Wyatt, a neighbouring farmer who had become accustomed to hiring a meadow which formed part of Leatherslade Farm. He wanted to know if he could make a similar arrangement with the new 'owner' of the farm. Bruce gave the visitor some cock and bull story about being at the farm to take care of redecorating the premises before the new owner moved in. He promised to pass on Mr Wyatt's request.

The day seemed endless. There was little interest in cards or other pastimes and it was difficult to concentrate to even read a book. Towards late afternoon we assembled in the kitchen to go through the plan one last time to make certain that everyone knew exactly what they had to do. Subject to getting the greenlight from the Ulsterman, we would leave just after midnight and travel as an army detail on night manoeuvres. Bruce would be dressed as the officer and would be carrying 'official papers' to show in the unlikelihood that we were stopped by Old Bill. Bruce's driver would be 'Corporal' John Daly and the rest of us (extra) ordinary soldiers. At Bridego Bridge, where the railway goes over a quiet country road just off the B488, two miles north of Cheddington Station, we would put dark blue boiler-suits on over the uniforms and go about our various tasks.

As night fell, we sat around in the dark swapping anecdotes and dirty jokes. Goody told us about an encounter he had once had with a gorgeous chick in a swanky London restaurant. She was alone - and so was Gordon. He beckoned the waiter over and had him invite the young lady to his table. It was almost love at first sight. They wined and dined by candlelight, they danced cheek to cheek, they kissed. Gordon paid the bill.

'You're place or mine?' he asked.

In the cab on the way to the young thing's flat, Gordon started to slide his hand up under her skirt and between his companion's legs. She stopped him. She had something to tell him: 'I'm not a girl!'

Gordon then gave a graphic description of how he ejected, somewhat prematurely, his perfumed partner from the taxi - whilst it was still in motion. More a question of crying shame than *Crying Game*.

During the fun, Bruce lit up one of a number of cigars he had in his top pocket. Bobby Welch, who was sitting nearby, asked Bruce for one and Bruce obliged.

'Give one to Pete,' suggested Bob.

'No, no,' said our stand-in train driver. 'If I had wanted one you'd give me one, wouldn't you Bruce?'

I could almost see Bruce smiling in the gloom.

'Don't worry, Dad,' he said taking a long drag at his cigar. 'If you wanted one - I'd give you one!'

Everyone laughed, including the old man.

'I like your friends,' Peter confided in me. 'They're such a jolly crowd.'

Just before 10 p.m., Goody slipped out of the farm to phone Brian Field from the phone-box in nearby Brill. He was soon back with the news we had been waiting to hear.

'There's an unusually big load on the train tonight - and, gentlemen, it's on its way.'

THURSDAY, 8 AUGUST 1963

Oh, the good life, full of fun seems to be the ideal
Mm, the good life lets you hide all the sadness you feel

It's the good life to be free and explore the unknown
Like the heartaches when you learn you must face them alone
Well, just wake up, kiss the good life goodbye.

Tony Bennett, "*The Good Life*"

Midnight came and went. I hardly had time to remember that it was my 34th birthday, yet by the end of the day it would certainly be the one to remember!

The night mail train from Glasgow, the Night Flyer, Up Postal, consisting of a high-powered diesel engine (D326 - 40126) and twelve coaches, had left Carlisle en route for London at 9.04 pm. At 12.30 a.m. the train passed through Crewe Station where driver Jack Mills and Fireman David Whitby had taken control. It was now our turn to leave Leatherslade Farm to meet with it. We finally got on the move slightly before 1.00 a.m. From what I remember it was a cool, dry, moonlit summer night with just a few scattered clouds. More importantly there was no sign of rain.

The gang set off in convoy and looked every bit the part of an army patrol on night manoeuvres we were meant to be.

I was in the lead Land Rover, which was driven by John Daly. Mr One drove the truck. Besides the driver my Land Rover was carrying Bruce, Roger Cordrey and, of course, Peter, who was my responsibility for the night. Most of the rest of the gang piled into the truck, with Roy James bringing up the rear in the second Land Rover with Gordon Goody, Jimmy White and Mr Two.

Bruce had given all the gang a number so that no names would be used. Bruce was number one.

The country lanes were deserted with not a sight nor sound of anything during the 50 minute drive to Bridego Bridge (Bridge 127) with the exception of a solitary hitchhiker. We backed the lorry up between the bridge and a pond so that it was in place to receive the mailbags. The Land Rovers were parked close by.

Our first task was to put our blue overalls on over our army uniforms, overalls being more appropriate for our trackside duties should we be spotted from a passing train or car. I then scrambled over the protective fence and up the bank to the track with Bruce and Peter. Markers were unrolled which would show Peter exactly where the train had to stop for unloading. We made our way up the track towards the gantry and Sears Crossing, a bridge which went over rather than under the track. Roy James left us to cut the telephone wires from the track side boxes and went off to help Bruce and John Daly to cut the public telephone lines that linked two nearby farms, Rowden Farm near Bridego Bridge and Redborough Farm near Sears Crossing, to the outside world. Bruce then went back to get one of the Land Rovers so that he could take up his position further down the track, where the road to Ledburn crossed under the railway, a mere 800 yards from Leighton Buzzard Station, from where he could warn us of the train's imminent arrival.

John Daly and Roger Cordrey had the most to do at this time. To them fell the responsibility of stopping the train. John's signal with an amber light would slow the train at the distant signal, the dwarf signal, while Roger's red light would stop the train altogether by the home signal on the gantry. A distance of some 1300 yards separated the dwarf signal and gantry.

We spent nearly an hour and a half trackside waiting for the train. During which time other trains sped by and one, a freight train, came to a stop directly under the gantry. Roger hid behind the signal while the rest of us crouched down on the bank listening to the conversation between the driver and his mate. Old Peter was so relaxed that he lit his pipe as he sat on the embankment. The match flared into the night sky. Charlie Wilson came scurrying over from the other bank but hadn't the heart to yell at Peter.

'Look at the old fucker. You'd think he was on his holiday,' was all he said.

It was just after three o'clock when Bruce's voice crackled over the walkie-talkie to warn us that the train was on its way. The light on the gantry switched to red and Roger scrambled down to join Buster, Jimmy White and Roy James, Bob Welch and Mr One and Three on the other side of the track to where I was waiting with Peter, Charlie Wilson, Gordon Goody, Jim Hussey Tommy Wisbey and Mr Two.

'My word!' said old Peter, as he saw the light turn to red. 'Your mates have thought of everything.'

The train came slowly, almost silently, to an 'armchair stop'. From where Peter and I were hiding there was only the sound of the diesel motor ticking over. A light went on inside the driver's cab, then a door opened and a shadowy figure descended from the train and headed to the foot of the signal gantry. It was David Whitby, the fireman.

Whitby went to the gantry to call the signal box and must have discovered that the line had been cut. He was starting back to the train when he saw Tommy Wisbey who he must have assumed was working on the track. He went over to talk to him and was grabbed by two members of the gang and unceremoniously bundled down the bank where he was handcuffed and told to keep quiet. We were on the move.

Roy James and Jimmy White took up their positions to start uncoupling the locomotive and the High-Value-Package (HVP) coach from the rest of the train.

Buster Edwards and Gordon Goody stormed the cab from different sides. The train driver, Jack Mills, reacted instinctively and kicked out at Buster as he was coming up the ladder. Gordon pinned Mills and spun him around to hand him to the biggest member of the gang, Mr Three, who in the heat of the moment coshed Mills once and once only. He fell sideways to his knees striking the back of his head against the cab wall.

Mr Three was chosen to take the train because he was big, because he was a professional. He wasn't the sort of bloke who goes mad. He wasn't a sadist. He wasn't into violence. He coshed the driver once.

Other members of the gang now swarmed into the cab from both sides.

'Get the old man up here!' a voice called. I recognized it as Gordon Goody. I led Peter across the track to the iron ladder leading to the cab.

The driver was back on his feet by now, looking groggy and bleeding from a head wound; Charlie Wilson, ever the gentleman, was mopping the blood with a white handkerchief while at the same time seeking to console him.

'You're okay, Dad,' I heard him say. 'You're not badly hurt.'

Peter had also witnessed the scene and threw me a troubled look - he hadn't bargained for anybody getting hurt, but then neither had I. The coshing was regrettable but it was one blow and not the heavy beating that the media likes to portray. The authorities, both at the trial and ever since, have manipulated it to turn public opinion against the train robbers. While force was certainly used to break into the HVP coach, you could never call the train robbery a violent crime compared with much that has gone on before and since.

The blood coming from Mills' injury seemed to have made people nervous in the cab and Goody took Peter by the arm and hustled him into the driving seat.

'When I give you the word, pull away,' he shouted. 'About a mile down the track you'll see the white marker. I'll tell you when to stop.'

Behind us Roy James and Jimmy White were waiting for the signal to complete the uncoupling of the engine and HVP from the other coaches; these housed some seventy two Post Office employees who were busily going about their business of sorting the regular mail, oblivious to what was going on just a few feet away. An express train whistled past on the inside track, nearly taking Roy and Jimmy with it.

The word was passed forward that the uncoupling was complete but during the procedure, and unknown to any of us in the cab, there had been a loss of break pressure. Goody gave Peter the order to get the train moving. The old man just sat looking steadfastly at the controls.

'I'm waiting for my break pressure to build,' he said by way of explanation.

It was now a case of too many chiefs and not enough Indians.

'What's the problem?' barked Bob Welch. 'Let's get going.'

'I can't take the break off until I've got sixteen inches of pressure,' Peter added quite matter-of-factly.

'Get him out of here and get the driver,' Goody exploded.

Peter began to protest, referring again to the necessary brake pressure.

'Fuck the break pressure,' stormed Goody. 'Get the driver up here.'

Peter was pulled out of the seat and Mills took his place. Goody waved his cosh under the nose of the injured driver.

'Listen,' he said. 'Get this thing moving - but not too fast - and stop when I tell you.'

The pressure built and in more ways than one. Finally the large diesel lurched into life and began to move slowly forward. Peter was not looking happy.

'I could have driven it. Why didn't they let me?' he protested. I told him not to worry, it was going to be alright.

Roy, who was riding on the outside of the cab, saw the markers first and shouted for us to slow the train. The large locomotive glided to a halt and the gang spilled out from the train onto the track.

Bruce was already standing waiting for us, cutting an elegant figure in his army officer's uniform rather than our blue overalls.

'Well done, chaps!' he said.

We stopped the train exactly at Bridego Bridge, which we knew was little used at night. The bridge was just 38 miles from Euston, the train's final destination.

'Take Peter and wait for us in the back of the Land Rover,' Bruce told me.

'And make sure the old chap doesn't take off into the boondocks.'

Peter and I did as Bruce said, scrambled down the grass embankment to the road and over the tailboard into the back of one of the Land-Rovers. At the same time members of the gang were taking Mills and Whitby off the train and getting them to lie down on the grass embankment.

From our position Peter and I had a clear and unobstructed view of the bridge and the paralyzed train. There was the sound of glass shattering as the assault team lead by Charlie got to work.

'My word!' said old Peter for the umpteenth time that night.

We sat in awed silence witnessing the sacking of the train. The gang worked swiftly, passing the mailbags by way of a human chain to Jim Hussey and Bob Welch who were loading the truck. I knew then that I was a privileged spectator to a historic moment, although at the time I did not know just how historic it was to be. The Great Train Robbery was now fact.

Dawn was approaching and Bruce called a halt to the plundering of the train, even though a few mailbags still remained. Mills and Whitbey were moved from the embankment to the HVP coach with the five HVP sorters. We removed our overalls and reverted to the role of soldiers. The 'work party' returned to the vehicles breathing heavily from their labours. The whole robbery - from the stopping of the train at Sears Crossing to leaving the scene - had taken less than 40 minutes, 24 minutes since stopping at Bridego Bridge.

Our small convoy made its deliberately slow progress back to the farm, the truck sluggish with the weight of the mailbags and the gang. As I had had it comparatively easy I was given the task of being radio-operator and tuned into Old Bill's wavelength on the portable VHF radio we had brought along.

In comparison to recent events the drive back was uneventful and as we drove up the lane leading to the farm a rooster crowed. As far as I was concerned it was a new day in beautiful, bucolic Bucks.

As we reached the gate to the farm the radio crackled into life for the first time that morning. It was a general call. A train had been robbed near Linslade. The time was around 4.40 a.m. The first senior police officer would get to the scene of the robbery at just after 5.00 a.m.

The truck backed up close to the door of the farmhouse and was quickly and quietly unloaded, the mailbags and their valuable contents being dumped unceremoniously onto the floor of the empty living room. One hundred and twenty bags all in all - nearly ten bags each! Later we learnt that it had been eight bags that had been left behind on the train.

I assumed we would have our work cut out separating the 'wheat from the chaff' and made a comment of this nature to one of the others. By way of an answer Charlie Wilson opened a pocketknife and slashed open one of the bags. He took out a tightly wrapped bundle and ran his knife down the length of it, laying it open and exposing a wad of blue five pound notes.

'It's wedge, Ron,' he said with shining eyes and an ear-to-ear grin, 'it's all fucking wedge!'

The truck was parked in a lean-to-shed - squashing a can of yellow paint in the process - and the Land-Rovers placed out of sight. From the air or from the main road nobody would be able to tell that the farmhouse was inhabited, certainly not by sixteen villains and some 120 mailbags that contained 636 individual packages.

Members of the gang were selected to go to various vantage points in the house and keep an eye out for unwanted guests. It had already been decided that if Old Bill did come calling they would be 'taken care' of and tied up. The coshes were hung up on a row of hooks near the door.

Charlie and Roger Cordrey were appointed 'accountants' to take care of the counting and distribution of the cash, but first it was decided that we should empty the sacks on the off chance that a homing device had been planted in any one of them. It took Bruce, Mr Two and myself close to three hours to empty the sacks and pass the money to Charlie and Rodger.

Old Peter was much more relaxed by now and smiling at one and all. He set about making 'a nice cup of tea' for 'his boys', as he now fondly called us.

When the accountants reached the magic million we were all called in to admire the stack. Appreciative sounds filled the air and jokes were cracked.

'If only that prick on Police 5 could see this lot!' said someone.

'Who said crime doesn't pay?' added James.

Gordon Goody was crooning one of his favourite Tony Bennett pieces, *'The Good Life'*, while Charlie Wilson was twisting to a rousing version of Gerry and the Pacemakers *'I Like It'*. Bruce thanked everyone in the Gang individually before catching some well earned sleep. Buster was to wake him in two hours.

Although there was general euphoria our guard didn't drop. There was always somebody monitoring the police traffic on the radio until Old Bill took to using a code after suspecting that we might be listening in on the line, even then we constantly monitored the news broadcasts.

Some of us not on lookout duty returned our attentions to the Monopoly set. A costly mistake, as it turned out. Charlie was once again the runaway winner offering £5000 for a 'Get Out Of Jail Free' card. Jovial Tommy Wisbey quipped: 'Bank error in your favour. Collect one million quid.'

The original plan was for us to sit tight at the farm for some time - possibly a week or more. We certainly had the supplies for it and the farm was well off the beaten track and set well back from the road. Police broadcasts and news bulletins were to change all that.

It was around midday when we heard on the radio that the police suspected that army vehicles had been used in the robbery. Another report spoke of the likelihood that we were held up in a farmhouse somewhere in the vicinity of the robbery, perhaps 'within a thirty-minute drive or thirty-mile radius of Bridego Bridge'. A 'senior police spokesman', Malcolm Fewtrell, announced that a systematic search of farms and outbuildings would take place immediately.

For whatever reason, the police told the press that we had got away with 'over £100,000'. By late afternoon we were staring at a pile of over £2,500,000 and that did not count the ten bob notes. According to the *Guinness Book of Records* and official records our total haul that night was £2,631,784 of which only £343,448 was ever recovered. That represented over $7 million at the time and over £44 million at current sterling rates. If we had invested the money in a bank it would now be worth over £120 million.

The money was split into sixteen equal 'whacks' after Peter's £40,000 and £100,000 to be split by Brian Field, John Wheater, and Leonard Field had been deducted. The extra whack was for the Ulsterman. Each person took his share and packed it into kit-bags, holdalls and suitcases. My whack filled two army kit-bags, more money then I had ever dreamt of, over £147,000, nearly £2.5 million pounds at today's rates. I gave Peter his money in a leather hold-all.

'My word!' said the old man. 'Is this all mine?' His retirement was suddenly looking a little bit more promising that the fifteen bob a week promised by British Rail.

Decisions were still being taken as to what we should do next. As time may not be on our side we started to throw the empty mailbags down into the cellar and the cleaning of the house began. Wrapping paper bearing the names of various well-known banks were incinerated in a small stove in the kitchen until Roy pointed out that the column of smoke pouring from the chimney on a warm summer's day might attract the attention of Old Bill. The fire was quickly put out.

It was also decided that after the story we had told the neighbour about being there to decorate there should be some signs of life at the farm, so two of the gang went to dig a hole in the meadow behind the farmhouse. Peter saw this activity from an upstairs window. There was more than a hint of concern in his voice when he asked me why the hole was being dug. I told him it was to bury the mailbags and rubbish.

'Oh!' he said with obvious relief, 'is that what its for?' Peter was still troubled by the fact that he hadn't been given the time to drive the train and he assured me more than once that he could have done the job had he been given the chance. Subsequently I've been told that the engine had been modified in the weeks before the robbery, something we did not know, and no amount of waiting for the pressure to build would have helped Peter.

Peter was a loveable old man and I am happy that he never had his collar felt by Old Bill. He would not have survived in the nick and it was nice to think that at least he and three other members of the gang got to enjoy the spoils from that night's work with their families.

While it was felt unwise to use the Land-Rovers we decided to carry on with painting the truck in case it was needed as a last resort. Jimmy White and a helper set to with brushes and a can of canary yellow paint to disguise the khaki truck. This yellow paint would be the undoing of Gordon Goody at the trial after samples from the crushed can at the farm had been matched to those found on his shoes, only the shoes the police presented at the trial which had been taken from Gordon's house had never been any where near the farm. You can draw your own conclusion.

Quiet, chain-smoker Roger Cordrey put it to the gang that he could nip out on the bike he had thoughtfully brought along, to see what was going on in the neighbourhood and buy a newspaper and some more fags.

He would also make a couple of necessary calls to set up his own escape. If Roger was anything he was unobtrusive, so there was no objection to him going for a spin, especially as we all had the concern of how we could get away from the farm. It was agreed he would return in the morning.

The gang gathered to discuss the options and what our next move might be. The original plan had been to lie low, passing a week or so in the sun. One thing was for certain. Old Bill was flat out on the case and the 'Heavy Mob' were involved. The unanimous decision was that we should get away from the farm and the general area as soon as possible. Bruce encouraged everyone to wipe the place down.

"No dabs are to be left".

As nothing could be done until the following day we sat around drinking warm beer. It was then that somebody remembered it was my birthday. Each of the gang congratulated me and I was asked what it felt like to finally have made the Big-Time?

It had been a memorable day. Many of us had been without sleep for nearly thirty-six hours and it was beginning to show. We bedded down for the night, but the atmosphere was not as it had been on the eve of the robbery. It was hot and it was difficult, despite the exhaustion, to sleep.

AFTERMATH AND CAPTURE

£1,000,000! Biggest Ever Mail Robbery

Evening Standard, 8 August 1963

Balaclava and the 40 Thieves

Daily Sketch, 9 August 1963

I was clearly nicked. They don't send a car unless you're nicked.

Ronnie Biggs

Roger Cordrey cycled to Oxford, some 12 miles from the farm, and booked himself into a small hotel. The Thursday evening paper told him everything he needed to know. He had been involved in one of the largest robberies ever. Given his reputation for being able to stop trains he knew it wouldn't be long before Old Bill was knocking at his door. And if Old Bill knew of his reputation so did some of his friends who went back on promises to help after seeing the papers and hearing the news.

Back at the farm we had awoken early from our fitful sleep. After a breakfast of eggs, sausages, bacon and more of Peter's tea the 'cleaners' got to work washing everything with great care and attention.

Early on Friday morning Bruce and John Daly set off on foot to hitch-hike or get a bus to Thame where they could arrange to get some sort of transportation to come out from London. Luck was with them and an elderly man soon picked them up. Needless to say, the conversation turned to the robbery, about which the old man had some strong views.

'The scoundrels should be horse-whipped,' he declared vehemently.

'Too good for them,' replied Bruce in a similar tone. 'They need to be given a taste of the cat.'

During the day we continued to listen to the news broadcasts. The police were now certain that we were still in the area. All police units had been mobilized to take part in a massive search which would cover a thirty-mile radius from the robbery site. The farm was just twenty-eight miles from Bridego Bridge by road and 17 miles as the crow flies. The public were invited to get in touch with the police if they had seen or heard anything of a suspicious nature about the time of the robbery.

We were becoming more nervous and there was further speculation about what should be done in the event of Old Bill turning up on the doorstep. The most important thing would be to put out their radio - a pick handle would do the trick - cop for the cozzers and tie 'em up, then hide the car. But then what?

Suddenly a car came racing up the lane to the farmhouse. Everybody took up their positions as it stopped in a swirl of dust by the front door.

'I thought that might make you jump,' said a smiling Roger Cordrey as he emerged from a Wolsey he had bought in Oxford to replace the bike. Roger was back for his whack, but the news was mixed. 'Old Bill's flying about all over the place,' he reported, 'but at least there are no road blocks.' He spread the evening and morning papers on the kitchen table.

'Look fellas. We've hit the headlines.'

After some discussion Buster decided we should club together and pay a man to take care of the farm after we had left - if necessary he should burn it to the ground. Sadly, for most of us, the police got to Leatherslade Farm before the 'dustman'. Without the evidence they collected or said they collected at the farm the Yard would have had no case, just speculation.

First to leave the farm were Roger and Mr One, travelling in Roger's newly acquired car.

Just after dusk Bruce and John returned to the farm driving an Austin Healey apiece. A middle-aged woman at the wheel of a van accompanied them. Bruce told Peter to get his bags; he would be travelling with John and the lady, who had been introduced to me as Mary Manson, who would take Bruce and John's share which was to be hidden amongst furniture in the back of the van. I would go with Bruce and my dough in one of the Healeys; the other one was to be taken by Jimmy White.

We made our hasty goodbyes in the hope of never seeing one another again. And then we were on our way, the nippy sports cars growling along the country lanes. Not a sign of Old Bill.

Happy days were here again!

On the way to Redhill, Bruce and I talked about our plans for the future. I visualized dribbling some money into my 'on a shoestring' building business. I needed plant such as ladders and scaffolding and perhaps, later on, a smarter looking van for Biggs & Stripp. And, of course, I wanted to make sure that my sons got a good education.

I asked Bruce if he was going to get out of the business.

'I don't think so,' he said with half a smile, 'I'll probably look around for something bigger and better.' He also spoke of the importance of a sound education for his son. 'I think I'd like him to become an eminent Queen's Counsel,' he joked.

We made a short stop near London Airport so that I could tell Charm that her loving lord and very clever husband was on his way home. In a relieved but anxious voice she asked me if I had recently been in the company of a friend who wore spectacles. I told her I had and that he was in the car.

'Now I know,' she said.

Mary Manson had followed Bruce's Austin Healey back from the farm and at Horley we stopped to go our individual ways. I shook hands with old Peter and wished him well. We agreed not to be in touch until the dust had settled.

Charm was all done up in her Sunday best when when Bruce and I arrived at 37 Alpine Road in Redhill. She gave Bruce a shy hello and eyed the two kitbags standing in the middle of her neatly-kept kitchen where she had even prepared something for us to eat.

'What's that?' she asked.

'Money. It's all money,' I replied yanking open the drawstring on the kitbag and pulling out a few bundles of fivers for her to see.

'What a clever husband! And what a clever friend!'

We were all took excited to touch the food and eventually Bruce left, promising to give me a 'tinkle' in the near future. I wouldn't see my good friend for another twenty-nine years, until we met again in Rio.

I would not see my brother Jack, either. Charmian waited for Bruce to leave before telling me that my brother - fifteen years my senior - had died of a heart attack on the eve of the robbery. His wife, Winnie, had been in touch to ask if I could attend the funeral. Charm told her that I was somewhere in Wiltshire engaged in a tree-felling job, the story I had given her and Ray Stripp to account for my absence. Winnie suggested that Charm should contact the Wiltshire Constabulary to see if they could find me. All I had told Charm was that I would be in the vicinity of Devizes. Charm had contacted Redhill Police Station and asked for help in tracing her husband. The call had been logged in the 'Occurrence Book' and a search had been carried out in Wiltshire but there had been no sign of Charmian's 'clever husband'.

The next morning after my first decent sleep in what seemed like weeks we tipped the contents of the kitbags out onto the bedroom floor.

'What would have happened to me and the kids if you had been caught?' Charm asked as the realization of what had happened sank in. 'We can't keep it in the house you know. Where are you going to hide it?'

I assured her that she had nothing to worry about and that everything had been thought of. It hadn't, of course. First, however, we had to go through all the money to make sure that none of the notes had any kind of identifying mark on them.

'It smells awful,' she said.

'But it looks divine,' I countered.

We went through the pile note by note setting to one side any that were in any way suspicious. With a little reluctance we had to burn a pile of more than £700 in the kitchen stove, that is over £10,000 at today's values, later digging in the ash around the rose bushes.

I packed £40,000 in blue five pound notes into a suitcase, £60,000 in mixed notes into another and the rest into a holdall. I had three 'minders' who I was hoping I could trust with my cash and made arrangements by telephone to meet these people the following day. Charm and I kept a modest amount to pay off some bills and to have a private celebration - for my birthday if anyone wanted to know.

Charmian's sister, Rosalind, was invited to baby-sit for us so that we could have our night out. We took a train to London where for the first time ever I was quite happy to join Charm window-shopping.

We were wandering around Soho when we saw a notice on a newsstand: 'Train Robbery Latest. Police Hunt the Weasel'.

Although Roy James' nickname had been The Weasel, this Weasel did not turn out to be anyone I knew, so I was not unduly worried. I bought the newspaper anyway. The Weasel was described as a well-known figure in the underworld and, as usual, the police were 'acting on a tip-off.' The news was not sufficient to put us off a splendid Indian meal. Wined and dined, we caught the last train back to Redhill without giving the robbery or the Weasel a second thought.

I was up bright and early on the Sunday morning and went out to buy all the newspapers, certain that they would give the robbery their full attention. From what I read Old Bill didn't seem to be making much headway with their enquiries, but much was being made of the 'battered' driver.

A friend in the building business turned up in his pick-up truck soon after 9 a.m. and the suitcase containing £60,000 was put in the back and covered by a tarpaulin. I gave my friend a carrier bag holding £5000 which was the amount agreed upon for him to baby-sit the money 'until further notice'.

I arranged to meet a second friend just after noon in the saloon bar of his favourite pub in Horley, a short distance from Redhill and not a million miles from old Peter's home. I called a mini-cab and casually handed the driver a suitcase holding £40,000 to put into the boot of the car. When we got to the pub my friend was waiting for me, greeting me with a strong handshake and a warm smile. He was also to receive a £5000 'drink' for his troubles.

I felt like a drink myself, so after the delivery I dropped in on one of my favourite watering-holes in Redhill. Sally, the barmaid, was ringing up a sale on the cash register as I approached. She was looking closely at a one pound note that a customer had handed her, comparing it with a list of serial numbers by the side of the till. The fellow wanted to know why.

'I've got a list of numbers of notes that were stolen from the train and this might be one of them,' she told the customer.

'I wish it was,' he laughed.

I complimented Sally and asked her for a double Scotch handing her a recently 'earned' five-pound note. She tucked the fiver straight into the till draw and was just preparing my change when the customer drew her attention to the fact that she had not compared my note with the list.

'I don't have to check money that Ron hands me, I know him too well,' she said.

With the money out of the house I started to feel more relaxed. I told Charmian to go and buy herself some new clothes and shoes from the £500 that I had won on the horses. Unbeknownst to me, Charms purchases in Bond Street were to bring my name to the attention of the investigating officers for the first time.

On the Monday I was back at work lying furiously about the tree-felling job that had paid so handsomely. My partner, Ray Stripp, had told our motley crew of workers about my good fortune on the horses and it was pints all round at lunch. There was a lot of joking about the train robbery and, like most of the country, we toasted the robbers.

That same Monday the police had been contacted by a farm labourer and told about a suspicious looking truck parked in a farm not thirty miles from the scene of the robbery. At first the police added the information to their list of calls but the caller was persistent. On the morning of Tuesday 13 August the police found the farm. PC John Woolley was the man to go in the record books as the first policeman to visit the farm.

'The place is one big clue,' the police told reporters.

The evening papers also announced that chief of the Flying Squad, Detective Chief Superintendent Thomas 'Tommy' Butler, the so-called 'Grey Ghost', was now in charge of the train robbery enquiry.

The following evening we hear on the news that Roger Cordrey had been arrested in Bournemouth.

Roger's capture, along with a man called Billy Boal, who I had never heard of, was a blow, but I still felt comfortable that I would not immediately be amongst the suspects. Charmian was not altogether sharing my confidence and when, a few days later, a suitcase containing £100,000 was found in the woods by Dorking - scant miles from where we were living - she really got an attack of the 'nadgers'. Worse was to come, as four days after the Dorking find the police discovered a substantial sum of money concealed in the panelling of a caravan in nearby Box Hill - and Jimmy White's fingerprints to boot.

In August 1963 it seemed as if everyone was talking about the train robbery. Mick Bone, a paper-hanger who had worked for me on several occasions, sidled up to me one day; he knew that I had been in prison.

'I bet you wish you had been in on that train business Biggsy,' he said. 'Two-and-a-half million quid! 'Old Bill will never catch those blokes, they're bloody pros - they're all out of the country by now and bloody good luck to 'em. That's what I say!'

Exactly two weeks after the robbery, on 22 August, Charlie Wilson was arrested at his home in London, The arrest came on the same day that Scotland Yard was circulating mug-shots of Bruce, Jimmy White, Roy James, Buster Edwards and Charlie to the press. Now Charm and I were tuned into all news broadcasts on the radio and television. Families and friends of the men who the police were hoping could 'help them with their enquiries' would most certainly be investigated and visited, and as I knew that I was on Bruce's prison record as one of his 'associates' it would not be long before Old Bill came calling.

Inspector Basil Morris and Sergeant Church were from Reigate police station.

They came to see me at 6.45 p.m. on 24 August just to make a few 'routine enquiries'. I tried to look pleased to see them and invited them through to the living room. Charmian offered to make a cup of tea and gave me a glum look as she went to the kitchen.

Inspector Morris lost no time in getting down to the nitty-gritty of his routine enquiries.

'Now, Ron, when did you last see this chappie Bruce Reynolds we're looking for?'

'Bruce? I haven't seen him for about four years or more,' I said, lying through my teeth. 'The last time I saw him was when we were both in Wandsworth. Bruce went out before I did and I haven't seen him since.'

The questions flowed and so did the lies. The inspector told me that the local police had been keeping tabs on me and that he, for one, was glad to see that I had 'settled down to life on the straight and narrow'. He said he didn't have a search warrant but would I mind if he had a look around.

He was a 'friendly' policeman with a disarming manner. He admired our kitchen but took the opportunity to check in the Bendix washing machine which, he said, he had been thinking of getting for his 'better half'. He also checked out the stove where Charm and I had recently sent 700 quid up in smoke.

He checked the bedrooms, opening cupboards and wardrobes, then expressed a desire to take a look in the loft. I got him a stepladder and a torch and held the ladder while he climbed up into my workshop.

'Any sign of Bruce, Mr Morris?' I joked.

'No, Ron,' he answered evenly. 'No sign of Bruce.'

Next it was the garden that attracted Morris' attention and he made a beeline for the coal shed. I had recently had half a ton of coal delivered and upon seeing it the friendly Inspector gave me a probing look.

'You wouldn't be trying the oldest trick in the book, now would you Ron?'

I admit a delivery of coal in early August may have been a little strange but my coal was clean, so to speak.

'I think you're on the level Ron,' Inspector Morris concluded. 'But I am going to ask you for a little favour. If this fellow Reynolds should get in touch I'd like you to string him along. He's on the run and he's going to need somewhere to hide and I think there's a good chance he'll be calling on you. If he does, give me a bell at the station. I'll make it worth your while. You help me and I'll help you. Have we a deal?'

I breathed a sigh of relief as they went on their way. I thought I had handled the situation rather well. Charm was less impressed by my performance. She said I had gone a rather interesting shade of green when I had opened the door to our visitors.

Unbeknown to me the police thought they had their man the previous evening when they had swooped on the Grand Hotel in Leicester after a tip of from the receptionist. They had dragged a man they believed to be Bruce from his bed at 2 a.m, only it wasn't Bruce, it was Gordon Goody. Gordon was taken down to Aylesbury and interviewed by Butler, but then to his surprise he was allowed to go. Butler even giving him a lift back into London.

Soon it was September and there was less and less mention of the train robbery in the media. As far as Charmian and I were concerned no news was good news. I went about my business as normally as was possible, returning to work on converting a house into three flats. Biggs & Stripp were in action anything from 'penthouses to pussy-flaps'. The days were still warm - these were almost the halcyon days.

On the afternoon of 4 September one of my painters, Joe, asked if he could borrow the company van to take his wife to the pictures. I had no objections as long as he dropped me home and picked me up in the morning.

He dropped me off outside my house. Alpine Road was deserted as I walked down the side of the house and went in by the backdoor. Two men were in the kitchen. Old Bill!

One of them reached behind me and locked the backdoor, putting the key in his pocket.

'We are police officers,' he announced matter-of-factly. 'We are in the process of searching your house - we have a search warrant. We want you to be present when we take up the floorboards in the front room.'

This was not a time to be clever. It was a time when silence is often golden. I caught a glimpse of Charm who was looking very distressed. She tried to say something but was told to keep quiet. I could hear Nicky kicking on the door of his room and calling for me. It should have been play time.

Burly cops with their shirtsleeves rolled up were attacking the living room floor with crowbars. The policeman who had greeted me in the kitchen identified himself as Detective Chief Inspector Frank Williams and began a search of my person during which he appeared to find nothing of interest.

'I want you to show me the contents of a cupboard on the landing upstairs,' he said. 'I believe that's where you keep the tins of paint?'

Slightly bemused by this request, I was none the wiser after he showed a particular interest in yellow paint. A number of gallon tins were taken from the cupboard and marked up.

Nicky could hear me talking outside his room and was now shouting for me to open the door. Like his father he did not like to be locked up. I asked Williams if it would be okay to say hello to my son.

'No,' he said firmly. 'You are to be taken to the police-station to make a statement.' Another cop was told to fetch the car which was parked close to the entrance of my house. Then, wedged between Williams and another beefy detective, I was bundled into the car and driven off.

Later I discovered that one of the policemen to visit my house that day was a young detective called Jack Slipper. A name that I was going to get to know rather well in the coming years.

After leaving Alpine Road we took the wrong turning to go into Redhill where the local police station was located. I pointed this out to Williams.

'I know,' he said, with just the slight trace of a smile. 'We are not going to Redhill, we are going to Scotland Yard.'

We drove along Frenches Road and past The Jolly Brickmakers. How long, I wondered, was it going to be before I saw these familiar sights again? I was clearly nicked. They don't send a car unless you're nicked.

'You're very quiet, Mr Biggs,' Williams said sarcastically as we sped towards London. 'Nothing bothering you is there?'

At the Yard I was taken directly to see 'Tommy' Butler, the so-called 'Grey Ghost', who was now in charge of the train robbery enquiry. He pointed to a chair in front of his desk.

'Sit down,' he said. 'I have here a questionnaire. I'm going to ask you the questions and write down your answers.

I told Butler not to waste his time.

'It's only for your antecedents,' he added hoping to make it all look routine. 'Have you ever heard of Leatherslade Farm?'

'Of course I have heard of Leatherslade Farm, it's been on television every night for the last month.'

'Do you know Buckinghamshire well?' he pressed.

'Yes, I was stationed at two different camps in Buckinghamshire when I was in the Royal Air Force,' I admitted.

Butler started writing. Williams was at his side as a witness.

'Look,' I repeated, 'I told you I'm not answering any questions.'

Butler looked mean and leaned forward. 'Alright, I know it's a big one and you've got to keep your mouth shut, but I'm going to charge you with the train robbery. I've got you by the bollocks lad and what I don't know I shall make up - do you understand what I mean?'

'Perfectly,' I nodded.

A fast car was ordered up and Williams was told to 'take this bugger to Aylesbury and charge him'.

Charged, I was and photographed and fingerprinted and locked in a dark, dank cell.

'Turned out nice again!' I thought to myself.

'Act smart!' hissed Mr. Butler, 'while you've got the bleeding chance.
'A prison cell's awaiting you, not the South of fucking France
'Now, turn against your mates, lad, and I'll get you off with ten.
'Just write down their names for me - here, use my fountain pen.'
'Do you know what you can do?' I said, scared shitless, grey but grim,
'Go and write a letter to your favourite fag,' and I pushed it back to him.
'Alright, I'm going to charge you with - er - conspiracy to rob.
'I know the phrase sounds fancy - but then, so was the job.
'You're going to prison for twenty years!' His voice rose to a shout.
'You'll be fit for Sweet Fanny Adams by the time they let you out.'
Well charged I was - and printed, my soul suffused with pain.
I'd gone from rags to riches - and back to rags again.
Then swiftly off to Bedford nick, into the Flowery Dells.
Late night, sombre silence, foul, familiar smells.

Ronald Biggs

Charmian and I on our wedding day, 20 February 1960.

Early mug shot.

Love Birds. With Charmian in 1958.

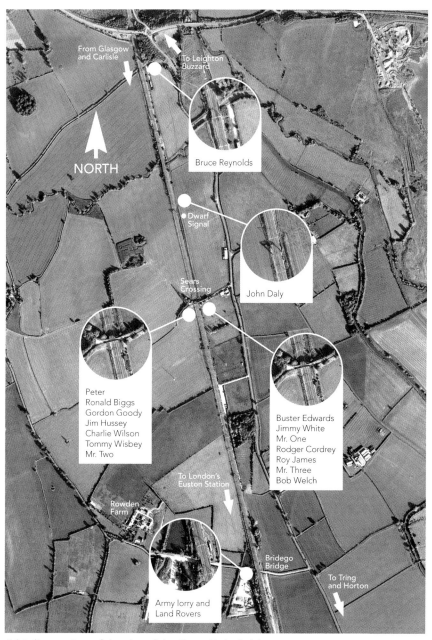

From Glasgow and Carlisle

To Leighton Buzzard

NORTH

Bruce Reynolds

Dwarf Signal

John Daly

Sears Crossing

Peter
Ronald Biggs
Gordon Goody
Jim Hussey
Charlie Wilson
Tommy Wisbey
Mr. Two

Buster Edwards
Jimmy White
Mr. One
Rodger Cordrey
Roy James
Mr. Three
Bob Welch

To London's Euston Station

Rowden Farm

Bridego Bridge

To Tring and Horton

Army lorry and Land Rovers

A bird's-eye view of the site of the Great Train Robbery.

After the robbery the train was taken down the line to Cheddington Station.

Leatherslade Farm was discovered on 13 August 1963. You can see the lorry and Land Rovers we left behind, the lorry now a nice shade of yellow!

Colour Plate 4

Monopoly money from the farm.

I am well and truly nicked!

Monopoly pieces from Leatherslade Farm used in evidence.

My prison file from HMP Wandsworth.   *Time to move. But I left the van behind.*

Free man. With Charmian in Bognor in October 1965.

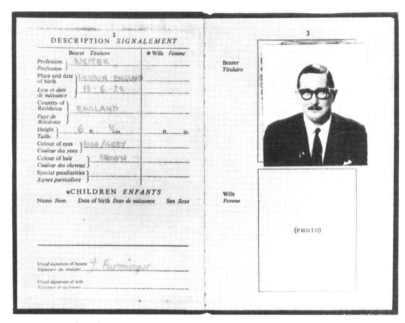

My passport to freedom as Terence Furminger.

Charmian and I (with my new face) reunited in Sydney in 1966.

What is it with boys and trains?

Reunited with Nick and Chris in June 1966

My new boy, Farley.

Charmian in the garden with Nick and Chris.

In the garden of our house in Melbourne. Very happy days.

The boys I left behind and subsequently lost. Chris, Nick and Farley.

TRIALS AND TRIBULATIONS

'And earthly power doth then show likest God's - when mercy seasons justice'

William Shakespeare, *'Merchant of Venice'*.

'Anyone for Anti-wank?' calls the cocoa-boy called, Smart
'It's made with milk and sugar tonight - cross me fookin' 'eart!'
'Evenin' chocolate's noorishin', the bromide meks the boobles.'
Guaranteed to cure the 'orn and all yer dickey troobles.'

Ronald Biggs

The next morning I was up before the beak at Linslade Magistrates' Court, where I was remanded in custody to Her Majesty's Prison Bedford. So convincing was Tommy Butler's manner when he gave his 'evidence' that he almost had me believing the things that I was supposed to have said. Under oath, he declared that when I had been asked about the farm I had replied: 'No. Never heard of it. I've got no interest in fucking farms.' He also told the magistrate that he had no idea as to why I had refused to sign my 'statement'.

As I was led away to my cell I heard a news report on the prison radio. It said that 'Ronald Biggs, a thirty-four-year-old-carpenter of Alpine Road, Redhill appeared before the Linslade magistrate...' I did not catch the rest as the screw conducting me down to the cell had butted in.

'We've got one of your mates here, Charlie Wilson,' he said.

'Charlie Wilson? Never heard of him,' I replied.

The next day when we were unlocked for exercise I saw both Charlie Wilson and Roger Cordrey in the yard. We ignored each other until the exercise was over. Charlie then said in a loud voice for all to hear: 'Aren't you the bloke who's been charged with the train robbery?'

'Yeah,' I said, 'but I had nothing to do with it.'

'Incredible,' said Charlie. 'I've been charged with that too. Bloody liberty.'

One by one the ranks of the 'innocents' swelled. First Jimmy Hussey, then Tommy Wisbey, who was quickly followed by Bobby Welch. None of us had any idea what evidence there was against us or how they came to pick our names. We were allowed visits, but we were all extra cautious as it was suggested that the visiting cubicles might be bugged.

Charmian came to see me and I was glad to see that at least by appearances she seemed to be weathering the storm reasonably well. During her second visit she told me that one of her friends, Jean Jarrard, was having a fling with a cop attached to Scotland Yard. He told Jean, after a bit of priming, that the evidence against us were the fingerprints found at Leatherslade Farm. Bob, Tommy and Jim, who had been three of the 'cleaners' at the farm, wouldn't hear of it.

'It's all bollocks,' said Bob firmly. 'If Old Bill produces fingerprints, then it's a fit-up.' Jim and Tom agreed, swearing that nothing had been overlooked during the clean-up operation.

They were almost right as even the forensic boys have admitted that the house was remarkably clean from having housed a gang as large as ours. It was only after they had dusted the more unlikely places, such as the Monopoly set, which we could easily have taken with us, that they found anything of worth.

The three of the gang who arrived at the farm wearing gloves and who had the sense and discipline not to remove them were never caught. What prints Peter may have left behind could never be traced as he had no previous record for them to be matched against and the Old Bill did not know that they were looking for a second driver. The fact that they did know which prints to look for, however, raises a few questions. It is almost certain that some disgruntled person who knew about the job but who had been left out pointed the finger. A finger that pointed to Bruce and by association to me.

A 'fit-up', by the way, is the introduction of false or manufactured evidence at the scene of a crime. Back in the mid 60s a certain detective by the name of Harry Challenor had grabbed three young lads during a street disturbance and charged them with 'Being in possession of an offensive weapon', the weapon being a piece of brick. The kids denied the charge saying that they were not found with pieces of brick in their possession when they were taken into custody. Not to be made a liar, Mr Challenor produced a brick and a hammer and broke the brick in front of the boys.

'An offensive weapon for you,' he said. 'One for you. And one for you.'

At the trial an alert defence lawyer noticed that the three 'offensive weapons' fitted neatly together. What did not fit very neatly together was the fact that until they had been arrested the three boys hadn't known each other, as they came from different parts of London. They were sent home and a little later Harry Challenor took his turn in the dock. He had been overworking, the court was told, and he really was a very fine officer having been awarded this, that and the other for his dedication in the fight against crime. He was sentenced to a spell in a rest home – which just goes to show that while we are all supposed to be equal in the eyes of the law a few remain more equal than others.

Gordon Goody was the next to feature in the news. The police had taken him in for questioning early on, when then hotel receptionist in Leicester had mistaken him for Bruce, but after being interviewed by Butler no case or charges were brought against him and he was released. Butler even drove him home. Gordon then surprised us by turning up in Bedford to visit Charlie. I'm not certain to this day why he took the risk but he had a message for me from Bruce and that was to let his solicitor, George Stanley, take care of my defence. Until then, as a poor, struggling carpenter, I had been granted Legal Aid. But I decided to take Bruce's advice.

During the time in Bedford I tried to get the group interested in an escape. The wall to the prison was not very high and there were more than enough of us to take care of the screws that supervised the exercise.

But everyone still thought that they had a good chance of 'slipping out of it' - even when told about the fingerprint evidence - so the opportunity was lost.

Somebody was obviously reading my thoughts, because very soon after my proposal to escape we were transferred en masse to Aylesbury Prison. The hospital wing had been cleared of patients and we were put into cells that had barred observation flaps on the doors. Experienced screws were selected from different prisons around England to take care of us. Security, at first, was tight.

Just before the transfer, solicitor's managing clerk, Brian Field, and his boss, John Wheater, were arrested in connection with the sale of Leatherslade Farm, and at the beginning of December, Bruce's brother-in-law, John Daly was arrested in Eaton Square. John had dressed the part and was wearing a bowler hat, city suit and sporting a prodigious black beard. After a brief court appearance he too was sent on to Aylesbury. A week later, on 10 December, it was the turn of Roy James to fall into Butler's grasp after what was reported to be a dramatic roof top chase in St. Johns Wood.

The police had even stumbled upon Bruce after a neighbour had reported a ladder propped up against a house. Frances Reynolds had opened the door to them, but Bruce had the presence of mind to take off all his clothes and play the part of the cheating lover. Franny explained to the slightly uncomfortable policemen that she was a married woman and her boyfriend had come to stay with her for a day or so, and that she would be ruined if his presence ever became known. The two policemen, thoroughly understood, took their names and gallantly withdrew. It was not until they got back to the nick to check the names that they realised the names were not only false, but they had just had the World's Number One Wanted Criminal and his wife standing in front of them.

With no Bruce in custody, but 19 other people being held on various charges, Butler told the media that he was ready to start the court case. After a time security in Aylesbury was relaxed somewhat and we spent our time playing cards and chess, listening to the radio and getting to know one another rather better than had been possible at the time of the robbery.

Our legal representatives visited us all regularly. George Stanley also had the professional pleasure of taking care of Johnny Daly's defence. Stanley confirmed that the main evidence against us was the fingerprints found at Leatherslade Farm. Stanley suggested that I should admit to having been to the farm prior to the robbery, but only in my capacity of a carpenter, to construct a whipping-post for 'kinky' parties. He told John to plead guilty and hope for leniency.

'George is right,' said John after we had spoken to him. 'If fingerprints have been found at the farm we haven't got a leg to stand on. I think I'll take his advice: plead guilty and hope to cop a shorter sentence.' We all begged to differ.

'You'd be potty if you pleaded guilty,' said Bobby Welch. 'Plead not guilty and you've got a chance - we might be able to knobble someone on the jury. If you plead guilty, you're fucked!'

We really had to work on John to make him see that he was making the wrong decision. Finally he agreed to plead not guilty. The only one among us who was obliged to plead guilty was Roger Cordrey, as he had been caught 'bang to rights' with his share of the loot.

The majority of the gang thought that they still had a reasonable chance of slipping out of the charges against us, a view that was not shared by Gordon Goody, Charlie Wilson and Ronnie Biggs! We began to put together an escape plan.

God knows how or why, but Charlie had been put to work in a small kitchen in the hospital wing. His job was to prepare snacks and hot drinks for the screws. Two officers patrolled the prison yard at night and were accustomed to getting a mug of cocoa passed out to them through the bars of one of the cells. It was decided that these two screws would have to be drugged to facilitate our plan. Once the guards were in the Land of Nod, friends would come over the wall and Bob's your uncle. Roger Cordrey, who had spent a large part of his life in the horseracing world, was consulted for information as to the best type of dope for the job in hand. He knew exactly what was required and from where it could be obtained: tasteless and colourless, satisfaction guaranteed. Charlie was enthusiastic: knocking the screws out by hand - or by dope - would give him great pleasure. That was until Brian Field appeared reading from his Archbold's Criminal Law and Practice: 'For administering a stupefying drug: up to fourteen years imprisonment.'

'Fuck that!' said Charlie. 'Back to the drawing board!'

The screws that took care of us in Aylesbury prison were changed every month. Most of them were an unhappy lot and being away from their homes didn't do much to improve their humour. One exception was Paddy, a fine fella from County Cork. One evening when he came on duty he looked into my cell and saw that my table was laden with a selection of cold meat and cheeses plus a couple of bottles of Carlsberg 'Special Brew' lager.

'Sure, you fellas are livin' like lords,' said Paddy, 'I think I'm in the wrong game.'

'Hello Paddy,' I greeted him, 'fancy a beer?' The Irishman took the slender bottle and slid it into a pocket at the side of his trousers where his truncheon should have been. He thanked me, saying that he would drink it later.

'Y'know,' he said, lowering his tone, 'I've got a lot of admiration for you and your mates.' I felt I knew what was coming next. 'I'd be prepared to help you lads - if you needed anything. But I wouldn't bring in any guns or dope.'

'Come off it, Paddy. You know that we're not into anything like that. But I would be interested in getting hold of a miniature radio.' So we talked about a price and a place where the deal could be done. As I knew Aylesbury fairly well from my days in the Royal Air Force I was able to arrange for a friend to meet Paddy outside a certain cinema at eight in the evening. He would pass over a tiny 'Ruby' radio and receive an envelope containing £100, now worth around £1500. Paddy was delighted - and so were Gordon and Charlie when I told them that we had a sympathizer in our midst. A contact was made with a legendary key-maker, known as Johnny The Bosh. He only had to know the make of the lock to come up with a blank key that was sure to fit. This information was duly passed out and the key was produced and handed to one of Gordon's pals. During the next couple of weeks, hacksaw blades, a one-inch wood chisel, a watch, the blank key and a set of needle files were smuggled into the Maximum

Security Wing of HMP Aylesbury. All that we needed to put our plan into operation was a copy of the key that unlocked the doors to our cells.

Security slackened off during the months we had spent on remand. The hearings at the Magistrates' Court were over and we had all been committed for trial. We associated most of the day, only being locked in our cells during lunchtime and after 9 p.m. The screws were generally easy to get along with, although some were not very happy about the amount of 'freedom' we were given. Friendly screws often played games of cards or chess with us, and it was during one of these fraternal moments that Goody was able to exercise his artistic skills.

As a guard and I sat facing each other, pitting our wits over the chessboard, Gordon came along, sketchpad in hand, and asked the screw if he had any objection to being drawn in this somewhat remarkable pose. Permission granted, Goody started sketching away, telling us how he planned to publish a book of his drawings 'when he got out'.

'Make a bomb!' he predicted.

The screw sitting across the chessboard from me was so engrossed in the black and white armies in front of him, that he paid no attention to the bunch of keys hanging from his belt: in the meantime Goody was filling in the details, from time to time complimenting my adversary on his strategic expertise. With the aid of his sketches and the needle files, Goody produced the key we needed overnight. The following morning, whilst someone kept the screws occupied with some trivial matter, Goody tested his handiwork on the door of my cell. It turned the lock first time!

It was a 'goer'!

Roger Cordrey, Billy Boal (whose only crime was to give Roger a lift and help him hide the money, and who had been arrested at the very beginning along with Roger) and Brian Field shared a dormitory at one end of the first floor of the hospital wing. The door was not like the cell doors, which were faced with sheet metal on the inside. The dormitory door was fitted with a flimsy mortise lock and there was no metal facing. Anyone on the inside would have little trouble cutting the wood and removing the lock altogether. As Roger and Brian were not anxious to participate in the planned escape, we reluctantly decided to invite Boal to join us.

Ever worried about the welfare of his wife and three children, Boal was only too ready to 'make one'.

All the arrangements were made. Charlie's 'firm' would leave a car at a spot near the back of the hospital. Bill would quietly cut the lock from the dormitory door and get out, unlocking Gordon's cell, which was next-door to the dormitory. Gordon would then unlock Charlie - who was on the same landing - and they would cop for the night watchman, tying him up. Then they would go down to the cells in the basement and unlock me.

Lying under a blanket, fully dressed, I heard the night watchman shuffling around, making his rounds. I could just imagine good old Bill Boal at work on the door - using the chisel as I had shown him. Somewhere a clock struck eleven, then twelve… one… two. At three o'clock I took my clothes off and got into bed: something had obviously gone badly wrong.

For whatever reason, Boal chickened out and laid wide the plot to the chief screw. The screws moved in with a massive search of the cells and their occupants. 'Association' came to an abrupt end and the screws were no longer friendly. Most of the items that had been smuggled in were found and confiscated. The cops were called in and wasted their time asking us questions. All privileges ceased, visiting time was curtailed and foodstuff coming into the prison was restricted to the permitted amount. And for good measure, a pig of a Principle Officer came to the nick to take charge during the Christmas period.

God Rest Ye Merry Gentlemen!

Roger John Cordery, Charles Frederick Wilson, Thomas William Wisbey, Leonard Dennis Field, Douglas Gordon Goody, William Gerald Boal, Ronald Arthur Biggs, James Hussey, Brian Arthur Field, John Denby Wheater and Robert Alfred Welch were charged on divers days unknown between the 1st day of May, 1963, and the 9th day of August, 1963 in the County of Buckingham conspired together and with other persons unknown to stop a mail with intent to rob said mail. Against the Peace of our Sovereign Lady the Queen, Her Crown and Dignity. For that they: Roger John Cordery, Charles Frederick Wilson, Thomas William Wisbey, Leonard Dennis Field, Douglas Gordon Goody, William Gerald Boal, Ronald Arthur Biggs,

James Hussey, Brian Arthur Field, and Robert Alfred Welch on the 8th day of August 1963, in the County of Buckingham being armed with offensive weapons or being together with other persons robbed Frank Dewhurst of 120 mailbags contrary to Section 23 (1)(a) of the Larceny act, 1916.

The trial proper began on 20 January 1964. The judge was one Mr Justice Edmund Davies, a Welshman and one not known for his leniency in dealing with the likes of us.

As the crime had been committed in the county of Buckinghamshire, the venue for the trial was set to be the county town of Aylesbury. The town's Assize Court was far too small to accommodate such a large number of accused, so the local Rural District Council Chamber was converted into the courtroom. A team of carpenters were called in to construct an enormous dock that would be big enough to seat all of us and then as many again to accommodate the accompanying policemen.

Every morning, Monday through Friday, we would be handcuffed and locked into small individual compartments in a police bus, commonly known as a Black Maria. Then with a massive escort which consisted of at least four police cars and a dozen or so motorcycle cops, we would make the ten-minute journey from the prison to the council chamber.

School-kids would wave and give us the thumbs up as we went to-and-fro; in complete contrast, the more elderly inhabitants of the area who would shake their fists as the bus passed.

Never had the town of Aylesbury seen anything quite like it, and I doubt they ever will again.

After the morning hearing we would return to prison in much the same fashion for lunch. At the time we were still having our meals brought into the prison from one of the town's better restaurants and served by the proprietor. One prison officer was heard to grumble: 'Isn't it bloody marvellous! You blokes are eating roast pheasant and jugged hare and here we are, lucky if we get some beans on bloody toast.'

At around 2 p.m. the routine would be repeated and we would be cuffed up and sent off to court for the afternoon session. On our arrival in the courthouse there was always one officious uniformed superintendent who would fuss around us like some giant mother hen telling us to do this and do that, to stop talking, to sit up straight. On and on he went. At one point, early in the proceedings, he produced some squares of cardboard with strings attached which he had numbered from one to twelve. He held one of the cards out to Tommy Wisbey.

'Here, hang this around your neck,' he instructed, 'so that you can be easily identified.'

'Easily identified?' replied Tommy indignantly. 'What do you think this is? A fucking cattle-show? Shove 'em up your arse!'

And that, so to speak, was that, at least as far as the cards was concerned.

The trial proceeded.

The court, packed with reporters, coppers, the public and the accused, would often become stuffy, particularly during the afternoon sessions. A string of bank clerks were early witnesses and they would be lead painstakingly through their earlier statements to the police by the junior prosecutor, Howard Sabin. The aim was for the prosecution to prove that beyond any question of doubt the train in question had been carrying a large sum of money which was subsequently stolen. At times it was hard to stay awake and more than once I saw members of the jury nodding off. My solicitor, George Stanley, had engaged Mr Wilfred Fordham, a barrister, to defend me. Fordham was a kindly old gentleman, highly respected in legal circles.

At one point Fordham's absence from the proceedings, as he catnapped in court, was noted by his Lordship who sat drumming his fingers as he waited for my defence counsel to rejoin us. Charlie Wilson spoke to me about the matter.

'It's really nothing to do with me,' he said, 'but old Wilfred spends every afternoon having a kip. Your liberty is on the line. If I was you I'd get myself someone who's a bit more on the ball.'

Charlie was right, so I spoke to George Stanley about it. Stanley argued in favour of sticking with Fordham - a fine man if it should come to making a plea for leniency, he said - but it was finally decided that a QC would be brought in and Mr Fordham would stay on to assist.

I remember feeling distinctly more optimistic after my first meeting with Michael Argyle, QC. At that time he was the Recorder for Leicester - dishing out bird! A young man, obviously well bred, exuding efficiency and Old Spice. This was more like it!

A hush fell over the court when Jack Mills, the train driver, entered to give his evidence. The judge glared in the direction of the dock as Mills made his way to the witness box and took the oath. He was invited by the judge to give his evidence seated and accepted the invitation. Aided by the prosecutor, Mr Mills described his misadventure when his train was stopped at a point on the line known as, Sears Crossing. The hordes of reporters scribbled away furiously, not wanting to miss a word of the driver's whispered and damming testimony.

Mills was the key figure in manipulating the 'monstrous' nature of our crime. Without him it would have been nigh on impossible for the judge to get away with the sentences he later handed down. I never met Mills personally, so I can only base my impressions on hearsay, but I do know that when the robbery was planned there was never any intention that anyone would get hurt. As Bruce himself has said of the coshing of Mills: 'I feel sorry for Mr Mills. Sorry for the injury he got. It was a mistake that should never have happened.'

One of the people most troubled by Mr Mills' performance in court was not a member of the gang but the wife of my lawyer, Peta Fordham. Mrs Fordham, who went on to write a book, *The Robbers' Tale*, revealed that in an interview with her five years before his death Mills had admitted to her that he had been warned that his 'pension would be affected' if he showed any sympathy in court to the gang or suggested that we had treated him 'like gentleman'. He was also not to admit under any circumstances that his worst head injury came from his fall against the curved steel dashboard which runs under the driver's window and not from a blow to his head from Mr Three. (Though as we were all wearing masks, Mills would not actually have had any idea which of us did cosh him).

After Mills' dramatic court appearance it was left to the guard of the train to provide the court with reason for laughter. He was a talkative witness and the prosecutor had his work cut out to stop him from rambling on about 'railway procedure' and like matters. Describing his duties in the event of his train coming to an unscheduled stop, he told the court that he had left the guard's van and went to place detonators on the line by way of a warning to any train that might be approaching in the same direction. But the gang also knew a thing or two about railway procedure and one of our number had already put detonators on the line.

'When I walked back down the line to place my detonators, what do you think I found?' asked the guard.

The prosecutor smiled politely,

'I am quite certain that the court is itching with curiosity to learn what it was you found.'

'Detonators! Someone had already laid detonators!' There was something else the poor man found; when he hurried to the front of his train he found that the engine and the High Value Package coach were missing!

On the fourteenth day of the trial, my old friend, Detective Inspector Basil Morris, appeared to give evidence. The cross-eyed cop stepped smartly into the witness box, seized the New Testament in his right hand and held it aloft,

'Detective Inspector Basil Morris,' he announced in a loud, clear voice, 'Surrey Constabulary, Reigate CID.'

It was the first time the gang had seen Mr Morris, and Tommy Wisbey, always ready to see the funny side of things, cracked up at the sight of the Inspector.

'Jesus Christ!' he said, sotto voce, 'It's Ben Turpin!' referring to the cross-eyed comedian in the old Mack Sennett movies. He dropped his head into his hands and began to shake with suppressed laughter. Those of us who had heard Tom's crack tried to keep straight faces. Once more the judge glared in our direction. The prosecutor was taking the Inspector through the evidence he had given before a magistrate when I was first charged.

'Did you, Inspector Morris, ask Mr Biggs if he knew any of the men wanted for the train robbery in Buckinghamshire?' he asked.

'I did,' affirmed the Inspector.

'And what did he say?'

'He said: I know Reynolds, I met him when we were doing time together.'

This reply took the prosecutor by surprise, it was not the reply he was expecting or wanted. To enable the jury to return an impartial verdict, it is essential that there must be no indication that the accused has previously been to prison. Telling the court I had 'done time' was quite wrong. Those in the courtroom who were aware of this, looked at Inspector Morris in disbelief, especially the Old Bill who were in charge of the investigation!

Brian Field, who was sitting behind me in the dock, laid a hand on my shoulder. 'Ronnie! You lucky so-and-so!' he said excitedly, 'That entitles you to a retrial!'

Gordon Goody grinned, 'You crafty bastard, Biggsy,' he said softly, 'You had that cozzer straightened!'

My lawyer hurried over to the dock to confer with me about 'the Inspector's unfortunate remark.' I didn't hesitate to tell him I wanted a retrial. I imagined that if I stood accused alone I would have a better chance than standing cheek by jowl with a bunch of obvious thugs. My counsel went off and entered into a whispered conversation with His Lordship, returning to say that the judge did not think that the jury had 'picked up' the Inspector's reference with regard to me having previously been to prison. But I insisted. I wanted a retrial.

The judge gave the order for the jury to be taken from the court then, when the last good man and true had left the council chamber, Mr Justice Davies turned his attention to the hapless Detective Inspector. I almost felt sorry for him, such was the dressing down he received from the judge.

'That the Inspector who, of necessity, must be a man of great experience in his duties, should have so far forgotten his duties as to bring in a phrase of that kind quite gratuitously is grossly improper and cannot be too strongly condemned,' Mr Justice Davies told the court.

I was then discharged from the present trial without a verdict and ordered to be held in custody until the date of a new trial. I nursed a hope that my lawyers could get the venue of my trial changed - perhaps to the Old Bailey - where friends could possibly 'get at' someone on the jury to hold out for a 'not guilty' verdict. But it was decided that to try such a move might well be prejudicial to my situation. It wouldn't do to piss His Lordship off.

So the next day, when the gang were carted off to court, I stayed at the prison, once more the odd man out. I was allowed to pass my days in the company of Roger Cordrey who was also not attending the trial because he had pleaded guilty. He was interesting, intelligent company, with an endless fund of anecdotes about his capers before the train robbery. Unlike myself, in twenty years Roger had only one previous conviction, for embezzlement, that had landed him in Borstal.

Three days after Inspector Morris had made his blunder, the case for the prosecution was closed. It was now up to the defence to make submissions to the judge and jury, offering arguments with regard to the innocence of their respective clients.

On Friday 14 February the defence began. The gang told their stories and produced their witnesses. If they were to be believed, few of the defendants should have been accused in the first place. Gordon Goody, for instance, couldn't have participated in the raid because he had been going about his business smuggling watches. Roy James, late on the night of 7 August, had engaged in a long conversation with a friendly taxi-driver which took them into the wee small hours of the morning of the 8th. And so forth. The trial drifted on into March.

One mid-morning Roger and I heard the main prison gate opening. We went to the window of the dormitory and saw a police car drive in. Minutes later Johnny Daly, the man who wanted to plead guilty, came to the door, trembling and pale faced,

'What's the trouble, John?' I asked, 'are you ill?'

'No, I'm not ill. I've been acquitted!'

'Christ! You've been chucked? That's fantastic!' said Roger delightedly 'How? Why?'

'Reaburn (John's counsel) made a submission to the effect that the Monopoly set could have been taken to the farm after I left my prints on it. The judge accepted that fact and acquitted me. I've just come back to pick up my belongings. I'm free! - but I can't believe it!'

Too bad I wasn't able to share the lucky Irishman's good fortune. My fingerprints were also found on the Monopoly set but also a sauce bottle (I never thought they would 'ketchup' with me). It was the sauce bottle that tied me to the farm. A previous resident at Leatherslade Farm was the key witness and he swore that no such item had been left there.

Most of the explanations given by the gang during the trial for their fingerprints being found at the farm were, at best, ludicrous. Jimmy Hussey's palm print, for example, was found on the tailboard of the truck that was used in the robbery. His story was that an acquaintance had pulled up outside his home driving that very same vehicle. His friend was 'delivering some fruit and veg down the country somewhere' and invited Jim to go along for the ride. Unfortunately, Jim's poor old mum was not very well so he had to take care of her. However, thinking that there might be a nice apple within easy reach, Jim rested his hand against the tailboard...the next thing you know, he's getting tugged in for the train robbery...what a liberty!

My fairy story was even more pathetic. Charmian and I, the court were told, had been given the chance to buy the humble little house we were renting in Redhill. The owner, a retired policeman, had told us that if we could come up with £500 as a deposit we could pay the rest off weekly instead of paying rent. During a trip to London to visit my ailing father, I ran into an old prison chum named, Norman Bickers. I told him about the 'golden opportunity' we had to buy our own home and that all we needed was the down payment. Norman was eager to help, after all we had been cellmates.

It so happened that Norman had been invited to join in 'a little piece of business' - down the country somewhere. He was not at liberty to give me any details, but he was sure that I could take part in the venture. I would be away from home for four or five days, so it would be necessary to concoct some kind of a story to tell my wife. The tree-felling job was Norman's idea. He knew where I lived and he knew Charmian. It would be no problem to convince her that a few days away from home would provide us with the cash for the deposit on the house. It was arranged that I would tell my wife about the job and Norm would pick me up in his car on the morning of 6 August.

Charmian (who had agreed to play her part in this pretty piece of perjury) waved us goodbye as we set out for 'somewhere in Wiltshire' to cut down trees. But instead of driving to Wiltshire we went to Leatherslade Farm in Buckinghamshire. The place was deserted when we got there; but we saw an army truck parked in one of the outbuildings. Inside the house, which was unlocked, we found a great amount of food, sleeping-bags and army uniforms. I didn't like the look of it. I imagined that there was some kind of plan afoot to attack a military installation. I got cold feet and wanted out. But, much like Goldilocks in the house of the three bears, we fixed ourselves something to eat. Hence my fingerprints on the ketchup bottle and a Pyrex plate. After the snack we looked around and found - of all things - a Monopoly set! I opened the box; I hadn't played Monopoly since I was a kid. We decided to get out and go straight back to London, where I spent the next few days with Norman's friend, Brian Morse - another ex-con - arriving back in Redhill on Friday 10 August.

Later, when called upon to substantiate my story before the magistrate, Brian and Norm lied skilfully and convincingly; working hard for the £1000 apiece they were paid.

By now the gang, particularly Hussey, Wisbey and Welch, were feeling less confident about their chances of 'slipping out' of the case. There was some speculation as to what the sentences might be in the event of us being found guilty. According to *Archbold's Criminal Law and Practice*, the maximum term of imprisonment for robbery was fourteen years, but there appeared to be no limit for 'conspiring to rob' the second charge against us. 'Conspiring to blow up a bridge', however, carried a maximum sentence of fifteen years, so it was thought that our conspiracy charge was infinitely less serious. Bob Welch, a shrewd, inveterate gambler, sadly hit the jackpot. 'If we go down,' he predicted 'We'll get thirties - mark my words.'

It was while that I was awaiting my retrial on 26 February that I lost my prized radio. I was lying in my bed quietly listening to Sonny Liston defend his world title in Miami against the then Cassius Clay. Clay won the fight and the title after the sixth round when Liston refused to come out for the seventh. When he did I gave a little whoop of joy, as not only did I like Clay but I had money riding on him with other members of the gang.

Unfortunately the screw outside the door heard my little cry and wanted to know what it was all about. At first I pretended that I could hear the radio being used by the screws in the yard outside my window, but I didn't think he was at all convinced. He wasn't, and the next day while they started pulling my cell apart to look for things that had been smuggled in. They found the radio.

The closing speeches for the defence began on 10 March and ended on Saturday 14 March. The following Monday the judge began his summing-up. It took six days.

On Monday 23 March the jury retired at 3.36 p.m., the 49th working day of the trial, to consider their verdicts, deliberating over their task for two whole days. With the exception of John Wheater, the solicitor Brian Field worked for, all the accused were found guilty on the conspiracy charge. Roy James, Charlie Wilson, Gordon Goody, Jimmy Hussey, Bobby Welch, Tommy Wisbey and Bill Boal (who was nowhere near the train or the farm), were also found guilty of robbery with violence. After hearing the verdicts, the judge decided not to pass sentence until my retrial had taken place.

On the morning of Wednesday 8 April I appeared once again before his Lordship, Mr. Justice Edmund Davies, but with a different jury and at the Assize Court rather than the Rural District Council Chamber. The prosecution went through all the evidence, some but not all of the witnesses were recalled.

Michael Argyle, peering over the top of his half-moon glasses, addressed the court with charm and eloquence in my defence, describing how I 'took fright' at the sight of the army uniforms at Leatherslade Farm.

My case was looking reasonably good until Norman Bickers was called to support my alibi. He had mysteriously disappeared. A private detective was hired to find the missing witness, but to no avail. In the meantime, the foreman of the jury seemed to have taken a distinct dislike to me. The feeling was mutual, whenever I caught his eye I returned his sneer. With my key witness missing I could see the chances of my acquittal were becoming less and less.

In his closing speech to the jury, Mr Argyle made a splendid effort to convince them of my innocence. But, in view of the fact that I had pleaded not guilty, Mr Arthur James, QC, prosecuting for the Crown, had the right to the famous 'last word'. And that word was, 'Bullshit!'

The foreman lapped it up. There was no doubt in my mind what the verdict was going to be if it rested with him alone.

Mr Justice Davies finally summed up, eulogizing at length my learned counsel's manipulation of the English language.

'But, ladies and gentlemen of the jury,' he went on to say, 'let us keep our feet firmly on the ground. What the Crown says is so-and-so. And what the Crown says is this, that and the other.' The jury gaped. Then, off they went to deliberate. It didn't take them long to come back with the verdict: guilty on both counts.

The next morning, 16 April, just over eight months since the robbery, we all left Aylesbury Prison in the Black Maria. This time we were not taken to the Rural District Council Chambers but instead were driven to the old Assize Court and locked into chilly cells beneath the courtroom. A steep, narrow staircase led up to the dock where, one by one, we were called to receive our sentences. Roger Cordrey, who had pleaded guilty, was the first up the steps.

'Roger John Cordrey,' said the judge. 'You are the first to be sentenced out of certainly eleven greedy men whom hope of gain allured. You and your co-accused have been convicted of complicity, in one way or another, of a crime which in it's impudence and enormity is the first of its kind in this country. I propose to do all within my power to ensure it will be the last of its kind; for your outrageous conduct constitutes an intolerable menace to the well-being of society.'

The judge went on at length with a prepared text which was obviously aimed more at the general public's perception of the case than the man in the dock. He referred to the robbery as 'nothing less than a sordid crime of violence inspired by vast greed' and he did not miss the opportunity either to mention the 'nerve-shattered engine driver' whose treatment by the gang had had such a 'terrifying effect on law abiding citizens.'

Mr Justice Davies did, however, recognize that within the gang there were two exceptions, one of which was Roger, which hardly prepared Cordrey for what came next.

'In respect of the four counts,' the judge announced, 'you must go to prison for concurrent terms of 20 years.' Prison officers hustled Roger from the dock and down a second flight of steps that led to a different line of cells as the court took in what the judge had said.

Little Billy Boal, who was neither a conspirator nor one of the robbers, was next to be called for sentence.

'William Gerald Boal,' said His Lordship, 'you, who are substantially the oldest of the accused, have been convicted of conspiracy to rob the mail and of armed robbery itself. You have expressed no repentance for your wrong-doing, indeed, you continue to assert your innocence but you beg for mercy. I propose to extend to you some measure of mercy and I do it on two grounds. Firstly, on account of your age, you being a man of 50, and secondly, because, having seen and heard you, I cannot believe that you were one of the originators of the conspiracy or that you played a very dynamic part in it or the robbery itself… In the light of these considerations the concurrent sentences you will serve are, upon the first count, twenty-one years and upon the second count, twenty-four years.' Boal was the second exception.

Charles Frederick Wilson followed. The judge, now warming to his task, told Charlie: 'It would be an affront to the public weal that any of you should be at liberty in anything like the near future to enjoy any of those ill-gotten gains. Accordingly, it is in no spirit of mere retribution that I propose to secure that such an opportunity will be denied all of you for an extremely long time. Nevertheless, the plea of Mr Wilfred Fordham for a gleam of light at the end of the long dark tunnel to be left for his client, is a plea I intend to heed in respect of all of you. On the first count you will go to prison for twenty-five years and on the second count you will be sentenced to a concurrent term of thirty years.' Charlie was taken down to join Roger and Billy Boal. It was my turn.

'Ronald Arthur Biggs, yesterday you were convicted of both the first and second counts of this indictment. Your learned Counsel has urged that you had no special talent and that you were plainly not an originator of the conspiracy. These and all other submissions I bear in mind, but the truth is that I do not know when you entered the conspiracy, or what part you played. What I do know is you are a specious and facile liar and you have this week, in this court, perjured yourself time and time again, but I add not a day to your sentence on this account. Your previous record qualifies you do be sentenced to preventive detention; that I shall do. The sentence of the court upon you in respect of the first count is one of twenty-five years' imprisonment and in respect of the second count, thirty years imprisonment. Those sentences to be served concurrently.'

The old boy's totally off his rocker, I thought to myself. Only spies get locked away for thirty years. With remission for good behaviour, I calculated, it meant that I was looking to do at least twenty years in the nick! Twice the amount of bird you might get for bumping somebody off, for Christ's sake.

Charmian stood above in the public gallery, pale and shattered. As I was led in the direction of the 'down' staircase I looked up and gave her a wave and a smile. I may have lost a battle but I knew the war was far from over.

'What did you get?' asked Charlie as I joined him and Roger and Billy Boal in the cells.

'Thirty!'

'Same as me. Bill got twenty-four and Roger got twenty on a guilty plea, for fuck sake.'

Wisbey, Welch and Hussey, all sentenced to thirty years, joined us in swift succession. Then came Roy James, bewildered with his thirty-year sentence.

'Who's dead?' he asked. 'Did we kill somebody?'

Swashbuckling, Gordon 'Checker' Goody came down from the court tight-lipped, also with thirty years. Bobby Welch had been right.

Brian Field was sentenced to twenty-five years imprisonment for conspiracy with a concurrent five years for obstructing justice. Leonard Field - no relation to Brian Field - who was paid £500 to 'buy' Leatherslade farm received a similar sentence. John Wheater, Brian Field's boss, who had been only marginally involved in the conveyance of the farm, was sent down for three years.

The gang was demolished. The villains had got their just desserts. Newspapers sold like hot cakes. Meanwhile, back at the nick, they were waiting for us. We were only given time to pick up our personal belongings and shake hands with each other. Then, handcuffed and under heavy police escorts, we were taken individually to different prisons around the country.

I wasn't told where I was going but from road-signs I gathered that my new home - at least for the time - was going to be Her Majesty's Prison in Lincoln.

At 'reception' I exchanged my sports jacket and cavalry twill pants for an ill-fitting 'Special Watch' prison uniform. The cons working in the area were friendly, almost reverent, - never before had they seen anyone with a thirty stretch. I could even feel a certain sympathy from the screws, and the prison medical officer made a joke that he and I could change places - for the right price.

At the time, it was recognized that Lincoln was a 'cushy' nick. The next morning I was presented to the prison governor, who turned out to be none other than the discipline-minded Commander Cook, governor of Lewes gaol when I had been sent there in 1949. It saddened him to see me in front of him under such unhappy circumstances, he said, and it was his unhappy duty to inform me that my earliest possible date of release was 16 February 1984. I laughed. 'The time will soon pass, sir.' I would be fifty-four.

'Really, Biggs,' said the commander in a voice I had never heard back in the old days. 'It's hardly a laughing matter. Now look, if there is anything you need, don't hesitate to ask - I'll help you all I can. And, Biggs, keep the chin up!'

For quite some time there had been various mentions in the newspapers about the possibility of a parole scheme being introduced into the British penal system. Under this scheme prisoners would be eligible for parole after serving just one third of their sentence. Remission, on the other hand, offered a third off the total sentence for good behaviour. Although it was clutching at a straw, and not, at the time, a 'Jack Straw', I told myself that such a scheme would come about, and this had been taken into consideration when the thirty-year sentences had been dished out. Perhaps I would see a light at the end of the tunnel after I had served ten years or so.

On the day we were sentenced, our respective counsels lodged appeals against the severity of the sentences. I didn't entertain high hopes that there would be any reduction - in fact, we were running the risk of having the sentences increased. For the time being, I decided to play it cool.

For the record the trial had lasted 51 workings days over a period of 10 weeks. Evidence had been heard from 264 witnesses and an estimated 2.5 million words had been spoken. The words filled over 30,000 pages of foolscap paper. The 12 jurors, who were paid 50 shillings a day, had examined 613 exhibits and listened to the questions and speeches of the 21 barristers.

In Lincoln I was allowed to exercise with other Special Watch prisoners and offers to help me escape were soon being made. The main wall around the prison seemed much lower than ones I had seen at other nicks, and it appeared to be reasonably easy to put an escape plan together. But I decided to wait until the appeal had been heard before making any moves to 'have it away'. In any case, after less than two weeks in Lincoln I was transferred without explanation to HMP Chelmsford.

At Chelmsford the wall was higher, but the food was better. A friendly prison officer, who was the physical training instructor, noticed that I was pretty much 'out of shape' and arranged for me to have daily workouts in the gymnasium. A fellow Special Watch con, 'Spider' Webb showed interest in my get-fit sessions and approached me with an escape plan that 'couldn't fail'. It sounded good but I told him that I was going to wait until my appeal had been heard before thinking about going over the wall.

Early in July, once again under maximum security conditions, the gang was reassembled in HMP Brixton. On arrival we were immediately placed on Rule 43, which meant that we were to be held incommunicado. We were allowed to exercise, but never more than two or three of us on the yard at any one time. We were supposed to walk separately, in silence, but we took little notice of the screws trying to impose this order. On one of these exercise periods, I found myself in the company of Gordon Goody and Jimmy Hussey. We kept 'bunching-up', as the screws put it, and from time-to-time one of them would stop us to space us out.

'Now keep a space between you, lads,' one said. 'If the governor comes by and sees you all walking together, I'm the one who's going to drop a bollock.' Spacing us out for the fourth or fifth time, the screw said, 'I've been standing here thinking: you three blokes are facing ninety years imprisonment between you!'

'That's right, guv' said Jimmy with a straight face, 'and half a million fucking quid!'

One member of the gang who decided to play it even cooler than I did was Charlie Wilson, who didn't even bother to appear at the Court of Criminal Appeal when the hearing began. Charlie had a plan and that plan included staying put in HMP Winson Green, Birmingham. If he attended the appeal he ran the danger of being transferred to another prison.

The appeals were over, Roger and his friend Bill Boal had their sentences reduced to fourteen years. In Boal's case, the court saw that his physique and temperament did not fit him for a part in the robbery.

The two Fields were 'lucky'. Their appeal against conviction on the conspiracy charge were allowed and they left the court facing only five years. The rest of the appeals were dismissed - including Charlie's, which was heard in his absence. The best was yet to come. The next day I was transferred to HMP Wandsworth, Britain's answer, at the time, to Alcatraz.

As far as HM Government was concerned this was to be my home for at least the next 20 years. Not a happy prospect if you want to get out with all your marbles intact. In the event, as history records, Wandsworth was to be my home for just a few days over one year.

'The same old screws with the same old bull;
'All correct, Sir! Three bags full!'
The same old chief - still scratching his balls,
The same old wit on the whitewashed walls;
'McGinnis was here, ten years hard labour,'
'Do thy bird and love thy neighbour.'
The same sharp cons, the same old slags.
The same old stench of mailbags.
The same old Padre with the same old text:
Make peace with God! - you might be next.

Ronald Biggs

Chapter Five

ESCAPE:
THE MAKING OF A LEGEND

All too soon the shouts of the Screws:
'Unlock the ones! Unlock the twos!
Empty your piss pots then bang up your doors.
Unlock the threes! Unlock the fours!
Downstair transfers to Dartmoor and Norwich.
'old out your plate lad. 'ere comes your porridge.'

Ronald Biggs.

'I have much patience and equanimity but I am rapidly losing both and, quite frankly, rather than finding it more difficult to escape, I am finding it difficult not to!'

Prisoner 2731, Biggs, in a letter from Wandsworth prison to Marcus Lipton, Labour MP for Brixton.

Had I not escaped from Her Majesty's Prison in Wandsworth, South London, there would never have been a 'Ronnie Biggs' to talk about and this is something that is sometimes overlooked.

At the time of the train robbery no one person involved was any more famous than any other. That is at least as far as the general public were concerned, although I am sure that the Yard had its favourites. Admittedly some of us did get a head start with the media: Roy James for being a promising driver, myself for the mistrial, and Bruce and Buster for still being at large at the time of the trial.

But while the man in the street could name the gang to a man during the trial of 1964, fifty years on - and thanks mainly to the media - the names to stick are Biggs and Buster. Those of the right age will remember Charlie Wilson for his escape to Canada and his murder in Spain, and Bruce Reynolds as the brain, but the other names have mostly been forgotten with the passing of time.

In just the same way, in 1966, the British public could name England's World Cup side. Today the players that are remembered are not remembered so much for what they did on the day, but for the combination of other moments that marked their career. One of the moments that marked my career was the escape from Wandsworth Prison in July 1965.

Now you don't have to be a contestant on Mastermind to realize that any man sentenced to thirty years behind bars is going to think at least once about how to escape. Normally, the thought went as far as getting over the wall, what you did after that as one of Britain's most wanted criminals was a bridge to be crossed when you came to it.

When I was first sentenced I was given about five minutes to talk to Charmian before being taken off to the cells. She was upset and crying, but I told her not to be like that as she, more than anyone, should know that I was not going to stick around and spend a lot of time in prison if I didn't have to. I would be out the first chance I got.

I wasn't being totally sincere with Charm or myself, however, as at the time I honestly did believe that a parole scheme would come about and if it only meant doing ten years then I was going to do those ten years and get them out the way as fast as I could. The only way to do that was to keep my nose clean. That is what I tried to indicate to the authorities when I got to Wandsworth, but I think they took it with a pinch of salt; given my record. The idea of Biggs keeping his nose clean, was a little hard for them to contemplate.

I think all the members of the gang knew that whoever escaped first would have the best chance of getting away with it, as once a couple of us had got away the security around the rest would become much tighter. Yet at the time, all of us would have considered that escaping from an HM Prison was something of a doddle. If it was easy to stop and rob a train it was even easier to escape from the nick. It was not a question of 'if' we would get out, but 'when'.

Charlie Wilson was the first to walk. And walk he did after being 'abducted' from Winson Green Prison in Birmingham on 12 August 1964. Three men, described as 'strangers', somehow got him over the prison wall and into a waiting car - wearing only his vest - without leaving the vestige of a clue. He was on the run for over three and half years before being recaptured in Canada. It was the capture of Bruce and Buster and the re-capture of Charlie that kept my picture and name in the press, and at a time when I was hoping to slip into a life of Australian obscurity.

On the same day as the appeal had been turned down I was transferred from Brixton to Wandsworth, a prison I knew well and hated. But being sent to Wandsworth had its advantages and I certainly knew its ropes.

In a very short time I had a miniature radio smuggled in and every Saturday afternoon Joe, the landing cleaner and a fellow con, would deposit a bucket of murky water with a floor cloth and scrubbing brush outside my cell door with a view to having a 'scrub-out'. Down in the depths of the inky water would be lurking a tin of crab, lobster, corned-beef, peanuts and half a bottle of whiskey. The empty tins and bottles went out the same way.

I was first put to work - for a few brief hours each day - in the mailbag shop, hand-sewing mailbags for the GPO. I was considered a 'security risk' and categorized as a Special-Watch Prisoner. There were thirty or more cons in this category, most of us with a history of having broken out of one nick or another. We had coloured patches sewn on to our jackets and trousers and we were denied certain 'privileges' such as evening-classes and 'open' visits. We worked immediately in front of a watchful prison officer. To relieve the tedium I became a bookmaker.

Almost as soon as I arrived in Wandsworth I began receiving offers from various cons to help me escape, but I turned them all down. One of these offers came from the prisoner who was working beside me, Paul Seabourne. Paul was on the tail end of a four-year sentence with less than a year to serve. He had a good reputation among the other cons and was known to be 'as game as a bygone' having escaped from Wandsworth during the sentence he was serving.

Paul and I became good friends. I liked his dry sense of humour. I turned down his first offer to get me out, using my argument about the introduction of a parole scheme and getting out legally after ten years or less.

'You're dreaming,' Paul said. 'There has been talk of a parole scheme for donkey's years. In any case, you can't be serious that you're prepared to face ten years bird?'

I assured him I was.

It eventually got to a point where Paul and I started to annoy one another, him wanting to get me out and me refusing. Finally he told me that he was simply against the idea that I had been handed a thirty-year sentence for robbing a train.

'It's a fucking diabolical liberty, that's what it is,' he said, 'and I intend to get you out. I don't want any of your lousy train money either. I'm a thief and I'll steal my own money.'

Paul loved the idea of getting me or anyone else out of Wandsworth. The idea of my escape really turned him on. I think to him it was a way to fuck with the authorities. To stick it to them on a grand scale.

On the Glorious Twelfth Charlie was 'spirited away' from Winson Green. I was delighted for Charlie and was not in the slightest bit surprised that Chas had 'had it away'. The Home Office was far less elated and orders were given to double up on the security with regard to the train gang, especially when less than a week later they uncovered a plot to free Gordon Goody from Strangeways Prison in Manchester.

A screw was posted outside my cell door full time peering at me through the Judas flap at fifteen-minute intervals. I could hear him coughing, sneezing, farting and humming to himself. His chair creaked with every movement, he would have conversations with passing screws or the night watchman and I could hear him messing with his Thermos flask and sandwiches. At first I asked him politely to make less noise but it was all to no avail, so I became more abusive.

As a result I started being subjected to frequent 'changes of location', sometimes at midnight or later - the 'idea' being that this would confuse would-be rescuers. Nobody seem to consider that it would have been all too easy to have hung some kind of marker from the window ledge to show my new location!

Wherever I went in the prison during the day I was escorted by two screws. I couldn't even take a crap without one of my vigilantes checking me out from time to time.

After a few weeks of the 'extra security measures' I felt that my health was being affected so I asked Governor 'Gusty' Gale to relax the pressure, showing him my trembling hands.

The governor was very sorry, he said, but his orders were from the Home Office and those orders were quite clear.

'I have to detain you in this prison Biggs - and detain you I shall. About turn. March out.'

Later, in the exercise yard I told Paul that if the offer was still open I wanted him to get me out.

From that moment in the yard, Paul and I started plotting, considering every possible angle to put a plan together that was going to work. Every exercise period would be taken up exploring the ways and means of getting me over the wall. I had to curb some of my friend's enthusiasm: at one point he suggested storming the gate lodge at night, tying up the screws and releasing everybody!

In the middle of our scheming an old friend, Dennis Stafford, came to Wandsworth with a six-month sentence to serve. Dennis had achieved notoriety when he escaped from the grim confines of Dartmoor prison back in the fifties Dennis was a very bright chap and a helicopter pilot.

Without knowing that Paul and I were already hatching an escape plan, Dennis was soon offering his professional aviation services. I passed this information on to Paul who glowed with the idea of 'riding shotgun' on a helicopter breakout of the exercise yard. But some time before I had been transferred to Wandsworth, during a short sojourn at Chelmsford prison, a helicopter had flown low over the jail during an exercise period. In an instant two screws were standing at my side and my stroll around the flower garden of HMP Chelmsford came to an abrupt end.

I have to admit that I rather liked the idea of an airborne exit from Wandsworth, but I was looking for something a little bit more practical and with fewer risks. Then one day the idea of a removal van came to mind and I asked Paul just how tall the average van was.

'Not tall enough to reach the top of the wall if that's what your thinking?' was his immediate answer. 'But I like the idea.'

We made some calculations using my experience in the building trade to find out the exact height of the prison wall by counting the number of brick courses. It was over twenty-five feet high.

'What about a platform on top of a furniture van?' I suggested.

'Charming,' he scoffed, 'Old Bill seeing us heading in the direction of Wandsworth nick in a removal van with a platform on top is never going to wonder what we're up to!' But he thought about it.

At this time another friendly face appeared in the Special Watch section of the mailbag workshop. His name was Eric Flower. Eric was a pal from the early days in the boob. We had been Young Prisoners at Lewes in 1949 at the time that I had met the young Post Office sorter by the name of Kitson.

Eric had been sentenced to twelve years for conspiracy to rob, armed robbery and robbery with violence, and had lodged an appeal against the severity of his sentence, while knowing full well that he stood little or no chance in having it reduced. As a prisoner on appeal, however, he was able to receive visitors on a daily basis and I immediately saw how this could be very useful with regard to passing messages in and out of the prison.

At first Paul was reluctant to include anyone else in our plan for fear of a possible leak. But I convinced him with the argument that if we didn't put Eric into our plan he would soon organize a plan of his own which could very well harm ours.

I didn't have to twist Eric's arm to 'make one' on our piece of business and I was more convinced than ever that with him aboard we were going to pull it off.

Another member of the mailbag workshop that I extended an invitation to do a bunk, was Roy Shaw. He had been sentenced to 15-year for the robbery of a security van, and a further three years for grievous bodily harm. Roy partly blamed the length of his sentence on the Great Train Robbery, with longer sentences becoming the norm.

I told Roy of my plan as we stitched mailbags, and that do be part of it he would need to come up with £10,000. Roy weighed up the pros and cons, but realised in the end that he would need a lot more than £10,000 to keep on the run. He wasn't wrong and by chance prior to my escape he found himself transferred to Parkhurst on the Isle of White and would not have been around on the big day. Next time I was to see Roy was going to be in Rio when we would both be as free as a bird.

During the weekdays Special Watch inmates like myself were exercised in a yard that was flanked by the main prison wall. On the other side was a narrow service road which ran around the prison and on to the main road and freedom.

Exercise took place in the afternoon in the form of two one-hour periods: two o'clock until three and three until four. A senior prison officer was always in charge of the exercise and he would appear in the workshop just before 2 p.m. to make the random selection of half the number of Special Watch cons for the exercise period. Those passed over at this time would then automatically be taken into the yard at three o'clock as the first batch returned to the workshop. As we could not guarantee being picked for the first period we would have to be 'missing' from the workshop at 2 p.m. on E-day.

As soon as I had decided to go over the wall I embarked on a get-fit program, as I was quite a bit overweight. I obtained some books from the prison library on yoga and physical training and had a one-hour workout every evening. At night I listened to my miniature radio tucked under my pillow and only just loud enough for me to hear. An Australian pop group, the Seekers, had a hit at the time which was my inspiration: it contained the line *There's a new world somewhere, they called the Promised Land.'* Years later I was to meet them in Melbourne when I was working as a carpenter at the Channel 9 TV station.

Charmian knew about the escape plan and was very excited about the possibility of seeing her loving lord in liberty. A month or so before Paul was due to be released, Charm received a communication from a friend of ours, Brian Stone. Brian was in Brixton Prison on remand facing some spurious cheque charges and needed some financial assistance. I gave

Charmian the green light to arrange a lawyer to defend our friend and soon enough there he was sitting beside us in the mailbag shop!

Despite the circumstances of our meeting Brian was 'over the moon' with the four year sentence he had received as he had been expecting to go down for a much longer stretch.

'If I can help you in any way,' he said as we shook hands, 'don't hesitate to ask.' He was to prove as good as his word.

I had figured that Eric and I were going to need a little help on E-day. There would be four screws in the exercise yard and it was a certainty that they would come running as we started scaling the wall.

I talked it over with Eric and Paul and it was decided that we would ask Brian to mind us as we went into action. Brian didn't think twice when I put it to him, but he suggested that there should be a second 'minder' to tangle with the screws. Paul was already uptight about too many people knowing about the escape, but he agreed that two minders were better than one.

I decided, at Brian's suggestion, to have a wee word with a young lad from Glasgow. I told him that I needed someone to help me go over the wall. I stipulated that I didn't want any violence and all he would have to do would be to grab a screw and hang on. I told him I would pay him £500, the equivalent today of close to £7500, for his help.

'I don't want your money Biggsy,' said the Scot. 'I'll do it for the prestige.' The brotherhood of prison life really does exist.

Days before Paul's release we were doing dummy runs, rehearsing ways and means of avoiding the first exercise period. Dwelling in the bog seemed to be sound, a 'sudden excruciating pain in the gut' was another sure-fire way to be taken to the prison hospital for a dose of 'white mixture', a concoction that was administered for practically everything. 'Guaranteed to cure coughs, colds, sore holes and pimples on the dicky,' as the hospital orderlies were wont to say. But a hospital visit was good enough to be missing from the workshop for half an hour or so.

As Eric was able to receive visitors every day, he got his friends and family to arrive at 1.30 p.m. on the dot, thus avoiding the first call. There was also a storeroom in the workshop where one could go to have a pair of scissors sharpened or get more mailbag thread and 'not hear' the first call for walkies. On one of his visits Eric was able to smuggle in the business part of a small ladies wristwatch that was to be vital for timing ourselves in the exercise yard.

It had been arranged that on the day Paul would go into action at exactly 3.10 p.m., giving us enough time to make sure we were in the yard. We discovered that it took approximately half a minute to get from the toilet block to the main wall at a point between the two screws.

The yoga started to pay off nicely. One evening a screw named Armstrong, opened my cell door and saw me doing press-ups.

'What are you doing, Biggsy,' he jibed. 'Getting ready for your release?'

I smiled at his little joke. 'Something like that Mr. Armstrong.'

'I bet you wish you were!' he guffawed as he walked on.

Not long afterwards a certain Mrs. Armstrong witnessed us coming over the wall 'full of the joys of spring', as she put it.

When I had finally given Paul the word that I wanted to escape he made two stipulations. Money to cover his expenses and an introduction to 'someone who you can call your friend.' I assured him there was cash available and he would be working with a very staunch friend, Mickey Haynes.

The eve of Paul's release arrived and there was the customary leg-pulling by the screws. 'You'll be back!' and so forth. The cons were sorry to see him go; he had been good company distinguished by his humour and indomitable spirit.

Paul lost no time in contacting Charmian and we soon began receiving 'progress reports' via Eric's visitors. Our 'bird' was dragging. E-day was set for Wednesday 7 July 1965.

As it turned out E-Day was a typical English summer day. The forecast was rain!

When my cell was unlocked soon after 1.00 p.m. the screw found me doubled up in agony, gasping for medical attention. To say it must have been something I ate wasn't that far fetched in Wandsworth! Two screws were summoned to escort me to the sick bay. The quack had seen it all before and as I had expected prescribed a good dose of 'white mixture'.

Miracles of miracles it worked and by 2.30 p.m. I was fully recovered and back in the mailbag workshop, sewing away.

Eric was smiling after having spent the last half hour with his loved-ones while Brian was looking relieved after having spent a similar length of time on the crapper. Wee Jock also looked confident as he emerged from the storeroom.

At 3 p.m., as expected, the call went up to put our work away and line up for exercise. Before five past three we were in the yard and conforming to regulations, were walking around the footpath in pairs. Eric and I together, Brian and Jock a few yards ahead. The wall was almost within touching distance.

Dark clouds lowered above us and it began to drizzle.

Fuck!

The discipline officer - the screw in charge of the exercise - gave a signal to the other three screws to take us back into the prison wing for 'indoor exercise.' I protested, pointing out that it was only raining lightly, but as I was speaking the heavens opened and it started to piss down. Eric and I exchanged dejected looks as we were returned to the workshop.

At the very same moment the escape team was trundling towards the prison in their converted furniture van. But when Paul saw the rain he knew from experience that we would be taken off the yard. Given Britain's inclement weather we had foreseen the situation and it had been decided that should rain 'stop play' we would carry out the same procedure the following day.

Happily nothing the escape team or us had done had attracted any attention so the escape was very much on. There was still the frustration of knowing that we had nearly done it and would have to do it all over again. We would all have to be missing from our place of work the next day when the screws chose the cons for the first exercise period. If it meant having a crap, sharpening our scissors, going special sick, or whatever, not one of the four of us could afford to be in the workshop until well after 2 p.m. I was logged on my prison record as arriving from my cell at 2.20 p.m.

The delay had given Paul some extra time and he decided to tour the phone-boxes in the direct vicinity of the escape and disconnect the mouthpieces to stop people telephoning our getaway to the police or reporting a suspicious looking van. We only discovered later that not even a prison of the size and importance of Wandsworth had a direct line to the police. When I did go over the top the screws had to call 999 like everyone else and this meant a twenty-minute delay until the cops arrived.

Thursday 8 July, one year and eleven months to the day since the robbery, the sun rose brightly over London and I sensed that this was going to be the day. Charmian, who must have been getting fed up of traipsing off to museums with the kids as an alibi, set off for Whipsnade Zoo in Bedfordshire. She also thought that after the disappointment of Wednesday this would be the day.

Never had the exercise yard look so good. The time was 2.30 p.m. I felt like peeing with pleasure - so after about half an hour we headed for the toilets, where - surprise, surprise - Brian and Jock were to be found just shaking the drops off as we arrived.

'Tell me, do you boys hang around here all the time?' I said. With his back to the screw, who was watching closely to make sure that no one was having a crafty smoke, Eric checked the time by his watch and gave a nod. It was close to 3.00 p.m. The four of us joined the other cons on exercise.

As we drew level with the wall I heard the sound of a heavy vehicle on the other side. I stopped to tie my shoelace, looking up at the wall. Suddenly a head in a nylon stocking appeared. A split second later the first of the rope ladders came snaking down the wall. As Eric and I made for them the screws came running, blowing their whistles. Brian and Jock went into action.

As I cocked my leg over the wall Paul, the man in the nylon mask, greeted me.

'Hello, you big ugly bastard!' I gave him a slap on the back and looked down at the mêlée in the prison yard. My boys were hanging on to the screws as if they loved them.

'You're too late,' Brian shouted gleefully, 'Biggsy's away.'

The truck was parked close to the wall, something that would be unthinkable today, so it was an easy matter to drop onto the roof. A large rectangular opening had been cut in the van to allow a five-foot hinged platform to be pushed up through the roof giving Paul those vital extra feet needed to reach the top of the wall and throw the rope ladders down. On the floor of the van were a number of old mattresses for us to jump down on to. A getaway car was parked nearby with Paul's trusty friend, Ronnie Leslie, at the wheel. Two other cons seized the opportunity to follow us over the wall and because of this Paul never got to burn the truck as he had planned.

Besides Ronnie Leslie, a motor mechanic who had worked on converting the van, there was a third member of the escape team, Ronnie Black, a Ron who I had had my doubts about.

Ronnie Black had spent time with me in Wandsworth where he had proved to be a bit of a hothead. The last thing I wanted was to have any kind of violence or guns. No guns and no violence was a strict rule and Paul had grudgingly agreed to go along with this. I got pissed off, therefore, when I heard the rules had been broken and there had been a shotgun involved. But Paul just offered to put me back inside. There is also a story that before we got over the wall Blackie had locked some screw's child in an outside toilet after he had emerged suddenly from a house.

As Eric and I scrambled into the car with Paul and the two Ronnies, the other two Special Watch cons, Robert Anderson and Patrick Doyle, came racing to the car looking for a lift.

'Let 'em in,' I shouted. They piled in and we zoomed off full of the joys of being sprung.

We had made it!

We had done it!

We had fucking escaped from Wandsworth!

Despite the initial euphoria we still had a long way to go. The car raced around the perimeter wall, all seven of us piled inside. It was the only route to freedom and the main road. As we sped off our route to freedom was nearly blocked by a prison work party with a dustcart. Happily the screw, not knowing who we were, pulled them off the road and waved us through. If he had left the cart in the road our exit would have been blocked.

We drove on, four of us desperately trying to tear off our tell-tell Special Watch prison uniforms. A police car passed us going in the other direction, but there never seemed any danger of being stopped.

Even without being chased or followed we went through with Paul's plan. It took us to a quiet cul-de-sac close to the prison where we dumped the first car and ran up a footpath leading to a second car. If Old Bill had been in pursuit we would have run down the alley and hoped they did not have a second car waiting.

As the second car had been hired on a dodgy brief we told the two opportunists they could use it after they had dropped us off and go as far as they liked until the next day, when a scream would go out for it. The first to be dropped off were the two Ronnies at Tooting Bec Station. The five of us then went on to Dulwich where Eric, Paul and I left the car close to our destination. Our final address was not something we necessarily wanted to broadcast to our uninvited guests who, without a plan, were more likely than us to get picked up.

When I was in hiding I read that our guests had been caught after three months. One of them, Robert Anderson, had been one of my heaviest punters in the prison and owed me ten ounces of tobacco when we escaped. As he dropped us I asked 'Hey! What about my ten ounces?' 'I'll pay you the next time I see you,' he replied with a wink. He still owes me.

According to Frankie Fraser, Anderson turned up on his doorstep. 'On the afternoon of the escape I was sitting in an office of our fruit machine and jukebox distribution company listening to the details of the escape on the radio and TV when there was a knock at the door. The door was opened, and standing there was Andy Anderson. He said he had been told that if he was in London and needed any help, to call at the office. Well, to say he needed help is a major understatement. There were more policemen on the streets of London than hornets in a giant hornet nest.'

Frankie welcomed Anderson into his office; raised some money, bought some clothes, and made a call to Scotland to Arthur Thompson and Mendel Morris to say Anderson would shortly be on his way north.

Even after all these years I can't help thinking about the king sized bollocking the governor at Wandsworth must have got for the manner of my escape. That was just fine with me because he had not believed me when I said I did not want any special treatment but wanted to be treated like every other con. He had said that it could not be. When I told him that everything he was doing was going to drive me over the wall, he saw this as insolence. I was not trying to be insolent, I was trying to be perfectly honest, man-to-man, and show that it would be too much for me to endure. In the end I think I proved my point.

Charmian heard of my escape on the four o'clock radio news when they first announced that four men had gone over the wall of Wandsworth, one of whom was 'believed' to be train robber Ronald Biggs.

Wandsworth Prison held Oscar Wilde in 1895 and was the scene of a sensational escape in 1965 by the train robber Ronald Biggs. Notable among former Wandsworth residents are the novelist William Makepeace Thackeray and the exiled French author Voltaire.

Encyclopaedia Britannica

ON THE RUN: LONDON-BOGNOR-ANTWERP-PARIS-SYDNEY

Yard probe the Great Escape. Train robber Biggs hunted after fantastic jailbreak drama… and the riddle is: Who helped on the inside?

Daily Mirror, 9 July 1965

The Train Robbers snatched another of their £2,500,000 gang from prison yesterday – at gunpoint, in daylight, in public, in the heart of London.

Daily Express, 9 July 1965

If Charlie's escape had been audacious, then Ronnie's was downright cheeky.

Bruce Reynolds

The hideout was the upstairs flat of a semi-detached house in a quiet Dulwich road. On that lazy summer afternoon the road was deserted and Paul, Eric and I appeared to be just three young men going about their business. Suddenly Eric noticed the barrel of the shotgun sticking out from a sports coat that Paul was carrying under his arm. Oops!

Two young people were at the flat when we arrived: Paul's brother-in-law, George Gibbs, and his wife Jean. Eric threw me a furtive glance indicating that he was far from happy about 'unknowns' being on the scene. 'George is sound,' Paul assured us, 'and so is the girl.' It was now just after 3.30 p.m.

'Open up the champers, for Christ's sake!' I exclaimed.

We celebrated and toasted Paul. Another bottle of champers was cracked as we sat around the telly to catch news of the escape. Exit Biggs and co. - enter Mrs Armstrong! They announced that it had taken Old Bill twenty minutes to get to the nick.

'If I'd known, I would've made you buggers walk,' Paul remarked with obvious pride.

Although for the moment we were safe, I could see that Eric wanted to arrange somewhere more secure for us to hole up. He had friends in East London, well connected friends, and as soon as it was dark he slipped out of the house to make a phone call to one of them, a certain Freddie Foreman. Eric had worked with Freddie, who I had never met, but he was already friends with Bruce, Buster, Tommy Wisbey, Gordon Goody, John Daly, and Jimmy Hussey. Eric returned looking elated – his friends would be arriving in less than an hour. Now it was Paul's turn to look troubled. He wanted to know more about Eric's pals.

'I promised to get you out and I did,' Paul said, 'and I want you to stay out. You would be as safe here as anywhere.'

Eric could not agree. 'Paul,' he said, 'Old Bill is going to turn over every drum in South London. They must know that we're not far from the boob. My people will have us safely down in the country by tomorrow morning.'

I had to admit that the idea of getting off the manor appealed and I was certain that Eric wouldn't be putting us in the hands of mugs. We also knew that Paul would be the number one suspect for putting together the escape. In the prison workshop it must have looked as if we were Siamese twins at times the way our heads were always locked together. Paul didn't seem too worried about the possibility of getting his collar felt, but as Eric was quick to point out, if the Old Bill were looking for Paul it would automatically lead them to us. We had also picked up that Paul and George's wife were on extra friendly terms - and George didn't look too happy about it. Ever super-security conscious Eric saw this as another good reason not to dwell in Dulwich.

With the arrival of Eric's friends the once spacious living room looked crowded. Both men, Freddie and Alf Gerrard, were twice the size of Paul and unmistakably villains. Paul was wearing his worried look again. He had recognised one of the men. When the chance came he drew me into another room.

'Look,' he said, 'I know Alfie and I can tell you he's bad news. They're not here to do you any favours and they know you've got lots of dough tucked away.' He produced a Walther pistol. 'Take this to look after yourself. You're out, now make sure you stay out. Use this if you have to.'

I refused to take the gun. I told Paul I didn't need it and that I could take care of myself better without one.

'Do you know what you are?' he said. 'A big, ugly bastard!'

Freddie and Alfie got into the front of the car which they had parked a short distance along the street. Moments later Eric and I slipped into the back and crouched down on the seat. We were tired, it had been a long, and to say the least, exciting day.

Morning noises filled the room but they were not country noises they were city noises. We were not 'in the country' but in a humble tenement building in Bermondsey. At least we were South of the River!

An elderly docker by the name of Tom was our landlord for the next few days. We were provided with clothes, loads of good grub and booze and a record player, plus a pile of LPs which had been knocked off from a shop in the Charing Cross Road a few days earlier. Life was starting to look considerably better than it had done a few days earlier.

If Lady Luck was looking after old Biggsy, she wasn't as kind to the other people involved. Days after we moved on from Dulwich, as Detective Chief Superintendent Tommy Butler and his Flying Squad crew were raiding every hang-out where he thought Eric and I might be found, Paul was arrested. Paul was to serve four and a half years for getting me out of prison, but many more indirectly for later crimes because the authorities were always out to get him for springing me from Wandsworth. Paul knew he would get caught, but he didn't care. My freedom was his reward. His only charges for getting me out of prison were expenses - which were virtually nothing - and some money for Ronnie Leslie. When I got over the wall I had to force £1000 on Paul as a show of gratitude, but he only took it because of his old lady.

Ronnie Leslie got three years for helping Paul, while Brian Stone and his mate Jock, instead of being picked for England and Scotland to strengthen their defence, were given an extra twelve months apiece for their rugby tackles on the screws.

A week or so later we were moved from Bermondsey to a new address, this time to a spacious apartment in Camberwell owned by Freddie's sister-in-law, Nellie. While we were there we were introduced to a friend of Alfie's named George. This sharp-looking fellow represented an 'organisation' capable of taking care of travel arrangements for people like Eric and myself. Thomas Cook they were not. With great self-assurance, George outlined a 'package deal' which consisted of temporary passports; a boat trip to the Continent, a car transfer to Paris, plastic surgery, ('complete facial reforming by one of the most famous names in European cosmetic surgery', was how he put it), real passports in our 'new image'; and airline tickets to 'anywhere in the world'.

The price?

A mere eighty grand. Over £1.2 million at today's prices. A bargain, George assured me, as a lot of people would have to be paid off. With a bit of haggling the price fell to £40,000. £20,000 down and the rest after the ops in Paris. There was also the question of a further £15,000 for the safe passage of Charmian, Eric's wife Carol, and the kids to join us at our final destination. A cool £55,000 was spent, nearly eight hundred and fifty thousand pounds at today's rates and roughly a third of what I had netted from the robbery.

In January 1996, under the Thirty Year Rule, it was revealed that in July 1965 the then Prime Minister, Harold Wilson, pressed for a novel way of preventing us train robbers from laundering our money. He suggested to the Treasury to secretly prepare replacement banknotes and suddenly withdraw all former currency. Banks would then ask customers to account for their money in order to exchange old notes for new. Wilson's idea was that the money we had all kept under the mattress after the robbery for a rainy day would become useless. Thankfully, the PM's idea was rejected out of hand by the Whitehall Mandarins as impossible to effect, so money, for the moment, was not my problem.

The 'organisation' I talk of had nothing to do with the train robbery - despite what people would like to believe - but is a body that helps those with the right connections. It almost certainly got Buster Edwards out of Britain, and more than likely Charlie Wilson. But I am only guessing. Freddie Foreman explained how he helped organise Buster's return in his biography The Godfather of British Crime.

My contact with Charmian was at first restricted to calls to phone-boxes in and around London, the numbers of which she had jotted down in the weeks before my escape. I have always assumed that Charmian's movements would have been monitored during this period but, despite the escape, Scotland Yard never contacted her directly.

As the preparations for the move to Paris would take some time our minders decided that we should make yet another move. Once again, just after dark, we were picked up and spirited across London to our new digs. This time we would be sharing a room with a private detective! An Irishman whom, for his current peace of mind, I'll call Mick. The apartment was in a house somewhere between Putney and Richmond which belonged to a pleasant couple, also friends of Alfie. Everyone was in the villainy business, including the Irish detective - and, as Alfie noted, 'Here you are among your own.'

Our host made us very welcome and the grog flowed. Mick entertained us into the wee small hours with hilarious tales about his clients and his work, which normally included observing wayward husbands while he got pissed on Guinness.

Mick insisted that Eric and I should sleep in his double bed and that he would be quite happy sleeping on the floor with his faithful friend, Prince, a docile German Shepherd. A thick curtain had blacked out the only window in the room.

'Sure we wouldn't want the neighbours looking in now, would we?' was Mick's only concern. Indeed we wouldn't and it meant that we could sleep late, more often than not being woken by the phone and one of Mick's more hysterical clients.

Now Mick was one of those people who had the knack of coming out of a deep sleep and being able to sound sensible and fully alert in an instant. He would come alive with the wildest line of bullshit imaginable.

'Mrs Parker?... Good morning Mrs Parker... Yes, it's a wonderful morning. I've very good news for you. Your husband is not meeting another woman... No! I hope that puts your mind at rest, Mrs Parker. Believe me nothing more than a few drinks with the boys and a game or two of darts... Thank you, Mrs Parker.'

With that he would roll over and show the true Mick we had come to know and love: 'God, my head! What's th' fuckin' time, Ron?'

Although we were enjoying the company of Mick and co, we were not getting any exercise to speak of. It was still summertime and I was hankering to feel the sun on my body. As we were, we were only improving our prison pallor.

Leafing through a copy of *The Evening News* one day, I spotted an ad: Bognor Regis: 3 bedrooms; garden; quiet, secluded neighbourhood. I showed it to Eric and he was as enthusiastic as I.

'If we could get that,' he said pointedly, 'we might even be able to get the girls down to take care of our needs!' We were both looking forward to something a little bit more intimate than the telephone conversations we had managed todate.

We put the idea to Mick, who promised to talk it over with Alfie. Alfie growled a bit when he heard our request but finally agreed to see what could be done.

All went well. After the trip to Bognor lying down in the back of Alfie's car, we found ourselves in a comfortable, fully furnished two story house, a little old fashioned, but exactly what we had been hoping for. There was a small garden surrounded by a high wooden fence with flowers and plants galore. This, we decided, was more like it. It was late July 1965.

A plan was made for Eric's wife to come down to take care of the shopping, cooking and washing. Charmian would be brought down if-and-when there was a chance.

With the arrival of Carol to take care of the chores life was almost idyllic. After a hearty breakfast - Carol was a good cook - we would lie in the garden sunbathing and listening to the radio. The Dave Clark Five were also feeling pretty good at the time as their song, appropriately entitled *Catch Us If You Can*, was riding high on the charts that summer.

Carol had arrived with their only child, Kim, a cute, blonde four year-old. Eric was looking quite mellow and content with his lot. I must admit that I felt the odd twinge of envy in my celibate state.

One night the door to my room flew open and a body landed on top of me.

'You're nicked, you bastard!' It was Charm. My cup runneth over.

Once again we were nearly one big happy family, although Charm for safety had left the kids back in London where they were being looked after by Mary Mason's son. The only thing Charm and I couldn't do, was go for a walk on the beach. But we talked and made our plans for the future. One of Alfie's friends, whom we had met early on, had been to South Africa and from what he said about the place we were leaning in that direction as the place to wind up. But I still hadn't forgotten that 'new world somewhere, called the Promised Land' that I had heard the Seekers singing about.

The second anniversary of the robbery came and went.

George from the organisation came to visit us on a couple of occasions to discuss details of the plastic surgery. He took photographs of Eric and me on the first visit and returned with suggestions from the surgeon who was going to wield the knife. Eric was only to have a nose job, I was going to have the works.

As you can imagine, I was somewhat apprehensive about the surgery and I asked George for more details.

'Don't worry about a thing,' he assured me, 'Liz Taylor has it done every couple of years. If you want to, you can even have the skin removed from your finger tips and then you could never ever be nicked!'

At a price today of around £17,000 a finger, I declined.

Our sojourn to Bognor was coming to an end George informed us, so we started making the necessary preparations to move back to London.

Sure enough in mid-September the 'holiday' came to an end and after three months of hiding behind net curtains it was time to move on. Little did I know that those early autumn days of 1965 were going to be the last time that I was to put foot on British soil until I returned 13,068 days later in May 2001.

Eric and I were eventually transferred back to the flat in Camberwell belonging to Freddie Foreman's sister-in-law, Nellie, minus the wives and kids. Now that we knew that we were on the point of departure the time seemed to drag. We wanted action.

Early one morning that October, Alfie turned up with two parcels of clothing. 'Put this clobber on,' he growled in his normal friendly manner. 'You're on your way.' The clothes were obviously second hand and consisted of flannel shirts, jeans, donkey jackets and gumboots. We were supposed to look like seamen.

We dressed quickly and were soon on our way in a black van which had been parked outside the building. Freddie Foreman, whom we had first seen at Dulwich, was at the wheel and from him came the instructions. 'When you 're dropped off, walk straight through the gate. The mate of the boat on which you're travelling will be waiting to meet you. He'll take you aboard and hide you.' He then produced an envelope which turned out to contain a couple of seasickness pills.

'Take these if you think you are going to have a problem,' he said. 'You'll probably have a rough trip across the Channel. Now however bad you feel, stay put. Even when the boat docks. The mate will tell you when it is okay to go ashore. When you leave the boat walk straight out of the dock gate and turn left. Keep walking. Someone will come along driving a yellow Daf and offer you a lift into the city. He will take you to a motel where George will be waiting for you.'

As we left the van close to London Bridge Freddie wished us well.

The mate, a Dutchman, was waiting for us just as Freddie had said. He spoke little English but had enough international sign language to get us to follow him. Other than the three of us there was no other sign of life. We went aboard the cargo ship unchallenged. Down in the hold we scrambled over sacks of what smelled like rubber and with the aid of a torch the mate conducted us through to the bow where a small area had been left clear. The mate indicated that this was to be where we would spend the journey and shone the torch on a whisky bottle full of water. 'No smoke,' he said. 'No food - only water.' We got into our deluxe accommodation and the mate left us, barricading the entrance with sacks of rubber as he went. It was the first sea trip for both of us.

After what seemed like an age, the boat's engines began to throb and we were under way. The trip was not as rough as had been expected but it seemed to take forever, especially as we had no idea of time.

Finally we became aware that the boat had docked and after a time the sacks began to fall away. It was our friend, the mate.

'Come. Leave now!' he beckoned in his faltering English. We clambered over the sacks on stiff legs and up onto the deck. It was early morning and the boat was as deserted as when we had embarked. The mate smiled and shook hands pointing to the dock gates as he did so. I don't know if he ever did know what, or rather who, his rather precious cargo was.

There was nobody to be seen and the dock gates were wide open just as the organisation had promised. We turned left, as per instructions, and before we had gone more than a couple of yards, along came a yellow Daf. 'Hello boys,' called the driver. 'Going into town? Perhaps I can offer you a lift?'

His name was Peter and it turned out that he had been the captain of our vessel. With typical heavy Dutch humour he asked if we had enjoyed the crossing. He laughed when we told him we did not even know where we were.

'Antwerp boys! You're in Antwerp. I'm sorry that we won't have time to stop and look around but your friend is waiting for us.'

Further on we stopped at a set of traffic lights and our attention was drawn to a pretty Belgian girl dressing a shop window. We made appreciative male gestures and the girl smiled and waved. We were also sorry that we couldn't stop and look around.

George was waiting at the motel. He was immaculately dressed with Lisa, his 'gorgeous piece of German crumpet', at his side. He wrinkled his nose as we approached. 'Christ,' he said disdainfully. 'You two look as if you've spent the night down a rat-hole.'

After a quick shower, a shave and some fresh clothing we were ready for action. The first step of which was a slap-up breakfast while George outlined the next leg of the journey, which would take us to Paris.

We would be travelling in two cars. Eric would be with George and Lisa in George's Mercedes and I would travel in a Ford Zephyr with an English couple - trusted friends of George - and their two young daughters. We were given false passports, mine in the name of Ronald King, a sports master by profession.

'We'll drive ahead,' George told us. 'When we come to the frontier the gendarmes will only be interested in one thing - Lisa's legs - and you'll be letting them see plenty, won't you darling?'

I was told that I would be in the back of the Zephyr with the kids and all of us were to be asleep.

George's friends, Bill and Veronica, and their children, joined us at the motel in the early afternoon and after lunch in a swanky restaurant - 'This is on Mr. King!' - we headed for France.

Crossing the frontier proved no problem. Bill presented the passports and a gendarme peered into the back of the car. It was by now way past midnight and the three innocents were fast asleep. Bless 'em!

We had made it to France where I could only echo the thoughts of Maurice Chevalier: 'Thank heaven for little girls.' After a brief pit-stop for a beer and a snack we pressed on for Paris.

Bill pulled up behind George's car in a tree-lined avenue with the Eiffel Tower looming high above us. A man stepped out of the shadows and went to George's car and got in. The Merc pulled away and we followed though the quiet Paris streets.

When I was released in 2009, a man claiming to be Bill made contact with the *Mail* to sell his story. Sadly I never did find out if it was Bill as he was asking far too much money for his story.

Our new hide-out in Paris was a fourth floor apartment on the Rue Vivienne and the person who would be taking care of us from here on was 'Henri', the man who had recently emerged from the shadows. Henri was well dressed and appeared to be in his mid-fifties. He was powerfully built, not the kind of man you would choose to pick a fight with. He had a bone-crushing handshake, a big smile, and an even bigger heart. He spoke English with a heavy American accent which made it impossible to pin down his origins.

'From here on I'm the Boss,' Henri told us as we surveyed our new surroundings. 'Ya gotta do everthin' th' way Uncle Henri tells ya, an' I don't want to find you guys sneakin' out t' get laid.'

The apartment was small but comfortable and well stocked with food and drink. Henri was to visit us daily with bread, milk and the newspapers.

Within a day or so George came calling and told us we would be taken to the clinic to discuss the forthcoming surgery.

It was cold and snowing heavily but Eric and I were thinking of sunnier climes, as after the ops we would be free to go anywhere. We both discussed the subject of where 'anywhere' would be until one Sunday afternoon I read an article in *The News of the World* describing the pleasures that Australia had to offer and in particular Bondi Beach and Sydney, and the sun kissed sheilas. I handed the article to Eric and without hesitation we both agreed that we could do with some of that. So Oz it was.

Eric and I began to look forward to Henri's daily visits. We could hear him as he hauled his bulky frame up the wooden staircase to the flat where he would arrive breathless. Every day he would follow the same routine, slumping into a chair from where would come the by now familiar phrase: 'God dammit boys! - I quit!'

Henri was quite a man. He could converse in seven languages, including Russian and Chinese. He told us he had been everything from a prize fighter to a pimp. At the time he had been asked to play nursemaid to us he was running a small sandblasting business and living beyond his means. He also collected money from a number of whorehouses for someone he affectionately referred to as his 'bors'. The boss, he told us, was the owner of the apartment that we were using. He also liked to talk about the 'broads' at the houses where he picked up the takings but declared that we would never touch any of them.

'The bors would bust my ass,' he added with obvious concern and respect for this unknown gentleman.

George turned up a couple of times, bringing mail and presents from home, where our wives were 'over the moon' with the progress we were making.

Although it was against our orders we did go out at night from time to time. We even went to see Les Folies Bergère where Eric was nearly selected to join the girls on-stage in the can-can. Mostly we would go to small bars and jazz clubs where we could pass unnoticed as a couple of British visitors enjoying the Parisian nightlife. Sometimes Henri would arrive in the apartment and see some telltale sign that we had been out of the apartment, like a box of matches. He would look at us suspiciously.

'Have you two been out tom-cattin'?'

'Not us, Henri!'

But one night I did go out tomcatting and the feline company I arranged was a little pussy; 'All the way from Greece,' she purred.

Finally we were taken to the Clinique Victor Massé in Henri's old Citroen Deux Chevaux (what else!) and he was clearly nervous about his 'hot-cargo'. Hunched over the wheel like the getaway driver in a bad B-movie, Henri's nerves took him through a red light on more than one occasion. Crack-driver Eric, crouched on the floor, could only grin and bare it.

Marcel, let us call him, would perform the operations. I had my doubts about him being 'one of the most famous names in European cosmetic surgery' but pressed on. He examined us and made a few notes. A date was fixed. We had three days to think about our new hooters.

When Henri came back for us on the appointed day he was beaming. 'Dis is it you guys. Lambs t' the slaughter.'

Our 'cover story' for the clinic was that we were a pair of Canadian tax dodgers - not that anyone seemed to worry. Whilst I was being prepared for surgery a doctor spoke to me in French. I apologized and told him that I did not speak any French. He looked bemused: 'But it says on your card that you are from Quebec?' I put on my best sick smile and explained that my mother had taken me to the English speaking provinces when I was a small child. I got a feeling the doctor did not altogether believe me.

My mobile stretcher was wheeled off to await my turn in the operating theatre. A sexy nurse dug a needle in my arm and hooked me up to some sort of contraption. She took my pulse, her hand was cool and efficient.

'You are very calm,' she said. 'That is good.'

'I am?' I swallowed.

'Yes, your pulse is quite normal.'

I was just about to invest further in this conversation when the doors to the theatre swung open and there was my old mate looking a very sad and sorry state. I wanted to laugh. Only his blood suffused eyes were visible - and they were visibly distressed - and two bloodied prongs projecting from the area that had been his nose. A muffled voice came from behind the bandages. 'Don't let them tell you it doesn't hurt'

Before you could say 'knife' or check my pulse I was on the operating table and starting to feel woozy. Bright lights, voices, someone breaking up the cartilage in my nose with what felt like a hammer and chisel. The blood was running down my throat. 'You won't feel a thing,' they had said. 'Liz Taylor does it all the time...'

Henri arrived the following morning to pick us up and take us back to the apartment. As usual he was smiling broadly, thanking and bull-shitting Marcel the surgeon. He looked at Eric and I sitting sore and glum with the plaster nose-cast taped to our swollen faces

'Hey! Ain't my babies lookin' beautiful?' My friend and I were not able to say much but Eric made a supreme effort and pleaded with Henri not to make us laugh.

Back at the apartment Henri set out our antibiotic tablets and painkillers, fussing around us like a mother hen. 'An' you guys are gonna have t' start eatin' a lotta yogurt. Don't tell me you don't like it cos that's all I'm gonna buy for ya. You babies are going to look so goddam beautiful when them casts come off that I'm gonna kiss ya!'

We tried not to look at each other for fear of laughing but in the end I cracked up when I saw Eric trying to eat yogurt with a table knife to avoid opening his mouth. Then we both started laughing. They say laughter is the best medicine, but on that day I was not so sure.

The pain from the first surgery eased off after a couple of days and eating and drinking became less difficult. George paid us another visit to talk about the second part of my surgery. A permanent face lift. He and Henri pooh-poohed my misgivings about further suffering. 'The worst,' they assured me, 'was over'.

'Anyone would think you were going to have your cock chopped off,' George added by way of encouragement.

It was about this time that our friend Henri told us that his name was not 'Henri'.

'That's the name that George chose for me. For Christ sake do I look like th' kinda guy that would have a dumb son-of-a-bitch name like 'Henri'? No! I'm gonna tell you guys my real name. It's Barney.' He gave us his best Anthony Quinn smile and stretched out his hand. 'Shake hands with Barney. An' don't forget it! Every time you guys called me Henri I felt like pukin''

Barney went with us to the clinic to have the casts removed and was very impressed. Looking at Eric in profile he said, 'It's amazin'. Ya went in lookin' like Jimmy Durante an' ya come out lookin' like Mickey Rooney.'

At first it was strange looking at and feeling my new nose. It wasn't and still isn't - after all this time - exactly what Marcel had promised, but if I had my reservations, Eric seemed to be more than happy with the results of his op. His nose had been quite a landmark.

Barney, who had suffered none of the pain, was in high spirits that everything was going so well and invited us out to lunch at his favourite Chinese restaurant. A second treat was in store. He insisted on taking us to see a movie. We looked in a newspaper and found a film that was in English with French sub-titles. It was called *The Brig*, the story of 24 hours in a US marine prison in Japan. Early into the film it became clear that Wandsworth had been a holiday camp by comparison. Some of the scenes were so brutal that Barney was moved to rise from his seat and shout abuse at a particularly unpleasant Marine screw.

'You mother-fucker!' he shouted at the screen. 'You goddam mother-fucker - I'd kill ya' We had to drag him back into his seat.

Far too soon I was back at the clinic getting a thorough medical examination before surgery. I could not help wondering why all the fuss if the worst was over. Suppositories were issued and administered with devastating results and once again I found myself in pre-op.

I regained consciousness at one point and found myself lying in a bed in a ward with the faithful Barney sitting beside me in a chair. Unbelievable pain was raging in and around my head. Pain like I had never experienced before.

Barney was smiling. 'You look beautiful, sweetheart,' he said just before I vomited into his lap and went into oblivion again. When I came around the second time everything had been cleaned up and there was no sign of Barney. The pain was unbearable, any and every movement sending shock waves of agony through my head. I could see French windows at one side of the ward and I began to think about getting up and throwing myself into the street. Luckily, just trying to sit up was out of the question.

I made a supreme effort and managed to press a bell push that was suspended above the bed. Somewhere a bell rang and at the same time a light came on in the middle of the ward. A door opened an inch or so, then a hand appeared and switched the light off. I rang the bell again and the same process was repeated. I gave up on the idea of asking for help and tried to sleep. Only Edgar Alan Poe could do justice to the night of torment that followed. If only I had taken the gun that Paul had offered to me I might well have used it that day!

Two days later I was released from the clinic. Barney was all smiles again, conversing with the nurses and my favourite surgeon. I was given a huge supply of antibiotics and Barney wrote down in what order they had to be taken. It was four of this, six of that and two of those. And more goddam yoghurt.

When Eric saw the results of the operation he was very impressed.

'Christ,' he said. 'You look like a bloody Chink. Nobody would ever recognize you now.'

He was right I did have an oriental look but as the days passed the swelling slowly left my face and I began to lose my Asian appearance. After a week I returned to the clinic to have some of the stitches removed - there were 140-odd in my face to tackle - and this was a fairly bloody business.

The healing was a slow and painful process.

When the swelling and discolouration left my face, Barney took us out to have our hair cut, telling the open-mouthed barber that I had just undergone brain surgery. From there we were taken to a photographer to have pictures taken for our new passports. The scars on my face were still vivid and a black pen was used to give me some sideburns and hide the tell-tale marks. The photographs were sent on to George and he turned up at the apartment a couple of weeks later with the 'goods': the new passports, crisp and freshly issued by the Foreign Office, plus a one way ticket to Sydney for Eric - it had been decided that he would go a couple of weeks before me as a trailblazer.

George also brought more mail from our wives, money and a Christmas present from Charm - a gold watch. She didn't know it at the time, but the organisation had planned their own present and that was for her and the boys to spend Christmas in Paris. I would finally get to see the kids for the first time since my escape.

Three days before Christmas it was time for Eric, now Robert Burley, to leave Paris. Eric set off for Sydney and one day later had rung through to say he had arrived safely.

'The place is fantastic,' he enthused. 'It's tailor-made for people like us. The beer's great and I've sun-bathed on Bondi Beach already.' This was excellent news and I began looking forward to joining him in the 'Promised Land.'

Charm and the boys arrived safely in Paris for Christmas. Barney brought me the glad tidings and told me that he would take me to meet them as soon as it was dark. Many precautions had to be taken to make certain that they had not been tailed.

Barney finally stopped the car near a cinema and pointed to a car parked nearby. It was the same Ford in which I had made the trip from Antwerp to Paris.

'There's your old lady and your kids,' said my friend reaching out to shake my hand. 'Merry Christmas! I'll see you guys later.'

Charm and the boys had been driven from London to Dover where they had caught the boat to Ostend before driving on to Paris. They were travelling on passports in Charmian's maiden name and did not attract any attention during the festive season.

It was wonderful to see Charmian and the boys again and there was much hugging and kissing. Nicky appeared to be a bit bewildered by his father's 'new look' and had to be convinced that I really was his father, but he was soon over it and chatting excitedly. When he could get a word in, Chris, now close to four years of age, also had much to say once he accepted it was his dad. It was Christmas and Father Christmas was on his way!

We booked in to a modest hotel, the Hotel Cécilia at 11 Avenue mac Mahon in the centre of Paris, and spent the next five days having family fun. We went to the parks and the zoo. In the evening a baby-sitter would come in so that Charm and I could do justice to the nightlife of Paris. We did our Christmas shopping and Charmian bought me a pair of very expensive crocodile shoes 'to travel in'. The shop assistant told me to take shoes that were half a size smaller than what I usually took, so that by the time I had worn them in they would fit more snugly. They felt tight, but I took the assistant's advice.

We were having a wonderful time: going to shows and eating at famous restaurants. This was the life, but I knew it could not last forever. Sure enough, just after Christmas, Barney appeared at the hotel with the news that it was my time to move on.

Early the next morning, Wednesday 29 December 1965, George arrived with my new passport and the ticket to Sydney. I had some misgivings about the passport as it was quite obviously brand new and didn't have any stamps in it whatsoever.

'How did Mr. Furminger get out of England and into France without a single stamp in his passport,' I asked George.

'You worry too much,' was his only reply.

With a butterfly or two in my stomach I said my goodbyes to Charmian and the kids and reassured them that we would all be together again and hopefully soon. Nobody was looking particularly cheerful - least of all Nicky who was coming down with the measles.

I also took my leave of my very special new friend Barney. Wherever you are Barney, thanks!

George and I set off alone for Orly Airport and the flight to freedom. It was goodbye Europe, hello brave new world. There seemed to be very few people at the airport that day and my misgivings about the passport returned. To make matters worse the official at passport control looked most unfriendly. George shook me warmly by the hand and I went to meet my doom.

To my surprise the official barely glanced at the passport and handed it back to me wishing me 'Bon Voyage'. I gave George a wave and headed for my flight to Zurich - the first leg of my journey 'down under'.

I travelled as the writer Terence Furminger, a man who had been paid £1000, about £15,000 today, for the use of his documents. To all intent and purpose Ronald Biggs no longer existed. I had perfected the escape. The only flaw to the plan was the crocodile shoes. They were already starting to pinch and I hadn't even got to the plane.

THE WIZARD OF AUS:
TIME DOWN UNDER

There's a new world somewhere
They call The Promised Land
And I'll be there some day
If you will hold my hand
I still need you there beside me
No matter what I do
For I know I'll never find another you

It's a long, long journey
So stay by my side
When I walk through the storm
You'll be my guide
Be my guide

The Seekers, *I'll Never Find Another You*

Ronald King - Terence Furminger - Terence 'Terry' King - Terence 'Terry'
Cook – Terence King-Cook - Arthur Robert Carson - Michael Haynes

The aliases of Ronald Arthur Biggs

"The weather is glorious, the opportunities are marvellous and the natives
are friendly."

Ronnie Biggs in a letter from Australia to Charmian

After a stifling stopover in Darwin to go through immigration formalities, the plane finally touched down at Mascot Airport in Sydney. It was New Year's Eve 1965.

I crushed my swollen feet back into my crocodile shoes and limped to the customs area. All that I could think of at that moment were all the more comfortable pairs of shoes that were in my suitcase.

'Anything to declare, sir?' said the official in an unmistakably Aussie twang.

'Yes,' I replied. 'These shoes are killing me. Please let me get at some old ones.'

I had already kicked off my crocodile shoes and was eager to make the change. Suddenly there seemed to be something more serious to deal with than my mutilated feet. Not only were the shoes made from crocodile skin - which put them in a special class - but even if they did let them into the country there would be import tax to pay.

'If you let me get at a different pair of shoes, you can keep these or throw them away,' I offered. 'I'll never, ever use them again.' The offer was enough. I was cleared through customs, shoes and all.

'Welcome to Australia, Mr Furminger!'

Now I was bouncing along in the old Hush Puppies. I had made it to the Promised Land. I was in bloody, beautiful Australia, a world away from Wandsworth Prison. Catch us if you can!

As I left the airport it started to rain. A sudden rust coloured downpour. But I wasn't worrying about the rain or its colour - I felt like Gene Kelly even with my aching feet.

I took a taxi to King's Cross and found the Wentworth Hotel where I had arranged to meet Eric.

'Mr. Burley checked out two days ago,' the desk clerk apologised, 'and does not seem to have left a forwarding address.'

Worse was to come. The hotel was fully booked for New Year's Eve. With a lot of persistence the staff managed to track down a room at a hotel nearby after some kind soul had cancelled their reservation. I left a message at the Wentworth in case Eric was to return. The message was to call Mr, Furminger 'as soon as possible.'

There was no air-conditioning at the hotel other than an old-fashioned fan that whirred above the bed. But the room was clean and spacious - and the fridge was well stocked with cold beer. Still doing mental handsprings I opened a 'tube' and guzzled the contents. Happy New Year, Ron!

After a long and much welcomed shower and a shave I got dressed and decided to look around 'the Cross'. Light years before, when I had been in Wandsworth, I had read a humorous book about the Aussies called They're a Weird Mob. Now I would be able to judge for myself.

With my scars and Paris pallor I probably looked a bit weird to the Aussies. I visited a few bars and found out all about 'ponies' and 'schooners' and 'grogged on' into the evening. By midnight I had joined up with some British sailors and their girlfriends, singing and sharing their champagne. We went from *Waltzing Matilda* to *We'll Meet Again* and back again.

I slept well and woke up early, the sun shining through the blinds on to my face. Today was a day to tour the city and get my bearings. I wanted to see some of the Sydney shoreline and especially the famous Bondi Beach.

I got the first taxi that came along.

'Where to mate?' the driver asked.

'I'd like to hire you for the whole day,' I said. 'Perhaps you could show me all the places of note in Sydney, but especially the beaches.'

'I'm your man,' said the driver enthusiastically. 'The first thing we will do is to turn off this bloody meter. I hope you'll excuse the smell of drink mate, but I've been on the piss for most of the night.'

There were no worries. I had also been on the piss too so I appreciated the man behind the wheel as my kind of cab driver.

The cabbie's name was Stan. Born and bred in Sydney, Stan was a family man with four kids. He had a keen sense of humour and soon we were chatting away like old friends. His passions were horse-racing and Chinese food, so once it had been established that I shared both these enthusiasms we decided that after the tour of the city we would go to a track called Randwick and then on to one of Stan's favourite Chinese restaurants for dinner.

I told Stan I was a writer and that I planned to stay in Australia for about six months. As I didn't have a fixed abode at that moment, I asked my new friend if I could possibly have my mail sent to his home. He readily agreed.

'I'll take you to a pub near the Cross where us cabbies get together. I go there practically everyday so everyone knows me and that's where I can hand over anything that comes for you.'

It was a beautiful, sunny day and I enjoyed the tour. The beaches looked great! Stan gave me a quick lesson in 'Strine' - the way fair dinkum Aussies speak the English language. I picked up a lot more when he took me to the pub where the cab-drivers hang out!

The races turned out to be something of a financial disaster. Neither one of us backed a winner but Stan kept the schooners coming and I loved every minute of it. By the time we got to the Chinese restaurant we were firm friends and we agreed that it had been a bloody beaut day.

When I got back to my hotel there was a message from Eric with a telephone number where I could contact him. We had a brief but euphoric conversation on the phone and an hour later my friend was knocking at the bedroom door.

'Bob Burley?'

'Terry Furminger? You made it, you old bastard!'

When Eric's funds had begun to dwindle he had found himself a room in a boarding house and had even got himself a job as a petrol pump attendant in a service station. Eric was looking a picture of health and already had a deep tan.

'I go to the beach every morning before going to work,' he said. 'We'll go tomorrow. Just wait until you see the crumpet.'

Eric was pleased to hear that I had already managed to establish an address where our mail could be sent safely.

It did not take us long to find ourselves a furnished house in Botany Bay (where else!) and settle in. Our next-door neighbours were the owners of the house and offered to take care of any chores. We bought an elderly Morris and spent some time tarting it up. Eric, who knew about these things, happily taking the engine to pieces.

Sunny and happy days, all that was missing were the wives and kids. At that same time, back in the UK a waxwork of Charlie and I had been unveiled at Madame Tussauds, while at the end of January 1966 Goody, James, Wisbey, Hussey, Welch, Cordrey were all being reunited by being transferred to HMP Parkhurst, on the Isle of Wight. Less than two weeks, later, on 11 February, John Wheater, the solicitor who had purchased Leatherslade Farm for Bruce, was released from prison. The first person convicted of the Great Train Robbery to be so.

As the cash was getting low at the start of 1966 I wrote to Charmian to send me more. We had decided that it was a bit unwise to transfer money via the banks for the time being so we opted for the old prison trick of smuggling in money and letters. Banknotes or letters would be tightly folded lengthwise until they became narrow strips. The strips are then glued between two pages of a bulky magazine. Charm was no stranger to these little subterfuges and soon enough my Aussie chum, Stan, was calling to say that there was mail for Terence Furminger.

The second time my dutiful wife sent me a copy of Country Life it unfortunately seized the attention of Post Office inspectors, who obviously were interested to know why anybody would send money in this fashion. The first hint of trouble was a call from Stan.

'Look Terry,' he said in a slightly worried tone, 'I've had the bloody demons from the Post Office down here. They're looking for you.'

Although Stan did not have our Botany Bay address he did have our phone number and that was enough to give Eric the nadgers. It was clear that we would have to 'shoot through' as Old Bill would certainly be wanting to have a little chat with Mr Furminger. Eric had thoughtfully bought the Morris in a false name, so there was no way the car could be traced and we hoped our landlord would not remember the car's registration number. We loaded up the Morris with our worldly possessions and headed out in the direction of Melbourne.

Eric was all for putting as much distance between us and the Sydney 'demons' as possible so that when we got to Melbourne we decided to press on.

It was late at night when we arrived at the outskirts of Adelaide, 860 miles from Sydney. Eric exhausted after the long drive pulled off the road and we slept in the car until daylight.

I liked the 'feel' of Adelaide immediately. It had a certain atmosphere of calm, especially at a beach area we arrived at called Grange. We bought a newspaper and scanned a number of ads for room and board. One was for 'Surfside', a guesthouse owned and run by a young Australian called Gavin Jones. His price was five dollars a week - in advance.

The other guests were a pretty mixed bunch. English, Australian and New Zealanders, mostly young, mostly nice. I have many fond memories of the time spent at Surfside.

Eric had kept the name of Bob Burley, but I was now operating as Terence King. We both got jobs without any trouble, Eric as a service-station attendant and me as a joiner in a furniture factory where I sweated for peanuts. But I didn't mind we were having a ball and as a life style it was certainly more appealing than HM Prison. The only thing missing (apart from the wives and kids) was female company. Nobody could explain to me why, but there was a noticeable shortage of sheilas in Adelaide. You had to be built like Mr Universe just to get it on with any girl that appeared on the beach.

Money having changed hands in England, the organisation was in the process of preparing travel documents and tickets for our families to join us. Charm would be travelling as Mrs. Margaret Furminger, which worried Eric somewhat.

Having 'lost' the Morris in a road accident, I bought another car from one of Surfside's boarders, an English fellow called Mike. It was a Holden, an Australian car, and in reasonably good condition. Once again Eric 'did a job' on the engine.

Word reached us in April 1966 that Carol, Eric's wife, had arrived in Sydney with their daughter. Eric drove like a man possessed as he raced to pick them up clipping hours off the time it had taken us to get from Sydney to Adelaide. There, at the Sunshine Motel, were Carol and Kim waiting to greet us.

Charm had taken the opportunity to send more funds and a letter indicating that she would be arriving herself in the next couple of months. We returned to Adelaide at a more leisurely pace.

It wasn't long before Eric moved out from Surfside and into a small flat close to the gas station where he was working. I stayed on and it was about this time that the cook was sacked for being drunk on duty. A fearless Australian lady took her place by the name of Anne Pitcher. Anne and I became good friends and not long after her arrival at Surfside we took over the management.

April had also seen the arrest of Jimmy White in Littlestone-on-Sea in Kent after nearly three years on the run. In June Jimmy was sentenced to 18 years for his part in the train robbery, a fact that reflected how unjust our 30-year sentences had been.

It was almost mid-June when I got the news that Charmian was virtually on her way to Australia. For security reasons it had been decided that it would be best for her to arrive in Darwin where I would go to meet her. From an Australian motel guide I found what would be the perfect place for her and the boys to book into, the Koala Motel.

The day that I was due to travel I became sick. I developed a high fever and arrived in Darwin feeling pretty groggy. I spoke to a number of taxi drivers but not one of them had ever heard of the Koala Motel. Later I discovered that the motel was still under construction. That's builders for you!

As there was some kind of convention going on in Darwin I considered myself lucky to even find a hotel room. I flopped onto the bed and promptly fell asleep.

When I awoke it was already past the time when Charm's plane was due to arrive. I grabbed a super quick shower, dressed and called a cab to take me to the airport. I was quite late and the passengers were already leaving the airport when I arrived. I looked about for Charmian and the boys, but there was no sign of them. I was thinking that they may have got a taxi and gone off in search of the Koala Motel when I saw her through the glass doors of an office. Charmian was standing by her luggage, talking to an airport official. There was no sign of Nicky or Chris. As I stood undecided what to do she turned and looked in my direction but gave no sign that she had seen me. She was looking troubled.

I turned away abruptly, telling myself that she had been detained. 'Jesus Christ!' I thought, 'now what?' I went out of the airport feeling sick and desperate. I hid behind a clump of bushes and waited. After what seemed liked hours a van with some people in it came through a gate at the side of the airport. I was convinced it was Charm on her way to be locked up for the night. Back at my motel I spent a fretful night wondering what the hell I should do. If it had been discovered that Charm was using a phoney passport, she would obviously be charged with something and possibly make a court appearance. Wild ideas were going on inside my head.

Early the next morning I called Eric in Adelaide and told him that Charm had been taken into custody. He was shattered by the news. If Charm had been nicked Old Bill must know that we were in Australia.

'What are you going to do?' he asked. I told him that I had been thinking about going down to the courthouse to see what I could find out. Eric didn't think that this would be a good move.

'Don't go anywhere near any courthouses, for Christ's sake - even if she is taken to court today there is nothing that you can do. Your best move would be to get back to Adelaide on the first plane out of Darwin.'

I told Eric that I would get back to him later and hung up. I had had an idea. I would call the airline and see what they had to say with regard to the whereabouts of one Mrs Margaret Furminger. I rang and got an efficient sounding female on the line.

'Hello, I wonder if you could help me? I'm trying to find out if a Mrs Margaret Furminger arrived on the BOAC flight via Zurich last night?' There was a suspicious pause.

'Hello...Yes, Mrs Furminger did arrive and she is staying at the Fannie Bay Hotel.'

I thanked her for her help and hurried out of the post office from where I had made the calls. The women had sounded a little too ready with the information for my liking and I had a sneaking feeling that she had not been alone.

Over a much-needed beer I studied a map of Darwin that I had bought the day before. I found that the Fannie Bay was situated on the edge of town. I made up my mind, I was going to go out to the hotel.

As I got out of the taxi the first thing I saw was Old Bill! There were plainclothes coppers everywhere! As I walked down the path to the foyer of the hotel I passed two beefy chaps with short haircuts. I was doing my best not to turn green. The receptionist smiled.

'Can I help you?'

I noticed other big men with short haircuts standing around talking. As soon as I asked for Mrs Furminger, I told myself, these bastards were going to pile onto me. 'Yes,' I found myself saying. 'Could you tell me if there is a Mrs Furminger staying here?'

'She is, sir. She's on the second floor - would you like me to call her for you?'

Nobody moved and a few brief moments later there was Charmian and the boys hurtling down the stairs and into my outstretched arms.

'Darling!'

'Dad!'

We hugged and kissed and cried with happiness, oblivious to the onlookers. Nicky and Chris were tugging at me for my attention, wanting to show me the drawings they had done on the flight.

I was right about the men with the short haircuts. Darwin was hosting a major convention for senior policemen, and that was the reason all the hotels were full. When I had seen Charmian 'look through me' she had been preoccupied with the fact that there was nowhere for her and the kids to stay and there had been talk that she would have to pass the night in the local police station! A vacancy at the Fannie Bay Hotel was found at the last minute. Earlier that morning when I had been biting my nails with anguish, Charm and the kids had been enjoying themselves at the beach until being scared off by a flasher!

It was fabulous being together again, all the agony of the previous hours now forgotten. We went to the beach where Charm had got her first glimpse of Aussie manhood. I swam and played with the kids, chasing them and giving them 'bear-hugs' when I caught them. Back at the hotel I phoned Adelaide and brought Eric up to date with the glad tidings.

'Thank God for that,' he said somewhat relieved. 'I was just starting to make plans to shoot-through again.'

Charmian had arrived in Australia with all that remained of my share of the train robbery cash - a little over £7000 (about £110,000 today).

After lunch we went to a number of banks and changed a couple of thousand pounds into Australian dollars and then went shopping for a car. We had decided that we would buy a station wagon and make a slow overland trip down to Adelaide. It would be our first holiday together since we went to Hastings five year earlier.

It did not take us long to choose a vehicle. A brand new, gleaming white, Holden station wagon took our fancy. As I didn't know how to drive a car at the time we went for a test drive with Charmian at the wheel. We would take it, we decided, and with all the extras. It came out about $A3000 including the tax and insurance. We loaded up with an array of stuff we thought we might need for the trip: blankets, jerry cans, water bottles, an ice-chest, and so on. Then we went back to the hotel and picked up the luggage.

We finally drove out of Darwin as evening approached, the sky streaked dramatically with red and gold. We stayed close to Darwin on the first night but the first big dot on the map was to be our target for day two. It was a place called Daly Waters.

As it got dark on our first full day behind the wheel we calculated that we must be somewhere near Daly Waters in the Northern Territory. We stopped where there was some light and sound coming from a bar of some kind. I went to investigate. The people in the bar stopped talking as I entered.

'Could you tell me where I might find the Daly Waters Hotel?' I asked politely.

The barmaid looked me over. 'You're in it, mate.' The laughs continued.

The Daly Waters Hotel made the Fannie Bay Hotel look like the Savoy. When Charm went to the Ladies she found somebody washing their socks in the only sink. The 'somebody' was a truck driver, a male truck driver to boot. Later as Charm pulled on the sheet I was hogging it ripped right down the middle! Welcome to Australia, Charm!

Early next morning we were on the highway and the sun was shining fit to bust. The station wagon had an automatic transmission so once we were out in the middle of nowhere I had my turn at the wheel. Soon I was zipping along Highway 1 - nothing to it - Charm gently nagging. 'You're doing eighty! Slow down a little.' The kids were loving it every bit as much as I was. It was hot and it was dusty but we didn't mind we were having the time of our lives marvelling at the flocks of coloured birds, the billabongs, the 'roos and the emus.

'There are only two things wrong with Australia,' I said at one point. 'Too many flies and not enough women.'

We trekked on across the Northern Territory on Highway 87 and everywhere we stopped Charm turned a few heads with her Pommy accent and beehive-hair-do.

Looking at a map I discovered that our route east across Queensland to the Great Barrier Reef would take us close to Mount Isa, a copper mining town where I knew a couple of my friends from Adelaide had gone to work. On the spur of the moment I suggested that we should make a bit of a detour and give my chums a surprise.

It was early afternoon when we drove into Mount Isa. After we had booked into a small but comfortable motel, I left Charm with the kids and went off in search of my friends, Mel Kidd and Dave Stone. I had no trouble locating the mine where they had told me they were working, but I got little or no help from the Personnel Department.

The department that day consisted of one bloke who was sitting behind a desk writing. He hardly looked up from what he was doing when I entered his office.

'Good afternoon,' I said, 'I'm trying to locate a couple of friends who work here - Mel Kidd and Dave Stone?'

'We don't give out information about our workers,' the man said flatly.

'But I'm a friend of these people,' I insisted.

'So you might be,' said the man, still writing. 'On the other hand, you could be a debt-collector or a copper. Sorry mate, can't help you.'

'Thanks very much! But if by any chance you should see either of my pals, would you please tell them that Terry King is staying at the Paramount?'

The man showed no sign that he had heard me or cared, so it was a pleasant surprise when later that evening Mel and Dave showed up at the motel.

Several years later, when I was hiding from the police in Melbourne, I considered making my way to Mount Isa. The policy at the mine, by then, rather appealed to me!

From Mount Isa we headed across to Cairns on the Great Barrier Reef. We stayed there for a couple of days, going off on tours in the glass-bottomed boats, oohing and aahing at the coral formations and the brightly coloured fish. The kids played happily on the beaches, already tanned and glowing with good health. It was a big improvement on Bognor. The motel where we were staying had a baby-sitting service, and in the evenings Charmian and I could go out to dine.

Somewhat reluctantly, we left Cairns and began the long trip south to Adelaide. We took the highway along the coast, making overnight stops in Townsville and Mackay, with an extended stopover in Rockhampton for three nights.

One early morning we 'discovered' a deserted beach at a place called Yeppoon, close to Rockhampton. The tide was out and there was not a footprint to be seen on the sand. We couldn't resist. We changed into our bathing togs and raced across the virgin sand in the direction of the sea. 'Last one in the water is a bad egg!' I cried. The sea was crystal clear and shallow, with hardly a wave. We were spread out as we gleefully splashed into the cool water, Charmian bringing up the rear some twenty yards behind us.

Suddenly, she turned back towards the beach screaming as she ran madly through the shallow water. Calmed down, but still white with fright, she described how a water snake had passed between her legs.

We continued our adventurous journey down the coast to Sydney, where we stayed the best part of a week, then across country to Adelaide via Melbourne. The trip had taken us just over a month - long enough for Charmian to get pregnant again!

We had a jubilant reunion with Eric and Carol, the kids resuming the brief friendship they had with Kim in the UK. A good friend from Leeds, Mike Cunnington, joined our company as did Anne Pitcher, my partner in the guesthouse at the Grange. One big happy family.

Soon after our arrival in Adelaide, we rented a spacious house in an area called Glenelg and spent nearly all our remaining cash furnishing the place. Wall to wall carpets, 'Danish' furniture and so forth.

It had been suggested that Charmian could take part in the activities at the guesthouse. Her job was to serve food to the guests and clear the tables, not ideal work for somebody in her condition, yet even despite the heat she managed to battle through until she was nearly seven months pregnant. But the guesthouse with or without Charm was not paying, so reluctantly I passed on my share of the business to Anne and found myself a job as a carpenter.

The kids had taken to their new life style like fish to water and soon made friends with other children in the neighbourhood. Nicky was six years old at the time and had accepted his new surname, King, without question. We had told him that I was on secret government work and it was necessary to live with a different name. He was a bright little chap and caught on quickly, never making any reference to his life in England. One day, however, when he was playing with the kids next door, I heard him shout, 'All right, you be the police inspector and I'll be one of the train robbers.'

Life was almost a bowl of cherries. With plenty of overtime I was earning good wages, setting money aside for Charmian's forthcoming confinement. At weekends we would go with the 'Burleys' to one of the many beaches in the area or to 'hotels', as the pubs were called, and grog on while the kids ran wild, appearing every so often for another lemonade or more crisps.

Farley Paul, our third son, was born in Glenelg Community Hospital on 21 April 1967. Paul being in honour of Mr Seabourne without whom there would have been no Farley. After a few drinks with the lads to 'wet the baby's head' I went to the hospital to visit my wife and the latest addition to the Biggs family. Charm was sharing a room with another lady who had also recently given birth. When I arrived, the other happy father was in the room, gazing proudly at his handiwork cradled in his wife's arms.

'Terry King' I said warmly, extending my hand to the fellow, 'Congratulations!'

Mrs Charmian 'Furminger' was quick to cover my blunder. 'You and your silly jokes, Terry! Why don't you tell the gentleman your proper name?' I laughed it off, but I saw how easy it was to slip up using an alias. I would have to be more careful.

Farl was a great kid. He rarely cried or made a fuss. We all loved him! But not long after Charm left the hospital we received a bit of a blow through the post. It came in the form of an anonymous letter. The police, it said in poor handwriting, were aware that I was in Australia. It was imperative that we should move out of Adelaide as fast as possible and change our names again. It was something of a mystery because we thought the only people who knew our address were immediate friends. I was all for ignoring the letter, but Charmian didn't want to take the chance. We discussed the matter with Eric and Carol. Charmian was right they said, we had to 'shoot through'.

Heartbreaking though it was, I went out the next day and sold the station wagon for $900 Australian dollars, getting gyped on the deal. At a different used car dealer, I bought a furniture truck for $600 that looked as if it had been fabricated soon after the discovery of Australia. But it suited my purpose and it left me with $300 for gas and other expenses. Soon after dark that very same day, Eric backed the truck into my garden. Then, as silently as possible, so as not to alert any of the neighbours, we loaded the truck with the major part of our belongings and stole off into the night and out of Adelaide - destination Melbourne. Charm and the kids went to spend the night with Carol.

Early the next morning Eric and I arrived on the outskirt of Melbourne. Eric was just about wrecked after the 500-mile drive. Without too much trouble we found a warehouse where, at an exorbitant price, I was able to leave the furniture. After a meal and a wash and brush-up, we set about finding new accommodation for my family.

In a local newspaper I saw something I fancied. It was a two-bedroomed house with a 'beautiful garden' and a telephone. I rang a number and made an appointment with the estate agent.

I introduced myself as Terence Cook, giving my profession as an architect. My wife and children, I said, were on their way to Australia from England and I was anxious to find somewhere nice and comfortable for them. I was very sorry, but I couldn't provide any references because I had only just arrived in Australia myself. The estate agent was uncertain, the owners had asked for someone who was able to furnish references, but as

I looked like an honest person he didn't think that would be a problem. He picked up a pen and asked, 'What is your full name?'

'Terence King.' I replied.

The man looked up in surprise, 'I thought you said your name was 'Cook''

'I'm sorry,' I stumbled, 'I have a double-barrelled name, it's King-Cook really. For practical purposes I mostly call myself Cook.' Mistake number two, but luckily the agent kept writing and an appointment was made to see the house in Hibiscus Road, Blackburn.

A pleasant Australian couple, Bert and Joan Shepherd, were the owners of the house. I told them much the same story as I had told the estate agent and was accepted as the new tenant without further ado.

I suggested to Eric that we pass the night in a cheap hotel, but he was all for getting straight back to Adelaide without a rest. We made better speed with the van now that it was unloaded. We had left a mattress and a couple of blankets in the back of the truck and I managed to crash out for a few hours. Eric woke me up when we were about halfway through the journey; he was unable to go any further. I would have to drive, he said. I had no experience of driving a vehicle with manually operated gears and I reminded my friend of this. I suggested that we should pull off the road into a lay-by and continue after Eric had slept a while. He argued that this might attract the attention of Old Bill, we had to press on, he would show me how to drive the truck - there's nothing to it, he promised

Sitting alone behind the steering wheel of the ancient furniture van, I found myself thinking of places where I would rather be. The headlights needed adjusting, and on full beam I was blinding on-coming drivers and being blinded in return. Enormous semi-trailers would go screaming by, seemingly inches away. I would have settled for the worse kind of nightmare, even more plastic surgery in Paris. Never had I been so happy as when the dawn broke.

Miraculously back in Adelaide, we both slept through the rest of the day at Eric's flat. That same evening we were going to pick up the rest of our goods from the house at Glenelg and repeat the performance. And, after another 500 bone-shaking miles in the 'beast', with Charmian, Carol and the kids following in Eric's elderly car, we trundled into Melbourne a second time.

Mrs Shepherd, our new landlady, had left the house spick and span and, by the time we got the furniture arranged, our new home looked very cosy. We had told the older boys that they were going to have a new surname, Cook, and before they went off to explore the neighbourhood we gave them a briefing. The next day, leaving Charm with the children, including Farley who was barely three weeks old, I returned to Adelaide with Eric and Carol. On arrival we took the truck to the dealer I had bought it from and swapped it for an automatic Ford Falcon, who's flying days were soon evidently long past. But somehow I got it - and myself - back to Melbourne.

As 'Charmian' was such an unusual name and we wanted to break off as many ties as possible with Adelaide, it was decided that Charm would change her name to 'Sharon'. So we became known as Terry and Sharon Cook. We made friends with some of our neighbours. Lawrie and Rhona Black, who lived next-door, were particularly friendly and helpful - always ready to baby-sit if Charm and I wanted to go out for the evening. The Williams family, neighbours on the other side of our house, were quite the opposite. Soon showing a hostile attitude to the 'bloody poms' who had moved in next to them, a hostility they would continue to be unfriendly to Charm long after I had gone. But we took the good and the bad in our stride. We had settled in nicely. The kids were in a school just around the corner and I had found myself a job as a carpenter. We acquired a friendly yellow Labrador bitch whom we named Sadie, and it looked as if we were set to live happily ever after.

We expanded our circle of friends. At work I palled up with other Brits, Aussies and the odd Greek (aren't they all!) and we held some wild parties - the Williams being startled from their slumbers at 3 a.m. one night by the Phantom Bugler. As time went on we exchanged the much-maligned Falcon for a smart green Holden - that too, coming and going, had annoyed our neighbours. Sometimes I would pick up the boys after school and drive them home doing 'screamies', a la Batman, much to their delight.

To 'help out with the housekeeping' Charmian bravely took on evening work, which varied from packing biscuits at the Brockhoff Biscuit Factory to packing tissues at Bowater Scott. She was none too keen on the work, but I think she liked the chance to have a natter with the other women.

For Christmas 1967 we drove down to Adelaide to spend the holidays with Eric and Carol and Anne. A good time was had by all, but perhaps foolishly we returned the following year for New Year when a surprise was awaiting us. Eric's mate Alfie Gerrard was also paying a visit, the same one who along with Freddie Foreman had taken Eric and me off Paul's hands when we had first escaped. Ronnie Everett and Jerry Callaghan who had fled Britain after a run in with the police accompanied Alfie.

'Nice to see you fellas again!'

It was getting a little too warm in Adelaide. So after a jolly New Year's Eve party, we made our goodbyes and went back to muggy Melbourne.

The old fortune-teller in Hastings had been more right than wrong to date and just as she had suggested I still had 'foreman trouble'. Much to Charm's distress, I changed my job on a number of occasions. I had a stint as a maintenance carpenter at the television studios of Channel Nine. At weekend beach events, the hard core of the maintenance crew, Bert and I, would erect the camera stands, perving shamelessly at the sunburned sheilas.

It was our economic situation that finally dragged me away from Channel Nine where there was rarely any overtime to be had. I found myself another erecting job at Associated Insulation, this time office partitions. The pay was better and the hours were longer. Another year slipped by.

During the time we had been in Australia, we had seen a number of news items regarding the train gang. In September 1966, Buster Edwards had given himself up to the police and had been subsequently sentenced to fifteen years imprisonment. Jimmy White was also nicked in the same year and was probably delighted to cop 'only' eighteen years. Mighty Paul Seabourne, who had been given four and a half years for getting us out of Wandsworth, didn't stay free for very long after his release. He went back with ten years for holding up an armoured truck. And about the same time, 'Gentlemen' George, the Mr Fixit who had made all our arrangements, was also given a long stretch for a piece of business that had gone badly wrong. Then, after we had spent a happy Christmas and

New Year, we heard the bad news that Charlie Wilson had been re-captured in Canada. That was 25 January 1968.

As 1968 got underway, I was working on suspended ceilings at an immense shopping centre that was under construction. I had teamed up with a likeable Dutch carpenter named Martin, and we were on piecework, working flat out. One morning, I noticed two men carrying a large sheet of glass. The fellow at the back looked a lot like my very good friend, Mike Haynes. I got down from the scaffold where I had been working and went to get a better look at the bloke. Sure enough, it was Mike! I couldn't believe it. I sneaked up behind him, grabbed his arm and said, 'You're nicked, Haynes!'

When I first got to Australia, Charmian had been so elated that she had gone to visit Mick and Jess Haynes to tell them the good news. But before she could say where I was Mick had stopped her. No one should be told, he had said wisely. The fewer people who knew of my whereabouts, the better.

We were both completely knocked out by our amazing chance encounter. Mick and Jess and their two children, Tracy and John, had emigrated to Australia only a short time before we met. During the lunch break we got together, still 'mind-boggled' by our encounter. That evening we all got together at Hibiscus Road - there was a lot of drinking to do and the girls had plenty to talk about! It turned out that the Haynes' had a flat not very far from where we were living so we got together quite frequently, becoming better friends than ever.

But there was more bad news to come. On 8 November 1968 Bruce Reynolds was caught in Torquay. Now I really was the odd man out. As in my case, Bruce's fingerprints had been found on the Monopoly board and a bottle of tomato ketchup. He pleaded guilty and in January 1969 received a sentence of twenty-five years imprisonment. Bruce's wife Frances had her story published in the *Sunday Mirror* in London and subsequently in March 1968 in an Australian women's magazine.

The magazine in question, *Woman's Weekly*, had been delivered to our home with the newspaper and Nicky was leafing through the pages. 'Look mum,' he said. 'Here's a picture of Dad!'

Charm hastily relieved Nick of the magazine, telling him that it was just somebody who looked like me. But she was worried - and so was I when I got home from work and saw the article.

A bright young Australian girl called Marjorie, who had been one of my guests at Surfside, also saw the story and she too thought that Terry King looked a lot like the photograph of one of the wanted men in the article. She showed it to Anne Pitcher's son-in-law, Max Philips, who agreed that there was a strong resemblance. Max was a newscaster with a small radio station near Perth and decided to announce his suspicions over the air, which resulted in a visit from the local demons who were more than interested in hearing whatever Philips could tell them about Mr King.

While we had been doing our thing in Melbourne, Eric had gone into business with Alf and his chums. They had set up a trucking company in Adelaide and were doing very nicely. The article in the *Woman's Weekly* didn't please them.

Without knowing that our clever little guest at Surfside had recognized me, they assumed that somebody would. It was just a question of time, they said, before Old Bill would find out that I was in Australia. Eric and his friends - who also had good reasons to avoid contact with the police - decided that it would be prudent to abandon everything and shoot through, advising us to do the same. Even though we knew that other people in the neighbourhood would see the article I was all for riding out the storm. The months crept by and we started to relax again. Eric and friends first tried Melbourne, against our wishes, and then moved on to Sydney.

I changed my job again. Still in the office partitions and suspended ceiling business, but this time as a foreman, cracking the whip over a fairly motley crew of thirty-odd carpenters and labourers. I tried to be a good foreman. I didn't dock anyone's time for being late or absent if they had a good excuse. I had been one of these poor buggers myself once. We played nine card brag' almost every lunchtime, frequently going over the allotted break time, especially if there was a big kitty that had to be won.

'You're very popular,' said my boss one day. 'Everyone's asking to be put in Terry Cook's gang.' But our output must have been satisfactory, as we were chosen to take on a big job at the new Melbourne Airport.

Charmian, was still working at the Bowater Scott factory, and we were becoming a bit like ships in the night as with only one car I would return home just in time for Charmian to shoot off for her night shift, having already prepared dinner for me and the kids and prepared Farley for bed.

I usually arrived home soon after six, looking forward to my nightly 'playtime' with the kids. Farley, now a fun-loving two year old, would begin rocking his cot against the wall of his room, demanding my attention. Most evenings we would all end up in the bath together, the kids clamouring to be the next 'depth charge.'

One October evening, during the fun and games, I received a telephone call from a friend who was aware of my true identity. He asked me if I had seen the six o'clock news. I told him I had arrived home too late to catch the headlines.

'Make sure you see the nine o'clock edition,' he said seriously, 'it concerns you - and the news is not good.' I got the boys to bed before nine and sat on the edge of a chair to watch the news.

Earlier that day, 16 October, a Reuters correspondent named Reeves had dropped in at Melbourne Police Headquarters in Russell Street snooping around for news. He happened to see a memo on a desk to the effect that it was suspected that I was living in Melbourne with my wife and children. Mr Reeves sent out this little gem of information as a news item and in no time the rest of the media had picked it up.

Channel Nine showed mug-shots of Eric and me, together with our general description and the information that the police believed I was working as a carpenter in Western Australia. The train robbery story was rehashed and the public was invited to contact the police in the event of having any information that might lead to our capture. This time, the shit had well and truly hit the fan.

Charmian paled when I told her the bad news. 'What are we going to do?' she asked. Once again I was all for 'sweating it out'. I was sick of running. I even considered giving myself up. But Charmian wouldn't hear of it.

'Never give up,' she told me. 'I'm going to pack a bag for you and in the morning we will decide what to do.'

Early the next morning, a Friday, Charmian backed the car out of the garage and drove to our local newsagent. She bought both Melbourne dailies and they told her more than she or I needed to know. Our story was all there including the name and ages of the kids, and that included Farley.

Charmian drove straight back to Hibiscus Road.

'Quick, kiss the children goodbye – it's all there in the *Age*,' she told me.

I grabbed my bag, kissed the kids and jumped into the passenger seat of the Holden. Our lovely little boys were still sound asleep when we left. I hoped and prayed that I would be able to come back to them. We had a plan. Charmian would drive me to a motel on the outskirts of the city. There I would wait to see if the situation got any worse - or otherwise. In the event of little or no reaction to the news, we would meet at eight o'clock at a certain Chinese restaurant.

A good foreman to the last, I had filled in the time sheets of the workers I was responsible for and took them to a fellow foreman, Andy, who lived close by. I was taking a chance as Andy may well have seen the news the previous evening. But Andy, a Scottish ex-commando, and I were pretty good mates so I didn't think there was a chance that he would 'dob me in'. We often drove to work together and he was surprised that I was calling on him at the crack of dawn. Without preamble I told that I was leaving town for a little while, perhaps for a long while, and there was a strong chance that I would never see him again.

'Look,' he said 'It's a bit early in the day for this kind of stuff. Sit down and have a cup of tea, and tell me what's going on!' But I shook hands with him, said goodbye, and left him standing open-mouthed.

Charmian drove me to the Alexander Motel in an area called Essenden, not far from the airport where I had been working until the previous evening. I kissed my tearful wife goodbye and watched her drive off, then turned and booked in at the motel under the name of Arthur Robert Carson.

In her heart Charmian knew it would probably be only a matter of time until the police found the house, but she decided to carry on as if everything was normal. Back at Hibiscus Road she got the kids washed and dressed and dropped Nicky and Chris off at Blackburn North School. She then drove to the hairdresser with Farley for her normal Friday appointment. If the staff had seen anything in the morning papers, they did not say anything.

Charmian returned to the house, but there was still no sign of the police so she went and picked the kids up from school and just as I had, she picked up a copy of the evening paper. The news was more a less a repeat of what had already been published and added nothing to what we had already learned. Perhaps we would be okay.

Charmian left the kids at home with Nicky in charge and drove to the nearest public phone to call me. She was put through to 'Mr Carson' and updated me on the lack of police activity or any activity, for that matter. A case of no news is good news and we planned to meet at the restaurant at eight o'clock as originally planned.

At around seven-fifteen, Charmian set out for the Chinese restaurant. She was going to bring me a few more shirts, my electric razor, that I had forgotten in the rush to leave the house, and some family photos. As she turned right off Hibiscus Road, all hell broke loose and about a dozen police cars converged on her from every direction. The doors of the car were pulled open and four armed officers, guns at the ready, piled in. They wanted me 'dead or alive', they said. Charm got cross at the sight of the firearms. 'My husband isn't here,' she told them.

After some discussion, Charmian, was allowed to return to the house to check on the children who were to be looked after by our neighbour. She was then taken first to Russell Street Police headquarters, Melbourne's equivalent of Scotland Yard for the Victoria Police, and then to 43 McKenzie Street, the headquarters of the then Commonwealth Police, Australia's equivalent of the FBI.

Ignorance being bliss, back at the motel I emptied out my case and packed it with the clothes and personal items I might most need. I planned to leave the motel when it was dark and keep my appointment with Charmian at the Chinese restaurant. I didn't plan to return, and even left an unpaid bill of £3 and a couple of suits. I wanted to travel light. When there was no sign of Charm by nine o'clock I guessed that she had been taken into custody. Now what?

I thought of turning up on Mike Haynes' doorstep, but dismissed the idea instantly: Old Bill was probably grilling him at that very moment. Finally I decided to grab a cab and pay a visit to the friend who had tipped me off the night before. He was not expecting me. In fact he got a bit of a fright when I tapped on his bedroom window. But he was more than ready to help and two days later I found myself in a cosy little holiday home called Blue Waters, high up in the Dandenong Mountains that flank one side of Melbourne.

I was provided with plenty of food, magazines and a radio. Much to my joy, I heard that Charmian had been released after spending the weekend in custody and reunited with the children. Then my friend came to visit with some further good news, Charmian had sold her story to the Packer group of newspapers for $A65,000, although the tax man was going to grab $40,000 of that leaving Charm with just $A25,000. The other not so good news was that the hunt was very much on. Victorian Chief Superintendent Jim Milner was in charge of the operation. He made frequent statements to the public - and me - via radio and television, telling us what moves were being made to catch the train robber. Railway stations and airports were under close watch. Roadblocks had been set up at strategic points. Biggs was desperate and without friends, according to Mr Milner, who promised that I would be locked up in the City Watch-house 'within twenty four hours.'

'Fresh evidence' was presented to the news hungry press corps when detectives discovered the clothing, including the two suits, I had left behind at the motel and a little later a much publicised home movie was shown on television in which - according to Mr Milner, who made the dramatic presentation - the wanted man could be seen on a beach in Spain, puffing away at a cigar. How either of these incidents could have been of any help in getting me in the City Watch-house I never discovered. Furthermore, I am a non-smoker and I have never set foot in Spain. But the net was tightening.

A few days later my favourite cop came on the radio and telly to say that the search was going to swing in the direction of the Dandenong Mountains, the 'perfect place' for someone to hide. My pal had also heard Jim Milner's pronouncement and soon showed up at my little hideaway in the hills. It was too bad, but I would have to find another refuge.

It was a Sunday evening when I knocked on the door of Mike Haynes' house.

'Christ Almighty!' exclaimed my old mate as he opened the door, 'I thought it was the Law! Come in!' They had kept up with the news, of course, and thought that Old Bill would be paying them a visit any moment. It would be very risky for me to stay with them. But they were friendly with a young English couple whom Mike thought could be asked to put me up for a week or two. He would speak to them the next morning before they went to work.

The couple, George and Janet, agreed to let me stay with them until the heat was off and that evening, when it was dark, I walked to my new digs. My hosts were clearly quite nervous about their lodger but, said George, they were taking the chance because I was Mike's friend. Janet prepared the spare room, hoping I would be comfortable, and then showed me where everything was that I might need. They both had jobs and would be out of the house all day. I would have to fend for myself.

The 'demons' were still very active in the area. Through the net curtains in the kitchen I could see patrol cars cruising around the neighbourhood. Then, much to my delight, a couple of desperados escaped from Pentridge, Melbourne's grim old gaol, and the police turned their attention to the capture of their fugitives.

Eric Flower, alias, Bob Burley, was arrested in Sydney on 24 October, one week after I had gone to ground. More bad news. Then, days later, Alfie Gerrard's friends met a similar fate. Soon it was Alfie's turn. A neighbour had spotted him sunbathing in the back garden of a rented house. The good lady, mistaking Alfie for me, phoned the cops and 'Biggs' was pounced on. Sorry about that, Alf!

About the same time, a certain Mr Ronald Biggs planned a sea trip. A trunk bearing his name had been delivered to the port awaiting the arrival of the owner. When he turned up to travel he, too, was pounced on and dragged away to the slammer. Sorry about that, Ron.

Eric, Alfie and his friends having been arrested were all extradited back to Britain. Eric was sent back to Wandsworth to finish his 12 years, while the other three stood trial for assault.

As the weeks passed the police pressure seemed to ease off. As the police had not visited the Haynes', we decided that it would be safe for me to move in with them. There was more room, a garden that wasn't overlooked by neighbours, and I would be with people whom I considered to be 'family'. My plan at that time was to lie low for a few months then make my way up north.

Thanks to the attitude of the personnel department in one of its mines, I was being seriously considering Mount Isa in Queensland as a place to head for.

Although Charm had been charged with illegally entering Australia, she was still permitted to go about her business and was being well advised by lawyers hired for her by the Packer group. The police kept watch on her, following her wherever she went, and a squad car could always be seen close to her house. But, with the help of friends, we managed to communicate, although it was to be nearly three months before we could physically meet, which had seemed like an eternity, and then at first it was just for one hour. I was thinking particularly of Charmian and the kids when Christmas came. Although there was a fine 'Christmas spirit' at the Haynes' and an abundance of everything, it was difficult to be 'merry'. New Year's Eve was even less jolly, as my friends went off to spend the evening with Charmian. At midnight I raised a glass of champagne to absent friends and loved ones, listening to the neighbours singing 'Auld Lang Syne'.

It was during this period that Mike Haynes very generously offered me his passport.

'It's yours,' he said, 'If you think you can do anything with it.' Well, that literally opened new horizons. Mike and I were quite similar in general appearance and height; the only real difference was the colour of our eyes, his being brown and mine blue. But it was an offer I couldn't refuse.

Once again I was in a position to go anywhere in the world. But where? Mike, Jess and I discussed the subject for hours while we played cards. I would have to think about a suitable disguise if I was hoping to get out of the country. I had gained quite a bit of weight since I had gone to ground so we decided that I would become a fatty. From then on, much to Mike's delight, we ate Spaghetti Bolognese practically every day.

I was still in a dither about where to go until one evening Jess arrived in the house with a pile of travel pamphlets.

'Here you are, Ron,' she said, dropping them on the dining-room table.

'See if you can find a place you fancy in this lot!' I picked up the brochure that was on the top of the pile. It was a VARIG Airline leaflet showing the beautiful Bay of Guanabara and Sugar Loaf Mountain. 'I want to go there,' I said without looking any further.

Mike looked at the pamphlet over my shoulder, 'South America!' he exclaimed. 'Of course! Why didn't we think of it before? There's a 100,000 Nazi war criminals hiding out over there - that's the place to go!'

All three of us had precious little knowledge about South America. All we knew was what we had learned from the Mission Impossible television series: cruel dictators, corrupt officials and incompetent soldiers. So it was decided. I was going to try to get to Rio de Janeiro.

A map was produced to work out the best way to get there. A boat to Panama, then a plane down to Rio - Mike made it sound so easy.

I needed a haircut and Mike, who had been in the army and had a bit of barbering experience, offered to do the honours. Soon I was sporting a 'short back and sides' that would have gratified the most demanding Company Sergeant Major. Jess giggled, 'now you look more like an escaped con than ever!'

Returning to the passport, I found - as good luck would have it - that Mike's photograph was quite loose and easy to remove. The difficult thing was going to be reproducing part of the embossed Foreign Office stamp which appeared on the bottom right hand corner of the picture. That evening, under the cover of darkness, Mike and I went to a shopping mall where I made a couple of dozen passport pictures. The next morning, at my instigation and expense, the Haynes family went off camping for the weekend. I needed to be alone to work on the passport. Having got Mike to stock up the refrigerator with beer before leaving, I got to work as soon as they were gone. I had never considered taking up forgery for a living, but by Sunday afternoon I was satisfied with my labours. The new Michael John Haynes had a passport. When Mike saw the result he was very impressed. It was bloody near perfect, even if I say so myself.

Charmian had been able to lay her hands on some cash that she was to receive for the story she had sold, but not too much or it would have raised suspicion. She had been told of Operation Rio and managed to get $2000 to me without too much trouble. With part of the money Jess went to a travel agency and booked a sea passage to Panama in Mike's name. I would be sailing on the RHMS Ellinis, a Greek liner of the Chandris Line, in less than a week.

During my time with Mike and Jess I had not totally wasted my time, and by putting pen to paper I hoped that I could leave Charmian with a little insurance policy. Over what would be 77 typeset pages, I told my story to date. Charm was to hang on to the manuscript, complete with my fingerprints and signature, and sell it to the highest bidder once I was safely away.

If they gave me a fortune
My pleasure would be small
I could lose it all tomorrow
And never mind at all
But if I should lose your love, dear
I don't know what I'd do
For I know I'll never find another you

The Seekers, *I'll Never Find Another You*

Chapter Eight

THE PACIFICS:
MELBOURNE TO RIO

Personally I think society has a right and a duty to eliminate these people (the train robbers) who have shown that they are not prepared to play according to the rule.

Alec Muir, Chief Constable of County Durham, February 1969

Biggs tricks police again

***Evening Standard*, 22 October 1969**

It seemed that the whole ship was singing 'Waltzing Matilda', roaring out the words of the Australian 'national anthem'. I couldn't sing. I had a problem with a lump in my throat. I had a feeling that I would never see this lovely land again - and I was going to miss it.

Ronald Biggs, 7 February 1970

As I had left most of my clothes at the hotel, I had precious little to put in the much-travelled suitcase which Mike produced for the trip. My bits and pieces just about covered the bottom of the suitcase but little else, so Mike threw in a sleeping-bag and all the old clothing that he and Jesse no longer needed. Thinking that it might come in handy, I packed the magnifying glass which I had been using to work on the passport. One of the locks on the case was broken, so we secured it with a piece of cord on one side. Not exactly what the well-dressed traveller would use, but at least it was functional.

When the day arrived for me to embark aboard the RHMS Ellinis - 5 February 1970 - both Mike and I were more than a little apprehensive. Fortunately, the ship was to sail in the evening so we would be able to leave the house under cover of dark. The plan was for Mike to go through passport control as the passenger, while Jesse and I went aboard as visitors to see him off. I had stuck Mike's picture lightly back into his passport. Once we were all on board I would take the ticket and passport, swap the photographs and assume my new identity. We opened a bottle of brandy 'to calm the old nerves', as Mike put it. I had a last get-together with Charmian to say goodbye. She was enthusiastic about the plan, but sad to see me go. It had been nearly four agonizing months since the police had raided the house.

Charmian and I had no idea when we would meet again. We kissed and hugged each other.

'You'll meet other woman,' said Charmian unhappily, 'but don't forget about us.' It would be four years almost to the day when I was next to see Charmian and that was under very different circumstances. I was also unaware that the previous day Jack Mills, the driver of the train, has succumbed to lymphatic leukaemia.

Everything went according to plan on the day. Mike had no trouble going through passport control and the ugly suitcase was taken from him to be stored in the cabin. Wearing horn-rimmed glasses and a check cap I went up the gangplank of the Ellinis with Jesse steadying herself on my arm. We met Mike on deck, all of us nervous but flushed with success and brandy. I took the ticket and passport from Mike and went off to find the cabin I would be sharing with three other people. As luck would have it, it was empty. I locked myself in the toilet and swapped the photographs in the passport, taking particular care in how I stuck down my photo. This was in the days when there was no plastic film over the photo, so I didn't want anyone to be able to see the pencil marks on the reverse side. I flushed the torn up pieces of Mike's picture down the toilet bowl and rejoined my friends on deck. Not for the first time, Mike said softly: 'Now make sure you keep your bins on at all times - we know you hate the bloody things, but keep 'em on. And keep yourself to yourself - play the part of a hermit, don't mix.' Sound advice from a caring friend, my 'brother' as Paul Seabourne had called him.

The Haynes' could not stay very long. They had made plans with Charmian to see The Modern Jazz Quartet and didn't want to miss the concert or the alibi. We said our fond farewells.

'Have a good trip, Mike and don't forget to write!'

I watched and waved my friends ashore, then mingled with the other passengers on deck. They were a mixed bunch as the Ellinis was bound for Southampton via Sydney, Auckland, Tahiti and the Panama Canal. The ship's siren blew and a general call went up for visitors to go ashore. Families and friends left the ship and gathered on the quay calling last minute messages to their departing loved-ones. As I walked to the rail to look down at the throng I found right beneath me and looking up was a foreman called Les, with whom I had been working a short time before I had gone to ground. He saw me, perhaps saw through me, but he didn't show any signs of recognition. I turned away from the rail and went to my cabin. The world was turning out to be far too small for my liking.

My cabin-mates were a lot younger than me; two Aussie university graduates, Bill and Greg, on their way to Canada, and Peter, a wiry Italian-Yugoslav, also Canada bound. Greg produced some 'coldies' and opened up the conversation. He was more talkative and humorous than his friend. Peter was quite a card and as friendly as only the Italians can be. He had been working as a labourer in Australia and rolled up his shirtsleeves so that we could see his rock-hard muscles. It soon became obvious that Peter was sex-mad.

The boat would be stopping at Tahiti and the vivid description Greg gave of the exotic delights awaiting us left our Italian friend with flared nostrils. Soon we were under way and the boat came to life; the evening meal was served and the bar was open. We opted unanimously for a liquid dinner and grogged on into the night, finding out about each other. After half a dozen tubes we were all getting along like long established chinas, and before the evening was over, Greg paid me the highest compliment that any Australian can pay to an Englishman: 'You're not a bad bloke - for a Pommy.'

I rose early the next morning and went on deck for a walk - I had to meet the public sometime. Other early risers smiled and said good morning; the disguise seemed to be working. A bell sounded which announced breakfast. After the walk I fancied a nice cup of hot coffee. The only person sitting at the table to which I had been assigned was a pretty young lady with fluffy blond hair, blue eyes and great tits. She reminded me of the sexy nurse in Paris.

With savoir-faire one would normally associate with Gregory Peck in his prime, I joined her.

'Mike Haynes.' I said, extending my hand.

'Blondie,' she said with a firm grip. 'At least that's the name I'm using while I'm on this boat.'

She was as Australian as Ayre's Rock, the kind of a girl who would have happily told Gregory Peck to go play with his marbles. On a scale of one to ten she probably saw me at that moment as a one, a right-one, a four-eyed, piss-weak, Pommy bastard. I raised my cup to take a sip of coffee. For a moment I wondered what had happened - I couldn't see a thing - my glasses had steamed over. Blondie thought it was hilarious as I groped around the table to find my napkin.

All too soon Frank, a shy Spanish fellow on his way to Caracas to join his brother in a restaurant business, joined us. Then along came an elderly English couple, the Harrisons, polite and kindly folk who had spent many years fruit-farming in Australia but who had not lost their frightfully posh Pommy accents. They were going back to England 'for one last look at the old place'. Miss Carey was the last to make up our group at the table, a crotchety old Irish lady, who, understandably, appeared to have 'missed the bus' at some point in her life.

It was heating up in the dining room and my glasses started to slide down my nose. The faster I pushed them up, the faster they slid down again until finally, with a crash, they fell off my face altogether and clattered onto my plate. I didn't say what I wanted to say, I simply wiped the glasses on my napkin and put them into my pocket, never to be used again. Fuck the glasses, I thought!

We were steaming towards Sydney, the first stop on the voyage. Greg and Bill were full of plans to go ashore and have a last gut-full of fair dinkum Australian piss. But I feigned sickness, making appropriately nauseating sounds in the bathroom.

'Sorry, boys,' I groaned, ' I wish I was well enough to go with you.'

Before I had gone aboard the Ellinis, I had imagined that my chief obstacle would be the Master at Arms. I had visualized an unpleasant snooper, in all probability an ex-detective, who would recognize me instantly from wanted notices sent to the ship. I needn't have worried, there wasn't a nicer person on board ship. He was an easy-going young Dutchman, courteous and friendly, who occasionally joined us for our informal parties in the cabin prior to dinner.

Well sloshed, my cabin-mates returned to the ship just before we were due to sail, abusing piss-weak Poms in general and me in particular. A little later, when I heard the blast on the ship's horn advising visitors to leave, I started to feel 'much better'.

'Typical of you useless Poms!' Greg ventured.

Crowds of people were on deck as the Ellinis slowly drew away from the quay. Other passengers had joined the ship and there was a similar scene to the one in Melbourne, with well-wishers waving and shouting from the dock.

There was a certain feeling of excitement in the warm summer evening air now that we were leaving Australia and New Zealand would be our next stop. A singsong started up and as we passed beneath the Sydney Harbour Bridge and it was not long until it seemed that the whole ship was singing 'Waltzing Matilda', roaring out the words of the Australian 'national anthem'. I couldn't sing. I had a problem with a lump in my throat. I had a feeling that I would never see this lovely land again - and I was going to miss it. The date was 7 February 1970.

The next morning volunteers were invited to participate in various cruise activities. Jimmy, as camp as a row of pink tents, was in charge of deck recreation and was allocating small jobs to anyone who was interested.

'Hmmm, you look nice,' he said when I stepped forward to be interviewed, 'I wonder if you would like to take care of ladies' deck sports?'

How could Jimmy have known that this was exactly the kind of job that I had been born for? The next morning I was handling a bunch of lovelies wearing brief tennis skirts and 'Gorgeous Gussie' knickers; leaping and cavorting under the approving - and roving - eye of their 'sportsmaster'.

I was not keen to go ashore in New Zealand either. It was still too close to Australia for comfort. But my cabin-mates and other people who I had chummed up with were going off to do a bit of rubbernecking and I was obliged to join them. It was a sunny afternoon, so I was able to put on a pair of shades for the outing. Blondie saw me leaving the ship and told me the 'sunnies' gave me a sinister air.

'You look like a Mafia hit-man,' she declared.

Back on the ship again Peter was all but doing handsprings; we were en route to Tahiti. That evening, so that the people could get to know each other for the Pacific crossing, the official 'Captain's Party' was held with everyone turning out in their crumpled finery. I stood at the side of the dance-floor with Greg and co, swigging Greek plonk from a paper cup, checking out the sheilas. Greg summed the ladies up as a 'fuckin' grim lookin' bunch', but an unaccompanied girl in a white dress caught my eye.

Unmistakably English, almost prim, not unlike a young Joyce Grenfell to look at. Her name was Molly Evans. When I asked her to dance, she warned me that she was not a very good dancer. She was not much of a drinker either and, a little later, she warned me again; she was not very good in bed. She was frigid, she told me.

We found a secluded spot on an upper deck and sat looking at the stars. Molly thought it was the right moment to tell me about 'John', the love of her life until a tiff had sent her running off to Australia. She missed him dreadfully and knew that he was missing her, so she was on her way back to England to see if there was a chance of reconciliation with her erstwhile lover. But, she sighed, she felt physically attracted to me - and Johnny boy was on the other side of the world!

The weather was perfect. Most mornings we would lie around one of the decks sunbathing and knocking back coldies. The dirty jokes out of the way, we turned to more profound subjects. A conversation arose about Australia's national hero, the outlaw, Ned Kelly, who was hanged in Melbourne jail. I remarked that I thought it was odd that a nation - one of our colonies - had chosen a criminal as their national hero. Greg, who was from the State of Victoria - 'Kelly' country - was swift to defend the Irish renegade.

'So I don't want to hear anyone havin' a shot at Ned Kelly... like this bloke, Briggs (sic), they're lookin' for back in Melbourne, no self-respecting Australian would ever dob him in.'

'I read somewhere,' I interrupted, 'that an Aussie newscaster near Perth was the person who put the police on to Briggs.'

'You're missing the point, mate.' responded Greg, 'I said; 'no 'self-respecting' Australian. Nobody back there wants to see him caught, even the Chief of Police is helping the bloke; he comes on telly all the time, telling Briggs his next move! It's a bloody comedy.'

A day or so later, sunbathing with Molly after a swim, she suddenly surprised me by whispering in my ear: 'I know who you are!'

Warning bells were clanging.

'Really? So do tell me, who am I?'

'You're Bruce Reynolds!'

'Bruce Reynolds! I think you'll find he's in jail for the train robbery.'

'Well,' Molly insisted, 'If you're not Reynolds - you're Charlie Wilson!'

'And if I'm not Charlie Wilson, I must be Ronnie Biggs?'

'Yes! That's who you are!' she said as her eyes brightened. 'But don't worry, I won't tell anyone, Mike - and I'll help you if you need money or anything.'

What a sweet girl. What an amazing girl!

It was just before dawn when the ship docked in rainswept Tahiti. The Aussies and I felt that we needed more sleep, but Peter was up and dressed, pacing the floor of the cabin, waiting for the gangplank to be lowered so that he could get to the girls. When the time came he was the first person off the ship.

Molly and I mooched around the island in the rain until we got bored and went back to the ship early for afternoon tea. To our surprise, Peter was sitting in the dining room, looking a picture of abject misery, nearly knee-deep in empty beer cans. I approached him.

'Hey! Peter. You make good fucky-fucky?' He looked disgusted.

'Don't make fucky-fucky. Don't make any fucking thing. All the Tahitian girls are fat pigs! One looks at me and says, 'hey boy, let's make fuck. Only five dollar' I tell her, 'Fat pig! I don't pay five cents to fuck you!'

The voyage progressed. We were on our way to Panama where I would be saying goodbye to all my fine new friends. Most of them were going onto the US, Canada and England. There were two I knew who would be leaving the boat in Panama, Frank, the Spaniard who shared my table, and an attractive but rather serious German girl, named Rosie, whom Frank had befriended. They were both en route to Caracas.

In October 2010 the *Mail On Sunday* published a couple of photos of me on the cruise that were taken by the ship's photographer. One photo showed me, Bill, Molly, Greg and Peter enjoying a drink, another of Molly and I getting some food. While the *Mail* had the year right, it being 1970, they did not quite spot the subtlety of my disguise of piling on the pounds. Instead they decided my beaming round face and trendy sideboards were 'swollen from plastic surgery.' I know the surgery in Paris was primitive, but I think after four years the swelling might just have gone down!

Just before we docked in Panama, immigration officials came on board to interview the travellers about to disembark, setting up a table in the dance-hall for that purpose. Offering up a silent prayer, I presented my passport to the agents. There was a problem: I didn't have a visa to land in Panama. I explained my reason for leaving the ship in Panama and said that I was unaware that I needed a visa 'just to pass through'. I was granted a stay of seven days but was obliged to pay a $200 bond, about $3000 today, which would be refunded when I could show the authorities an airline ticket out of Panama.

Two hundred dollars was about all the money I had and I needed that to cover the cost of a flight to Rio. The official was adamant; he would have his bond. I was wondering how I was going to manage when there was an announcement over the Tannoy address system that Michael Haynes was wanted in the Purser's office. I dragged my feet. Had somebody recognized me? Was I about to be arrested, as Dr Crippen had been in 1910, after a radio message had been flashed across the ocean to Captain

Henry Kendall of the SS Montrose? There was a message, but it was from Charmian who had managed to radio to the Ellinis a further $200 and which was now at my disposal. The gods were smiling on Biggsy.

I picked up my battered suitcase and prepared to leave the ship at Panama. It was early evening and many passengers were going ashore just for a look around. There was much hustle and bustle of people coming and going. Suddenly I heard someone calling the name, John, several times. It was Mr. Harrison, the polite Englishman.

'John Haynes?' he said holding up an envelope. 'Here's a letter for you!'

Sure enough, the letter was addressed to Mr John Haynes, c/o SS Ellinis.

'I thought you said your name was Mike,' said Mr. Harrison. 'You can't fool me! What are you up to, old lad - running away from a woman?'

'My name is, Michael John Haynes,' I told him, 'and I'm not running away from a woman, I'm running away from her husband!'

The playful Englishman slapped his thigh with delight. 'You old rascal!' he chortled. 'Anyway, may God take care of you wherever you go - I like your spirit!'

We shook hands and wished each other luck. The letter wasn't for me; there was another Mr Haynes aboard the Ellinis!

Molly, Greg and Bill went ashore with me. After I had booked in to a ramshackle hotel and unburdened myself of my equally ramshackle suitcase, we went off to a bar for a few last jars together. We were not too impressed with Panama City. Steel-helmeted police, armed to the teeth with machine guns and grenades, patrolled the streets in pairs, looking distinctly unfriendly.

After handshakes and back-slapping, my Aussie friends returned to the ship to give Molly and I a last chance to be alone. During those last few weeks, Molly was feeling less and less like returning to the love of her life. She fancied the idea of going on to Rio with me.

At the hotel where I had booked in there was a problem: the senhorita could not be allowed to accompany me to my room. There are none so stupid as those who want to be. Molly and I didn't have a clue what all the fuss was about. We turned from the agitated hotel receptionist and went hand in hand straight up the creaking staircase.

In spite of Molly's insistence to join me on my South American adventure, I managed to get her back to the boat before it sailed. She was young and pretty, I told her. She should go back to England, marry John and settle down to the kind of life that she was obviously cut out for. Like many of the people I have met on my journeys, I have often wonder whatever happened to her. Jack Slipper claims that he did track her down and interview her in South London after my arrest in Rio. He described her as "a very smart, respectable woman in her thirties." She did not hide from Slipper that we had become close.

Molly and all the friends I had made on the crossing from Australia gathered at the stern of the liner, waving and shouting their goodbyes as the ship slowly inched away. The Pommy contingent was singing, Maybe it's Because 'He's' a Londoner. The quay was quite deserted and suddenly I felt very alone.

I made my way back to the hotel, flopped out on the lumpy mattress and fell into a deep sleep. In the morning I was woken by the rattle of a snare-drum. Jesus! I thought, a public execution is about to take place! I jumped out of bed and peered out of the grimy window which overlooked a square below. A detachment of soldiers was getting into line. Somebody blew a number of notes on a bugle and the soldiers snapped to attention.

An officer took a couple of paces forward and saluted. Then the Panamanian flag was run up on a flagpole and everybody disappeared as quickly as they had arrived.

Later, that same morning, I met Frank and Rosie at the KLM office where they were in the process of arranging their flight to Caracas. Frank invited me to stop off at Caracas on the way to Rio and spend a week or two with him and his brother. So the ticket I bought was for Caracas, Rio and Montevideo. Montevideo was to serve as a red herring if and when the police traced me to the Ellinis and as far as Panama.

With the ticket in my hand, I went to the immigration office to collect the 200 bucks that I had left as a bond. The agent who had gone aboard the Ellinis attended me, wishing me good luck on my trip south.

When I arrived at Caracas Airport the first thing I noticed was a lot of policemen. Many of them were wearing plain-clothes, but it wasn't difficult to pick them out. They would have made perfect extras on any Mission Impossible set. However, I went through customs and the passport checkpoint without a hitch and joined my friends, Frank and Rosie, who having arrived a couple of days earlier were at the airport to meet me. I found out later that the cops had been on the lookout for a Commie terrorist of some kind and had no interest in a mere British train robber.

I arrived in Caracas on 26 February and stayed for two weeks, enjoying the hospitality of Frank and his brother, Carlos. As Frank had started work, I found myself in Rosie's company a fair bit and we became fond of each other. She had split up with her husband in Australia and was seeking a new life in South America. She wanted me to stay in Caracas and I was tempted - I had even been offered a job, together with a work-permit and other papers in the name of Michael Haynes. But nothing could change my mind: the plan was to go to Rio de Janeiro and to Rio de Janeiro I would go.

MR HAYNES SETTLES IN RIO

Wherever you are and whatever you are doing, sit down. Our darling son Nicky has been killed in a road accident.

Charmian Biggs, 5 January 1971

Lonely was Ned Kelly,
Lonely am I
In a crowd of other people,
Lonely is a wife without a husband,
Lonely is a lost child
In the street,
Lonely is a parent without a child.

Nicholas Biggs, 9 years old, December 1970

Vai, minha tristeza, e diz a ela
Que sem ela não pode ser
Diz-lhe numa prece que ela regresse
Porque eu não posso mais sofrer
Chega de saudade
A realidade é que sem ela não há paz
Não há beleza, é só tristeza
E a melancolia que não sai de mim
Não sai de mim, não sai

Tom Jobim / Vinicius de Moraes, *'Chega de Saudade'*

On Sunday 11 March 1970, I landed at Rio de Janeiro's old Galeão airport after the overnight flight from Caracas. It was early in the morning, sunny and already very hot. Once again I felt my heartbeat accelerating as I stood in line for my passport to be examined.

During the flight I had struck up an acquaintance with an elderly American gentleman named Bill and now, trying to appear quite at ease, I was chatting away nineteen to the dozen with the old chap as we waited our turn behind a group of nuns. Subconsciously, I think, I hoped the nuns might bring some added heavenly protection. I need not have worried, my passport was stamped and returned with hardly a glance from the immigration official. I was in Brazil. I had done it again! I felt the same rush of adrenalin and euphoria that I had experienced when I escaped from Wandsworth and when I first arrived in Australia. It was the beginning of another new phase to my life.

Bill was only going to be in town for a couple of days. He was on his way to Argentina and had broken his trip to deliver a letter to a friend of his wife who lived in Rio. Bill was already booked into the Luxor Hotel on Avenida Atlantica, the Copacabana seafront, and suggested that I should find a room at the same place. In the taxi we drove along Botafogo Beach, which in places seemed within touching distance of the massive Sugar Loaf Mountain. It was that very same view that had first attracted me to Rio on the VARIG Airline brochure I had seen in Melbourne and every bit as impressive. It was unbelievable.

The prices at the Luxor were equally unbelievable. I left my case with Bill and went off to find something more down-market and within my limited means. A couple of blocks back from the seafront I found exactly what I could afford: a fleapit, the Hotel Santa Clara, at three dollars a night. The doorman-owner was a swarthy Portuguese who smelled of sweat. After we had laboured over a sign-language deal, a bulky black lady, also smelling of sweat, showed me to a room. The window looked out onto the wall of a neighbouring apartment building. The furniture was old, the washbasin was cracked and there was an unpleasant, sweaty-sock smell in the air. But it was all I could afford and I had known worse. It was to be 'home' for the next couple of months.

I lunched with Bill and afterwards went with him to deliver the letter to his wife's friend, who lived within walking distance of the hotel. Nadine Mitchell was her name, a beautiful American lady in her late fifties (I think she would settle for that). A Christian Scientist and an English teacher, Bill had described her as 'quite a gal.' Later she confided in me that she had been in show business, dancing with the Ziegfeld Follies at a time when gangsters regularly made passes at the girls. She had been 'married' to a Brazilian army colonel who had died and so she now considered herself to be a widow.

When she heard that I had spent some time in Australia she told me about a young Australian fellow, Rob, who had left Rio just before my arrival. Rob, she said, had come to Rio with a 'serious drinking problem' and she was happy to tell me that she had cured him. Now, no self-respecting Aussie I had ever met would let some sheila get between him and his grog, so I thought this bloke had to be a bit of a wimp. Nadine said that he was travelling in the north of Brazil but would soon be back and she wanted me to keep in touch so that she could introduce us.

When Bill left, apart from Nadine, I knew no other English speaking person in Rio and it was no easy matter getting to grips with the Portuguese language. Asking for a beer, I was offered milk, wine and Coca-Cola. The taxi-drivers, it seemed, found it more difficult to understand my Portuguese than anyone else. If ever I wanted a grand tour of Rio I only had to ask to be taken from one end of Copacabana to the other. I was pleased, therefore, when I met Adauto Agallo, a clerk at the American Express office in downtown Rio. He was a young Brazilian who could speak English fluently and we soon found that we had a mutual interest in jazz.

I had gone to the Amex office to see if I could receive mail there. The smiling, helpful Mr Agallo told me there was 'no problem, man.' By a happy coincidence, he lived only a stone's-throw from the flea factory where I was staying. Sunday afternoons, Adauto told me, were dedicated to serious drinking and jazz so I took him up on his offer to visit him at his home.

I met and liked his family and friends, particularly a young medical student called, Mauricio, who laughed a lot and could also speak fairly good English. He called me, 'Gringo'. One evening, following an afternoon of slugging back a goodly number of gin and tonics, I agreed to go with Mauricio and a couple of his friends to a 'special' night club. We roared off into the night in Mauricio's Karman Guia coupé. The club was way out in the sticks and I didn't have a clue where we were, but it appeared to be a popular place. The 'Gringo' was introduced to the young proprietor, who spoke a little English, and a table near the raised dance floor was quickly arranged. The music pounded, the strobe lights flickered and the booze flowed. I was enjoying myself immensely. Mauricio drew my attention to a slender young girl dancing alone and smiling in our direction.

'Hey, Gringo,' shouted Mauricio, 'I think that girl wants you to dance with her.'

When I awoke the next morning, I found myself lying on the floor of a hotel bathroom. I remembered the smiling girl and dancing with her. I remembered taking a couple of drags at the cigarette she was smoking and telling myself that it was marijuana ... Never again, I vowed.

Nadine contacted me a few days later to tell me that Rob was back in town and invited me to meet him over dinner at her apartment. Rob was from Adelaide and seemed like a decent sort of a bloke. After a superb dinner, washed down with water, Nadine said that she would like to read to us from the Bible. Hours later Rob and I left the apartment together.

'Christ!' he said when we were out of earshot, 'I need a bloody drink after that!'

'I thought you had stopped drinking,' I said. 'Nadine told me that she had cured you of a serious wine-drinking problem.'

'Cured me of drinking wine, my arse,' scoffed the Aussie, 'I gave up drinking wine because I discovered cachaça!'

Cachaça, I knew, was a cheap, potent white spirit produced from sugar cane. The original elixir of life.

'Speaking of cachaça'' Rob went on 'I'm going to take you to the Bip-Bip bar! You are going to love it!'

The Bip-Bip bar was in nearby Ipanema, specializing in drinks made from fruit juices and cachaça. The choice was wide and exotic to a newcomer to the tropics. We started with tangerine and then went on to passion fruit, followed by strawberry, lemon and tamarind.

Around midnight, and now back in Copacabana, we decided to go for a swim. The surf was up! Quite pissed and completely starkers we threw ourselves into the foaming breakers. We sobered up a bit when we came out of the water as we couldn't find our clothes. During the time we had been frolicking in the sea, the current had taken us further down the beach and away from where we left our stuff. We eventually found it untouched and went dripping back to my hotel. Rob hoped that he would be able to crash-out in my room, but the Portuguese doorman-owner, who never seemed to leave his post, even to sleep, wouldn't hear of it. I was already in his 'black book' for being a couple of weeks in arrears with my rent so there was no point in arguing with him.

Nadine had got us to promise that we would go with her to church the following Sunday morning.

'Fuck that!' said Rob when I phoned him at his hotel to remind him of our obligation 'I'm going to the beach.'

So I went alone and was rewarded with a warm smile from Nadine. After the service she introduced me to a number of the congregation, including Werner and Joyce Blumer, a Swiss stockbroker and his wife, leading lights in Rio's Christian Science community.

Everyone was very friendly, especially the Blumers. When Werner learned that I knew a thing or two about carpentry he immediately invited me to his house to take care of a number of things that needed repairing. He had a fully equipped workshop, he told me, so tools would not be a problem, I jumped at the chance to earn some extra cash. Apparently satisfied with my work, Werner suggested that I should move in with them and be part of the family. There were only two rules, said my new boss; no girlfriends and no alcoholic beverages on the premises.

It was about this time that I met an attractive mulatta named Edith. She was Adauto's sister-in-law and worked for General Electric as a bilingual secretary. She was twenty-seven. We started out as 'just good friends', but when our relationship developed into an intimate one I told her my story, including the fact that I had a wife and children in Australia. We became closer friends than ever. Edith wanting, above all, to see me reunited with my family.

A month after my arrival in Rio, on 20 April 1970, Detective Chief Superintendent Tommy Butler, the Grey Fox, died. Even on his retirement from the force a year earlier he had vowed that he would still search for me. Forgotten and unnoticed, Bill Boal also passed away. He died in prison having been accused and sentenced for the train robbery. His misfortune was to be with Roger Cordrey at the time of his arrest. Unfortunately for Boal, the only evidence they fitted him with was the same "yellow paint" that had magically found its way on to a pair of Gordon Goody's shoes that had never been anywhere near the farm. Admitting Boal was innocent would have brought into question much of the prosecution's evidence against Gordon and the rest of the gang.

As fate would have it, on the day that Butler died *The Sun* newspaper in London finally published the 77-page manuscript that I had left with Charmian in Melbourne. Charm had managed to get a lawyer to negotiate a good payment from the Murdoch paper. The money, Charmian sensibly turned into a trust fund for the boys that would help go towards paying for part of their education. She always was far more sensible with money than me.

Not surprisingly the publication of my story in *The Sun* stirred up a storm on both sides of the equator, with the authorities still assuming I was hiding out in Australia. A furious commissioner of police in New South Wales, Norman Allan, called Scotland Yard when he learnt the Yard itself had confirmed to the paper that the manuscript was genuine. He expressed amazement that Scotland Yard had supported *The Sun* in this way and pointed out that, whilst police in both countries still could not find me, a solicitor had been able to receive a manuscript with my fingerprints and signature on it. In Allan's opinion, the Yard were helping to finance my escape and even "giving comfort and aid to an escaped prisoner."

Six months after arriving in Brazil, and still living with the Blumer family, the time came for me to renew my visa. I did not want to attract the attention of the Brazilian authorities by over staying my welcome and that meant that I would have to leave the country, if only for a couple of hours. After consulting a map, I decided to take a bus trip to Argentina - I thought it would be a nice little jaunt. Werner provided me with an advance against my salary which enabled me to buy the bus ticket and still have money over for other expenses.

I got off to a bad start on the trip, finding that my seat on the 1000-mile journey to Porto Alegre was next to a very fat Brazilian lady. During the night, when she stretched out to sleep, she overflowed over into my seat, making it impossible for me to get any shut-eye. I spent the night sitting on the steps by the door of the bus. At Porto Alegre, in the south of Brazil, I had to change busses and I was grateful to find myself on a much less crowded one. It was still many hours and over 650 miles to Buenos Aires, but at least I would be able to get some sleep.

It started to pour with rain as we left Porto Alegre. The bus lurched and shimmied on the muddy highway, finally slipping off the road altogether and into a ditch. All the hombres were called upon to get the bus on the road again, even the sleeping Gringo in his suede shoes.

Treading warily, I made my way to the rear of the bus and joined in the heaving and shoving. We were winning!

Push!

Suddenly and without any warning the driver hit the gas and the bus slewed back towards the ditch. I leapt aside to avoid being knocked over and landed up to my knees in soft, wet red mud. Soaked and muddy, I returned to my seat in the hope of catching an extra forty winks while I dried off.

By my calculations, we would arrive at the Argentine border about five o'clock in the morning, an hour, I told myself, when frontier guards could be caught napping. Leaving Brazil presented no problem. The bus driver collected our passports and other documents and took them away to have 'saída' stamped into them. I relaxed - it was going to be easier than I thought. The driver soon returned and the bus proceeded across a bridge into Argentina, stopping at the Argentinean checkpoint. Here we were all taken off the bus and herded into a large, well-lit office where we stood in line waiting to be attended by a solitary official who was sitting behind a small desk.

The line moved quickly, the official appeared to only give a cursory glance at the documents before stamping them. When I reached the table and held out my passport, however, he gave me a long, hard stare. He took Michael Haynes' passport and began going through it slowly, page by page.

He returned to the page with the photograph, looking from the picture to me. He did this several times. He then picked up a paper knife and attempted to raise the corners of the photo. Still not satisfied he went through the passport a second time, stopping at a page where there was an entry written in red ink. At one time, the real Michael Haynes had crossed from India into Pakistan and had been suspected of trying to smuggle a

Land-Rover, hence the entry in red. The official pointed to the page, said something in Spanish, and looked at me enquiringly. I shook my head.

'I'm sorry,' I said, 'I don't speak Spanish.' Then, with a flourish, he stamped the passport with an 'entrada' and scribbled his initials beside it. He fixed me one last time with a long, hard stare, tapping the passport against his hand for what seemed like an eternity before handing it back to me without further comment.

Leaving the office I looked around for a toilet; the incident had given me an urgent desire to relieve my bowels!

The trip continued without further drama and I arrived in Buenos Aires looking a picture in my by now dry pants which were pink from the knees down with shoes to match. One of Nadine's friends in Rio, an Argentine lady by the name of Fanny, had kindly suggested that I could stay with her relatives in BA, and had given me some small presents to deliver to them. I found the address without much trouble and received a warm welcome from Fanny's sister and her husband. They took me around to places of interest and various bars and restaurants, but there was a serious language barrier as neither one of them spoke any language other than Spanish and my Portuguese was still not up to much. My funds were low and the weather had turned cold, so I didn't stay much longer than a week in BA, returning to Rio by a bus that was taking a different route to the one that I had arrived on. I didn't fancy a second encounter with the border official who had literally scared the shit out of me!

Back in Rio and the bosom of the Blumers, I picked up from where I had been before my excursion. I wrote to Charmian, describing my 'near thing' in Argentina and it's laxative effect. At that time, Charmian and I were kicking around a few ideas and making uncertain plans to reunite at some stage. We had written about the possibility of me sneaking back into Australia and for that reason it was necessary for me to keep my passport ready for action.

One of Werner's partners in the stock market was a middle-aged American named Scott Johnson. He was also in need of a carpenter and I started working for him at weekends. We became pretty good friends and frequently went to the samba clubs that abound in Rio. Scott was pretty well off, drove a Ford Cutlass and was extremely popular with the dusky young girls who flocked to the escolas de samba, as the clubs were called. I really enjoyed these evenings at the samba schools. The beer was cold and the prices were as friendly as the girls. I also happened to like samba.

I spent most of Christmas 1970 with Edith and some of her friends, one of whom was a detective who went around with a gun tucked down the front of his trousers. Like many of his kind, he believed that all thieves - with the exception, of course, of detectives - should not be allowed to live. Despite his presence and views we still managed to have a jolly time and celebrated Christmas Day by eating feijoada - a traditional Brazilian stew of black beans and hunks of fat salted pork and meats, served with rice, kale, pork crackling and slices of fresh orange. A truly superb dish which was one of my all time favourites.

Everything seemed to be going well. With the extra money I had been earning by working for Scott I was able to buy myself some new clothes and other small luxuries. Although I was quite happy with the Blumers, I was keen to rent a place of my own and regain my personal freedom. Scott had told me about an apartment in Copacabana which belonged to one of his friends. He was confident that he could get it for me at a really low rental.

One sunny morning in February 1971, I received a phone call from my friend Adauto Agallo. A letter had arrived for me at the American Express office and he had taken it to his home for me to collect. His wife would be there if I wanted to go by his apartment and pick it up. I told the Blumers I had something important to take care of and took the bus to Adauto's home. His wife, Olga, all smiles as usual, handed me a fat envelope bearing Charmian's unmistakable handwriting. Not wanting to be away from my job for too long, I thanked Olga and left, happily tearing the letter open as I went. The opening line of the letter stopped me in my tracks: 'Wherever you are and whatever you are doing, sit down... our darling son Nicky has been killed in a road accident...'

I felt physically sick and faint, completely stunned by the terrible news. I don't know why but I felt I had to talk to somebody about it. Like someone in a trance, I got to a bar and sat down. I tried, but it was impossible to read any more of Charmian's letter. I could only cry silently. I saw a pay phone on the wall of the bar and got up to phone somebody - anybody. I dialled a number and heard Adauto's voice, 'Hello - hello? American Express - hello?' I did all I could to force myself to speak, to say Adauto's name, but I was unable to utter a sound. I hung up and stumbled out of the bar. Still in a trance I wandered aimlessly down the road. Then, through the haze, I knew what I was going to do. I would go to the British Consulate and give myself up.

A fifteen-minute bus-ride later, I found myself standing outside the British Consulate in Flamengo. The journey, however short, had been time enough for me to get over the initial shock and partially regain part of my composure. I went to a bar close to the Consulate and quickly gulped down two large brandies. From where I stood, I could see the Union Jack hanging in front of the Consulate building. All I had to do was walk in through the door and announce who I was. Instead, I crossed the road and sat down on a bench in Flamengo Park and read Charmian's letter from beginning to end.

Charmian gave me details of the accident, which had occurred on 5 January, and said she felt heavily responsible because she had been driving when the tragedy occurred. She was in no way responsible. The crash had happened less than thirty yards from the Haynes' front door. Charmian had just dropped Mike and Jess off after the New Year break when the car was hit by another vehicle going straight across a junction which was Charmian's right of way. Charm's car somersaulted twice. Farley had been badly cut in the crash and his left eye and forehead gashed, while Charmian and Chris were both badly shaken. Nicky, however, had been hurled from the car and landed on the side of the road. Blood was pouring from his mouth and Charm realised he must have suffered terrible internal injuries and cradled his head in her lap. It took over 20 minutes for the first ambulance to arrive which took Nicky, Charm and Farley to the hospital while Chris stayed behind with Jess Haynes who, along with Mike, had witnessed the crash. Mike went in the ambulance with Charm, who was sure that Nicky had died during the drive to the hospital. A fact confirmed by the doctors who could not resuscitate him at the hospital.

Charm was numb, but had little time to feel sorry for herself. She had to turn her attention to Farley who was in considerable pain and being stitched up, but thankfully he would be all right and recover in time.

I sat in the park for a long time thinking things over and re-reading the letter and came to the conclusion that the last thing I should do was to give myself up. I felt it was not what Nicky would have wanted.

The Blumer family had no idea that I had a wife and three children on the other side of the world and I had never given them any reason to believe that I was anyone but Michael Haynes. When I returned to the house they could see that I was very unhappy and naturally wanted to know why. I thanked them for their concern and invented some lie.

Life continued, but Nicky's death at the age of ten had left me devastated. I found it hard to garner any enthusiasm for anything. When Carnival came around, my first in Rio, Edith got tickets for us to see the parade of the samba-schools. I was not really in the mood to watch a Carnival parade but Edith and her chums insisted that I needed something to lift me out of the doldrums. I'm glad I went. It was - and is - a wonderful and moving experience.

Each day, however, I thought more and more about getting back to Australia and to do so I had to keep 'my' passport up to date. To do that, and not attract unnecessary attention, I had to make a second trip out of Brazil.

I had been in Brazil for almost a year. Loath to return to Argentina, I decided in March 1971 to take a bus to Corumba, a town on the Bolivian border.

During the long, dusty journey, the military and civil police stopped the bus at least half a dozen times. The police either boarded the bus or took us all off for a more thorough search, whichever method they chose they always demanded to see every passenger's identity and travel documents. When I had chosen Brazil as a refuge, I was quite unaware of the fact that the country was under a strict military dictatorship. A Communist witch-hunt was on and anyone found without some kind of identification was hustled off to the nearest delegacia for some heavy questioning or worse.

One evening in Rio when waiting for a friend, I was approached by a couple of Colombian hippies who showed me a piece of paper and made it clear that they needed money. As they were going through their routine, two cops appeared out of the shadows with guns in their hands. 'Documentos!' said one in an unfriendly fashion. I froze. I didn't have my precious passport or any other identification with me. The hippies showed the cops the piece of paper they had shown to me but the policemen were clearly far from satisfied and the Colombians were marched off at gunpoint, leaving me standing holding my breath. The police had obviously thought they were trying to shake down a British tourist. Even though I had been in Brazil a year, I was still very much the innocent abroad. It was to be one of many close calls.

It was only when I got to the police post in Corumba and saw the photographs on the walls of the cocaine busts that had recently been made, that I realized that I was using a well-trodden South American drug trail. This explained at least the number of searches, but I still had to return the same way!

At the Brazilian-Bolivian border a friendly Brazilian policeman stamped the 'saída' into my passport and advised me to stay on the other side of the border for a couple of days before re-entering Brazil. He was clearly used to 'tourists' who needed to re-validate their visas.

A bus took me over a bridge into Puerto Saurez on the Bolivian side of the border. It was very different from my arrival in Argentina - I was in Bolivia and I had not even been asked to show my passport. I found a cheap hotel and booked in. With great difficulty, I asked the proprietor of the humble establishment where I should go to get an 'entrada' stamped into my passport. Every evening, he told me, the man responsible for the border could be found at a nearby bar where he had his dinner. This was the hombre to speak to.

I had no trouble spotting my man, another Mission Impossible type. I soon discovered that he was running a nice little scam shaking down 'tourists' like myself who required his initials in their passport so that they could return to Brazil for another period of six months. He started out at $100 for the 'entrada' and 'salida' stamps - plus his initials - but grudgingly settled for twenty when he found I was not kidding about my worldly wealth.

Two nights at the Mosquito Motel had been two nights too many; I was glad when I got back to Corumba and caught the bus back to Rio, even if Rio was over 1200 miles and a number of police searches away.

Soon after my return from the Bolivian trip, thanks to Scott's diligent work, I moved into a twelfth floor, fully furnished apartment in Rua Prado Junior in Copacabana, a short walk from the beach. I was still unhappy, but gradually the pain of losing Nicky eased and I picked up the pieces of my life. I worked long hours during the week and relaxed on the beach at the weekends with Edith and her friends.

About the middle of 1971, Edith went off on a long vacation to England and the US, so I started frequenting Adauto's Sunday afternoon jazz sessions again. On one of these visits I was introduced to a lively, friendly Brazilian fellow called Paulo. He spoke English quite well, having lived in the US for a couple years and I found him interesting company. He was also a samba enthusiast and we made an arrangement to go to his favourite club, the Bola Preta, (the Black Ball) the following Friday.

The Bola Preta is situated in downtown Rio, the business heart of the city, next to the Municipal Theatre. It has a reputation for 'hot' samba and is very popular with people of all ages and all colours and creeds. We got there early so that we could be sure of getting a prime table near the dance floor and ordered a couple of beers. Among the dancers I noticed a small young woman with long black hair and an enchanting smile. A young Brazilian guy accompanied her, but before the evening was over I had a chance to exchange a few words with her. Her name was Raimunda Nascimento de Castro, she said, with the same wide smile and she would be happy to meet me at the club the following week.

It was a fine romance until the day that Edith was due back from the US. Raimunda had left her baby-doll nightdress on the bed and I suggested that she might like to take it with her in case Edith, who had a key to my apartment, turned up without warning. Raimunda exploded, giving me the ultimatum that I had to make a choice between her and Edith. I chose Edith and the fiery Raimunda stormed out of my life in a huff.

Whilst I had been dallying in Rio, Edith had not been wasting much time in New York and had met and become fond of a hotel manager, something she made no mention of on her return. I noticed, however, a distinct change in her. She spoke enthusiastically about New York and said that she would be going there again for her next vacation.

Unwilling to make another trip out of Brazil after my previous experiences in Argentina and Bolivia, I allowed the validity of my visa to expire in September 1971. Charmian was still nursing the hope that I would be able to get back to Australia, but the more I thought about it the less likely it seemed to be a good idea. My return to Australia, even if it were possible, could only be disruptive as far as Chris and Farley were concerned. They were both at school and leading reasonably orderly lives, my presence was sure to create complications. I outlined these misgivings in a letter to Charmian who wrote back saying that she saw my reluctance to go back to Australia as an attack of 'cold feet'.

Edith's holiday was coming up and she was going off to the States again, but promised to be back in time for my birthday on 8 August. I took her to the airport with a number of her cronies, one of whom jokingly teased her that she was going to take 'good' care of me whilst she was away. But Edith hugged me and told her friend to back off - she would be back soon, she said, to claim 'her man'.

Another of Edith's friends, who was always referred to as 'crazy', was a Brazilian airline steward by the name of Magalhães. He was crazy because he smoked marijuana, something that Edith strictly disapproved of. Magalhães was enthusiastic about his vice and on more than one occasion he invited me to share a joint with him. But I remembered my first and only experience and turned down his repeated offers.

A few days after Edith's departure Scott gave me a call and discovering that Edith was away, suggested a night out at one of the samba clubs. I was all for it and we made arrangements to meet at the Bola Preta on the weekend. As always, the club was full but Scott bribed one of the waiters and a good table was soon made available. A couple of pretty mulatta girls at a neighbouring table were showing obvious interest in the two big gringos and at Scott's invitation they came across and joined us. The one that I took a fancy to was called Ana Paula. She was very attractive with high cheekbones, white teeth and a good figure. We drank and we danced and eventually went back to my apartment to get to know each other better!

August 8 came and went and there was still no sign of Edith. I telephoned her home and her sister Zelia answered. Zelia was Edith's eldest sister and it was obvious from the start of our affair that she didn't approve of Edith being involved with a married man. She had even resorted to macumba, the Brazilian voodoo, to try and get us to stop seeing one another. I asked Zelia if she had any news of Edith.

'Haven't you heard?' she asked, in a friendlier manner than I was accustomed to.

'I haven't heard anything,' I replied. 'Edith said she would be back before 8 August but I haven't heard anything. What's going on?'

Zelia could hardly wait to tell me. 'But Ronnie, Edith got married last week. Didn't you know?'

'What! Who to?'

'A German, someone she met when she was in New York last year.'

I was amazed by the news. Edith had mentioned meeting a German and it had crossed my mind that she might have had a fling with him, but I found it unbelievable that she had actually gone and got married. Zelia must be lying, I thought.

But Zelia wasn't lying. Edith flew back to Brazil a week later to collect her clothes and to quit her job. She phoned me before returning to New York and said tearfully that she had made the decision to marry on the spur of the moment. She hoped that I would understand. I said I did and wished her good luck and much happiness. She had been a fine friend and I was going to miss her.

It was a Saturday and although we were well into winter it was a warm, sunny day. I had just finished tidying up the apartment when someone rang the bell. I opened the door to three young hippies, one of them sporting a large Afro hairstyle. He had heard that I was looking for a carpenter and was applying for the job. Some time before I had been needing help with some work and I had spoken to various people in the building trade about a carpenter. When he called I had little work on, but I invited the group in so that I could write down his name and address in case I needed someone in the future. I opened a couple of beers and asked Afro about his experience as a carpenter. If it had rested solely on the look of the chap I doubt very much if I would have hired him. Out of the blue he asked me if I had any objection to him rolling a joint and I told him to do his own thing, no problem. He rolled a long thin 'cigarrinho'.

He told me that his name was Marcelo and he lived in Ipanema. The joint finished, he lit up and took a couple of long tokes before passing the cigarette on to me. I hesitated for a second, then took the joint from him and took a drag on it. I passed it on to Marcelo's pals; it duly came around again and I had another puff wondering if I was doing the right thing. The joint was smoked down to the end and the hippies got up to leave. I thought they looked a bit uneasy on their feet and asked myself why anyone bothered to smoke the stuff. All I felt was a slight nausea. When they had gone I cleared away the beer bottles and glasses and put on a record. It was Jazz Samba with Stan Getz, Charlie Byrd, and Luis Bonfá, a record I particularly liked and often played. Then I stretched out on the settee to relax.

What followed defies description. I've been told that I went on an 'astral voyage', whatever it was it was no ordinary trip. I was omnipotent - until it was time to turn the record over. The floor had turned to cotton wool.

The experience was so extraordinary, if that's the word, that the next morning found me knocking on Marcelo's' door for more of the shit. I was hooked.

It was Ana Paula's birthday on 8 September. I was going to take her to dinner and we had arranged for her to arrive at my place around seven o'clock. About six the doorbell rang and I presumed that Ana Paula had arrived early, but it wasn't Ana Paula, it was Raimunda with her wide smile.

'Como vai, seu vagabundo? (How are you, you bum?)', she asked.

In no time we were on the bed and talking about old times. I was really getting carried away when I remembered Ana Paula. It was ten to seven. Hastily I explained the situation to Raimunda and asked her to come back the next day. She called me a son of a bitch, but promised to return. Through the spy hold in the front door I watched her walk down the corridor to the lift. Almost as soon as she got there the door opened and out stepped Ana Paula.

She entered the apartment sniffing the air like a pointer. 'I can smell a whore,' she said. 'You've had a whore in here. I just saw her getting into the elevator.' I tried to talk my way out of it but Ana Paula was a bright girl and she knew very well what the score was. We talked about our relationship over dinner and we decided quite amicably to go our separate ways. Two days later Raimunda moved into my apartment and my life.

Until her arrival, the apartment was - to say the least - untidy. In one day, while I was at work, Xuxu (shoo-shoo, a small, green vegetable) as I called her, had the apartment clean, polished and in apple-pie order. As I looked around admiring her handy-work, she appeared with a glass of cold beer and invited me to sit down and switched on a table-lamp. I was surprised to see that the white bulb had been replaced by a blue one. Then she put on a lazy samba record and began to dance to the music, letting down her long black hair. Artistically, she stepped onto the marble coffee-table and slowly started to strip off her clothes. We got on very well together and she was fun to be with. At what I thought was an appropriate moment, I told her my true name, the reason why I was in Brazil and the fact that I had a wife and children in Australia. Raimunda took this piece of news in her stride and it appeared to make little difference to our relationship. She showed a lot of interest in my children and told me that she herself had a young son who was living with his father, a doctor, in Maranhão, in the north of Brazil.

Around the end of 1972 I received word from Mike Haynes that he needed his passport back: he was planning to return to England with his family the following year. He had applied for a new passport, claiming that he had lost his old one, but for some reason his application had been turned down. He would have to find the old one, he was told.

I was wondering how I could get the passport back to Mike as its not often you meet people travelling between Brazil and Australia, when at a party I was introduced to a Brazilian girl called Dilse who worked in tourism. She told me that she would be taking a group of Brazilians to Australia in February 1973. I explained to her that I knew the country quite well and had friends there - perhaps she would be kind enough to take some small presents to them for me. She agreed readily and when she travelled she took a small package with her which among other things contained Mike's well travelled passport - minus the pages relating to my exit from Australia and the subsequent trips around South America. When Mike finally received his passport he mutilated it further and scribbled in it with coloured pencils before presenting it for renewal. It had fallen into the hands of his young son, he explained, and was believed!

Mike and his family returned to the UK in July 1973. Like Molly he received a visit from Jack Slipper after I had been found in Rio. Slipper says he even found the passport! Mike was questioned and made to give a lengthy statement, but was never prosecuted in Britain.

The months passed, bringing financial ups and downs. More than once the power was cut off when I failed to pay the light bill on time, so I was very pleased when the Blumers called me into work on an art gallery they were in the process of setting up. It was during this period that I met Joyce Blumer's sister-in-law, Phyllis Huber, an attractive and intelligent lady in her late twenties. She had been well educated and spoke English with an American accent.'

Hi,' she said when we met. 'You must be Mike Haynes - I've heard a lot about you.' She invited me to dinner where I was introduced to her hippie friends, Brazilians and Americans, who of course were all 'heads'. After the meal we sat around talking, drinking cheap wine and smoking grass. I enjoyed the company and I became a frequent visitor to Phyllis' apartment. It was there that I met a young Englishman of White Russian extraction by the name of Constantine Benckendorff - 'Conti' to his friends. Over a joint or two we became quite pally and started going around together. He got interested in a stoned-out idea that Phyllis and I had to set up an interior decorating business we planned to call 'Planet Venus'.

I had told Phyllis my real name and why I was in Brazil but she wouldn't believe me! 'Don't freak me out, Mike' she had said when I told her my real name was not Mike Haynes. I also trusted Conti enough to reveal my identity to him. It blew his mind but he said that he was ready to help me in anyway possible.

A little less than a year after she had moved in, Raimunda asked me if I minded if her mother came to stay with us for a while. There was only one bedroom in the apartment but Raimunda said that her mother would be quite comfortable on the settee. We wouldn't even notice she was there, she promised. So I agreed.

A couple of weeks later Dona Maria arrived in Rio after close to three days on a bus, accompanied by Rosangela, Raimunda's 15-year-old adopted daughter, who would also be quite happy to sleep on the floor of the living room and go 'unnoticed'. It soon became clear that all three of the ladies had the same insatiable thirst for the Brazilian television soap-operas, which further induced me to seek the company of my grass-smoking friends. The 'blue-lamp' cabaret had sadly closed.

One evening I returned home to find Raimunda, her mother, Rosangela and two other females who I didn't even know, all soaking their feet in bowls in preparation for a manicure session. The air was a mixture cigarette smoke and nail-varnish remover fumes and the telly was going full blast. The next morning I had a bit of a showdown with Xuxu and ended up by saying that the time had come for Dona Maria and Rosangela to return to Maranhão. Raimunda's reply was along the lines that if her mother and her adopted daughter had to go, then she would go with them. A few days later I took all three of them to the bus station and waved a sad 'goodbye' as they set out on the long journey north.

Scott Johnson had just bought a rooftop apartment and planned to make extensive changes, so I was invited to take charge of the job. We started going to the samba clubs again at the weekends and it was on one of these jaunts that I met a nineteen year-old bank clerk named Lucia. Pretty, long-legged and sex-mad. It was something of a whirlwind romance and we spent as much time as possible together, mostly in bed. She didn't move in with me but she did bring some clothes to the apartment and left them hanging in the wardrobe.

Around this time, I received a desperately unhappy tape from Charmian telling me how much she and the boys were missing and needing me. There was further mention of somehow me getting back to Australia. The content of the tape left me very depressed and thoughts of giving myself up began to enter my head again. Charmian and my children were unhappy and so was I. The only way to put our lives in order, I thought, was to go back to prison.

I talked the matter over with Conti, who thought I had to be potty to be thinking of going back to the nick. But he knew I was serious. During the time I had been free the long awaited parole system had become a reality in Her Majesty's Prisons. In theory, certain cons would be considered for release on parole after completing one third of their sentence. By this time the members of the gang who had been sentenced to thirty years were already eligible for parole and their cases were no doubt being 'considered'. Had I not done a bunk in 1965 I would have been standing alongside my colleagues, also cap in hand. Now, if I went back to jail voluntarily, I decided, it could weigh heavily in my favour in front of some future parole committee. Roy James, by-the-way, was the first of those to receive a 30-year sentence to be paroled. He was released in August 1975 having spent nearly 12 years in prison. Prior to him, Roger Cordrey had been released in April 1971, while Buster and Jimmy White, who had been convicted after the rest of the gang, got out in April 1975.

Conti was going back to spend the Christmas of 1973 in England. I asked him to do me a favour.

'When you get back to London,' I said, 'I'd like you to make a few discreet enquiries to see if you can find a paper interested in buying the story of my return to HMP Wandsworth.'

'If that's what you want, I'll do the best I can,' said Conti, 'but I still think you're mad.'

One evening, after a not very happy Christmas, I arrived home to find Raimunda sitting in the living room. She said she had decided to come back to me, she was 'my women'. However, she wanted to know what was the 'shit' hanging up in the wardrobe. Inadvertently I had left the front door open, and almost on cue, Lucia came into the apartment with her best friend, Ana. I sensed that an ugly situation was about to develop and herded Lucia and her friend out of the apartment. I apologised to Lucia about the unexpected turn of events and told her that I would explain everything the following day. Then, while she waited in the corridor, I put her clothes into a suitcase and took it out to her. Raimunda's anger had subsided and I found her weeping when I went back into the living room. A long conversation followed, during which, I told her of my decision to give myself up, outlining my reasons. She said that she knew that I was unhappy and that I had to do what I thought was best. But she wanted to be with me until I left Brazil, she loved me.

Xuxu, was back in my life!

Oh, but I watch her so sadly
How can I tell her I love her
Yes I would give my heart gladly
But each day when she walks to the sea
She looks straight ahead, not at me
Tall and tan and young and lovely
The girl from Ipanema goes walking
And when she passes, I smile - but she doesn't see (doesn't see)
She just doesn't see, no she never sees me…

Tom Jobim / Vinicius de Moraes, *'The Girl From Ipanema'*

My friendly shipmates.(L to R) Me, Bill, Molly, Greg and Peter.

The real Michael Haynes.

A Murdoch cover boy and girl.

The Trocadero Hotel in Copacabana where Slipper found his man.

Raimunda with her mentor, Fernand Legros.

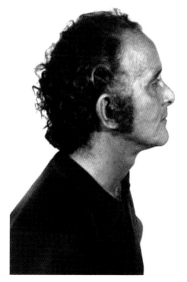

Rio mug shots from February 1974.

Two's company! Raimunda and Charmian put on a brave face.

Mike's birth certificate.

With a pregnant Xuxu.

Colour Plate 12

The young Mr Biggs.

With the crew of HMS Danae in April 1977.

I was a good parent. Honest! Ask Mike.

Once found by the media, they became my source of revenue.

Playing myself in a Japanese TV film.   *Rio beach bum.*

The special relationship.

Raimunda and Ulla.

My best friend in Rio. Ursula 'Ulla' Sopher.

Even in Rio the police kept an eye on me. Even at my local bar.

Modestly I can say I did throw some very good parties, and the press were always welcome to come along and join in the fun..

With my nemesis, John Miller, the man who tried to kidnap me twice, and failed miserably on both occasions.

The Roda Viva Restaurant, under Sugar Loaf, from where I was kidnapped on 16 March 1981.

CAUGHT:
SLIPPER DROPS THE CATCH

When a prisoner escapes, there are always reports of sightings. Each one has to be looked at. With Biggs the sightings filled twenty-seven files.

Jack Slipper, 1974

There are times when the hardest part of a police officer's life is having to hold his tongue. In my twenty nine years of service, it was never harder than when, as operational head of the Flying Squad, I flew out to Rio de Janeiro to arrest the last of the Great Train Robbers, Ronnie Biggs, and failed to bring him home.

Jack Slipper, 1980

In January 1974 I received an excited phone call from Conti. He had met a *Daily Express* reporter named Colin Mackenzie at a cocktail party in London and it was almost certain that his paper would be interested in buying my story. He handed me over to Mackenzie, who asked certain questions to verify that it was the real Ronald Biggs on the line. Satisfied with my answers, he said that the *Express* was ready to send him to Brazil just as soon as he presented some written evidence. The paper wanted some concrete proof that I really was who I said I was because it had recently been left with egg on its face over another hunt for a fugitive in South America. The fugitive in question had been, or rather turned out not to be, Hitler's number two, Martin Bormann.

I sent Mackenzie a letter bearing my signature and a copy of my fingerprints. The letter read: 'Hi, Colin, Perhaps not the best set [of fingerprints] that have been taken, but certainly as good as those found on the Monopoly box and the sauce bottle! Convinced?! R.A. Biggs.'

I was somewhat uneasy about dealing with the Daily Express as I was well aware that it was the newspaper that had been partly responsible for the capture of gang member Jimmy White. But I was going to give myself up, so I ruled out the possibility that anything could go wrong with the business in hand.

My letter having been received, Mackenzie sounded ecstatic on the phone. It was a great story, he enthused, and there would be no problem with regard to the 'bread'. Everything was being kept top secret, he assured me, as did the *Express* News Editor, Brian Hitchen, who also came on the line. The date was 24 January. Only Colin and Conti would be travelling to Rio, Hitchen assured me, while only the very top brass on the paper were in on the story.

Early on the morning of Wednesday 30 January there was a phone call from Conti informing me that he and Mackenzie had arrived safely in Rio and were comfortable installed in room 909 at the Trocadero Hotel [now the Arena] on Copacabana beachfront - a stone's throw from where I was living.

I had made an arrangement with Lucia, with whom I had still remained friendly with despite the presence of Raimunda in the apartment, to meet her at the beach that morning. I picked her up at her flat, told her what was happening and took her with me to meet the man from the Express.

When the door to room 909 opened, I saw that there were two men besides Conti in the room. They were introduced to me as Colin Mackenzie and Bill Lovelace. I reminded Mackenzie that I had been assured that only he and Conti would meet me in Rio, I wasn't very pleased to see a third person.

'Don't worry about Bill,' Mackenzie said disarmingly, 'you can trust him with your life. We must have photographs for the story and Bill is the best.'

Lovelace was already taking pictures, suggesting poses that I should take with Lucia, murmuring the appreciation of her charms all the while.

'By God, Ron, she's beautiful! Where did you find her?'

When Lovelace stopped for a breather, I asked Mackenzie how much I was being offered for my story?

'How much do you want?' he asked.

'£50,000,' I suggested.

'My office has only authorized me to go as high as thirty five,' Mackenzie said, looking me straight in the eye. I reached out to shake hands with the representative of the *Daily Express*.

'It's a deal,' I said. 'I'll settle for that.'

I went on to explain to Mackenzie exactly how I wanted the *Express* to handle the money. Part of it was to go direct to Charmian and part to Raimunda. I asked if there was anyway of avoiding paying tax on the sum and Mackenzie assured me that it would all be taken care of.

I had imagined that the *Express* 'team' would want to rest up after their overnight flight from London, but Mackenzie was all for getting started on the story immediately.

'Let's get the work out the way, Ron. Then we can relax,' he suggested.

Lovelace went off to get some shots of the local scenery and Conti was volunteered to take Lucia to the beach, a chore he jumped at. Mackenzie and I worked on my story for the rest of the day, only taking a short break for lunch. Early the next morning, Thursday, I was back at the Trocadero with a new round of revelations for Mackenzie. Again we worked through the day and into the evening. I felt like a little light-hearted entertainment after all this work and suggested to Mackenzie that we should go out to a nightclub or something of that nature. But the reporter made a face and said that he must have eaten something that had disagreed with him, he had an attack of 'tourist tummy' and would prefer to retire for the evening.

The following morning, as I was getting ready for day three in front of Mackenzie's tape-recorder, Raimunda announced that she thought she might be pregnant. She had been pregnant a couple of times before and a friend of hers, who is a nurse, had been called upon to take care of the problem. I saw it as a complication I could well do without and suggested that she should visit her friend and take whatever steps were necessary to terminate the pregnancy, should her suspicions be confirmed.

When I arrived that Friday at the Trocadero, Lovelace was already taking photographs of Lucia who was wearing a tiny bikini, the type known in Brazil as fio dental (dental floss). Conti and Mackenzie were watching and drooling, the latter showing no signs of his malady of the previous evening. Lovelace wanted some shots of me in beachwear and so I changed into a pair of blue and white striped bathing trunks that belonged to Conti.

Not long after the end of the photo session there was a knock at the door which I took to be room service. Conti went to open the door. A much taller person who I recognized immediately as Old Bill propelled him back into the room. I was sitting on the floor, still wearing Conti's swimming trunks and, regardless of what has been written or reported in the past, I simply said, 'Oh, fuck!'

To give him his full title, it was Detective Chief Superintendent Jack Slipper, head of Scotland Yard's so-called Flying Squad who had stalked into the room.

'Hello Ronnie,' he said, 'I think you know who I am? I certainly know who you are and I'm arresting you.'

He swung around on Mackenzie and continued. 'You've overstepped the mark this time, my lad. You're in trouble.' He turned back to me. 'Where are your clothes?'

'In the bathroom.'

'Right, let's go there.'

In the bathroom as I was getting into my clothes, there was a conversation between Slipper and I that went something like this: 'Look Ronnie, there's no point in you and me putting questions to each other. As far as I'm concerned, you're going back to London. You've got a prison sentence you've got to finish over there. The only thing we have to talk about is when you go. You can bugger us about for a time over here by arguing, or you can come quietly now; so if you simplify it for us, we can help you.'

It reminded me of a conversation I had had many years earlier with Inspector Basil Morris in Reigate.

'You're not going to believe this,' I said, 'but I was trying to give myself up. It would mean a lot to me not to go back wearing handcuffs.'

'I don't know about that,' Slipper said doubtfully. 'If I was to go back to England without you I'd be looking for a new job next week.'

'I'll go back without giving you any trouble,' I promised Slipper, 'but if I go handcuffed it will look as if I have been nicked and I've already told you that I was going to give myself up. Ask the reporter in the other room if you don't believe me.'

'I can't promise anything just yet,' said Slipper. 'We'll have to see.'

When Slipper had marched into room 909 of the Trocadero to 'nick' me (acting without any official power in Brazil whatsoever), he had been accompanied by a fellow policeman from Scotland Yard, Detective Inspector Peter Jones; the British Consul General, Henry Neill; his Brazilian Vice-Consul, Francisco Costa; and the Rio city police commissioner, Dr Ivo Raposo, and his assistant.

Back in the bedroom Slipper gave Jones, who had been taking down the particulars of everyone else in the room, some orders with regard to our exit from the hotel, then he produced his handcuffs.

'If you don't want me to give you any trouble,' I threatened, 'don't even think about putting those cuffs on me.'

A short argument followed which was interrupted by the Commissioner, who opened his gabardine jacket to reveal the handle of a gun tucked down the front of his trousers.

'Oh, great,' said Slipper. 'That's great.'

'What's so great?' I demanded. 'This son of a bitch might shoot me and you think that's great? I don't think it's all that great.'

Up until that point Raposo had not uttered a single word. I was unaware that he could speak English and certainly had no idea that he was a Commissioner.

Raposo, which appropriately means 'fox' in Portuguese, looked mean and took a step towards me. 'Did you call me a son of a bitch?' he hissed.

'Yeah, I called you a filho da puta. I'm unarmed and you might just shoot me. Sure your a son of a bitch!'

Slipper stepped into the arena. 'Calm down, Ronnie. No one is going to get shot.' He put his handcuffs away and took a firm hold of my belt. 'All right, we'll go down to the car like this. Peter get the lift.'

With Slipper hanging onto my belt we left Mackenzie, Conti and Lucia in the room and departed the hotel in silence. On the way down in the lift I was trying to work out exactly how the police had arrived on the scene. When Slipper had entered the hotel room Mackenzie had appeared to be as surprised as I was, so I had not suspected foul play as far as he was concerned.

The vice-consul's car, a chocolate coloured Austin Maxi, was parked in front of the Trocadero and as we approached it Bill Lovelace ran up and began shooting pictures of my 'arrest'. I glared angrily in his direction; the evening before we had been drinking and chatting together like old chums. I was put into the back of the car between Jones and the commissioner's number two, Slipper got into the front with the Commissioner and the vice-consul who was acting as the driver. Henry Neill was to follow in his car with his driver.

As we pulled away, Slipper turned to face me. 'We're going first to your flat, Ronnie, so that you can pick up some warm clothes,' he said. 'It's bloody cold in England at the moment so you'll need a jacket or a sweater - and you can also collect any personal stuff that you may want to take back with you.'

At that moment I resigned myself to the fact that I had been nicked and there was little point in not co-operating. During the journey to my apartment the Commissioner apologized for threatening me with his gun and I in turn apologized for calling him a son of a bitch. With Slipper once again holding onto my belt we went up to my twelfth-floor apartment in Avenida Prado Junior. There was no sign of Raimunda.

Keeping a close watch on me, Slipper made small talk while I got together the things I wanted to take back with me to Britain. He indicated that he was not keen on Brazilian food and was looking forward to getting back home to some 'decent grub'. With one last look around my Brazilian home we headed back down to the car.

We proceeded from Copacabana to a grand old building known as the Catete Palace in Flamengo. At the time, part of the palace was being used by the federal police as its headquarters in Rio. Between 1896 and 1954 the palace had been used as the official residence of the Brazilian President: that was until President Getulio Vargas shot himself to death on 24 August 1954.

The police chief, or delegado, was Inspector Carlos Alberto Garcia, a flashy character with a pearl-handled gun showing above the waistband of his pants. Puffing on a cigar, he received Slipper and his party, listening intently to the details of my capture and identity from the British Vice-Consul, Costa. Leaving me in the care of Peter Jones, Slipper, Costa and Garcia retired to the delegado's office to discuss the matter further. Jones appeared to be as anxious as his superior to get back to London; he and Jack, he confided, had plans to take their wives out for dinner the following evening. It was only later that I discovered that the night out was to celebrate my return to prison!

A federal agent, probably acting on Garcia's orders, appeared from nowhere and slapped a pair of handcuffs on my wrists. Moments later Henry Neill arrived in the charge-room puffing and panting. Having witnessed my reaction to handcuffs when Slipper wanted to put them on me, he protested on my behalf, speaking to the agent in Portuguese.

'Take these things off this poor boy. He's not a common criminal!' He explained who he was and the handcuffs were removed.

Neill sat down beside me and told me what he thought would be the best way to treat my present situation. 'I'm most anxious,' he said, 'that you should do everything to avoid spending any time in a Brazilian prison. I have visited one and I can assure you that it would horrify me to see you pass even one night in such a place.'

He explained that I would have to make a statement to the Brazilian authorities, but to be certain that I could leave the country without a hitch I would have to be careful what I said. If I was asked how I arrived in Brazil, said the British Consul General, it would be better if I didn't mention the fact that I had entered Brazil on a forged passport; such an admission might well result in up to six months in a filthy Brazilian prison before being sent back to England to serve my time there. The best thing, he advised, was to say that I had entered the country from Paraguay, having crossed the border without a passport. It sounded like good advice, and when I was called to make my statement I explained my arrival in Brazil along these lines and signed my statement.

From that moment on, I was considered by Brazil to be in the country illegally - I was no longer 'on the run' - and, as a result, it was necessary to take my fingerprints forty times. I asked the cop why he needed to make so many copies and he simply said that it was normal in cases of 'expulsion'.

That didn't sound so good.

Raised voices came from the delegado's office and a little later a disgusted Jack Slipper came out to say that nothing was going to happen until after lunch. I was left in the care of two Brazilian cops who promptly put me back into handcuffs as soon as Henry Neill was off the premises.

The afternoon session was much like the morning one: another shouting match. Jones was pacing up and down, glumly looking to his watch as the hours ticked by.

'It doesn't look as if we're going to catch our plane,' Jones said with a worried frown at one point 'And there isn't another one until tomorrow morning.'

Finally Slipper emerged from the delegado's office looking distinctly miserable. 'We won't be flying back tonight,' he said dejectedly. 'The chief has got to wait for instructions from Brasilia.' I sensed a slender ray of hope.

The delegado came to speak with me, telling me that I would have to spend the night locked up. He seemed quite friendly and shook hands with me as he was leaving,

Late that evening I was taken under a heavy armed escort to a tiny prison located in Praça XV, close to the docks. It wasn't really a prison, it was a very old police station that had half-a-dozen cells in its basement. But it served as a 'special' prison where, it was said, political prisoners had been taken for interrogation. 'The Presidential Suite', as one cell was called, was under several inches of water. Henry Neil had not exaggerated when he had described a Brazilian prison earlier that day.

I was put into a cell which already housed three other prisoners, all awaiting trial. One of them, Mario, a middle-aged taxi-driver, was a friendly fellow who wanted to know how and why a gringo had landed in their midst.

There were no beds or mattresses in the cell and the prisoners were expected to make do with newspaper and cardboard to lie on. Whilst I told them the outline of my story Mario prepared a place for me to sleep, taking paper and cardboard from the three existing makeshift pallets. The Brazilians listened carefully to what I had to say, finding it difficult to believe that anyone involved in the robbery of the trem pagador (pay train, as it's called in Brazil) should be sharing their cell. Mario had an immediate answer to my problem.

'You've got to arrange a Brazilian child,' he said emphatically, 'Buy, borrow or steal one if necessary, any colour, any age - the only way to get out of the fix you are in is to get a kid and say it's yours. Do you have a girlfriend? Would she help you?'

I told them about Raimunda and mentioned that only that morning she had told me that she might be pregnant.

'Que beleza! (How beautiful!),' said the taxi-driver. 'You lucky son of a bitch! If you've got a Brazilian girl who's expecting your child you've got it made! Puta que pariu! If you father a child in Brazil you will never be made to leave!'

Mario's words were cheering and the slender ray of hope broadened, but I was still a long way from being 'home and hosed'. It occurred to me that Raimunda might not be pregnant, or might not want to have the child even if she was. Perhaps Slipper would get me on a plane the next morning before I could get to see Raimunda.

The following morning, with my predicament in mind, I filched the razor blade I was given to shave with and hid it under the lining of one of my shoes. I had read an article in a magazine about an American con who had avoided a number of court appearances by swallowing razor blades wrapped in bread - I, for one, was ready to give it a try if it kept me off the plane. If I declared that I had a razor blade for breakfast I would be rushed to the hospital and not to the airport.

By the time I was transferred back to the Federal Police Headquarters, Slipper, Neill and the delegado were already involved in yet another heated discussion and it soon became clear that it would be impossible to get me to the airport in time to catch the morning plane.

The session ended with Slipper and Jones being told that, as it was Saturday, nothing more could be done until the following Monday or Tuesday. Even though I was sitting handcuffed I was delighted with this piece of news.

Not long after they left the delegacia Raimunda was escorted into the room where I was being held. When she saw that I was handcuffed she broke into sobs and began protesting in a loud voice. The chief came out of his office, no doubt wanting to know what all the noise was about. He managed to calm Raimunda down, giving her his handkerchief to dry her eyes.

'Now, you come into my office and tell me everything you know about your boyfriend. Stop crying, and I promise to help you all I can.' Garcia put his arm around Raimunda and led her into his office, talking to her like some kindly uncle.

I could hear some of the conversation between Raimunda and Garcia from where I was sitting and Raimunda was clearly doing her best to let the delegado know what a wonderful and kind person I had been to her and her family. Garcia now wanted to hear what I had to say, from the time I had arrived in Brazil 'till today. I began by telling him that the statement I had made the previous day was not true, mentioning the fact that the British Consul General had advised against telling the true story to avoid complicating my return to Great Britain. After I had told my tale the delegado repeated his desire to help us in any way he could, indicating that he had not exactly fallen in love with his visitors from Scotland Yard.

After a fresh and lengthy statement, I was given time to have a private conversation with Raimunda. She was pregnant and she was certain that she wanted to have the baby whether I went back to England or not. At that time, I assessed my chances of staying in Brazil as close to zero but, even so, I also wanted Raimunda to have my child.

All the time our little drama was going on inside the delegacia, a horde of reporters and photographers, many of whom had flown in overnight from England when word of my arrest had got out, were struggling to get to see us. But the good Dr Garcia had given strict orders to keep them at bay - he had a special presentation of his own in mind.

At the time of my arrest the most popular television programme in Brazil was a Sunday evening series called *Fantastico! (It's Fantastic!)* on TV Globo. The programme combined news, current affairs and entertainment with a weird and wonderful mix of events from around the world. Dr Garcia had come up with the idea of putting Raimunda and me on the programme with a view to letting the Brazilian public see us 'in the flesh' - and, at the same time, collecting a few cruzeiros for his trouble. The filming took place in the delegado's office, Raimunda and I sitting side by side on an ancient settee. As the camera rolled Dr Garcia stood to one side assuming the role of director, making signs for us to snuggle up together, to hold hands and kiss.

'Let the Brazilian people see that you love each other!' he said. 'Smile! Look happy!'

When I got back to the dirty little prison, my cellmates were delighted when I told them what had transpired during the day. Mario, the taxi-driver, kept repeating his favourite oath, *'Puta que pariu!'* An oath which is certainly more poetic in Portuguese than in English as it roughly translates as 'Whore that gave birth to you!'

Dr Garcia's production was shown on television the following evening and although I didn't get to see it, I heard that the program created a lot of public sympathy. The delegado's superiors were not as impressed, however, and Garcia was later demoted for allowing the filming to take place in the delegacia.

On the Monday morning, with the razor-blade still in my shoe, I was taken once again to the Catete Palace. A decision was expected with regard to my position and the mob of reporters and photographers were pushing and shoving at the front gate as we drove into the palace grounds.

Raimunda was there, now a celebrity after her appearance on *Fantastico!* and a weekend of giving interviews to the press. So were Slipper and Jones, neither one of whom was looking particularly cheerful. Colin Mackenzie, I was told, was taking care of Raimunda and had given her some money to buy some clothes. My friend Constantine was also being helpful by 'taking care' of Lucia.

At that time I was still unaware of the *Daily Express'* double-cross, believing that Mackenzie and Lovelace had been followed to Brazil. I had not seen the issues of that particular newspaper following my arrest and I was foolish enough to believe that the £35,000 'deal' I had made with Mackenzie was still on. The Brazilian newspapers that I had managed to get hold of gave no indication that the *Express* had put the Yard onto me.

There was, however, much criticism levelled at the British police for the manner in which they had arrived in Brazil unannounced and brought about my capture.

Mackenzie swore later that he had no idea that his superiors at the Daily Express had contacted the Yard. According to Slipper in his biography, 'Slipper of the Yard', the Express had tipped off the Yard from the word go, but did not tell Mackenzie at first, in case he took the story to the Daily Mail. But Slipper and Jones did meet with Mackenzie in London prior to the trip, along with Hitchen and the Express' legal advisor, Andrew Edwards. Finally, in 2011, Mackenzie admitted that he had actually met up with Slipper and Jones at their Rio hotel the night before my arrest.

At six o'clock on Monday 4 February Garcia made an announcement. I was to be detained in Brazilian custody for ninety days pending further enquiries. Slipper and Jones, without their man, returned on that night's British Caledonian flight to Gatwick to a cruel reception from the newspapers who had not got the goodies. In Britain an enquiry was already underway as accusations and excuses began to fly between Scotland Yard, the Home Office, and the Foreign Office.

It was on the flight back that the famous photo of Slipper sitting next to an empty seat was taken. It was not, however, as the press liked to make out, my empty seat, but was taken when Jones had gone to the toilet. Slipper was learning the hard way about how the press played their game.

A few days later I was on a plane but with a federal police inspector as my escort and flown to Brasilia where there was a special prison for foreigners. Apart from the inspector and I, the only other people on the flight besides the crew were a reporter and a photographer from the Brazilian newspaper, O Globo. That was the newspaper, one of the most influential in Brazil, which had run a front-page story on the day following my arrest, telling the population that the man who had been taken into custody had shot the train-driver three times through the head at point blank range.

Soon after we had taken off, the Globo reporter showed me a copy of the Daily Express with screaming headlines of my capture. Reading on, I soon discovered that I had been well and truly shafted and the Express was not about to come up with any money for my story. These tidings plunged me into a black mood, but a little later I was cheered up somewhat by a conversation I had with the inspector. Back in 1974, he explained, there were quite a large number of left-wing Brazilians who had sought political asylum in Great Britain, some of whom were wanted for alleged acts of subversion. Even though there was no Treaty of Extradition between Britain and Brazil, the Brazilian authorities had approached the British government, seeking the extradition of certain individuals, but Britain had steadfastly refused. With that in mind, said the inspector, he found it hard to imagine that Brazil would hand me over to the Brits.

'Inspector Helio,' I told him, 'you have made my day!'

At Brasilia Airport the inspector and I parted company and I was handed over to another federal policeman named Vivaldo, who spoke with a stutter and who, I later discovered, was the jailer at the 'special' prison. Still handcuffed, I was put into the back of a closed police truck which must have been standing in the sun for hours before I arrived; it was like getting into an oven. On arrival at the steel and concrete jail where I was to pass the next three months, I was greeted by an educated voice coming from one of the cells.

'Good afternoon, Mr Biggs. How was your flight from Rio?' Before I had time to reply or see who it was who had spoken, Vivaldo had unlocked an empty cell and hustled me inside.

I was relieved of everything except my underpants, with Vivaldo carefully inspecting each item and passing it to a trustee who stood holding a cardboard box. There was a wafer-thin mattress on one of the beds which Vivaldo flung into the corridor with a 'Puta merda!' A newspaper had been concealed under the mattress and when Vivaldo saw it he started shouting and stuttering at the trustee for not having removed 'everything' from the cell, as he had instructed.

'Filho da puta! Do I have to do everything myself?'

Well, I thought, Mr Vivaldo and I are going to get along just fine. He slammed the gate of the cell and locked it, then shook the gate to make sure it was locked.

'Welcome to Brasilia, Mr Biggs.' said the same refined voice when the jailer had left the area. 'Please don't let Vivaldo disturb you. He's really quite nice when you get to know him.'

There were eight cells all on the same side of the corridor, so it was impossible to see who was speaking to me. He introduced himself as, Fernand Legros, a Frenchman and, according to what he told me, a wealthy art dealer, unjustly accused of selling paintings that 'turned out to be' forgeries. He was awaiting extradition to face charges in France.

There were five other prisoners there beside myself, most of them also waiting to be 'repatriated.' Every evening, Monsieur Legros had dinner sent in from a nearby French restaurant, Le Paysan - for everybody. He would go from cell to cell with a menu from the restaurant, taking the orders.

'I am sorry that it is such a poor menu,' he said, when he first appeared at the gate of my cell, 'But we must remember that we are in Brasilia. How does steak and chips sound?'

My mattress had been returned and I was given a thin blanket that didn't smell too pleasant. But I stayed in my underpants for the first three days; no clothes, no comb, no toothbrush. And the food was served without knives, forks or spoons, obliging me to eat with my hands.

Late in the afternoon of the third day, Vivaldo appeared bearing the cardboard box containing my clothing and other items. He unlocked my cell and handed me the box.

'Get yourself ready quickly,' he ordered, 'Your wife is here to see you.' He went away and returned with a razor-holder and blade. 'Here. You need this,' he said 'You must make yourself look tidy!'

My wife had arrived! I almost felt friendly towards Vivaldo for bringing me such wonderful news. I shaved and got myself ready - without a mirror - in record time while my jailer waited poker-faced. Then he led me out of the cellblock, across a yard where a number of police vehicles were parked, and up a staircase and into another building.

Without knocking, Vivaldo opened an office door and nodded for me to enter. I found myself in a large room full of seated people with notebooks on their laps. Close to where I had entered the room, there was a desk and a chair...but no sign of Charmian. I had been conned into giving a press conference. Son of a bitch!

Most of the journalists were Brits, wanting to know how I was being treated and that kind of stuff. I was feeling somewhat hostile about the way I had been tricked, so I wasn't really in the mood to answer a dumb bunch of questions. When the interview came to an end, Vivaldo made a sign for me to stay seated until all the journalists had left the room. One of the last to leave was a reporter dressed in a safari suit who came to the desk where I was sitting and said, 'I have a message for you from George: he asked me to tell you that he has moved from number 30 Grand Avenue to number 9.'

'Thanks,' I said, 'That's wonderful news!' The message let me know that the last £30,000 remaining from the train robbery money was now worth less than £9000. A great investment!

I was just thinking how gratifying it would be to see Vivaldo drop dead when another visitor came through the door. It was Charmian.

She was glad to see me but she was very unhappy. Firstly she had been given no warning that the press would be in the room for our meeting. Secondly, for me to be living with another woman was one thing; to be having a child with her was something entirely different. With Vivaldo and a federal police public relations officer, who could speak English, hovering within earshot, it was not easy to discuss our situation. But, said Charmian, what was more important than anything was for me to keep my freedom. I explained that I would need to divorce her so I could marry Raimunda. Charmian was in shock but she said she was prepared to divorce me if it would strengthen my case. If I should be sent back to England at the end of my spell in Brasilia she said she would also return to England so that we could live again as man and wife when I had 'paid my debt'. A week later, on 16 February, we were jointly interviewed by the press before Charmian returned to Australia.

I was allowed to keep my clothes and other possessions - and I was surprised to see that the razor blade was still concealed in my shoe! Life was much more pleasant now that I could eat my food with the handle of my toothbrush. I was allowed the 'privilege' of buying certain foodstuffs from my 'private cash' and I was permitted to join the rest of the prisoners for an hour or so in the sun each day.

Colin Mackenzie and Raimunda had taken rooms at a hotel in Brasilia and became frequent visitors at the prison. When I had learned that the Express had called Scotland Yard to bring about my arrest I was reluctant to see Mackenzie, believing that he must have known I was being set up. He swore to the contrary and said that he had been 'devastated' when Slipper had entered the scene. Bill Lovelace, he went on, a case-hardened Fleet Street photographer who had captured many a heart-rending moment on film, had 'cried like a baby' when I went off as Slipper's prisoner, although Slipper has subsequently said that it was Lovelace who signalled to him from the hotel window that I was in the room.

Mackenzie was interested in writing a book with me. He felt that I had been treated unfairly; he too had been betrayed by his own newspaper. He also said that the proceeds of the book would ensure that Charmian and Raimunda could be taken care of financially if I eventually went back to do my time. In view of the fact that I had already given him a large part of my story before Slipper's arrival, I agreed to work with him in putting a book together. All he wanted for his labour, he said, was thirty per cent of whatever the book might net.

One day he turned up at the prison with a wide smile. Granada Publishing had advanced him £65,000 pounds on his book.

'Colin,' I said, when I heard the news, 'I need a lawyer!'

A week later Dr José Paulo Sepulveda Pertence, a highly respected Brazilian attorney whom Mackenzie had engaged to fight against my possible deportation - for $10,000, visited me. I was not too impressed with him on his initial visit; he looked and acted bored, frequently examining his nails. He drove a red Porsche convertible. But after receiving half his fee he started to shape up and one of his first moves was to get me before a Family Court, where I duly swore that I was the father of Raimunda's expected child.

Raimunda was looking radiant in her pregnancy and was a familiar figure in the Brazilian newspapers. She made a lot of friends and won people over with her smile and her cheeky repartee. Fernand Legros, who met her during visiting hours, admired her, and asked if he could 'have the honour' of becoming the godfather to our child. We accepted. In March he was deported to France where, although found guilty on some charges, he was set free because of the time he had already spent in prison in Brazil awaiting his deportation.

Back in the cells, the days and weeks dragged on. It was stinking hot, and just as Fernand had departed the much feared, Dr Brito, the Superintendent, had returned from his holidays and was back in charge. Radios and tape-recorders that had been permitted by Brito's stand-in were promptly removed. Visiting time was reduced and cells were searched daily.

Vivaldo was reduced to a stuttering mess; such was his fear of his boss. Most evenings, Dr Brito would visit us, going from cell to cell, tugging at the padlocks on the doors. He would often come to my cell and stand glaring at me. I would glare back, neither one of us saying a word. He gave me the impression that he wasn't all there.

It was coming to the end of my ninety days and I knew that Dr Pertence, my attorney, was standing by with a writ of habeas corpus to get me out of jail when my time was up. In the April he had managed to get confirmation of paternity from the Family Court.

On the morning of 6 May Pertence arrived at the prison to visit me, but was not allowed to enter. I wondered if it could mean that my case was before the judges at the Supreme Court. An agent took me from my cell to the adjacent office block where he took five copies of my fingerprints. I asked the man if he had any idea what was happening in my case, to which he said he knew nothing. I mentioned the fact that when I had been fingerprinted in Rio, forty sets had been taken.

'Forty sets are taken in the case of expulsion.' the agent told me.

'Well,' I said, 'as you've only taken five sets that must mean that I'm not going to be expelled from Brazil!' My case had been heard. I could feel it in my water!

During the afternoon, Vivaldo came to my cell and said mysteriously,

'Biggs. You should prepare your soul for a journey.'

'What do you mean by that?' I asked.

'Nothing. Just prepare yourself.'

'Vivaldo,' I said, 'you know something! What you mean is, that I am going to be released!' I was almost dancing around the cell by now.

'I don't know anything,' Vivaldo insisted, 'If Brito knew I was down here talking to you, I would lose my job.' Then, to my amazement, he put his hand out to shake mine saying, 'Good luck, Biggs. Go with God.'

A short while later, the second-in-command, Barbosa, paid me a visit. 'Get yourself ready, Biggs. You're being taken to Rio de Janeiro in half an hour.'

'Has my case been heard?' I asked. Barbosa was a decent bloke and had often come down to the cells to shoot the breeze with us, so I knew he would tell me what had transpired.

'It has,' he told me. 'You're going back to Rio tonight and tomorrow morning you will be released on conditional liberty.'

'Are you taking me to Rio?' I asked hopefully.

'No.' said Barbosa. 'Your escort will be Dr Brito.'

Even though I was going to Rio to be released, Brito insisted that I should make the journey in handcuffs. When I protested he said that once we were on the plane he would remove them, but he never did.

The press had got word that I was travelling to Rio and a small army of reporters and photographers were already on the plane when I got on with my loony escort. Colin Mackenzie and Bill Lovelace were among them and immediately started talking to me.

'Ron, you're free!' said Mackenzie delightedly, 'Why the handcuffs?'

Before I had a chance to say anything, Brito shouted at the reporters. 'No talking! No pictures!'

'Who's the idiot?' someone asked. Brito had picked up a blanket and was holding it up in front of me.

'No pictures!' he repeated.

The press were as baffled as I by Brito's attitude and I found myself thinking that some kind of trick must be taking place, perhaps I was being taken to Rio to be deported after all. The press, mostly Brits, were not intimidated by Brito's order for silence. Mackenzie began telling me that he had been present at the hearing of my case and at that moment I was free. Brito had had enough. He told me to get up and marched me to the back of the plane to sit in one of two jump seats normally used by the cabin crew during take-off and landing. I was sitting beside one of the rear doors of the plane, within easy reach of the door handle. Brito was still glaring in the direction of the mob from Fleet Street when I drew his attention to the fact that I could easily open the door whilst we were in the air and have him sucked out along with Fleet Streets' finest. Brito thought for a moment about what I had said and then hurriedly called a stewardess who confirmed what I had said.

'We are going back to where we were sitting,' Brito decided. 'You will not talk to anyone! If you don't respect this order your release can be cancelled. I want no conversation.'

Our return to our original seats brought a volley of piss-taking cheers from the press and rude remarks were made about the angry Dr Brito. When we finally touched down in Rio, Brito insisted on waiting until everybody had left the plane before taking me off. We went down the steps of the aircraft with Brito holding the blanket over my head and shoulders. But the Fleet Street pros knew all about taking pictures under these circumstances. One of them simply put his camera under the blanket and got the shot he wanted.

A car was waiting to take us to the federal police headquarters at the Catete Palace. When I entered the charge-room where the drama had begun to unfold three months earlier, the first person I saw was Inspector Helio, the cop who had taken me to Brasilia. We exchanged greetings and then he asked me, 'Why are you handcuffed?'

I looked towards Brito, 'I don't know. Perhaps this gentleman can tell you.' Brito produced the key to the handcuffs and removed them. His mission was accomplished. Hopefully I would never see the arsehole again.

Inspector Helio told me that I was free to go but, he pointed out, there was a large crowd of newsmen waiting at the front gate and it was going to be virtually impossible for me to get away from them. He suggested that I pass the night in the delegacia, in a room that had no bars at the window so that I would not feel that I was still being detained. He would instruct an agent to wake me at five a.m., by which time, we hoped, the mob would have dispersed, and I could be driven anywhere I wanted to go. I was given the night watchman's room where there was a bed with a comfortable mattress - and the windows were wide open. But I was too excited to sleep. I was free!

CELEBRITY STATUS:
LIFE IN THE SPOTLIGHT

"It is outrageous that any criminal should make a profit out of his crime and today's announcement that the train robbers are to form a company to sell and syndicate their story is an outrage to the many industrious, hard working, clean living people who are the backbone of our country."

Tory MP, Nicholas Fairbairn, 5 April 1976

God save the Sex Pistols they're a bunch of wholesome blokes
They just like wearing filthy clothes and swapping filthy jokes
Ronnie Biggs was doing time until he done a bunk
Now he says he's seen the light and he sold his soul to punk

Sex Pistols, *'No One Is Innocent'*, June 1978

It was the beginning of a beautiful morning as I was driven out of a side gate of the Catete Palace on my way to Copacabana. It was a new day, a new dawn and I was feeling good! I was back in Rio and this time as Ronald Biggs. Michael Haynes had had his day in the sun. The date was 7 May 1974.

The *Daily Express*, still interested in getting every last little scrap of news on the 'Biggs' story, had rented an apartment in Copacabana for their team of reporters, which consisted of Mackenzie, Lovelace and a friendly Irish fellow by the name of Michael O'Flaherty. Raimunda was also staying in the apartment, but when I got there she was out. The lads from the *Express* had been up late celebrating my release. After much backslapping and hand shaking, O'Flaherty, whom I was meeting for the first time, told me that he was 'indeed honoured' to make my acquaintance. He put a tumbler of whiskey into my hand and we drank to 'freedom!' - what else!

It soon became clear that the *Express* was still trying to keep the 'copy' I could provide as their exclusive source of copy. My attitude at that moment was 'fuck the *Express!*' Mackenzie was now saying that he thought I should 'string along' with the *Express* for the time being. He was only staying on, he said, because he wanted to be in a position to take care of the 'little matter' of £35,000. I was hoping he could make the 'bastards' cough up.

I ran a bath. I felt like having a long relax in the tub to get the stink of prison and travelling off my body. Jesus! It was good to be out of that shit-hole in Brasilia.

I was stretched out in the warm sudsy water, probably humming The *Good Life*, when Mackenzie brought the telephone to the bathroom. Charmian was on the line, happy to know that I was a free man but glum at the implications. She supposed it meant that I had gone back to my 'Indian whore'. I had asked Mackenzie to get tickets for Charmian to come to Rio and she told me that she would be arriving in Rio with Farley and Chris a week hence and that a booking had been made for them at a seafront hotel in Ipanema. Whilst I was talking on the telephone, Lovelace pushed open the door and snapped a picture; another 'scoop' for the *Express*. The following week the picture appeared as a centrefold in the Brazilian magazine, Manchete, and apparently pissed-off a lot of people in high places. The Feds advised me to adopt a lower profile.

Raimunda arrived, bringing with her an entourage of reporters and photographers, some of whom managed to push their way into the apartment. Lovelace and O'Flaherty went into action, physically ejecting their uninvited guests with a rich assortment of bad language. Xuxu looked a picture of health and happiness, laughing delightedly at the wild confusion she had caused. We were pleased to see each other, hugging and posing for Lovelace, who was still breathing heavily after his struggle with his brothers from Fleet Street.

During the morning, Dr Pertence paid us a visit and outlined the findings of the court. I had gained a victory disguised as a defeat, he explained.

An order had been made for my deportation that gave me thirty days to look for a country that would accept me. But, there was a rider to the effect that it had to be a country that did not have an extradition treaty with the United Kingdom. Pertence went on to explain that deportation would mean extradition and the letter of the law - which was also to help me later when in Barbados - clearly stated that the father of a Brazilian child could not be extradited. He advised me to comply with the order and go through the motions to see if I could find another country willing to accept me. The Daily Mirror took this chore off my hands. There appeared to be only two countries in South America that did not have an extradition treaty with Britain - Venezuela and Costa Rica - and when approached by the Mirror they were swift to decline my company. The Venezuelan authorities had by now learnt that I had passed through Caracas Airport on a false passport and would be happy to charge me with that offence should I choose to visit them again.

As the news of my arrival at the apartment in Copacabana began to spread, the press started to gather in the street in front of the apartment building and the commotion brought residents to their windows to see what was going on. Some photographers had talked their way into apartments across the road and waited with cameras at the ready. More than once Lovelace told me to keep away from the windows. But I'd had enough. I had just spent three months cooped up in a prison with rats and cockroaches for company and now I wanted to feel my freedom. I wanted to walk along the beach, see people, drink a beer at a bar and visit my friends. The *Express* men whined about losing their 'exclusive' story. But I wasn't interested, I wanted out.

Outside was worse than I had imagined. Questions were being thrown at me from all sides in Portuguese and English. Flashbulbs blinded me. I tried to reason with the mob, which was a complete waste of time. I managed to get into a nearby bar, but it was immediately packed out with reporters and photographers, all desperate to buy me a drink. By now the *Express* gang had joined me in the confusion. Mackenzie suggested that we should get into a taxi to get away from the pack. But the pack took taxis too, and followed us in a wild chase down Copacabana. Finally I decided that I would have to talk to the journalists and let them get their precious copy and photographs. Then, mercifully it was all over - or so I thought.

It was early evening when I got back to the apartment where Raimunda was preparing a meal. We were alone and had a chance to sit down and talk. She had been busy during the three months I had been away. She had knitted and crocheted a lot of baby clothes and had even found time to crochet a beautiful black and white poncho for Mackenzie's wife, Tina, who had visited Brazil soon after I was sent to Brasilia. Although Raimunda was only a little over three months pregnant, her belly was already quite distended. But she carried it well and was obviously happy with her 'lump'.

By now Raimunda was well established in the hearts of the Brazilian people, many seeing her as a heroine who had saved the hapless gringo. That's certainly how I was beginning to see her!

There was a light tap at the front door and I went to investigate. It was yet another reporter, notebook in hand. His name was Harold Emert, he said, an American reporter for British newspapers resident in Rio, he would like to ask me a few questions. I turned him away. I couldn't take any more punishment. I've seen Harold many times since that day and, it's funny, he always calls on me when the other reporters have gone home.

He did, however, overstep the mark when he was found sneaking around my house with a camera after I had suffered a stroke. The cook, Rosa, took a broom to him, and he never did get his exclusive photo of me unconscious in my bed.

During the early days following my release I met many journalists and found out a lot about them. The journalist's motto, one told me, was, 'Never let the truth stand in the way of a good story.' The Brazilian press, never far behind their Fleet Street colleagues in terms of inventiveness, had declared that I was *O Cerebro*, the brain of the hold-up of the 'pay-train', providing me with instant celebrity status in Rio.

It was a strange sensation meeting up with my old friends again, especially the ones who had only known me as 'Mike Haynes'. The Blumer family had said kind things about me to the press while I had been away and received me with open arms, offering me their home if I needed somewhere to stay. Fine people. Scott Johnson, who I had at one time thought might be a CIA agent, had found it hard to believe that his carefree friend was a fugitive. I looked up my hippie friends, of course, and bent the law with them, listening to Dylan and Pink Floyd. Far out, man!

Shortly before I met up with Constantine, Phyllis Huber had introduced me to one of her best friends, an attractive mother of three young children, named Ursula – or Ulla – Sopher, and she and I had got to know each other. Ulla was also very surprised when she heard that I had been taken into custody for my involvement with the train robbery, but it didn't affect our friendship. We became closer.

Thankfully, the press interest in Raimunda and me began to taper off with time and most of the newsmen disappeared from the vicinity of the flat. Mackenzie and co. stayed on, awaiting Charmian's arrival.

Eager as I was to see Charmian and the boys, I had serious misgivings about the pending encounter. When Charmian and I had met in Brasilia, she had said that if I was allowed to stay in Brazil she would be ready to come with the children and live with me. And even though she had spoken of divorcing me, she was not going to hand me over to Raimunda on a silver platter - my head, perhaps, but not the rest of me! She certainly did not even contemplate or countenance my idea of a ménage-à-trois.

My wife and sons arrived on 16 May, the eve of Charmian's thirty-fifth birthday, and booked in at the Hotel Sol Ipanema on Ipanema Beach. Farley was now seven and Chris was a stocky eleven year-old. Seeing my kids and being able to hug them for the first time in four years was a great treat but there was a certain amount of uncertainty on their part when I met them.

Although Farley was gabbling away excitedly, Chris was much less effusive, answering my questions in monosyllables. Charmian's attitude was friendly enough, but somewhat frosty. During the day, however, the initial stiffness wore off and we began to enjoy ourselves.

Within the terms of my Conditional Liberty I had to be 'home' by no later than 10 p.m. My plan, therefore, was to spend my days with Charmian and the boys, returning to the apartment in Copacabana each night in time to beat the curfew. Raimunda was aware that Charmian had returned to Brazil and was not exactly enthusiastic about me passing the days in my wife's company. I had asked Mackenzie to give Raimunda extra attention during Charmian's visit and he bore the brunt of Xuxu's displeasure until I got home.

As it was planned for Charmian to spend at least two weeks in Brazil, Mackenzie arranged a two-bedroomed apartment in Copacabana for her and the boys that was within walking distance of the apartment I was sharing with Raimunda. He also hired a maid and these expenses, he explained, would be coming 'off the top' of his book, which was nearing completion.

Mackenzie also wanted to spend time with Charmian as she had a lot of information about our lives that I had forgotten, as well as material for the book, such as family photos.

The weather was still hot and much of the time we went to the beach where Charmian and I would discuss our complicated situation at length while the kids played and swam. Charmian said again that she would give up everything in Australia and come to live with me in Brazil, but we both knew that this was not a practical solution or even a possibility. The more we talked about the subject, the more bitter Charmian became until one evening when I was preparing to leave to meet my ten o'clock deadline she put her foot down.

'I've had enough of this,' she declared angrily, 'I'm your wife and I demand my rights! I'm going to that apartment with you and I'm going to sleep with you - whether your Indian is there or not!'

As good luck would have it, Raimunda was not at the apartment when Charmian entered the flat with her sleeves rolled up, ready for action. In the bedroom that Raimunda and I were using, Charmian noticed a baby doll nightdress draped over a chair together with the poncho that Raimunda had made for Tina Mackenzie. She picked it up between finger and thumb and dropped it instantly as if it was going to contaminate her.

'I suppose this is something you bought your Indian?' Charmian sneered.

'No,' I replied truthfully, 'that was a present from one of the Express reporters, Mike O'Flaherty.'

I could see that Charmian was in an ugly mood and offered to make tea, leaving her in the bedroom to cool down. While I waited for the kettle to boil I was praying for Raimunda not to return to the apartment, I didn't fancy the idea refereeing the fight of the year. I was pouring the tea when Charmian appeared in the kitchen doorway, almost snorting with rage.

'I'm not staying here another moment,' she announced belligerently.

'I can't stand the smell! Please have the decency to take me downstairs and find a taxi.'

Hiding a sigh of relief, I went to the bedroom to get my shirt. As I was about to leave the bedroom I noticed a piece of black and white material on the floor beside the bed, and I stooped down to pick it up. Then I saw more pieces of the same material under the bed, and some pieces of pink fabric as well. To my horror, I realized that Charmian had cut up Raimunda's nightdress and Tina's poncho into small pieces. Jesus Christ! I put everything into a plastic bag and went back into the living room where Charmian stood smiling maliciously.

'Charm,' I said. 'That was an insane thing to do.'

'Perhaps it was,' she said viciously, 'but it's only a small token of what I would like to do to that bitch!' I tried to calm her down as we went down to the street and stood waiting for a taxi. I knew that she was hurt and frustrated and I did everything I could to console her, but she was not to be mollified and left in tears.

Xuxu arrived the next morning having spent the night in a small, first floor kitchenette which she had rented in one of Rio's busiest thoroughfares, Avenida Nossa Senhora da Copacabana. She had found the place a few weeks before I was released from Brasilia and had rented it principally for herself, knowing that she would not be able to afford the high rent of the *Daily Express* apartment when the pressmen left. With Mackenzie's help she had bought some second hand furniture and a refrigerator. All the kitchenette needed, she said, was a coat of paint. Suddenly, she asked, 'Where is the poncho I made for Tina?'

'Oh. I forgot to tell you,' I began to lie, 'Bill Lovelace flew back to London last night and I asked him to take it to give to Tina.'

'You should not have done that,' Raimunda said, sounding put out, 'I wanted to send a letter with it... and where's my nightdress?'

'Isn't it hanging on the chair by the bed?' I asked, looking into the bedroom, playing out the charade, not overeager to tell her I had thrown it down the rubbish chute the previous evening.

'I don't understand,' she said, 'I left it on the chair together with the poncho.'

'Do you know what must have happened?' I said speciously. 'Bill must have picked it up with the poncho without realizing it. But don't worry, we can go out and buy another one.'

My story wouldn't have convinced the sleepiest jury but Xuxu accepted my version without question.

Later that day, when I went to the apartment where Charmian and the kids were living, I was pleased to see that Charm had recovered her composure. Her vandalism of the previous evening was not mentioned and as it was sunny we decided to have another afternoon at the beach. There, Charmian told me that she had reluctantly resigned herself to the fact that she would be facing her future without me. It was not what she wanted, but she would divorce me, as she had said during our meeting in Brasilia, so that I would be free to marry Raimunda and give the child my name. And, she hoped, it would also enable me to keep my freedom. We loved each other - as we still very much do - but, under the circumstances, we could only be friends.

When Charmian and the boys left Brazil at the beginning of June, I moved into Raimunda's tiny apartment in Copacabana. There was a double and a single bed, a dining room table and four chairs and the refrigerator in the principal room. There was a minute bathroom and an even smaller kitchen. The rent was $50 per month.

The front window looked out onto the roaring Copacabana traffic, seemingly within touching distance. There was a bus stop immediately in front of the building where busses would stop with a squealing of brakes and pull away again with high revs, leaving a wake of black smoke. When the window was raised, it was possible to see the smoke and fumes creeping into the room. Cockroaches outnumbered the tenants in the building by at least a thousand to one and then there were the rats.

I set to with sandpaper, filler and paint and in a week or so I got the place looking bright and cheerful. One of my hippie friends, 'Stainless'

Steve Able, painted a huge blue butterfly on the wall where we planned to install the baby, and one of the Blumer children, Linnie, did a beautiful job of painting a golden lion on a facing wall because she knew that the new arrival would be a Leo. Ulla's young daughter, Carla, also came and painted some animals on the wall of the 'nursery'. Raimunda had put herself into the hands of an obstetrician - a certain Dr Paulo - and he had estimated that the baby would arrive in the second week of August.

Although Raimunda seemed perfectly happy with the apartment and did her best to keep it clean, I started to look around for somewhere more salubrious. One afternoon, not long before Raimunda's confinement, I found myself in a lazy-paced, picturesque fishing village called Sepetiba. It was about forty miles south from Rio and could easily be reached by bus. I liked the place and made a mental note of the name.

It was about this time that I met John Stanley Pickston, a fellow-Londoner a few years younger than myself. Highly entertaining and always ready for a laugh, we soon became firm friends. He was - and is - married to a Portuguese lady named Maria Emilia (known as Lia) and lived only a couple of blocks from our apartment. We found we had a lot in common, both having the same working-class background. And, of course, we both liked a pint. We visited each other frequently, Raimunda always happy to entertain.

Raimunda and I had already agreed on names for our offspring and Michael Fernand Nascimento de Castro Biggs, to give him his full name, was born at 10 a.m. on 16 August, with Dr Paulo taking care of the Caesarean delivery.

Reporters had renewed their interest with the new twist in the Biggs' story and were vying for the first picture of the new Baby Biggs with offers of a thousand dollars for an 'exclusive'' shot. But a wily nurse at the hospital beat us all to it and had her palm greased by a Brazilian freelance photographer who was let into Raimunda's room a few short minutes after the baby was delivered.

As we did not have a telephone, an arrangement had been made with a neighbour - a lady by the name of Lena - to receive a call from the hospital the moment the baby was born. When Lena knocked at the door to tell me 'It's a boy!' I was as delighted as I had been when my other three sons had been born. Our apartment was full of friends and reporters waiting for the news and, after 'wetting the baby's head' with beer and a bottle of champers, I grabbed a taxi to the hospital to visit Raimunda and our new little Brazilian. Newborn children are rarely up to their fathers' expectations but Raimunda thought he was lindo (beautiful) and I had to agree. The old fortune-teller had been right again; I had had a child with a woman with long black hair.

Back at the flat, the booze was still flowing and the newsmen were waiting for my comments on fatherhood and my future plans with Raimunda. Was I going to marry her? At that time, the terms of my Conditional Liberty did not permit me to marry and it was to be eighteen years before this restriction was rescinded. It was to take me 28 years before I made an honest woman of Raimunda, or rather before she and I made an honest man of our son, Mike. We eventually married in July 2002 in the salubrious surroundings of Belmarsh Prison.

As I was not allowed to work in Brazil either, it was difficult to say what my plans were for the future. I could only hope that Mackenzie would come through with enough of the proceeds from his book to keep us going. He was still in Brazil but once we moved into the kitchenette, we saw little of him.

A couple of days later I picked Raimunda and Mike up at the hospital and brought them back to the flat. Neighbours and friends soon arrived with presents and congratulations, cooing and baby-talking. Mike was a great little kid with lusty lungs and a healthy appetite, slurping away at feeding time.

By Christmas, at four months, Mike - or, 'Mikinho' as we all called him - appeared to be making good progress, but I was not altogether happy about bringing him up in the pollution that surrounded us in Copacabana. I decided to take another trip to sunny Sepetiba to see what I could find by way of alternative accommodation and found exactly what I wanted; a house with a big sandy garden, about fifty yards from the beach. The house had not been lived in for some time and was badly in need of decorating. But the rent was only slightly higher that the shoebox in Copacabana, so I closed a deal with the Portuguese owner of the property and returned to Rio delighted with my good luck. Raimunda was uncertain about making the change. I had done so much to our flat, she said, and we would be so far away from our friends.

'But Xuxu,' I said, 'you'll love it when you see it!'

I took Ulla to see the place, driving to Sepetiba in her car. We took cleaning material and cleaned the house from top to bottom between us. Afterwards we passed a couple of hours relaxing at a bar on the tree-lined seafront and, later, became lovers.

Fernand Legros, the fraudulent Frenchman, had made contact with us soon after Mike was born. He had read of the event in the newspaper, he told us, and wanted very much to keep his word in regard to becoming Mike's godfather. Xuxu had been very impressed with Legros' claims to fabulous wealth and liked the idea of having someone like Mr Legros to look out for her son's spiritual requirements. Legros suggested that Mike should be baptized in France - at his expense, of course - and so it was agreed. About the same time a certain David Cohen became interested in Raimunda and Mike and approached her with regard to making some kind of a story for *The News of the World*. A deal was made to take them both to England with Mr Cohen acting as a chaperone. Raimunda was to be paid a thousand pounds. So, at the beginning of January 1975, she, Mike and Cohen flew to London. Shortly afterwards, Xuxu, the little half-indian girl from the interior of Brazil, showed her beautiful tits in a "world exclusive" on the front page of the world's largest selling Sunday newspaper.

It was a picture spread that I later learnt had particularly upset Charmian, as she believes it was a catalyst that had contributed to her father's suicide.

Within a few days of Raimunda leaving for England, I hired a van and took our bits and pieces to Sepetiba; I moved in, glad to be away from the noise and grime of Copacabana. Once again, I got busy with tools and paint and set about fixing the place up, calling in a good friend, Valmir, to give me a hand. I made a giant playpen and a cot with built-in coloured lights and a lift-out wicket fence at the front. Harrison Ford could not have done better. I renovated our furniture and shaped up the garden, enjoying the hard work.

Twice each week I had to take the bus into Rio to sign a register at the federal police headquarters. And twice a week I spent the night with Ulla who I was now becoming deeply involved with. Although Raimunda and I lived and slept together following my release from Brasilia, we had not resumed an intimate relationship. Furthermore, she knew of my affair with Ulla.

From England, Raimunda and co. moved on to France for the much-publicized baptism of Mikinho. Fernand Legros spared no expense to turn the event into an unforgettable experience for Raimunda and introduced her to artists and show-business friends. Champagne! Bright lights! And phoney promises. Xuxu was enchanted. The godfather bestowed heavenly protection upon his godchild in the form of a diamond studded gold cross, which turned out to be as snide as the canvases he was dealing in. But Raimunda would not have a bad word said about Monsieur Legros. She saw him and his friends as people who would enable her to become an artiste. They could open her *caminho* (or road), to stardom.

I met the party at the airport on their return to Brazil. David Cohen was smiling, Raimunda was using French perfume and Mike was just beautiful! Raimunda was also looking beautiful, and elegantly dressed in expensive-looking clothes. We parted company with Cohen and went by taxi to Sepetiba. I had hired my friend Valmir's sister as a maid and when we got to the house it was clean and polished as well as being freshly painted. Xuxu was pleasantly surprised. Mike's room was ready, with a white mosquito net hanging in place over the 'dream bed' I had built.

So Raimunda was back and we continued to live together. With the ease with which she made friends, Raimunda was soon mixing with the neighbours, inviting them in for a cafezinho and a spot of gossip.

Dona Maria Jose was our immediate neighbour and very simpatica. She had a gang of kids of her own to take care of but she was always ready to look after Mike if ever Raimunda and I had to go out. Her youngest - adopted - daughter, Renata, was about Mike's age and as they grew up they became sweethearts and sparring-partners. Raimunda also made friends with a very fat couple, named Borges, who ran a small general store around the corner from where we lived.

Borges and his wife were involved in a religion known as Candomble, often described as macumba. Candomble, which was brought to Brazil by the African slaves, is widely followed in the country and involves many weird and wonderful rites which, it is claimed, can bring about good fortune, good health and spiritual fulfilment. It is Brazil's voodoo, if you like, but more established.

Mr Borges said he thought that Raimunda and I should submit to one of these Candomble ceremonies and 'seek out our true destinies'. Raimunda was all for it and I - after my experience with the fortune-teller - agreed to go along, more out of curiosity than anything else.

The first part of the ceremony took place in the front room of a house close to where we were living in Sepetiba. We had been told to arrive at the house wearing old white clothing, bringing with us a clean set of clothes, also white, to change into later. After Raimunda and I had been introduced to the *mae-de-santo* (spiritual mother), decked out in her traditional voluminous white clothing, she asked us what it was that we were looking for in our lives. What were we asking of our saints? Raimunda had answered that she was looking for the road that would lead her to a career as a professional entertainer. My request was to receive a 'document' that would enable me to stay in Brazil legally. We were instructed to kneel on two rush mats that were placed side by side. A *pai-de-santo* (spiritual father), also taking part in the ceremony, and a female acolyte, a form of Candomble altar girl, began chanting while the mae-de-santo 'sprinkled' Raimunda and I over our heads and shoulders with a mixture of cubed fruit and vegetables which she took from two earthenware dishes. Any pieces that fell outside the area of the mats were gathered up by the altar girl and put back into the dishes. Then, two live black chickens where produced and, with the assistant holding them, the mae-de-santo cut their throats in turn, letting the blood flow over the fruit and vegetables in the two dishes. This part was an offering to Exu, the devil, and was put into a locked chamber at the side of the room where the ceremony was taking place.

Then, with Mr and Mrs Borges, who were going to be our 'witnesses', plus the *mae* and *pai-de-santo*, we were taken in a van to a secluded, wooded area where there was a waterfall. Here all four of us took off our clothes down to our underwear and threw them into the fast-flowing water which, we were told, would take all our worldly problems out to sea. It was all I could do not to laugh as Mr and Mrs Borges floundered around in the water looking like a pair of beached whales. With no apparent warning, Mrs Borges went into a trance and shrieking threw herself into the torrent of the waterfall, falling down with the impact of the water. After 'cleansing our bodies' in the icy water we were instructed to get dressed into our clean dry clothing. Then we were led to a flat rock where the assistant, who was also by now in a trance, was preparing for us plates of sliced apple covered with honey.

On the way back home in the van, Raimunda's eyes were shining. As far as she was concerned it had been a hundred dollars well invested; within a year she became a striptease artiste and, I imagine, a good one.

A month after Mike's first birthday, Raimunda took off on her second trip to Europe; this time alone. She said she would be away for three months. I was left holding the baby. But I didn't mind in the least: Mike and I got along fine. The only blot on the horizon was the fact that funds were running low and Mackenzie had not responded to an SOS for more cash which I assumed was still forthcoming from our deal. I started buying goods on credit from Borges' store, running up a hefty bill. Then, when I had a number of bills to pay, I borrowed money from Ulla to get by.

Things were tough from a financial point of view and I reluctantly dismissed the maid, Lucia, when I could no longer afford that luxury. I took on the housework, washing clothes and nappies and doing all those other interesting domestic tasks. Mike got accustomed to seeing me do the housework and started to call me, *mae* - almost pronounced, 'mine' - meaning mother! After a fall, he would pick himself up bawling, *'Mae-eh!'* Patiently I would wipe the sand out of his mouth and tell him that I was his *pai*.

Living in Sepetiba without a telephone, I was somewhat cut off from the outside world, but I was thoroughly enjoying rural life and my anonymity out of the spotlight. I liked the people in the area, who were simple but friendly, and I got on very well with them. Everybody, it seemed, had a kindly word for 'Biggies' (as I was known) and Mikinho. At weekends, a small group of musicians would gather at a nearby bar and play samba music, with everyone singing along and having a good time. There was always someone having a barbecue, or a feijoada, and I was frequently invited to these informal parties. Most days, when the weather permitted, I would take Mike to the beach for a couple of hours. I especially liked the peaceful atmosphere of the beach early in the morning. Friends often came down for the day. Johnny Pickston was a regular visitor - and so was Ulla, now that I was unaccompanied by Raimunda. She would sometimes bring her children, Alex, Felipe and Carla, and stay for the weekend, enjoying the relaxed life-style that was Sepetiba on-the-rocks.

Over the next few years there were many financial ups-and-downs. There were numerous offers of 'big money'. Merv Goldfinger - for want of his real name - invited me to join him for dinner at the Copacabana Palace Hotel to put to me a deal for the film rights to the story of my life. It looked good: $100,000 at the signing of 'the contract', $100,000 at the beginning of the filming and the rest when the film was in the can. But Merv was only one of a string of people who wanted to make some kind of a deal with me in the hope of a quick buck.

I was facing a fairly bleak Christmas 1975 as Roy James, Jim Hussey and Gordon Goody looked forward to their first taste of freedom after thirteen Christmases in the nick. I was wondering how I was going to put a turkey on the table, when a television crew from Argentina turned up at the front gate wanting to interview me. I told the producer a story of Yuletide hardship and charged $200 for the interview. The word must have been passed around that I was tucked away in Sepetiba as I was quickly sought out to give interviews by TV networks from Germany, Japan, Belgium and Australia. Now I had raised my price to $2000 an interview, and soon I was able to hire another maid and pay back Ulla the money I had borrowed from her.

There were other visitors to our house in Sepetiba, besides the newsmen. Total strangers, some from abroad, would manage to find their way to Sepetiba and the home of 'Biggies'. Often they would just be looking for a chat and the chance to pose beside me for a photograph, others had a more professional interest. One such person was a lady named

Maria Ippen who had escaped from custody in Vienna and got to Brazil to 'consult' with the person whom she considered to be the 'leading authority on escaping and staying free'. A young runaway from Scotland also turned up on my doorstep with a 'wee present' of twenty odd paperback books about famous criminals and crimes. He also wanted to know how to stay 'one step ahead of the law'.

One visitor, who came uninvited to a birthday party at my house, was a Rio resident and tour guide, Clive Wilson. A pompous young fellow, with a face that was set in a permanent sneer, I took an instant dislike to him. At the time I did not know that he would later give me ample opportunity to continue to dislike him and for rather better reasons.

During early 1976 most of the rest of the gang were released from prison, only Bruce and Charlie Wilson were still inside. Then, one morning in July 1976, I received a visit from a smooth-tongued South African named Gary van Dyk. He told me that he had been sent over by the gang and had a letter for me that had been written by Bobby Welch. Bob's letter was to introduce van Dyk and went on to say that the gang were in the process of putting a book together with a writer called, Piers Paul Read, who had done well with a book called *Alive*, about a disaster in the Andes. I had read the book and I knew that Mr Read was a very competent author indeed. Bob suggested that I should throw my lot in with the 'boys', as most of them had come out of prison hard up, as their 'minders' had scarpered with the dough they had been taking care of. Gary van Dyk was 'one of us', Bob wrote, and I could put my trust in him. I agreed to join forces with my colleagues and van Dyk, so I found a lawyer and signed the contract which van Dyk had brought with him.

I didn't like van Dyk, especially when he told me that he had killed eighteen men when he had been a mercenary in Angola. He had a dangerous look about him that didn't go with his glib tongue.

He told me that various members of the gang had tried unsuccessfully to get the story of the train robbery published and he, van Dyk, had come up with the idea that had got W. H. Allen, the publishing company, to do business. There was going to be a new angle introduced into the story; the robbery had been financed by a group of Germans, one of them being,

'Sigi', who was said to have been with us at Leatherslade Farm. For their investment the Germans, supposedly lead by one Otto Skorzeny, an officer in the Waffen-SS who had rescued Mussolini from the Marshal Badoglio government, had 'creamed off' a million pounds from the haul and the gang had divided the rest. I thought it sounded a pretty stupid idea and said as much to van Dyk, arguing that someone with Piers Paul Read's ability could write a sensational book by simply sticking to the facts. But van Dyk's plan had been approved by the gang and just like in the votes taken before the robbery, that was the way it was going to be done.

Soon, van Dyk told me, I would be visited by the author with a view to substantiating the German angle and I would have to be 'letter perfect' with what I told him. He would write, he promised, giving me the full details of the plot. He left, leaving me with $1000 which the gang had 'scraped together' for me. With regard to the proceeds from the book, said the South African, I would be in for a 'full whack' of £14,000.

I heard nothing more from van Dyk, Read or the gang for over three months, then I was called to attend the telephone in the neighbour's house. It was van Dyk. He hadn't been in touch for various reasons, but now the 'business' was very much on and he would probably be arriving with Read within a couple of weeks. I protested that I had no idea of what I was supposed to say, but van Dyk promised yet again that he would write, filling me in with all the details, before the arrival of the author.

Another three months went by without further contact from van Dyk. Then, sometime in January 1977, I received a telegram from a certain Jeffrey Simmons, representing W.H.Allen, inviting me to telephone him to discuss the book business and the pending visit from Piers Paul Read. I was wondering what I should do when van Dyk contacted me out of the blue. I told him about the telegram and reminded him that I still didn't know what I was expected to say. He told me not to worry, he would be back in Brazil before the author got there. Under no circumstances should I phone W.H. Allen. But I did phone and I got in touch with Jeffrey Simmons.

During our conversation, Mr Simmons asked me if I had received the £2000 from Mr van Dyk. I assured him that the only money I had received up until that moment had been $1000 - and that had been a handout from my old pals. Mr Simmons insisted that I must have received the £2,000. He had personally handed that amount to Mr van Dyk with the instructions to pass it on to me in Brazil.

'Our intention,' Simmons said, 'was to pay you between £4,000 and £10,000, depending on what you are prepared to tell us. We understand that there are certain things that only you and Buster Edwards know about and we will pay you the full £10,000 if you can confirm what he has told us.'

I wasn't surprised to hear of van Dyk's little deceit and I suddenly lost interest in the whole business and told Mr Simmons that I would be pulling out of the deal. He pleaded with me not to.

'Just meet our author at the airport,' he said. 'Have a few words with him and if you still want to forget the matter, put our man on the next plane back to London. If you will do just that we will pay you a further £2000 - do we have a deal?'

I reluctantly agreed, and a couple of weeks later Ulla drove me to the airport to meet Piers Paul Read. We went to his hotel, the Castro Alves, in Copacabana, where, without preamble, I told him he was being hoaxed and that there was no truth in the German connection. Up until that moment he had been the essence of self-confidence, chatting away about the 'fine bunch of lads' he was working with.

'What do you mean, no German connection?' he asked. 'Wasn't the whole thing financed with German money?'

'There was no German involvement whatsoever,' I told him. Read looked and sounded disconcerted.

'No Sigi at the farm?'

I shook my head, 'No Sigi at the farm.'

He dropped his head into his hands. 'Oh, those bastards! Those dirty bastards!'

I could see that he didn't want to believe me and later, when his book, *The Train Robbers*, was published in 1978, he went so far as to say that he thought the 'German connection' had paid me a visit and told me to say that the whole thing was a hoax. Ulla's Germanic looks seemed to have strengthened his suspicions. He wrote to the effect that he didn't feel safe in Brazil and could imagine himself being flown over the Mato Grosso in a light aircraft and thrown out.

Read paid me my £2000, packed his bag and lost no time in returning to London. Later he sent me a copy of his book and wrote in it that he hoped it was the better book that we had both talked about.

Unfortunately, it wasn't.

The federal police HQ had moved from the Catete Palace and was now in a dockland area of Rio known as Praça Maua. It was here that a squadron of British warships docked in April 1977. I had been to sign in at the delegacia, and I was on my way to a bar to have a beer when I noticed a couple of uniformed British sailors standing around a newspaper kiosk.

They appeared to be buying postcards and were having a bit of a problem with the Brazilian currency. Mr Nice-guy stepped in.

'Can I be of any help to you fellows?' I offered. The sailors looked at me.

'You speak English?'

'Yes. I am English.'

The sailors looked harder. 'You wouldn't be Ronnie Biggs by any chance, would you?' one of them asked.

I confirmed that I was.

'Blimey!' We only came off our ship not ten minutes ago and I said to my mate here - joking like - we might run into Ronnie Biggs, and we've done it!'

We got the postcard business out of the way and stepped into one of the numerous bars in the area. The sailors, Harry, a signaller, and, George, a cook, told me that they were off a ship named the HMS Danae, and that the squadron was in Rio for naval exercises with the Brazilian fleet. George mentioned another cook on the Danae known as 'Slinger' Woods who was on duty and unable to get ashore. George described him as a 'great fan' of mine and said that he was going to be pissed off if he didn't get to meet me. Harry suggested that I go aboard the Danae with them to 'meet the lads'.

'I can't go on board,' I said. 'I wouldn't be allowed in the dock without an identity document.'

'You don't have to worry about that,' Harry insisted. 'You're dressed in civvies. If you walk in with us, the blokes on the gate will think that you're one of our officers. Come on - me and George will take care of you.'

I allowed myself to be persuaded, even though I realized that I was taking a bit of a risk.

We went through the dock gate without being challenged, then onto the flagship, the HMS Tiger, which we had to cross to get aboard the Danae anchored alongside. As we boarded the Danae the lowering of the flag ceremony was in progress, so we stood waiting silently until it was over. The officer in charge of the proceedings then turned to me and said, 'I know you. You're that fellow, Biggs, aren't you?'

'Yes, sir.' I replied.

'Well, welcome aboard lad, but if anyone should ask you how you got on the ship - I don't know anything!'

I went down a steel companionway, with Harry and George leading the way, until we arrived at a room where a number of sailors were sitting around writing letters etc. Harry spoke. 'We would like you all to meet our friend - Ronnie Biggs!' The sailors all looked up, registering surprise and pleasure. A lad with an unmistakable Liverpool accent put a can of warm beer in my hand.

'Nice to meet ya, Ronnie. Here, have a can of Her Majesty's duty free beer - I'm sure she would approve!'

I was talking to the lads, drinking the duty free booze and signing autographs when George reappeared at the cabin door.

'Sorry to have to tell you this, Ron, but the word has gone around that you are on board and the Top Brass are in a bit of a panic. Perhaps you had better go ashore. Me and Harry are coming with you - and if anyone wants to join us I'm sure Ronnie won't mind.'

About a dozen of us invaded one of the clip joints in Praça Maua, grogging on until it was time for me to meet my curfew. I still hadn't met 'Slinger' Woods so, at Harry's insistence, I agreed to meet them at the same bar the following morning when 'Slinger' would be off duty.

I spent the night with Ulla, and when I got to the bar the next morning, there was a whole mob of sailors waiting to meet me. The beer began to flow. Harry told me that he had been up the best part of the night sending and receiving messages to and from the Admiralty.

'They've gone potty about you being aboard one of our ships,' he told me. 'They want to know why you were not arrested and put in irons!

What seems to have pissed them off more than anything is the fact that you were drinking our duty free beer! But fuck 'em, that's what I say!' I was inclined to agree.

'Slinger' Woods turned up at the bar - and he didn't care who knew it; I was his bloody hero. Another round was called, then another.

I had planned to get back to Sepetiba during the afternoon to spend some time with Mike. Ever the genial host, I invited some of the ratings back to Sepetiba with me and five of them agreed, including 'Slinger'. We went by bus.

Smothered in tattoos, the boys off the Danae were certainly a hit in sleepy-time-down-South Sepetiba with their rousing sea shanties. They were having a lot of fun and a lot to drink. It was a great party, but the next morning the sailors had to be at their posts. I called on a local taxi-driver, Agusto, to take them back to Praça Maua, in Rio. A price had to be agreed. With the driver there would be six of them in the vehicle, the roads were bad, the passengers were drunk - and they had passed the best part of their money over to Mr Borges at the bar.

Predictably, perhaps, the taxi broke down and the HMS Danae sailed off on manoeuvres without the help of 'Slinger' Woods and his mates. They had to be flown out to their ship by helicopter and were no doubt up before The Old Man. Back in the old days they would have been flogged.

When the ships returned to port to let the jolly jack tars have one final fling in Rio before heading for calmer waters, they were issued a notice: 'All personnel are advised against making contact with Ronald Biggs.'

The incident was blown up by the press, of course, and much talked about. Stories in the press included one about a rating making a citizen's arrest and the Brazilian navy threatening to blow the British ships out the water if they tried to leave Rio with me on board. Pure fantasy, as were stories that the incident caused a major diplomatic incident between Britain and Brazil. The British Navy is still a regular visitor to Brazil and when I was in Rio you could normally find a group of ratings and officers enjoying the hospitality of the Biggs' household. My snooker table was proudly covered by a Union Jack that was presented to me by members of the crew of the HMS Campbeltown.

Mike, who was now going on for three years of age, had heard reporters talking to me about the Danae incident and had some idea of what had been going on. By now he was a cute little chap and not a bit shy, opening conversations with perfect strangers. He made a point of telling everyone who I was.

'This is my dad, ' he would announce in a loud voice, 'Ronald Biggs. He stole a British ship! Isn't that right, dad?'

As far as Mike knew, quite a few of my friends smoked, 'English tobacco' and from time to time he would see me smoking the same stuff. One day, when I took him with me to sign in with the federal police, a cop offered me a cigarette. Ever ready to help, Mike put up his hand, refusing for me. 'No! My dad only smokes English tobacco.' Such a dear little boy! By the time Mike was five, he was already correcting my Portuguese - something he has done ever since!

Raimunda returned to Brazil. She had been away for two and a half years rather than three months, thrilling European audiences with her 'exotic dancing', and had plans to return. She now appeared to be very worldly-wise and could speak French well, but she was still a country-girl and obviously happy to be back in her own country. She had arrived with presents for everyone, including Mr and Mrs Borges, whom she saw as instrumental in her success abroad. Raimunda and I were still 'the best of friends' and she lived with us in Sepetiba until she went back to France to continue her artistic career.

In January 1978 the punk rock group, the Sex Pistols, had fallen out during a tour of the US. Johnny Rotten, the singer, and Sid Vicious, the bassist, decided to pull out of the group. The Pistols' manager, Malcolm McLaren, took their desertion in his stride and in February headed for Brazil with the two remaining members of the group, guitarist Steve Jones and drummer Paul Cook.

McLaren, always one with an eye for publicity, planned to reform the Pistols in Brazil with two of the world's most wanted men: Nazi war criminal Martin Bormann and little ol' me. Realizing that it might be difficult to make contact with Herr Bormann, McLaren hired the services of a Hollywood bit-player, dressed in uniform and jackboots, as a stand-in. Once more the gentlefolk of Sepetiba had reason to raise their eyebrows when the punks arrived with their clothes held together with safety pins. Even the poorest locals looked well dressed alongside the tatty lads from London.

Over drinks at the bar, McLaren invited me to 'join in the fun' with the boys, outlining what he had in mind. They had been filming their antics during their trip to the US and McLaren's plan was to turn the footage into a film, which was subsequently released under the title, *The Great Rock'n'Roll Swindle*. If I participated in the film, said McLaren, I would be paid a fee of $2000 and if I sang on a record with them a further $1000 would be coming my way. I pointed out to McLaren that, although I came from a talented family, I was not much of a singer.

'So much the better,' he declared. 'That's what 'punk' is all about!'

Well, $3000 was an offer that I couldn't refuse and I didn't dilly-dally in signing a contract with them.

Having listened to the Pistols *Never Mind The Bollocks, Here's The Sex Pistols* I felt that I could write something in a similar vein and suggested as much to McLaren. I wrote a piece which I called *'A Punk Prayer'* and recorded it with Steve Jones and Paul Cook in a studio in Rio. It was later released on 30 June 1978 as the Sex Pistols' fifth single under the title *'No One Is Innocent'* and sold over seven million copies worldwide, reaching number six in the UK. What happened to the royalties I should have received is something that I would dearly have loved to talk to Mr McLaren about, but sadly the Grim Reaper got to him before I could.

On 18 December 1978 Charlie Wilson, who had escaped to Canada, was released. After serving 12 years of his 30-year sentence, which included a loss of six months remission for his escape. Charlie was the last of the main gang to serve his time.

KIDNAPPED

Nips In and Out Like Ronald Biggs

British Leyland poster campaign for the Mini, February 1979

"It's a crying shame. The people who snatched Ronnie are nothing short of animals. I'm sick about it all."

Buster Edwards, Great Train Robber, April 1981

'Ronnie! Long time - no see!'

The cliché came from Clive Wilson, the Englishman to whom I'd taken a dislike when I first met him. He had lived in Rio for many years working off an on as a tour guide. Until Clive's appearance I had been enjoying a Saturday afternoon barbecue in Rio.

'Ronnie, look, I've got this journalist chap with me and he'd like to do an interview with you and perhaps take a few pictures.' Clive had sat himself down at my table and was warming to his subject. 'It's for *National Geographic* and the fellow can pay $200. What do you say Ronnie - a hundred for you, a hundred for me?'

'You piece of shit,' I wanted to say - but I needed the money so I let it pass. 'Okay,' I told Clive, 'invite your friend over in the morning around eleven.'

I have met many reporters and photo-journalists over the years before observing this one at work and I had a feeling, right from the start, that something was wrong. He didn't have a tape recorder or a note-pad.

Neither did he have the brash line of bullshit particular to newsmen. He was not at all professional with a camera - and he only had the one. But for the amount of time the 'interview' took, a hundred bucks was money for old rope even if he wasn't a reporter from *National Geographic.*

The reporter, who went by the name of Patrick Richardson King, paid me. Smiling and looking a good deal more relaxed than before the interview, he told me that his wife would be joining him in Rio the next day. He asked for a suggestion for a restaurant and a show he could take her to and then asked if I would care to join them.

The following day would be Monday 16 March 1981, the eve of St. Patrick's Day. As I had nothing else planned, except for my weekly signing on with the federal police, I thought why not?

The Sugar Loaf Mountain is one of Rio's most magnificent and best known attractions. The peak is reached by a two stage cable-car trip, a trip that was made internationally famous by James Bond's struggle with Jaws on top of the cable car in *Moonraker.* The first leg of the journey takes visitors to the top of a neighbouring rock, Urca Mountain. Both summits have the usual souvenir shops and ice-cream kiosks while on Urca there is also a restaurant and a semi-open air amphitheatre where samba shows were, at the time, a weekly attraction. This was my suggestion for Patrick and his wife. I arranged to meet with them at 9 p.m. at Roda Viva, a barbecue restaurant at the foot of Urca Mountain. I was also expecting John Pickston and some of his guests from London to put in an appearance. If not at the restaurant then at the show afterwards.

I arrived ten minutes early and took up a place a few tables away from the entrance to the restaurant so that I would be easy to spot when Patrick and his wife arrived. I need not have worried, as apart from one couple at a nearby table the place was quite empty. I ordered a beer.

A few minutes after I had got myself settled a young fair-haired man who I noticed had his right leg in a plaster cast joined the couple. He spoke briefly to the couple, looked around the restaurant and left. I ordered a second beer and looked at my watch. It was 9.10 p.m.

Suddenly and without warning, I was grabbed from behind in a chocking necklock. I reacted and struggled for air. A second person ran at me and started punching me in the pit of my stomach. I kicked out and managed to break free from the person who was holding me around the neck.

Instinctively I ran for the exit. Thoughts raced through my head and they told me that I was being attacked by the Brazilian police. But why?

As I flew, half falling, through the door of the restaurant I was grabbed by strong hands, overpowered and forced into a VW Kombi van that was parked close to the entrance of the restaurant. I was pushed, struggling into the van a hand appeared in front of my face. I bit the person's thumb and bit it hard. I tasted blood. They had me pinned face down on the floor of the van, it was then that I heard a Scots voice that I could never forget: 'It's us again, Ronnie! This time we got you bang t'rights - an' if you don't do everythin' I tell you to the letter there is every chance that you won't see your wee kid again - so just fucking behave.'

The voice belonged to the man who had tried to kidnap me two years earlier, ex-Scots guardsman John Miller - sometimes known as John McKillop.

The van pulled away from the restaurant under the noses of some armed sentries guarding a nearby naval establishment. Miller gave an order. 'Driver, keep the speed down. We've got plenty of time.'

While Miller was talking and giving orders he was taping my hands behind my back. It was obvious that he knew what he was doing. I was then gagged and blindfolded and bundled into a sack which I later discovered had been tailor-made for the operation and was equipped with four handles to facilitate carrying. Miller continued talking.

'Your old friend Fred is with me Ronnie. You remember Fred, don't you Ronnie? You've given him quite a nasty bite on the thumb an' he doesn't seem very pleased about it. He's right here beside you an' he's holding a nice big cosh which he'll be very happy to use if you try and give us any trouble. Give Ronnie a tap with the cosh Fred to let him know I'm telling the truth.' Fred dutifully gave me a whack across the legs. 'Now listen up, Ronnie. We are going to drive around for a wee while then we are going to transfer you to another vehicle. Don't try and make any noise - I don't want to have to give you an injection to knock you out - and let's not forget that we have got wee Michael.'

It had been exactly two years since I had first met Miller. At that time, March 1979, I was still living in Sepetiba. Miller had arrived in Sepetiba in a small yellow Volkswagen with two hefty friends whom he had introduced to me as Fred Prime and Norman ('Norrie') Boyle. Miller was well over six feet tall, powerfully built and sported a small diamond earring in the lobe of his left ear. They were all ex-Scots Guards, he told me, and they were in Rio as a second unit film crew doing fill in shots for Lewis Gilbert's Moonraker, which had recently been filming there. Miller presented himself as the cameraman, Norrie, who was about Miller's size, was the sound technician and Fred, a shorter, smiling fat man, with a huge curved beak like nose, the boom operator. They had read about my exploits over the years, they said, and admired my deeds of derring-do. Fred presented me with a bottle of Johnnie Walker Black Label telling me as he squeezed the life out of my hand that there was plenty more to come as long as they were around.

Although Fred had been a regular in the Scots Guards like his two mates, he was clearly a Londoner. He said he had been a boxer and a physical training instructor during his years in the army. Norrie, like Miller, was a Scot. He told me that he had held the rank of Company Sergeant Major before being demobbed. He appeared less boisterous than his friends and said very little. The quiet type, he enjoyed playing with Mike - who was four at the time - declaring that he loved kids and had two of his own.

Miller was quite clearly the leader of the little band, exhibiting brash self-confidence. Towards the end of his army service, he said, he had been a plain-clothes undercover agent in Northern Ireland, posing as an IRA sympathizer. The earring had been installed to provide him with a more devil-may-care appearance.

A little later, at a nearby bar, a curious local asked me why the big 'gringo' was using an earring. I relayed the question to Miller.

'Och!' explained the brawny Scot, ' Tell him I'm queer and that Fred here is my husband.' With that he grabbed Fred and kissed him full on the mouth. 'You great sexy thing! Ronnie just look at Fred's nose. Have you ever seen anything like it? It's not a nose, it's a sail. With a nose like Fred's you could sit in a boat and sail around the fucking world.' Fred took it in good spirits and laughed, obviously accustomed to his friend's rather ribald sense of humour.

'He's like this all the time, Ronnie, never serious.'

Over a lunch of giant prawns, Miller told me that their work on the film would be taking them down to Argentina the next day, but they would be returning to Rio soon. They wanted to be back in Brazil to celebrate Norrie's birthday on Wednesday 4 April.

'We'll get you nice and pissed that night,' Norrie promised.

Not even a week had gone by and Miller was on the phone to say they were back. 'Fred hasn't stopped talking about you. I reckon you've got a friend for life there. So when are you coming into town next, Ronnie?' Miller asked. 'We're staying at the Copacabana Palace and we would like to invite you and wee Michael to come and have a spot of lunch around the pool. Would Friday at one be okay?' It was, so I signed off agreeing to meet them at the hotel at the end of the week.

Something bothered me, however. Miller was being just a bit too friendly for comfort. I already had a feeling he was up to something, but I needed to find out exactly what. I telephoned Armin Heim, a German friend of mine, and a respected photographer. I outlined recent events to Armin and expressed my suspicions. Finally I asked him if he would come along and meet the friendly 'film crew'. Armin, good friend that he was, was all for it.

When I arrived with Mike at the Copacabana Palace, Miller and co. were already holding a small but somewhat noisy party around the hotel's pool. The group's behaviour was certainly not what would normally be associated with a hotel of such old world charm. Besides my three new friends, there was a young English couple, a blonde Canadian lady of ample proportions and the tour-guide, Clive. Now it became clear how Miller had got my address in Sepetiba. The big Scot pumped my hand and put his arm around my shoulders.

'Glad you could make it, Ronnie. Let me first introduce you to these fine people. Are you ready for a drink? I've got some great news for you. I've got you a part in the film - you big handsome brute. I'll tell you the details later.'

It was clear that Miller was in fine form. The wording of his t-shirt said it all: *I'm So Happy, I Could Shit.* I sat next to Fred who was effin' and blindin' away, his voice echoing off the granite walls of the normally sedate hotel.

'You should have been 'ere last night Ron,' he said. 'We was all nice and pissed. I was fuckin' paralytic. Norrie here chucked the fuckin' night porter in the pool!'

'He slipped,' Norrie corrected 'I was just trying to save him.'

Fred chuckled and lowering his voice, as if to reveal some terrible conspiracy, went on: 'The Canadian bird sitting next to 'im was all dolled up t'go to some fuckin' samba party an' when she had a go at Norrie about chuckin' the porter in the pool 'e chucked 'er in as well. What a fuckin' laugh.'

I noticed that Norrie and the Canadian lady were holding hands so she was obviously not bearing a grudge for her unexpected bath. Armin arrived at this point with his cameras - I had told him that I wanted to get some shots of the Miller gang - and he was soon enjoying the high jinks and free-flowing grog.

Over lunch Miller told me about the film part he had arranged for me. When he had been in Argentina he had told his boss, the film's director, Lewis Gilbert, that he had had the 'privilege' of meeting me. He had mentioned that I was on Conditional Liberty and not allowed to work and was badly in need of a 'few bucks'. Apart from being something of a fan of mine, Miller said, Gilbert was apparently quite sympathetic with regard to my impoverished situation and had come up with the 'great idea' to give me a small part in his next film which was also scheduled to be shot in Brazil. It would only be small cameo role, a chase scene in which I would escape my pursuers by jumping into a rowboat and rowing out to a yacht.

'Shouldn't be too difficult for you,' Miller said. 'I have also taken the liberty of telling Mr Gilbert that you would require $10,000 for participating in the film. I hope that will be enough.'

Work was to begin on the film soon, but not in Rio, rather in Porto Alegre in the south of Brazil. I pointed out to Miller yet again that under the terms of my Conditional Liberty I could not leave the State of Rio de Janeiro.

'Och, I don't think we need worry too much about that wee detail,' said Miller. 'One way or another we'll get you on location.'

The Canadian lady rose from the table. She was leaving Rio that evening and had a number of things she needed to do before she left. Norrie escorted her to her room. Suddenly Miller was on his feet.

'Grab your cameras Armin. Let's get ourselves a few candid snaps of Norrie humping the Incredible Hulk.'

On the second floor, where Miller and the boys had taken two adjoining suites, Miller discovered that the doors had been locked from the inside. The large Scot backed down the corridor and then came flying at the nearest door executing a near perfect double drop-kick. The door, the door frame and the architraves burst into the room, taking the plaster with it and ripping the wall-paper from the walls. I was getting a close look at the Scots Guards in action! Norrie and the lady were caught in the act as Armin clicked away through the rising dust.

Miller later apologized to the hotel's management for the 'dreadful accident' on the second floor. People in show business, he explained, were inclined to get a wee bit rowdy from time to time. He would, of course, pay for all the necessary repairs.

I went back to the Copa the following morning with Mike. He wanted to see the 'crazy men' again. Miller asked me to be at the hotel around ten o'clock as he was expecting a call from Gilbert. I invited Armin to come along for the ride.

On arrival we found the gang had been moved to rooms on the third floor. Drinks were poured by Norrie who was showing no apparent sign of resentment towards his friends for the previous day's invasion. He laughed when I mentioned the subject.

'John's fuckin' shell-shocked. We're accustomed to that kind of thing,' he said by way of an explanation.

At 10.30 a.m. the phone rang. Miller picked up the receiver. 'Is that you Lewis?... Aye, Ronnie's sitting right here in front of me... Aye, he's quite willing to take part in the film but there's a wee problem, he's not allowed to leave Rio... you can't change the location? Och! that's too bad... aye, I understand. I'll talk to him, Lewis, and get back to you later. Bye for now.'

Miller replaced the receiver. 'Ronnie there is no way that Lewis can change the location for the shoot. He just explained that it would cost far too much to bring the cast and crew back up to Rio - we've just go to get you down to Porto Alegre.'

'Forget it,' I said. 'There's no way I'm leaving Rio. I'm just not willing to take the chance. I can't afford to.'

'Listen, Ronnie,' Miller insisted. 'You could get a short haircut, put on a pair of shades and nobody would recognize you. Christ, look at me! I don't have to tell you of all people how to nip in and out of places. We could get you a plane and fly you down to Porto Alegre. You don't need any documentation for a private plane. You do your piece of acting and your back in Rio in three days and with ten grand in your pocket. Think about it, old son. You can even bring Armin if you want.'

'I don't have to think about it,' I replied firmly. 'I'm not leaving Rio - not even for a hundred grand - no way in the world.'

'Is that your final decision Ronnie?'

'Yes, that's my final decision.'

Miller broke the building tension with a new idea which had nothing to do with the film. Clive had told him about Paradise Island, also known as Jaguanum, and a boat trip offered to tourists where they could see crystal clear water, white sandy beaches, tropical birds and exotic plants.

'I'd like to take you, wee Mike and your pal Armin to the island tomorrow. Let's have some fun. Fuck the film deal! What do you say?'

Mike said yes!

That night I took the boys off to the local British pub, the Lord Jim.

While John set about hooking up with one of the many young ladies who was in the bar, Fred and I stood at the bar and talked about London.

'Don't let me ever see you wiv yer 'and in yer pocket,' Fred said as he organised yet another round of drinks.

Miller having picked up a cute blonde called Lucia and suggested, at the young girl's instigation, that we move onto Dancin' Days, a popular disco on Urca Mountain. As we emerged from the cable car the lights were flashing, the Bee Gees were belting it out, and the young Brazilians were getting it together.

While Miller took Lucia off to the dance floor I continued my chat with fat Fred.

'Ronnie,' he said, 'I just want to tell you that you've got a friend for life. That's no bollocks - I fink of you as a bruver and if you ever want anyone taken care of over in London you only have to give me a call.'

Our conversation was interrupted by a rather sweaty Miller. 'Och!', he said, 'are you two going to stand there all night making love? Come on, Biggsy, let's boogie a wee bit.' And boogie we did. Miller, in fact, probably boogied rather harder than he should which ended in a scene as we left after Miller had been accused by one of the other Brazilian customers of being a 'bad man' for the way he was treating young Lucia on the dance floor. In true Miller style, Miller laid his critic out splitting his knuckles in the process.

Despite the late night we all met outside the Copacabana Palace the next morning, Sunday, and took the tour bus to the coastal town of Itacuraça. The sun was shining and there was a clear blue sky. Everyone was in high spirits. Fred had arranged a case of cold beers from the hotel for the journey and Mike was sitting on Norrie's lap, chatting away. Miller explained that the hotel had been far from happy in letting Lucia up to his room, but he had simply slung her over his shoulder and told the night porter that she was a registered nurse who had come to dress his damaged hand. At Itacuruça we boarded a traditional saveiro, a type of schooner, which would take us out to the island.

All in all it was a jolly day, swimming and playing football on the beach, the visiting 'gringos' against the locals. We ate well and drank many a caipirinha, a drink made from limes, sugar and cachaça. Ulla's brother was at the island when we got there and he fell in with our group. He shared my opinion that Miller and co. were 'up to no good' and suggested that I should be on my toes. They are too good to be true, he said.

During one of the drinking session, Norrie asked me if I had ever taken Valium. I told him that I hadn't. Fred offered the information that Valium, when mixed with alcohol had a 'fuckin' devastating' affect. He knew, he said, because he had 'fuckin' tried it'.

Miller's physical strength was obvious. During the fun and games in the sea, Miller had grabbed me around the waist and stripped me of my bathing trunks in just a few seconds. At a later date somebody sent me the front page of a Scottish newspaper, the *Sunday Mail*, with a picture of John Miller in training for my kidnapping. He was photographed jogging in a park while carrying somebody across his shoulders.

That evening Mike and I returned to the relative peace and calm of Sepetiba, close to Itacuruça. Even though I trusted the gang less and less, I was now even more curious to find out exactly what they were up to. With his arm around my shoulder, Miller had told me what 'a great guy' I was. He didn't want to be a nuisance, but could he and the boys see me again before they left Brazil - they would be leaving at the end of the week. I said that I would see them again on Tuesday, two days later.

I arrived at Ulla's apartment in Santa Teresa (about twenty minutes by car from Copacabana) at around seven o'clock on Monday evening.

'Hey!,' said Ulla when she saw me. 'Guess what? You are supposed to have been kidnapped and on your way back to England on a chartered boat!

'I have just had a call from some man called Chris Buckland, who said he was a reporter with the *Daily Mirror*,' Ulla went on to explain. 'He told me that you had been grabbed by a group of ex-Scots Guardsmen and were now on your way back to England in an ocean going yacht. He called from New York and I told him I was expecting you so he said he was going to ring back later. For God's sake, Ron, what's going on?'

I brought Ulla up-to-date with regard to what had been going on with my Guardsmen 'buddies', the film offer and the conversation Miller had had with 'Lewis Gilbert'. We discussed the whole thing at length. Why would they want to kidnap me? Why the cock-and-bull story about a movie deal? Why Porto Alegre - which was way down south - when Rio had a port and numerous places where a yacht could be moored.

As promised, Buckland returned his call confirming everything that Ulla had told me. The ex-Scots Guardsmen had indeed been highly trained for the job, he told me, and their plan was to get me aboard a yacht and return to England with me as their prisoner. He wanted to know if this information coincided with anything that was going on in Rio at that moment. I gave him a brief account of recent happenings and he said that he was going to speak to his editor in London to see if he could fly down to Rio from New York to cover the story, possibly booking in at the Copacabana Palace to see if he could befriend the would-be kidnappers. He didn't make it.

A little later Ulla's sixteen-year-old son came home. He told me that earlier in the day he had answered the telephone to somebody by the name of Kenny Lynch, who was staying at the Inter-Continental and had left his room number so that I could call him. I wondered if it could be the English entertainer Kenny Lynch, so I rang the hotel. Sure enough it was the real Kenny Lynch. He was in Rio with his friend Bobby Moore, the great England footballer and captain from the 1966 World Cup winning side. This, at least, was a pleasant surprise. Lynch said that he and Bobby were both fans of mine and would like to get together with me while they were in Rio for a 'meal and a chat'. He suggested the following Saturday as he and Bobby were in Rio for a pro-am golf tournament and had to be on the course every day till then - so we agreed to meet at their hotel for lunch.

Ulla thought I was crazy, but I decided to go to Copacabana the next day to meet Miller and co. as arranged. In a strange way I was starting to enjoy our little game of 'cat and mouse'.

When I got to the Copacabana Palace on the Tuesday the boys were already around the pool, grogging on. Big John told me that he had just got back from Fortaleza, a city in the north of Brazil that is nearly twice the distance from Rio as Porto Alegre, having flown there the previous day.

'Aye, it was a hell of a journey, Ronnie, but Lewis was up there and wanted me to look over a new location for the film.' Miller had even found time during the past two days of travel to check out Rio's domestic airport, Santos Dumont.

'The film offer is still open, Ronnie,' Miller went on. 'I went down to Santos Dumont and looked it over. It would be dead easy to get you on a plane and fly you to the shoot. Don't say 'no' just yet. Just come down to the airport and see for yourself - would you do that? I would just love to see you score the ten grand.'

Before leaving Ulla's apartment I had phoned Johnny Pickston. I had not seen him for some time and as he only lived a couple of blocks back from the Copacabana Palace, I invited him to join me for a drink. I told him about Miller and co. and that I was due to have lunch with Kenny Lynch and Bobby Moore at the weekend. John expressed envy as he was and is a fervent West Ham supporter and a great fan of Bobby Moore. Next I called Armin and filled him in on the information I had received from the *Daily Mirror* reporter. I asked him to appear at the hotel as well.

Soon after I got to the hotel, John and Armin arrived together. We sat around and had a couple of beers and then Norrie suggested going up to his suite on the third floor for 'some serious drinkin''. There were still a couple of bottles of Johnnie Walker Black Label remaining. As Norrie poured generous measures of whisky into six tumblers, I enquired if it wouldn't be a better idea to keep the booze until the following day reminding him that it would be Wednesday and his birthday.

'My birthday is on Thursday, Ronnie. The 5th. Don't you remember?'

'I remember,' I said as Norrie passed me a full tumbler of whiskey.

I finished my drink, now feeling quite drunk, and decided to go down and sit by the pool again. Armin and John joined me. Suddenly, I made a decision.

'I'm going out to the Inter-Continental! I'm going to go and see if I can give Kenny and Bobby a nice surprise.'

Miller came hurrying up as John, Armin and I were staggering into a taxi. 'Where are you lot off to at this time of night?' he wanted to know. When he discovered, he wanted to come too, making out that he was a big fan of Bobby Moore.

The gang followed us out to the Inter-Continental in a second taxi. By the time we reached the hotel it was just past midnight. As luck would have it we found Moore and Lynch sitting alone in the hotel's nightclub, the Jakui Bar. Most of the lights had been turned down and it was quite gloomy. We all shook hands and then my two friends and I joined them at a table. John soon made it known that he was a football buff and launched into a conversation with Moore while Armin and I talked 'show-business' with Lynch. Miller and co. sort of hovered around the table saying little, if anything.

The visiting VIP's were still a little jet-lagged, but said they looked forward to our lunch on Saturday. It was time to say goodnight as they were expected early at Gavea Golf Club for the pro-am.

Outside the Inter-Continental, Miller drew me aside from the others and had yet another go at getting me interested in the 'film deal'

'The boys and me think the world of you and wee Michael', Miller went on. 'Go for the bread, old son - ten grand is ten fuckin' grand.'

'Okay,' I said. Years of criminal cunning coming to the fore. 'Five grand up front here in Rio and five grand at the end of the shoot.'

'I won't promise, Ronnie,' Miller said, 'but I'll do my best.'

I got a cab and headed over to Ulla's place in Santa Teresa to spend the night.

Miller phoned early the next morning. 'Ronnie, its fuckin' heartbreaking, but we've only got a day or two left in Rio,' he began. 'Look come by the hotel for lunch and bring wee Michael as Norrie's got a present for him, the walkie-talkies we've been playing with. We're covered, Norrie will just say they were stolen when we get back. Better still he'll say you nicked 'em!'

I told him that I had to go and sign on with the federal police, but Miller was most insistent that I come over and have lunch first.

'Look Ronnie, I'll even drop you off after lunch and as we are in the area you might as well get a look at Santos Dumont. See you at noon.'

I had left Mike with my neighbour in Sepetiba, so I went over to the hotel alone. I wasn't really interested in having lunch or seeing the 'boys'. My main interest was to see if I could make Miller part with some money up-front. A sort of reward for all the trouble they had put me to.

After lunch we took a taxi down to Praça Maua where the federal police are located. The gang went into one of the local clip joints to wait and I went into the delegacia to sign on. At that time it was a ritual that had to be followed on every Wednesday and Friday. Then I joined them at the clip joint. Again Miller broached the subject of the filming, urging me to go with them to Santos Dumont.

'The only place I am going,' I told Miller, 'is on a bus back to Sepetiba. There is absolutely no point going to the airport because I'm not going to go ahead until I get paid something up-front. At least two grand because before I start putting my liberty at risk there are a few debts I want to clear up first.'

'Ronnie, old son,' Miller interrupted earnestly, 'I promise I'll ring Lewis as soon as I get back to the Copa and I'll have your bread by Friday. You have my word on that.'

I rose early the following morning in Sepetiba and took Mike to the beach. While he played in the sand I sat thinking. It was not very likely that Miller would come up with the money - but he might just. If he did I could try and grab the money and run. Soon after we got home from the beach there was a call from Ulla. She had just received a call from an editor on a Manchester newspaper. A Scotsman called McGovern or McCartney, he had given Ulla much the same information that *Mirror's* Buckland had provided, emphasizing the fact that I should avoid contact with the Guardsmen at all costs. He described them as 'extremely dangerous' and wanted me to call him just as soon as I could.

I called Manchester, I think it was the *Daily Star,* and got straight through to McGovern. I told him I was calling in regard to some 'dangerous' Guardsmen.

'I'm sorry,' he said to my surprise, 'I'm unable to help you.'

'But didn't you just call and speak to my girlfriend and tell her that I should avoid some ex-Scots guardsmen at all costs?' I asked.

'I'm sorry,' he repeated, 'I know nothing about the matter.'

To say the least, I was baffled. I decided to ring Ulla back and tell her what had happened.

'Come back to Rio,' she urged. 'In Sepetiba you are a sitting duck.'

I knew she was right so I started to prepare to head for Rio that very night with Mike.

Minutes later, as if he had been listening on the line, John Miller called. 'Ronnie! How are you this morning you old reprobate? Did you get a good night's rest?... That's magic, Ronnie. Look, I rang Lewis as I promised and he is sending down the two grand. That okay for you?...You'll be coming into Rio tonight for Norrie's birthday party, won't you?... Och don't say you can't, you've got to come to Rio tomorrow anyway to sign in, right?... If you can't make it for Norrie you'll have to come and have a spot of lunch at the hotel.

About one then?... And listen Ronnie, what I'd like to do is for you to come straight up to my room when you arrive. We've got to have a serious talk about all those bastards that have ripped you off over the years. I want you to give me a list of everything that is owing and I'll go and get the bread for you. You've got my word on that Ronnie... See you tomorrow, old son - oh, and by the way it might be as well if you were to leave wee Mike at home, as we do have business to discuss.'

I had a feeling that Mr Miller was preparing to pounce. But why did he now want to get me to Fortaleza?

I was still far from happy about the conversation I had had with the editor in Manchester so I decided to call him again. The same Scottish voice came on the line. He was glad that I had called back. He explained that when I had called earlier there had been someone in his office and he was unable to speak freely. He endorsed all the things he had told Ulla and went on to say that Miller and co. were being financed by a wealthy jet-setter, an Englishman who spent most of his time abroad.

He said he knew the identity of this person but he was afraid to name names. He was not a brave man, he said. He was also unable to tell me why Miller wanted to abduct me.

If I wasn't confused before, I certainly was now. Who was the mysterious Mr Moneybags? What was his interest in having me kidnapped? Why did an editor on a Manchester based newspaper, and a Scot to boot, want to play Mr Nice-Guy to Ronald Biggs? One thing was for certain, it was time to stop putting my head in the lion's mouth.

I phoned my mates, Armin and John Pickston, and brought them up to date with the latest twists to the 'plot'. I suggested that they might like to go to the hotel the next day for yet another free lunch - but not to be surprised if I didn't put in an appearance. Then I called Big Ziggy, a heavyweight all-in wrestler who the boys had met at the Lord Jim, and invited him to join me for lunch. Then Rick, the 'rock-wrestler', a landscape artist who was a friend of mine and who had a formidable appetite.

'And take your friends', I told them, 'Mr Miller is a big-time spender.' With that organised I packed my bag, grabbed Mike and headed for Rio.

As 'my gang' gathered poolside at the Cop Palace with Miller's gang, I was having a quiet lunch with Ulla. The pieces were beginning to fall into place. A friend had called from London to say that he had been in touch with Lewis Gilbert's production office and they were quite certain they had no film crew operating in South America nor had Gilbert ever heard of John Miller. I had made a decision that was quite foreign to my nature - I was going to call the cops!

Before doing anything I had to go to the police to sign in. If I saw a certain friendly cop - Barradas - I would tell him the story and ask for his advice. As I went into the delegacia about an hour later, the very same Mr Barradas was standing in front of me.

'Hello, Biggs! How's the shrimp in Sepetiba?'

'You,' I said pointing at the smiling cop, 'are just the man I'm looking for. Can we step across the road for a cafézinho or something stronger?'

I told Barradas about my big 'friend' John Miller, giving him a detailed description which included the diamond earring.

'And now, you - the thief of the century - are asking the Brazilian Federal Police to protect you? I don't believe it,' laughed Barradas. 'But let's go back to the delegacia and you can tell the very same story to my boss - give him all the details and he'll decide what needs to be done.'

Dr Bizzo, a dapper fellow in a pale blue gabardine suit was the chief or delegado, as they are known in Brazil. I told him how Miller had been trying to lure me out of Rio, mentioning an offer of $10,000. Bizzo listened intently to my story, making notes on a pad on his desk and occasionally asking questions for clarification.

'Find these clowns and bring them in,' he instructed as I finished my story. 'Biggs, you stay here, I might want you to make a statement.'

Barradas left the room and was back within five minutes. 'You're not going to believe it but we've got the big son-of-a-bitch with the earring,' he announced. 'He was standing across the road from the delegacia.'

Bizzo asked me where I was staying and at what number I could be reached. I told him I would be with Ulla.

'Go there now and stay there,' Bizzo said. 'I'm going to ask this fellow some questions and it will be better if he doesn't see you.'

I left the delegacia a happier man knowing that Miller was out of circulation. I made contact with John and Armin, who recounted the lunchtime episode at the Copacabana Palace. Seven of my friends had turned up for lunch at Mr Miller's expense, a host who had been as genial as could be until it became clear that I was not going to put in an appearance.

'Where the hell is Ronnie?' he had asked the boozy congregation with obvious agitation. He had then gone into a huddle with Norrie and Fred before excusing himself, saying that he had to make some important phone calls. John, on the pretext of going to the gents, had followed him out of the hotel and saw him hail a taxi.

Ulla also had her own story. Shortly after I had left her flat to head down to the federal police, Norrie had called. He wanted to know if Mike or I was there. When Ulla said I wasn't he was most insistent that he wanted to drop around with Mike's walkie-talkies. Ulla told him to leave them at the desk but he kept wanting to know where Ulla lived. Miller, Norrie and Fred had, in fact, once dropped me off at Ulla's but thankfully they had forgotten to make a note of the address. In Santa Teresa, where Ulla lived and where I would live for many years, if you don't know where you are going you can spend weeks looking for the right road.

Later, after Miller and his friends had left Brazil, we also discovered that the gang had booked out of the Copacabana Palace at midday on that same Friday and booked rooms in the Gloria Hotel, just a stone's throw from the Santos Dumont airfield.

A federal agent - aptly named, Cobra - worked as a clerk at the same delegacia as Dr Bizzo. He spoke English quite well and had been the interpreter when the delegado interrogated Miller. Cobra was in charge of the file which I had to sign twice weekly and frequently had a number of questions to ask as he was eager to perfect his English. I had recently explained to him what 'a piece of cake' signified.

When I went to sign in on the following Wednesday, he told me what had happened to Mr Miller and his two friends. Fred and Norrie had been tracked down to the Gloria Hotel and had also been brought in for questioning. All three of them had denied all knowledge of a film deal involving me. They went further and said that they had obviously heard a lot about me and their only intention was to meet me and have a good time. They had been due to leave Rio that same evening and had hired a Lear jet to take them up to Belem in the far north of Brazil, where they had a yacht waiting for them to sail back to Britain. They had been cleared and released and Cobra had personally escorted them to Santos Dumont to catch their plane.

'Tell me something,' I asked Cobra. 'Would it have been easy for them to get me on that plane?'

'It would have been a 'piece of cake', Mr Biggs,' he winked.

Miller and co. were probably saved by their passports which because they had only recently left the Scots Guards, still showed their occupation to be 'government service'. Given the manner in which Slipper and Scotland Yard had tried to grab me in 1974, the federal police probably thought it was just another bungled attempt by the British Government to get hold of me. Rather than start another diplomatic incident they simply sent Miller packing without taking any further measures.

Shortly after Miller and the boys had left Brazil I ran into Clive Wilson in Copacabana and put it to him that he knew exactly what the ex-Guardsmen were up to and that he had given them my address in Sepetiba. He was offended. The last thing he wanted, he assured me, was to see me come to any harm.

I never did get to have my lunch with Kenny Lynch and Bobby Moore either. When I rang their hotel on the day we had arranged I was told they had gone travelling. Happily, I had not.

A CARIBBEAN EXCURSION: BARBADOS AND BACK

Kidnap or stunt riddle of train robber. Where is Mr Biggs?

Daily Express headline, March 1981

Nemo Me Impune Lacessit - No One Assails Me with Impunity
(Nobody fucks with me and gets away with it.)

Scots Guards' Motto (John Miller Translation)

That had all been two years ago in 1979. Now they seemed to have pulled it off. Inside the bag I was seething. Clive Wilson had obviously set me up for the phoney interview with Patrick King. My guess was that I was being driven to Santos Dumont to take the trip I should have made two years earlier. I tried to control my rage. Miller could well be bluffing about having grabbed Mike, but I could not afford to take that gamble.

'You're probably wondering what this is all about, Ronnie,' Miller said breaking into my thoughts. 'Well, I'll explain everything to you in good time. First we're going to transfer you to another vehicle.'

The other vehicle, as expected, turned out to be a plane. The gang unceremoniously bundled me into the back of it as a piece of luggage.

The jet engines started up and in a very short time we were airborne. The air pressure rose rapidly as we climbed, painfully popping my ears in the process. I was in a very uncomfortable position and squirmed around in the bag trying to stretch out and find the most comfortable position. My movements alerted Miller and brought him back to the bag. He spoke in a low voice.

'Just take it easy, Ronnie. Keep yourself quiet and still. I don't want to have to give you an injection but I will if I have to.' He gave the bag a couple of light taps and moved away.

Exerting all my strength in the confined space, I tried to get my hands free. I clenched my fingers, forcing my wrists apart. Suddenly there was a sharp snap. I had managed to break one of the tapes which secured my wrists behind my back. I rested, hoping that the sound had not been heard by anyone but myself above the sound of the plane's motors. I could feel more freedom in my hands now. I made a further mighty effort and the other tape snapped. My hands were free! Now, when we arrived at wherever the gang was taking me, I would tear the gag off and start screaming bloody blue murder.

Unknown to me, one of Miller's men had been sitting close enough to hear the sound of the tape snapping. Miller must have been given some sign as to what was going on. He came to the bag and loosened the rope that held the side laces together. I could guess what he was going to do so I clasped my hands together. Miller's hand probed into the bag taking no time to discover the fact that I had freed my hands. His face was close to mine, so close that I could smell his breath.

'You're being very stupid for someone with a reputation for being so smart,' he said softly. 'Another stunt like this and I'm going to have to give you a little jab of sodium pentathol. If I do, there's is a very good chance you'll vomit into your gag and fuckin' choke to death. Think about it, Ronnie!'

As Miller talked he pulled my hands from behind my back and roped them to my belt. He gave my bonds a tug. Satisfied, he laced the bag up again. If there was a consolation it was that my new position was marginally more comfortable than the previous one.

In all my life I had never ever felt the urge to kill somebody. But with Miller, I decided to make an exception. I fell to planning Miller's own death. It would have to be slow, perhaps through daily injections of his own sodium pentathol.

After several hours the plane landed and taxied across an airfield before coming to a stop. I could hear Miller giving orders, then talking to someone whom I assumed must have been our pilot. He was thanking the person and congratulating him on a 'smooth and pleasant' flight. Then, with Miller supervising, the canvas bag and its contents were dragged and heaved from the plane. I was being carried again and as I was, I heard someone speaking Portuguese. I figured that at least, for the time being, I was still in Brazil, perhaps in Fortaleza.

From what I could tell from within the confines of my bag, the gang met with little or no resistance in getting me out of the airport and into a waiting car. I was lying on my back, stretched out along the seat. Someone placed a heavy bag of some kind on my face making it almost impossible for me to breathe. I struggled desperately for air, trying to shake the weight from my face. Someone patted the bag. As the driver started the car, the radio came to life.

'Rádio Belém. Uma hora da manhã...'

The radio was turned off abruptly, I imagine by one of the gang, but at least I knew I was in Brazil, but it was Belem, Brazil's northernmost seaport and not Fortaleza as I had thought. Belem, which is just south of the Equator, is 975 miles northwest of Fortaleza and over 2,000 miles north of Rio which, I calculated, meant that I was a third of my way back to Blighty.

There was no conversation made by the gang between the airport and what I later learnt to be our destination, the Belem Yacht Club. On arrival at the club I was dragged from the vehicle in my bag and put on the ground. I heard the car drive off. I discovered later that the gang had left a car at the airport but could not find it and had to use a taxi instead. These boys were a class act!

Miller and a voice I did not think I had heard before started bawling the name, Greg. They shouted several times before I heard any response. After a short time I heard the unmistakable splash of oars and I was dragged into what I imagine must have been a dinghy. Miller, still giving the orders, told everyone to take care not to overturn the boat. When we reached their yacht, Miller unlaced the bag.

'Ho-ly sh-it!' a voice exclaimed in a rather stupid hill'billy accent. My gag and blindfold were unceremoniously removed.

'From here on in, Ronnie,' said Miller as he stood over me, 'you can have it hard or you can have it easy. It's going to be entirely up to you. We're going aboard the boat now and then I'm going to tell you all about our little operation. Trust me.'

The 62-foot motor-yacht, the Nowcani II *(Now Can I Too)*, had been hired by Miller and co. in Antigua in the Caribbean. It was roomy, comfortable and fully equipped with up-to-date sea going devices. There was a saloon, with a U-shaped seating arrangement around a dining table, at the end of which was a drawer containing cutlery. I was sitting at this table facing my kidnappers. Besides Miller and Fred Prime, there was a fair-haired guy with his leg in plaster, who I recalled had made such a brief appearance at the steak house just before the gang struck. His name was Thorfinn Maciver - another Scot, this time from Hawick - and he was the skipper of the yacht. There were two other men in the team, both in their mid-twenties. Anthony 'Tony' Marriage, of medium but wiry build, and Mark Algate, a tough looking character who was quite obviously into body building. On one of his arms was tattooed: 'I have only loved one woman in my life and that was another man's wife. My mother.'

Miller was the essence of good humour by now thanks to the apparent success of his operation. He was standing drinking from a can of beer. He offered me one.

'You look as if you could do with a wee dram, Ronnie.'

I ignored him.

'Perhaps a drop of brandy or a whisky? You can have anything you like, you know? We have your best intentions at heart.'

'Where's Mike?' I asked sharply.

'Wee Michael? Och, as far as I know, he's with your babysitter where you left him. That was all cobblers about having grabbed him. I knew you wouldn't dare call my bluff. But don't worry about the kid, we haven't laid a finger on him. However, I expect you are still a little pissed off with me, Ronnie, and I have to tell you, you have every right to be. But let me at least tell you what this business is all about and hopefully you'll see I'm not the total asshole you think I am.

'As I told you it is not our intention to hand you over to the cops. There wouldn't be any point in that as there is no longer any reward for your capture. Simply, we're going to sell this story to the highest bidder - after all we did the job that Scotland Yard failed to do. We're going to make a shit load of bread, Ronnie, and if you play your part and co-operate then you're in for a share of the proceeds. Fred only came along this time on that understanding, Isn't that right, Fred?'

Fred, his thumb now bandaged in a handkerchief, nodded. 'That's the Gospel truth, Ronnie. I promise.' There was no mention of Norrie Boyle and why he had decided to forego the pleasure of coming back to get me.

Miller ran through his plan. Unfortunately, he said, he wouldn't be making the trip with us, but Fred would be taking care of my every need. He was not able to tell me where our next port of call would be, but I figured that his plans included as my final destination a branch of HM Prisons.

Before he left he promised that we would not land anywhere for the present. 'Any deal that's made, will be on this boat,' he said, 'and outside territorial waters.' He elaborated, talking of flying a film crew out to the yacht to prove to the world that he really did have me. 'One thing is for certain, Ronnie, you're going to come out of this little drama as the hero. We're going to be seen as the villains. Mark my words.'

Miller got some more beers from the refrigerator and passed them around. I waved him away. Then, almost casually, Thorfinn, the skipper, tossed a clear plastic bag onto the table in front of me. 'Perhaps you would prefer to roll yourself a joint?' he suggested. 'It's pretty good weed.'

Well this was a different matter, if ever I had needed a joint it was now. 'Go ahead,' prompted Miller, 'you're in good company. We're all heads, except for Fred.'

Just as Popeye can take on overwhelming odds with a can of spinach, I felt that I could better face my situation after a few puffs of the proven panacea.

I rolled a fat one and lit up. The gang sat quietly as I silently dragged away on my joint. The captain was not wrong, it really was good weed. Miller who was standing some feet away, held up a sheet of foolscap. All I could see on it was an emblem of some kind in the form of a circle about three inches in diameter.

'You see this piece of paper, Ronnie?' Miller said as he waved it in the air. 'With this in my hand we sailed through Santos Dumont. The boys were carrying the bag, with me walking in front of them holding up the paper. Doors opened like magic!'

The doors of my mind, with a little help from the weed, were also beginning to open. We were still in Brazil and while I was in Brazil there was hope.

'I'll tell you something else, Ronnie.' Miller went on. 'Before we came to Brazil I had a good heart-to heart chat with your old friend, Jack Slipper.'

'Really? Why did you do that?' I inquired.

'I wanted to find out what our position might be in the event of getting caught during this operation.'

Since the kidnapping, I have been involved in several interviews with Jack Slipper. I tried to approach him about Miller's statement on more than one occasion. He was always evasive, but he never denied knowing Miller who thanks him for his help in his book.

'The most I will ever tell you, Ronnie,' he said on one occasion, 'is that shortly before you were kidnapped, I did meet a group of likely lads - more than that I'm not prepared to say.'

Obviously, the 'likely lads' were Miller and co. and I feel certain that Mr Slipper had knowledge of my kidnapping before it took place. And if Jack Slipper knew I was going to be kidnapped, who else did? That is a question the media, over the years, has chosen to overlook and ignore.

In fairness to Slipper, when *Odd Man Out* was first published in 1994 he tried to clarify his position in a newspaper article. He said that he had met Miller two years prior to the kidnapping and he told him of a plan involving fast planes and boats. Slipper asked him what it would cost and who was going to pay? Slipper says he was convinced that Miller was a

Walter Mitty dreamer, yet still reported the meeting to the Flying Squad. 'It wasn't until I heard Biggs had been kidnapped,' Slipper wrote, 'that I thought of Miller again. If I chased up every nutter I talked to I'd have done nothing else.'

'Have you got any questions before I leave?' Miller asked me.
I looked at my captors. 'Which one of you grabbed me from behind in the restaurant?'

The muscular fellow gave a sheepish grin. 'That was me, Ronnie. I hope I didn't hurt you too much.'

During the voyage, 'Muscles', as I took to calling Algate, informed me that he had been sent to prison for three years for blinding somebody. He had poked his fingers into the person's eyes during a fight. He had been released on parole after serving one year and, he claimed, he was in bed with his parole officer after their first meeting.

Miller was leaving, shaking hands with the rest of the gang. He whispered a few words to Fred then, in a louder voice said, 'Show Ronnie to his quarters - and don't take your eyes off him! That's an order!' To me he said, 'Use your head, Ronnie, don't try anything heroic - and before you think of jumping over the side of the boat, remember that you'll be in shark-infested waters!'

My cabin was equipped with two bunks, small but comfortable. Fred fastened the door open and stood 'at ease' on the threshold, very guardsman-like, with his hands behind his back. 'Why don't you sit down?' I suggested. 'Or do you plan to stand there all night?'

'That's right, Ronnie. I'm on duty.'

'How's your thumb?'

'A bit sore, Ronnie.'

'I wish it had been your fucking nose!'

Fred smiled, 'I bet you do, Ronnie.' Nothing more was said for a while, then Fred broke the silence. 'I'll tell you what, Ronnie, that bloke, Bizzo, sold you right down the river - him and Cobra, the one who can speak English.'

'What do you mean?' I asked, pretending to be only vaguely interested. Fred opened up.

'When we tried to get you two years ago, Bizzo told John that if he really wanted to get you out of Brazil, he should come back and do it with his help.'

'So what did Bizzo do to help?'

'He gave John the paper he showed you. But it nearly didn't happen - he wanted more money than we could afford, he's a right greedy fucker.'

'So how much did he settle for?'

'I won't tell you how much, Ronnie, but it knocked a hole in our expenses!'

With the knowledge that Mike was not in any kind of danger I started to calm down and with the gentle rocking movement of the boat plus the soporific effect of the grass, I finally fell asleep. When I awoke, I found myself being guarded by Muscles, who gave me a friendly 'Good Morning.' He hoped I had slept well. I was invited to use the toilet, but I was 'under orders' to keep the door open.

At the breakfast table I saw a slim, blond youth who I hadn't noticed at the gathering the previous evening. It turned out that he was the fellow 'Greg' who the gang had been calling to pick them up. Later Greg Nelson was to tell me that he was not one of the kidnappers, but a deck-hand from North Carolina who had been hired with the yacht.

Preparations were made to sail on the afternoon tide. There was some speculation that the Brazilian customs and immigration officials might come aboard and Muscles informed me that if that happened I would have to be tied up and gagged again. But perhaps, he said, it wouldn't be necessary as they had 'made friends' with the port officials on their arrival in Belém, handing out bottles of whiskey. They were hoping to make an exit in the similar fashion - this, unfortunately, turned out to be the case.

Soon we were chugging towards the mouth of the Amazon and the open sea. If I had any ideas about jumping over the side of the boat once we were sailing it would have been difficult. Fred had returned to duty and stayed close to me at all times.

'Once we are out of Brazilian waters,' Fred said, 'you'll have the run of the boat - until then you won't be allowed to show your face on deck.'

I thought it was best to try to give the impression that I had resigned myself to the situation. I conversed with my captors in a civilized manner, drank a few beers and smoked a joint or two.

There was a moment later in the voyage when I found myself alone with Greg, who was also fond of a smoke. As he was rolling one he said: 'Mr Biggs, the other night when I saw you smoke a joint in front of your kidnappers, I just knew that you were a cool dude, and,' he lowered his voice, 'if I can help you in any way, I will.' Sadly he never could.

My minder, Fred, was always anxious to have a chat. Out of the blue, during a conversation, he said: 'Major Ferguson is going to be pleased to see that we've been successful in grabbing you this time.'

'Who's Major Ferguson?' I asked.

'Major Ferguson is one of my old officers,' Fred said proudly. 'Two years ago, when we went back empty-handed, I saw the major, and he said, 'Sorry to see you back in Britain, Fred, without your prisoner, Ronald Biggs.'

'Did this 'old officer' know that you and Miller planned to kidnap me from Brazil?' I asked.

'A lot of people knew, Ronnie. John went to half a dozen newspapers, trying to find one to finance us.'

My thoughts returned to the conversation I had with the newspaper reporter by phone two years earlier. 'So who did finance you - then, and now?'

Fred smiled, 'Ronnie, if I was to tell you, you wouldn't believe me!'

Fred never did tell me nor did any of the other members of the gang but I still started mulling over what Fred had been saying as I lay in my bunk.

What was it to his 'old officer' Major Ferguson if I returned to Blighty or otherwise, I asked myself. From what Fred had said, it would appear that the major did have knowledge of what Miller and his army chums had been up to in Brazil. But who had told him, and why? As one of Fred's old officers, I assumed that he also must have been a Guardsman. Then I remembered having read somewhere that a number of prominent MPs had also served in the Scots Guards and I wondered if they also had an inkling of what had been going on. If Major Ferguson, 'half a dozen newspapers', and assorted MPs knew about the plot to kidnap me, who else could have been in on it?

Whatever thoughts I was having on the second morning out of Belem were broken by the noise of a Brazilian Air Force spotter plane as it flew low over the Nowcani II several times. The gang rushed on deck, waving and pretending to take photographs. Fred stationed his bulky frame in front of the companionway, warning me not to 'try anything'. I had got a glimpse of the plane from a porthole in the galley and felt a sudden surge of hope. Perhaps the game was up for my kidnappers and the Brazilian cavalry was on the way. When the plane flew off, Muscles descended into the main cabin with a worried look on his face.

'It was a Brazilian spotter.' he announced.

'Hooray!' I joked, 'I'm saved! And you lot are nicked.'

Tony Marriage joined us, he also looking worried. 'What do you think?' he asked Muscles.

'I think there's a good chance they're onto us,' his friend answered, 'and if they are, they'll probably send a fast patrol boat after us.'

He addressed me. 'Now, if we are intercepted, there are three options open to you. One; we can tie you up, gag you and hide you. Two; you can hide yourself. And three; you can meet whoever comes aboard and declare that you want to continue the voyage with us and return to England.'

'There's a fourth option,' I interjected. 'Meet whoever comes aboard and declare that I want to go back to Brazil!'

I had started to write a log in a notebook and I read aloud my latest entry: 'A Brazilian Air Force plane has just flown over the yacht. My kidnappers are in a state of panic!' Muscles didn't seem to find it funny. He told Marriage to get together all the stuff they wouldn't want to be found so that it would be ready to be thrown over the side if anyone approached. The 'stuff', as far as I could see, consisted of several canisters of army-issue mace; passports, probably false; and at least one rifle.

'What do you think the penalty would be in Brazil for kidnapping?' Muscles inquired.

'Anything from thirty to fifty years.' I said sincerely.

My kidnappers were most certainly in a panic and the order was given for 'full speed ahead' to get out of Brazilian territorial waters as fast as possible. Thorfinn Maciver, the skipper, calculated that we could be out of Brazilian waters as early as the following morning if the engine was kept at full throttle.

During my stay with the Blumer family, I had learned the meaning of 'metaphysical work', applying the power of the mind to any given situation so I started to think like a Christian Scientist to beat my abductors, calling upon the supernatural for help!

The following morning was sunny and there was a stiff breeze, favouring the course of the Nowcani II. The gang were all smiles as it became clear that we would soon be out of reach of the Brazilian authorities. To be on the safe side, the land-lubbers-turned-sailors tried to hoist the spinnaker to make even better speed, but they were unsuccessful. In fact their efforts turned into something of a pantomime, prompting the clearly irritated skipper to say: 'Never, in all my time at sea, have I ever seen anything quite like it!'

A few hours later Thorfinn calculated we were now safely out of Brazilian waters and so I was allowed on deck. As Miller had promised, I now had the complete 'freedom' of the boat. I could make my own meals and do my own thing, although Fred warned me that he would still be keeping a close eye on me.

Ripping across the water, with Brazil now far behind us, my shipmates were becoming more liberal in their behaviour and attitude, especially with their intake of booze. During their days of high jinks in Rio, the gang had been turned on to caipirinhas and what could be more suitable to serve on deck? The skipper, I noticed, was quite fond of the potion. And so was I. He was also a 'head', as I was, and wasn't averse to having a wee drag.

The party livened up, with the usual horseplay among young men. Tony Marriage and his bosom pal Muscles locked in 'deadly combat' and wrestled on the deck. Marriage lost and got up breathless and saw that I had been watching.

'You have a go at him, Biggsy,' he suggested, 'you're bigger than I am!' A friendly wrestle? Why not? Moments later, well remembering an earlier encounter with Muscles, I had him in a necklock, giving him stick! The more he struggled, the more I choked the shit out of him!

'Do him!' spluttered Muscles, 'Do him, somebody! He's doing me!'

When I let go, Muscles sprang up, rubbing his neck. 'You cunt!' he threatened, 'If you try anythin' like that again I'll fuckin' swing for you!' He addressed the others, 'He's not old and fucked-up like the rest of the gang - he's strong! Tie the fucker up, he's a dangerous bastard!'

However, the incident blew over with the breeze and I went back to the afterdeck to sunbathe.

Now that I was beyond help from Brazil, I thought it was only a matter of time before I got to England. I would probably never set foot in Brazil again. I worried about Mike, hoping that Raimunda would be able to get to Brazil to take care of him. For myself I was not worried; I was trying to work out a way to sink the yacht. I was still doing my metaphysical work and that evening the refrigerator packed up! Muscles and Tony tried to fix it, but without success. A lot of beer was going to get warm and a lot of foodstuff was going to spoil, so the order went up to eat, drink and be merry!

With nothing better to do that same evening, I picked up a pack of Tarot cards I found and began looking idly through them. I had heard of Tarot cards but I had never handled a pack until that moment. I soon found the card that I thought suited me down to the ground: The Fool. Thorfinn Maciver, 'the youngest skipper at sea', saw me going through the cards. He told me that he had studied the subject at length and was now convinced that it was an infallible 'science'. If I wanted him to, he said, he would 'read the cards' for me before the end of our voyage. I held up the card depicting The Fool.

'This, must surely be me.' I suggested.

'That's a better card than you might think,' Maciver explained. 'The Fool, in a manner of speaking, has God's Protection.'

On the fourth morning at sea I woke up early and immediately noticed that the boat was strangely silent. The engine was not running and we were becalmed. Suddenly, the skipper shouted, 'All hands on deck. We're sinking!' I was probably the only person on board who was pleased to hear Maciver 's urgent cry. And we really were sinking. My only regret was that Miller was not with us to go down with his mates! I was almost rubbing my hands with glee.

Overnight a lot of water had flooded into the Nowcani II and I went on deck to watch the crew feverishly baling out with pails and saucepans. Fred looked up from his labours at one point and said: 'I reckon you're doing a bloody Uri Geller on us, Ronnie!'

'I'm working at it!' I replied.

To this day the people who were on board the Nowcani II probably think I did something to stop the engine and sink the boat. If I did, it is all a credit to positive thinking.

By late afternoon, the 'engineers' had made the necessary repairs and got the engine going again. The voyage continued. By now the beer in the refrigerator was quite warm and eventually all the meat and poultry had to be thrown to the sharks. During a relaxed moment on the fifth day, Thorfinn offered to read the Tarot cards for me and I agreed. While I was shuffling and cutting the cards as he instructed, he repeated his conviction that the Tarot cards did not lie and I could believe what they were about to reveal.

I had no idea what Maciver was seeing in the cards as he turned them over one by one but whatever it was, he was quite obviously puzzled. 'It's amazing,' he said incredulously, ' here we are just one day from our destination and, it would appear, that you have already got one foot in Great Britain. Yet the cards clearly show that you are going to come out of this situation as the winner.' He sat looking at the cards shaking his head. I don't know if he knew it, but his prophecies had certainly given my flagging morale a much needed boost. It was also good to know that we were only a day away from our destination - wherever it might be.

There was excitement in the air on the morning of our last day at sea, 23 March, and everyone seemed extra friendly even though the engine was again playing up and what headway we did manage was made mainly under sail. The skipper made radio contact with someone, somewhere, but I was not permitted to hear what was said. I assume the conversation was with Miller who was planning to rendezvous with us.

As it might well be my last meal aboard the Nowcani II, I decided to prepare my own lunch. While I was searching in a cupboard for some condiments I came across a full bottle of Grand Marnier, a liqueur that I am particularly partial to. I opened the bottle and started pouring myself healthy nips. After lunch, without being told why, I was confined to my cabin so I took with me the book I was reading, the grass and rolling papers and the Grand Marnier. I could see no reason why I shouldn't enjoy my last hours aboard; after all, they might be my last hours of 'freedom' for some time.

Fred Prime came to my cabin for a little chat, perhaps to off-load his conscience. We were going to be parting company soon, he offered by way of explanation, and he just wanted to say that he hoped I wouldn't have any hard feelings towards him. He really liked me and he was going to make sure that I got my whack out of 'John's bit of business.' I was rather drunk by this time and I only vaguely remember the events that followed that day. I fell asleep but awoke to hear raised voices and shouting. Tony Marriage was shaking me.

'Biggsy! You're needed on deck! Right now!'

As I lurched on deck I saw, to my surprise, a huge grey gunboat close by, bristling with armaments and people.

'Who's the man in the red cap?' called someone from the gunboat with a loudhailer.

'It's Ronald Biggs!' shouted Algate. 'A fugitive from Great Britain.'

The voice from the gunboat announced that we were going to be towed into port. A Barbados coast guard vessel put the Nowcani II under tow.

The next thing that I remember clearly was being in the middle of a sea of perspiring black faces all gabbling away excitedly. A tall man wearing a light-coloured uniform and a cap with a lot of 'scrambled egg' on the peak, was holding me firmly by the arm saying, 'This way, Mr Biggs.' Later I discovered it was a gentleman by the name of Henrick Hutson, who was the Chief of Immigration. The rest of the events of that evening are far from clear in my mind, but I remember being fingerprinted and examined by a doctor who announced to whoever that I was in a 'state of shock'.

I woke up in a single bed in a small room. There was a table and a chair, where a middle-aged black man sat reading a newspaper, and a window with six vertical bars. It brought back memories. I was in a cell of some kind. The man put down his newspaper and we exchanged polite morning pleasantries. I discovered that I was in the Bridgetown police station in Barbados. I was feeling a little bit hung over and asked my guard if there was any chance of a wash and brush-up. There was 'no problem'.

Breakfast of coffee and croissants was brought to me in my 'cell' and this was followed by a visit from Mr Hutson, who politely asked me how I had passed the night and was there anything I needed. Mr Hutson was a very pleasant individual with impeccable manners. He explained to me that, for the time being, I was his responsibility, having landed on the island without a passport. But every effort would be made to ensure a pleasurable stay on the island. He promised to have me removed to more comfortable quarters as soon as I was officially handed into his care.

I was taken to the office of the Assistant Commissioner, another very dark person, by the name of Whittaker, which he pronounced, 'Widdiger'.

He was, more business-like than the affable Mr Hutson and very much a policeman. Early on in the piece, it was evident that Whittaker wanted to see me returned to Great Britain. He made some enquiries about the kidnappers and explained that in due course I would be appearing before a magistrate who would decide my fate.

My kidnappers, who had been held in the same police station, had been released to take the yacht on to Antigua, Whittaker told me. It was not considered necessary for them to be in town for the hearing with the magistrate.

Miller's original plan, I was later told, had been to rendezvous with the yacht off Barbados so that he could have his moment of glory by sailing into English Harbour in Antigua with me on board. The Nowcani II sailed into English Harbour, alright, only Miller and I were not on board.

Before leaving, however, Mr Prime had thoughtfully left a hundred dollar bill with Whittaker to take care of whatever needs I might have.

As soon as I was back to my room from seeing Whittaker, another visitor was announced. It was a certain Mr Ezra Alleyne, a lawyer, bespectacled and also very dark skinned. I began to wonder if there were any other white people on the island. He presented his credentials, adding that on the island he was known as the 'Perry Mason of Barbados' having never lost a case.

'You sound just like the man I need,' I said, not really interested in the services of a lawyer at that moment. 'But I have to tell you that I have arrived on the island penniless.'

'Let us not think about money,' said Mr Alleyne in a most un-lawyerlike manner. 'Let us just think about getting you back to Brazil!' He saw my smile. 'You don't know me from Adam,' he went on, 'but I know you very well. When the train robbery trial was in progress I was in London, studying law with Mr Ellis Lincoln - does that name ring a bell?'

I knew the name very well. Mr Lincoln was the solicitor who had handled the defences of Wisbey, Welch and Hussey. 'Sunshine,' as I had called Mr Alleyne back in 1964, had been a regular presence at the original trial as part of the Lincoln & Lincoln legal team.

'Mr Lincoln taught me something that I will never forget,' continued Mr Alleyne. 'It doesn't matter how difficult a case may appear to be - there is always a loophole. And, if you will allow me, I would like to find the loophole that will enable you to return to Brazil.' I shook hands with Sunshine for the second time and accepted his offer.

While I was still talking to Mr Alleyne, a man who the *Jornal do Brasil* was to describe as a mixture of Sidney Poitier and Gilberto Gil, yet another visitor was announced. A Mr David Neufeld was waiting to see me. Neufeld turned out to be a smartly attired lawyer from New York. David Levy, a writer who I had collaborated with on a book called, *'Ronnie Biggs: His Own Story,'* shortly before I was grabbed in Rio, had retained him after speaking with Charmian. The book was being serialized in the *Sun* and, at the time I was grabbed, many people, including the Brazilian authorities, thought my disappearance was all part of an elaborate plan to hype the launch. It was not, although even Miller gave this as an explanation once the media had tracked him down: he had flown to Miami from Belem to build himself an alibi in the days after I had been grabbed.

Mr Neufeld explained that he was in Barbados to secure the services of Mr Frederick Smith. Q.C., a former Barbados Attorney General, who would take care of my case. He showed little interest in the fact that I had just engaged Barbados' Perry Mason. He had his 'instructions' from Mr Levy and he wasn't about to settle for anyone other than Frederick Smith. We were facing something of an impasse until I made the suggestion that Mr Alleyne and Mr Smith might possibly like to work together. Ezra Alleyne was instantly agreeable. Frederick Smith, he said, was an extremely competent counsel. But Neufeld, who was to be expelled from the island for not having a work permit, grumbled that he wasn't keen on the idea.

But Alleyne and Smith it was - with the very able assistance of Mr Alleyne's partner, Alan Shepherd. The hearing before the magistrate was set for 5 April giving my team just a few days to prepare the defence. In the meantime, the immigration chief had me moved into the middle of a dormitory that housed about twenty of his agents, all nice lads who stood in line for autographs!

Every morning, propped up with pillows in bed reading the paper, the police chief, Whittaker, and Mr Hutson, visited me. The latter always enquiring if I had any complaints. Did I need more books? Writing paper? Anything from the supermarket?

'And what would you like for lunch today, Mr Biggs?'

'Flying fish?'

'Of course we have flying fish, Mr Biggs!'

I could order breakfast - anything I fancied - and have it served to me on a tray in bed, together with a copy of the local daily newspaper.

There was a PA system in the dormitory and during the day music and Bajan comedy programs were played. One afternoon, I found myself listening to the country and western tune, 'Lucille' and remembered my German friend in Rio, Armin, who played and sang that particular piece often and well. I was singing along in my mind, *'You picked a fine time to leave me Lucille…'* when one of the cops came into the dormitory holding a piece of paper.

'Do you know a person by the name of Armin Heim?' he asked. 'He's here to visit you.'

Armin had convinced a German newspaper that he could get a photograph of me in custody in return for his expenses to Barbados plus a nice few German marks on top. He had also convinced Whittaker that as my close friend he was on some kind of 'mercy mission' in Barbados, to get 'just one' photograph of me for my son, Mike, who was asking for a picture of his daddy. Armin would have sworn on a stack of Bibles that it was not for publication. As he said, he had to get to see me somehow.

It was a great tonic to see the big kraut. The great news was to know that Mike was safe and sound and had been delivered into the tender care of my friends, John and Lia Pickston. Mike was missing me, said Armin, but the Pickstons were doing a top job of keeping him happy. John had sent me a kind, humorous letter allaying my worries and a copy of *Ronnie Biggs: My Own Story.*

Armin casually got his Nikon out of his camera-bag and had shot half a dozen frames of me before Whittaker could get a protest together. A true pro.

On the day of my first appearance before Mr James King, the magistrate, a great crowd assembled around the courthouse and a cheer went up as I stepped handcuffed out of a police car. My 'hand picked' escort hustled me towards the court, one of them stumbling in the process, losing his gun from a shoulder-holster.

The confusion was much like it had been on the evening of my arrival in Barbados. It seemed to be the same sea of black faces around me. A fat lady with few teeth and a hat full of imitation fruit was calling to me in a loud voice: 'Mr Biggs! I'm praying for you! I'm praying for you to go back to Brazil and your son! You're going back because it's God's will!' At every subsequent court appearance I made that fat lady was there to tell me that she was still praying for me.

An aisle divided the courtroom with rows of benches on either side. To the left, facing the magistrate, sat the prosecution and the big noises of the Royal Barbados Police Force and the immigration department. To the right the goodies, plus two of Whittaker's armed cops who sat a bit too close to me for comfort. My legal team sat at a table behind me with a fine array of law books. The prosecution brought one.

Every day the courtroom was crowded to capacity. The international press pack, enjoying this winter break in Barbados, were standing by, notebooks at the ready. Many of them had already been in the West Indies to cover the England cricket tour.

Shortly after my arrival in the courtroom on the second morning, I heard someone behind me making hissing noises, trying to get my attention. I turned around to look straight into the smiling face of one Ronnie Leslie. There was no mistaking those pissholes in the snow! It was the same Ronnie Leslie who had helped Paul Seabourne to spring me from Wandsworth!

In town at the expense of *The News of the World,* Ronnie was allowed to exchange a few words before the cops stepped in and put the block on further conversation. Needless to say, the News of the World was hoping that Leslie would be allowed in to visit me so that they could put together some kind of an 'exclusive' story. I would have been only too happy to help my good friend, God knows he had helped me - and had served a three year prison sentence for taking part in my escape. But the headline in the local newspaper the following morning ruined whatever chance he might have had of being allowed to visit me. 'What is Ronald Leslie Doing in Barbados?' it screamed.

The prosecution, which was lead by Elliot Belgrave QC, an ex-student of Frederick Smith's, opposed my application for bail, stating: 'If Mr Biggs is released on bail, I'm quite certain that he will make a bee-line for the Brazilian Diplomatic Mission and then we'll never be able to get him out.' Once again I called upon my ability with regard to 'specious and facile lying', and swore that the idea had never entered my head. But it was to no avail. I had to remain locked up.

Whittaker, the police chief, gave evidence describing my arrival on the island and pertinent facts relating to my story. He made it quite clear to the magistrate that the police were seeking my return to Great Britain.

'Brazil!' boomed Mr Frederick Smith, for the defence, 'This poor man must be returned to Brazil! He was kidnapped from that country! Taken forcibly, against his will!' How sweet it sounded - especially in Bajan, 'Mr Biggs should be put on a plane and sent back to Brazil today!'

The court adjourned. Mr James King, the magistrate, wanted time to think.

During the hearing, Mr Alleyne and his partner discovered a certain omission on the part of the police. A document, relative to my presence on and possible exit from the island, should have been prepared by the police and handed to a certain parliamentary official. The official was then responsible for passing the document on to whatever department of the government required it. The police, however, had neglected this small chore. Mr Alleyne tracked down the parliamentary official and brought the fellow to the hearing. The official went to the stand and took the oath, going on to describe his job and his duties. With regard to a document concerning me he said that he had received nothing. Yes, he was quite sure. And, yes, it was customary to receive such a document.

'Thank you very much, sir. Your witness!'

The next day the police prepared and submitted the missing document. I asked 'Smithy' why so much importance had been given to the oversight on the part of the police if they had been able to prepare the document and hand it in a day later.

'The police are just wasting their time,' Mr Smith reassured me. 'It's not retroactive!'

Towards the end of the hearing, Scotland Yard sent a couple of beefy coppers over to Barbados in the hope that they would soon be returning to England with me.

It looked as if they were going to get their way. The magistrate's findings were that I should be handed over to the British authorities and returned to prison in Great Britain. I was given time to appeal against his decision. Without loss of time, the cops took me off to the cells at the back of the courtroom. Whittaker paid me a brief visit while I sat waiting for a car to take me back to the police station. He was all but smiling when he asked: 'Well, Ron, and how you feeling?'

I was in a mental slump but I was not about to let Whittaker see it. 'I'm okay, Mr Whittaker.' I replied, 'It's only the end of the first round.'

The police chief laughed indulgently, 'You're right, Ron. It's only the end of the first round.'

Hutson was at the police station when I got there, looking more serious than usual.

'Mr Biggs,' he said 'I am sorry to say that you are no longer in my care. As far as I'm concerned you are free to go but I don't think Mr Whittaker is going to let you go very far.' We shook hands. It was nice knowing you, Mr Hutson.

Hutson was right. Glendairy Prison was not very far at all. From the clang of the front gate to the stink of 'receptions' I was thinking, I've seen this film before. The same old screws with the same old bull.

'One on sir!'

'Thank you, Mr Peacock!'

It was Wandsworth all over again.

There were two screws in charge of receptions. One of them was sitting behind a desk that had a waist-high wooden balustrade in front of it. Open, on the desk, was the familiar huge ledger, into which my 'property' would be duly recorded. The second screw, who looked to be in his early sixties with a thin pencil-line moustache, was standing bolt upright at the side of the desk staring straight ahead, with a swagger-stick tucked under his left arm. The screw behind the desk recited: 'Stand on the line in front of the rail and empty your pockets. Do you have any valuables? How much cash do you have in your possession? What religion are you?'

More than a bit pissed-off and preoccupied with recent happenings, I didn't hear or understand one of the questions. I leaned forward to ask the screw to repeat the question, resting my hand on the balustrade. Like a striking cobra, the screw at the side of the desk whipped his swagger stick from under his arm and rapped it three times on the balustrade, making me jump.

'Get your hand off there boy!'

I gave him my best 'drop dead' look. This goon had somehow made sergeant, which entitled him to his little stick. The screw behind the desk continued his monologue, '... now take off your clothes and stand on the scales...'

Finally, Sergeant Goon led me through to the end of the main prison cellblock where a locked iron gate led to an area where there were ten more cells. A guard on the other side unlocked and opened the gate for me to enter.

'One on, sir!' snapped the sergeant.

I was shown to my new address: 'Cell 10. Death Row. '

The cells were tiny and dirty, with precious little space to move around. There was a bed with the traditional lumpy mattress, and a foul-smelling wooden commode in a corner. The door was a stout wooden frame, faced on the inside with heavy gauge iron mesh that was fixed with staples. I could see across a narrow corridor to the cell immediately in front of me, occupied on my arrival by a young burglar named Pedro Weekes. Pedro introduced himself and the other tenants of Death Row who I couldn't see, telling me their sentences and why they were segregated from the rest of the prison. Four of our number were 'waiting for de rope', Pedro told me, while the other were considered to be 'security risks.'

Sometime later Pedro wrote a full list of the inmates and their crimes and passed it to me during an exercise period. I asked my neighbour where the black door at the end of the corridor led. He grinned.

'Oh, man! That door leads to Paradise Island! And you don't need a passport to get there, man! But the only problem with going to Paradise Island is, you never come back!' It was, of course, the 'topping-shed'.

Many would argue that the man who should have been heading for the topping shed was one John Miller, but instead he was being tipped off by a man from the British High Commission to get as far away from Barbados as possible. Funny that!

Another man said to be holidaying in Barbados at the time of my arrival, and at the exclusive Sandy Lane resort, was none other than Sir Hugh Fraser, whose family at one time owned Harrods. He also chose not to stay around for the court case.

My time on Death Row gave me ample time to think about my kidnapping, yet it has only been in more recent years that the pieces of the puzzle have come my way which have formed a picture that suggests that the plot to kidnap me was known by some of the very highest in the land, including at least one member of the British Cabinet. Whether these gentlemen backed and supported my kidnapping because they believed they were righting a wrong, or for other motives, I simply don't know. This is something for the media to discover, should they wish to.

Miller, himself, has said that the first kidnap attempt was paid for by a German business colleague based in London, a nephew to a German steel millionaire, Baron Heine Thyssen, who put up the necessary £50,000. *The Sunday Time's* Insight Team would, however, have me believe that Miller's benefactor the first time around was one Baron Steven (sic) Bentinck, the wealthy son of a Dutch Ambassador.

The second, more expensive attempt, Miller credits to Sir Hugh Fraser, a fellow Scot, who conveniently died on 2 May 1987. With Fraser's death I will probably never get to know who else was behind or knew of my kidnapping and if indeed Fraser was involved or got the official approval of his political friends. What is certain is that while Miller shopped the first attempt around the newspapers, something he lived to regret, for the second kidnapping he was more discrete, making far better use of his Scottish connections and those of the Scots Guards. I have also heard that Miller tried to use a few of his entertainment industry contacts to round up the necessary cash.

Another name that keeps cropping up is Patrick Anderson, at the time the heir to the International Carpets fortune. Anderson had visited Brazil on a couple of occasions and, I am told, even had a few problems with Old Bill at Heathrow Airport for trying to carry certain substances into England that he shouldn't. Anderson, it is said, played the role of the mysterious reporter, Patrick Richardson King, who I was set to meet at the Roda Viva the night of my kidnapping. Miller would have us believe that 'King' got cold feet and hurried of to Miami. Others have told me that it was 'Anderson' who hotfooted it to England to try and sell the story to the press.

In a further twist in 2005, after Miller had milked my kidnapping for all that it was worth, Patrick King emerged from the shadows to claim in an ill thought out and untruthful TV documentary that he, and not Miller, was the brain behind my kidnapping. King's documentary and book should, like Piers Paul Read's *The Train Robbers*, be filed firmly under fiction. King claims all sorts of links to the "security services", and the murky world of MI5 and MI6, but I think in his and Miller's case, it is more about the M25, and going around in circles!

Whatever was going on behind the scenes in Barbados, the other cons in Glendairy Prison showed me much sympathy and friendliness. Everyone was convinced that, despite what Miller might have planned, I was going to be sent back to Brazil. With a few exceptions, the screws were friendly too, and agreed that I wouldn't have to return to England. One morning, when the shifts changed, a screw told me that he had heard on the radio that the Brazilian government had asked for me to be returned to Brazil. I couldn't believe it! I was sure the screw had got it wrong, but later in the day, when Smithy paid me an official visit to discuss my appeal, he confirmed the good news.

I started to receive a lot of mail from friends and well-wishers from different parts of the world. Some were simple and to the point, 'Keep your chin up, Ronnie, our whole family is rooting for you to get back to Brazil!' And, 'Don't worry if the worse comes to the worst, Ronnie. You can now get good Afghanistan Black in Wandsworth!' Some of the letters were deeply touching and beautifully written. 'Liz' from Belfast sent me various letters and a huge black cat card 'for good luck' - plus a monetary donation when she read in a newspaper that I needed cash to pay my lawyers. To all those people who wrote, expressing their love and support then and since, I most humbly and sincerely thank you.

The lads on Death Row were not permitted to attend church services in the prison so they conducted a religious service among themselves, with Mark Young, my next door neighbour who was serving time for shooting a policeman, leading the prayers and choosing the hymns. Everybody joined in, singing lustily - even the screw on duty. Pedro Weekes sang nearly all the time, and not a day would go by that he didn't sing his favourite piece, *'Diana'*. One evening I heard him singing, *'The Whole World in His Hands'*, putting in some words of his own: *'He got de great train robber in His hands...'* I was hoping that I would be in His hands when the day arrived for my appeal to be heard.

In a dank but spacious dungeon beneath the court, I paced back and forth contemplating my fate. It was exactly a month since I had landed in Barbados. What was it to be? England and cold comfort? Or sunny Brazil? I would soon know.

A jailer came and unlocked my cell. 'Okay, Mr Biggs. You're on next!'

The courtroom was packed. The appeal was going to be heard by two judges from the High Court, Barbados Chief Justice Sir William Douglas and Deputy Chief Justice Denys Williams, who had not yet taken their places on the bench. Smithy came over to the dock with a warm greeting and some words of comfort. He was confident that we would win. Mr Whittaker, bristling with self-importance, was standing to my left, no more than a yard away from the dock. He also looked confident.

'All stand!' The two black judges, looking somewhat incongruous in their white wigs, entered the court and took their places. When everyone was settled, the Clerk of the Court rose to say his piece and the hearing began. I was invited to sit down. Mr Smith got to his feet and ran smoothly through the story of my arrival in Barbados.

My appeal had been carefully prepared and was based on twelve different points. The judges listened attentively, interrupting from time to time with a question. As Smithy warmed to his work, outlining the points of the appeal, one of the judges stopped him. They were interested in hearing the details of point number eight: the one about the document that the police had failed to deliver to the parliamentary official. Mr Smith was quick to provide the details, indicating that the witness was in court should he be needed.

The judges also focussed on if the 1979 Barbados Extradition Act was in fact legally valid. Another potential loophole that had been spotted and raised in court by Mr Alleyne. Sunshine had spent several days researching the records of the House of Assembly to unearth the constitutional point of law relating to the Extradition Act.

He was asked by Smithy to present the argument to the judges that although The Act was valid due to significant legal reasons of interpretation, The Designation Countries Order was invalid and that included for Great Britain.

After a short conversation with their heads together, the judges withdrew from the court to discuss the matter between themselves. There was a small hubbub when they left, everyone wondering what this signified. Smithy knew. He hurried over to the dock again.

'Now look, Ron,' he said with conviction, 'if those boys are out of the court for more than ten minutes, you're going back to Brazil.'

The 'boys' were absent from the court for twenty-five minutes and when they returned I could see by their faces that Mr Smith was right. One of them addressed the court, speaking at length about the laws existing on the island and the necessity to observe those laws to the letter. It was quite clear that the procedure with regard to the document in question was imperative. The procedure had been neglected - and Mr Biggs was free to step down from the dock and leave the court.

The Barbados Supreme Court also ruled that the Barbados Parliament had not yet ratified an extradition treaty with the United Kingdom so the 1979 Barbados Extradition Act had not yet become law. It looked as if Miller had taken me to the only island in the whole of the Caribbean that lacked a valid extradition agreement with Britain!

The decision set off a commotion in the court, with people coming from all sides to congratulate me and shake my hand. I stood rooted to the spot in the dock, almost disbelieving the verdict, uncertain what to do next. A smiling David Levy appeared in front of me.

'Come on, Ron!' he exclaimed, 'Let's get out of here! You're a free man again!' Whittaker, who was standing within touching distance, didn't look at all happy. I offered him my hand in the time honoured gesture of gentlemen.

'End of round two, Mr Whittaker!' I said. But the police chief declined to shake my hand.

A crowd had gathered outside the court and people were milling around, patting me on the back and shaking my hand. Levy was trying to get me through the multitude to a taxi, wanting to get me to the house of the Brazilian Consul. Suddenly I found myself in the embrace of the lady with the missing teeth.

'I knew you would be freed!' she cried between rum-flavoured kisses. 'I knew because I've been praying for you day and night!' Tears of happiness were running down her brown cheeks - and mine!

At the Brazilian Consul's house there was the same degree of euphoria, everybody pleased that I had finally been able to make the 'beeline' that had previously been denied to me. From the moment I arrived, the telephone did not stop ringing. Levy monitored the calls, anxious that I did not speak to any journalists. He had hopes that a major deal could be made with a newspaper and he did not want me to leak any part of the story of my release. In my elation, and with a beer in my hand, I was ready to tell everybody who was willing to listen - quite free of charge!

By late afternoon, a televised telephone call to Mike was organized, but when the time came to speak to him I was so overwhelmed with emotion that it was almost impossible to speak. I could hear Mike on the line saying excitedly, 'Dad! Is that you? Are you coming back? Dad! Are you coming back today?' but I could only blubber a few words to confirm that I really was going back to Brazil.

Levy and Neufeld had contacted a friend in Miami and arrangements were being made to charter a Lear jet to pick me up in Barbados and fly me on to Brazil. All we needed was $16,000 but Levy had already received two offers from television companies interested in covering my return to Brazil - ITN from London and TV Globo from Rio de Janeiro - and they were each happy to contribute $7500 towards the flight. Levy covered the remainder. A temporary passport - a laisser passez - valid for 23 April to 2 May 1981 was prepared by the Brazilian Consul to enable me to make the trip. I would be entering into Brazil legally this time and as a Brazilian!

My old friend Whittaker turned up at the house with my bits and pieces of 'property' which he had had picked up from the prison. He had regained his composure and went so far as to shake hands with me and congratulate me on my good luck.

The Lear jet had arrived in Barbados stocked with champagne and caviar - this was not going to be an ordinary trip! Then, still unable to believe that it was all happening, I was driven to the airport with Levy in the car of a friendly Brazilian diplomat.

It was all a bit like Casablanca updated. It was dark, the tarmac was slick from recent thunderstorm and the sleek jet plane stood waiting. Come on, I thought, let's get out of here before someone issues an order to cancel the flight! I could well imagine Whittaker and a couple of his heavies turning up at the airfield with a warrant for my arrest. But we took our places in the plane and my fears dispersed as we sped down the runway and rose smoothly into the sky.

The sounds and the smell inside the plane brought back memories of the trip I had made tied up inside the canvas bag. But this time it was different. This time I wasn't seething with murderous rage. As I sat talking to the two reporters from ITN and Globo who were helping to finance the flight, I felt benevolent - even towards Miller and co!

In Glendairy prison, lying on my lumpy mattress, I had fantasized more than once about the possibility of a miracle happening that would permit me to return to Brazil and Mike. And I had made a promise to myself that if that miracle ever happened I would kiss the ground on my arrival! Short hours later, as I looked out of the window of the plane, I could see the Brazilian coast below, red in the first light of dawn. The miracle that I had prayed for was happening! Minutes later, the Lear jet touched down at Belem airport. It was the morning of 24 April 1981, forty days since I had been grabbed in Rio.

As soon as I stepped out of the plane I kept my promise, dropping to my knees like Pope John Paul II to kiss the ground. I wanted to embrace it! My trusty photographer friend, Armin, was waiting on the observation deck, camera in hand, but he had missed the shot.

'Do it again, Ron!' he bawled out. I was only too happy to oblige!

My triumphant return from Barbados to Rio on 24 April 1981.

A star is born. Mike at one of his Maracana shows.

Mike walking in the shadow of his father.

Mike has always had a love affair with the camera. In front of Sugar Loaf.

Mike (right) and his friends from Balão Magico. Together they sold over 10 million albums.

Eat your heart out Sinatra!

Giving Sting a few musical tips.

In session with the Sex Pistols and their manager Malcolm McLaren in February 1978.

My cellmates in Belmarsh and Norwich never ever looked this good!

Up Corcovado with director Lech Majewski, not a paddle in sight.

Keeping an eye on Prisoner of Rio. Paul Freeman, who played me, drying his hair.

Lunch with Charmian in Rio.

Step brothers, Mike and Chris in Rio.

Family time. Charmian, Farley, Mike and I.

My American mate, Diamond Dayne Henry.

Reunited at last. Paul Seabourne visits Rio in 1990.

Perhaps it was our age, but Paul and I decide to tackle a lower wall on this occasion!

Bruce Reynolds and I at my 70th.

Nick and Bruce Reynolds. Two of the best.

What was it Tony Bennett said about the good life? In my pool with Bruce.

I could have taken him! My great mate, Roy 'Pretty Boy' Shaw.

Time can heal most things. Mike and I with Jack Slipper in my flat in Rio.

A STAR IS BORN: MIKE BIGGS

Tears of joy for Biggs' son. My Dad is coming home.

Daily Express, headline, 24 April 1981

'When they (kidnappers) took on Ronnie Biggs they took on Dame Fortune – she's been courting Ronnie for years.'

Jimmy White, Great Train Robber

'Life is a big roulette wheel for Ronnie, and most of the time he wins.'

Bob Welch, Great Train Robber

Superfantastico!

The Magic Balloon Gang

For most of the flight down to Rio from Belem - on a commercial jet - I was pinned down in my seat by Brazilian journalists who were clamouring for details of the kidnapping. All I wanted to do was to look out of the window and appreciate beautiful, bountiful Brazil that was passing below, but it was not to be!

David Levy, who had accompanied me from Barbados along with his lawyer, David Neufeld, was doing his very best to hold back the reporters but he was not nearly as successful as Dr Brito had been on my flight from Brasilia to Rio in 1974. Levy, like Brito, had his reasons.

'Every word you tell them, Ronnie,' he warned, 'it's another grand off the value of your story!'

Later in the flight, once the journalists were satisfied that they had got their pound of flesh in advance of their colleagues awaiting my arrival in Rio, I was finally able to gaze out of the window and reflect upon the miracle that had allowed me to be on my way back to Rio - and with the blessing of the Brazilian government.

Writing in a British paper in 1994, Jack Slipper wrote: 'My personal view is that Biggs was rightly returned to Brazil after the kidnap, as it was illegal and our use of that illegal act would have condoned it.'

Cruzeiro flight 251 from Belem arrived a few minutes early at Rio's new international airport, touching down just before 10 a.m. A few minutes later, as I passed into the baggage claim area, I saw Mike on the other side of the sliding glass doors that separate the passengers from the people awaiting their arrival.

Mike was with John and Lia, waving his arms excitedly. They were not alone. There was a huge crowd of journalists and photographers who were jostling around them. A kindly federal agent, seeing Mike's predicament, opened the glass door and pushed him through into the baggage area.

Mike came running.

'Pai!'

As I picked him up and hugged him to me, he asked me through our tears, 'Dad, why do people cry when they're happy?'

As I had no luggage to speak of and had already legally entered Brazil on my arrival in Belem, I passed quickly through the airport formalities. Then, with Mike sitting on my shoulders, I went through the sliding doors and faced the army of newsmen. John and Lia were there, pushing through the crowd in an effort to get us to their car. Mike was shouting, 'Let my dad through!' while I tried to calm the impatient press corps. In all it took us some ten minutes to cross the airport's arrival hall, something that on a normal day with all the chaos you associate with airports, would take less than a minute.

As we scrambled into the Pickstons' Opala the press rushed to their cars so that they could follow us into Copacabana. A similar scene of confusion greeted us at the entrance to the building where the Pickstons lived. Lia went in first, wielding her handbag and laid open a path for us through the crowd of newsmen and curious onlookers. Finally we arrived at the apartment on the ninth floor and could start to celebrate my return to Rio with a nice cup of tea.

As I sipped at my tea and caught my breath, Mike sat on my lap and showed me my name 'tattooed' in big letters on his chest. You would have thought that I had never been away.

My friends had done a wonderful job of looking after Mike while I had been taken off to Barbados. At first, when it was known that I had been kidnapped, John and Lia had tried to keep the news from Mike but it was an impossible task given the media attention the incident had generated. Once Mike discovered the truth it must have been very difficult for the Pickstons to reassure him and keep his mind occupied. But John Stanley Pickston, who had not doubted for one moment that I would get back to Brazil, is a born funny-man and, among other things, he can make kids stop crying with his false nose and moustache. Nor is he the British community's favourite Pantomime Dame for nothing, so during his time with Mike he taught him a number of song and dance routines he brought to Brazil from England which included one based on *'Knees Up Mother Brown'*.

My thoughts of Mike and John were broken by the noise of the frustrated press corps who were now banging on the door demanding an audience. Finally - much to Levy's despair - I agreed to hold a press conference in the play area on the first floor of the building. Once that was over, I wanted to enjoy my freedom and went with Mike and John to the beach. But the reporters were not about to lose interest in a story that had dominated the press over the last forty days and they followed us at close quarters, asking more questions and taking endless photographs. Finally, we decided to take refuge in the Copacabana Palace, the hotel where so long ago, as it now seemed, I had begun the drama with Miller and his men. The same kindly and attentive waiters were there ready, as always, to make a fuss over 'their little prince', Mike.

A few days later I met up with Levy who declared that I had 'thrown away' whatever chance we might have had of writing a story about my kidnapping. He was returning to England that same evening, as he now saw no reason for him to stay on in Rio. He had been staying at Le Meridién, one of Rio's best and most expensive hotels, and there was one night remaining on the booking that he had made and paid for. He suggested that I make use of it.

Thinking that there might be some cash forthcoming from our book that had recently been published and which had sold well, no doubt helped by the publicity the kidnapping had brought, I asked Levy if he could leave me with some money. He laughed without mirth and told me the bad news: the expenses that I had incurred during my little adventure in Barbados were in excess of $50,000 which more than took care of my earnings. He was kind enough, however, to leave me with $200 and the keys to his room before catching a taxi to the airport. I was not to see David again for some 17 years when, back in Rio for a conference, he dropped by to see me in January 1998.

I had already spoken to Ulla; now I called her again and asked her to meet me at the Meridién hotel for a get-together. A week or so before Miller had grabbed me, Ulla and I had had a bit of a row and we were not exactly on speaking terms when I left the scene unexpectedly. Now seemed like a good time to forget our little squabble.

A few days later Charmian turned up in Rio with Farley. To help Levy with the legal bills, Charmian had managed to raise $10,000 by agreeing to do an exclusive story with Rupert Murdoch's *Melbourne Herald Sun*, and that included a reunion with me in either Rio or the UK, depending on the outcome of the court case. Happily it was in Rio, but unhappily my mind was elsewhere and after four days Charmian left to return to Australia.

About a year before my kidnapping, Mike (aged nearly six) and I had moved into a rather luxurious apartment on the eighteenth floor of a building that overlooked the bay of Guanabara and the Sugar Loaf Mountain. It offered the same picture postcard view that had first attracted me to Rio when I was in hiding in Australia, but at a price.

When I got back from Barbados, I found myself facing school, electric light, gas and telephone bills, plus $1000 in rent for the nearly two months that I had been away. Things were tough and I had to borrow money from friends to make ends meet. Little did I know, however, that certain things that had happened with Mike while I had been away would be the solution to our current financial crisis.

TV Globo, who had shown a great interest in my kidnapping from the beginning, had visited Mike at the Pickstons while I was in Barbados with a view to interviewing him for their Sunday evening prime time show Fantastico!, the same program that his mother and I had appeared on seven years earlier when I had first been arrested. Given the opportunity, John Pickston prompted his protégé to go through his 'Knees Up Mother Brown' routine for the TV camera. Mike ended his performance with a heartfelt plea to the Brazilian authorities to do something about getting me back to Brazil. He knew that the Queen of England wanted me, he said, but he needed me more in Brazil to take care of him.

By a happy coincidence, the then Minister of Justice, Ibrahim Abi-Ackel, was in the Globo studio waiting to be interviewed and saw Mike's section of the program. When he appeared on the screen he was smiling and said words to the effect that an effort must be made to bring about my return to Brazil. With the minister's words the great wheels of state and diplomacy were put in motion, all of which helped my speedy return.

Another gentleman who got to catch Mike's performance, and who was equally impressed, was a Spaniard by the name of Tomas Munoz. At the time, he was the president of CBS Records in Brazil.

The day Munoz knocked on my front door I was just thinking about moving to somewhere less expensive. Munoz saw Mike as an 'extremely talented child'. If I had no objection, he said, he was interested in making a record with Mike and two other youngsters. He had come up with an idea to create a children's vocal group. Auditions were already taking place, but he knew he wanted Mike. We asked Mike what he thought of the idea and he agreed without hesitation!

I had nothing against Mike participating in a musical group, providing, I said, that it didn't interfere with his education. At the beginning,

I suppose, I thought it might be fun for him, but not for a moment did I think it would develop into anything serious or financially rewarding.

Until Munoz's arrival on the scene, I had only ever heard Mike sing snatches of my best-seller *'No One is Innocent'* and the first few notes of *'Oh! Suzana'* when playing 'cowboys and Indians'. I mentioned this fact to Mr Munoz, but there seemed to be no problem; in fact he liked the idea of *'Oh, Suzanna'* as a piece for Mike to start rehearsing and it was to be included on the band's first album. The following day I went down to the CBS office in Praia do Flamengo and signed a contract.

When the group was formed it was given the name of *A Turma do Balão Magico*, or The Magic Balloon Gang. Besides Mike, two other extremely talented kids were chosen from the auditions: Simony, a six year old, and Toby who was eight. With the release of their first long playing record the group was an overnight success with the kids; the record's sales rocketed, a fat cheque was deposited in my bank account and the kids of the Balão Magico were presented with their first gold record!

Tracks from their first album were heard every day on the radio, even on programmes not aimed at the normal Balão Magico audience. It did not take long until the group was invited to participate in variety and music shows on all the major Brazilian television networks.

CBS Records appointed a capable young Brazilian lady named Monica Neves to manage the group for them, and soon after the first record was released the kids began to travel around Brazil, doing live shows as well as making promotional visits to shopping centres and record shops. The terms of the contract with CBS allowed for one parent to accompany each child and, after the federal police had given me permission, I travelled with Mike on most of the journeys the group made.

At first the audiences at the live shows were small, but before long the fans of Balão Magico were filling football stadiums from one end of Brazil to the other to see the talented trio. At Christmas time, the Globo network, which is the world's fourth largest, took over the gigantic Maracana Stadium in Rio de Janeiro to stage a free show which is televised live to millions and millions of homes throughout Brazil. The show features acrobats, clowns and other traditional circus acts alongside show business personalities and singers who entertain the crowd. The arrival of Father Christmas in a helicopter is the delirious finale.

As the audience is largely made up of children, the Balão Magico was a natural choice to take part in these shows as one of the main attractions. Each Christmas from 1982 to 1985, Mike, Toby and Simony sang and danced, without any show of nerves, in front of a live audience of close to 200,000 people.

The group's second album in 1983 was an even bigger hit than the first. One of the songs was called 'Superfantastico' and on this track the kids were joined by one of Brazil's top recording artists, Djavan. This catchy tune became a great favourite with the public and it was used to wind up the group's shows, they were invariably called back for an encore!

'Superfantastico' earned the Balão Magico a second gold record and their first platinum disc, as well as an even fatter cheque! The shows continued, with the kids giving as many as three performances over a weekend. Doting mothers would bring their children to the hotels where we were staying so that they could see the group up close and get autographs.

Simony was from a large family who had spent most of their lives in the circus. They were rough and ready folk and the girl's mother, Maria, was tough and avaricious. From the moment that the Balão Magico was formed, she tried to get a larger cut of the proceeds from the record sales and the shows for her daughter. She argued that Simony was the most talented in the group and should receive half the total amount, with the two boys left to split the remaining half. Toby's mother, Dona Rosa, and I did not agree. Monica Neves, who was managing the group, also sided with us.

It was during one of our weekend tours that a row flared up between Monica and Maria over the issue of Simony's pay. It resulted in Maria threatening CBS that she would take her daughter out of the group unless Monica was dismissed. Not to upset the apple cart, or the goose that laid the golden egg, CBS Records sadly bowed to Maria's wishes and gave Monica the sack. An impresario from São Paulo took her place; a slick and devious fellow by the name of Paulo Ricardo.

Paulo Ricardo was on very close terms with Simony's mother and soon they were calling the shots and banking the shows, paying the expenses and splitting the profits down the middle.

Each parent in the group was, in theory, free to bank at least one show each month. But Dona Rosa and I waived the concession so Paulo Ricardo and Maria were raking it in.

Flying back to Rio after another weekend of shows, Ricardo dropped into the empty seat beside me and started buttering me up with a load of old cobblers about his interest in Mike's career. He felt like a brother towards me, he said. Then he came up with an offer that common sense should have made me turn down on the spot.

'Senhor Ronald,' he said. 'We've got three shows lined up for next weekend. One in Santa Catarina, one in Joinville and one in Blumenau. Now, I know that you've never banked a show before, but I would like you to bank these three shows with me. Do you fancy taking a gamble? You could take home at least twice the amount you usually do.'

There was one obvious snag in banking a show: in the event of the show being rained off or not taking place for whatever reason, all the expenses - including the $500 for each child for each show - fell upon the shoulders of the person doing the banking.

Even though I knew that there had to be some sinister motive behind the impresario's offer, I decided to have a little flutter. Not for the first time, nor probably the last, Ulla thought I was mad. The area where the shows were scheduled to take place was down in the far south of Brazil and it was the rainy time of the year down there.

'You'll lose your shirt.' Ulla predicted.

It looked as if she was going to be right as it was a cold, grey and rainy Friday that greeted the Balão Magico as we flew into Santa Caterina the following weekend. It was raining when we landed and it was still raining when we got up the next morning - with the first show scheduled to take place at 11 a.m. Yet miraculously the weather cleared up and the sun appeared. The show was on!

I went to the stadium to look at my 'investment' and, in no time at all, the stadium dried out and the public began to come through the turnstiles.

Thank heaven you can always rely on a Brazilian audience to leave everything until the last minute!

It turned out to be a good crowd and a good show, in fact it was Superfantastico! Maria and the myriad members of her family, who had commiserated with me when we had arrived, were now grudgingly congratulating me on having 'backed a winner'. Maria tried to look pleased for me.

The next two shows, in Joinville and Blumenau, were also put on under ideal weather conditions before thousands of happy, cheering children - and I was in there cheering with them! Altogether – in addition to the lucrative aspect - it was a very pleasant weekend. In Blumenau, the German community had been celebrating their Oktoberfest - so my cup runneth over!

When the time came to settle, Paulo Ricardo was wearing a stiff smile. He asked me how much I 'thought' there was to come to me for the three shows. With Mike's payment included, I estimated that I was due to receive around $5500, but I accepted a thousand dollars less without argument.

About this time a Japanese team from NTV came to Rio to make a documentary film with me called, *Long Time No See, Ronnie*, a reference to what Slipper was supposed to have said when he met me in Rio. The film was to include Mike and 'my old adversary', who were both flown to Tokyo to participate in the production. Ulla was invited to go along as Mike's chaperone and, of course, jumped at the chance.

The Japanese producers were very anxious to have Mike's recording fame known to their viewers and a special record sleeve for the Balão Magico's latest album was produced for the Japanese market, with a portrait of Mike filling the back cover in place of a group shot. Meanwhile I was called upon to act out my own part in Rio with Brazilian actresses playing the roles of Charmian and Raimunda.

The money was now flowing in from Mike's work with the Balão Magico so I made an investment with a couple of friends. The investment resulted in a nightclub in Copacabana called Crepúsculo de Cubatão which became one of the hot night spots in Rio, especially with the 'darks'. Crepúsculo eventually ran its course and became the Kitschnet which had a similarly successful run before finally calling it a day in 1993. Towards the end, Kitschnet hosted a number of very successful male strip shows for the ladies and became Brazil's answer to the Chippendales.

The Balão Magico was now a household name and in 1983 TV Globo gave the kids their own breakfast-time program. The first of its kind in Brazil, it was the show which paved the way for Xuxa (Meneghel) to become one of Latin America's most famous media celebrities. Her morning show for children on Globo, Xou de Xuxa, made her one of the world's highest paid entertainers.

The recordings for the Balão Magico's shows were made at the Globo studio in São Paulo, which meant that Mike had to fly down there four or five times a week. I would pick him up at his school at midday, take him home for a quick shower and something to eat then rush off to get the two o'clock flight to São Paulo. The recording sessions often ran into late evening and we would return to Rio on the last flight, getting home after midnight. Homework was neglected and Mike started getting poor marks at school. The program was very popular, however, and thousands of fan letters poured into the studio each day.

At the height of Balão Magico's popularity, CBS Records decided to add another child to the group to keep the momentum going. He was a handsome and highly talented little coloured kid named, Jairzinho. A little younger than Mike, Jairzinho seemed to me to be an asset to the group. His father, Jair Rodrigues, was and is a well-known samba vocalist and Jairzinho had certainly inherited his father's talent. My view, however, was not shared by Simony's mother or Paulo Ricardo. When CBS first announced that they were considering Jairzinho for group, Maria called a meeting of interested parties to discuss the situation. We had fought hard to put our kids where they were, she argued, and she didn't think it was right that another kid should be allowed to walk into the group at the peak of its' success. To make matters worse, Maria went on, Jairzinho was a 'neginho' and it was unthinkable that our kids should share their hard-won fame with a black boy.

When I was invited to give my opinion, I argued in favour of Jairzinho joining the Balão Magico. A large part of the Brazilian population is made up of black, brown and beige people and I saw Jairzinho's admission into the Balão Magico as a certain way to increase record sales and balance the group. But I stood alone: even Toby's mother, Dona Rosa, didn't think a fourth member was necessary. But, after many bitter and heated arguments, CBS, who paid the piper, won the day and little Jairzinho joined the group in 1984 in time to record the band's third album.

The kids, who had not taken part in the discussion, couldn't have cared less about another child entering the group, it gave them someone else to play with during the tedious flights to and from the shows. Mike palled up with Jairzinho immediately and they worked very well together on the television programme. Conversely, Mike had never really hit it off with Simony and the two of them frequently squabbled. Provoked, one day, tough-as-nails Simony called Mike, 'the son of a thief'. Mike didn't hesitate with his reply: 'And you're the daughter of a bitch!' There's no business like show business, they say!

After John Miller and co. had tried to grab me the first time in April 1979, Ulla had suggested that Mike and I should move in with her and her children in Rio; she said I was a 'sitting duck' in Sepetiba and I tended to agree. She said the gang might try to get me again so obeying a law that Murphy would have been proud of I sold off my bits and pieces in Sepetiba, paid the rent and moved to Santa Teresa, one of Rio's most historic, bohemian and beautiful neighbourhoods. Ulla's apartment, which her father had bought for her, was situated on the middle floor of a fine old house that had been built in 1943 and been converted into three apartments. An elderly tailor and his family, who were the only tenants in the building with access to a large but run-down and overgrown back garden, occupied the ground floor. I used to look down with a certain amount of envy at the abandoned area beneath Ulla's bedroom window and imagine what I could do with the place if it were mine. I reminded myself that it didn't cost anything to dream.

Sometime later, in early 1980, Ulla moved from Santa Teresa and let her apartment to a young Brazilian couple, while I moved out to Botafogo.

Then, in the February of 1984, I heard that the apartment beneath Ulla's was up for sale. I immediately took a taxi over to the house, where I found the owner of the apartment at home. The place was shabbier than I had thought and it was obviously going to take a lot of time and money to fix it up. But at $16,000 the price was very attractive. Without haggling, I gave the old tailor a cheque for half the amount by way of a deposit and arranged to pay the remainder within twenty-eight days. I bought the apartment in Mike's name but I said nothing to him about the deal. I wanted to refurbish the place and present it to him as a surprise. Within days of signing the contract, I arranged for a team of tradesmen and labourers to start work on the renovation.

It was exactly a year later, in January 1985 when we finally moved into the apartment in Santa Teresa at Rua Monte Alegre, 470. The work wasn't finished but it was nearing completion and I, the ex-foreman, wanted to be around to supervise the final touches. The old tailor who had sold me the apartment would never have recognized the place. The worm-eaten flooring throughout the ground floor had been ripped out and replaced with white marble; all the old woodwork, cupboards and doorframes had been burned and been replaced with dark, polished hardwood, a seven meter by four slate-lined swimming-pool had been installed and Mike had his own suite, decorated with the colours of his favourite football team, Botafogo. We bought a beautiful Rottweiler puppy that we named Blitz and, a little later, Lua a miniature pinscher bitch. As well as the dogs we also had a number of birds, including a magnificent blue and yellow macaw named Fred.

So finally, thanks to Mike - and, indirectly, to John Miller, without whose 'help' Mike's talent might never have been discovered - we had our own home and castle. Biggsy's bolt-hole in Brazil.

The popularity of the Balão Magico continued, with Jairzinho now being tagged 'the Michael Jackson of Brazil'. Two more albums were produced, one of which sold half a million copies and earned the group a double platinum disc. The group were called upon to advertise various products and contracted by one of Rio's best-known entrepreneurs, Chico Recarey, to put on a series of weekend shows at his 'emporiums of entertainment'. Every Saturday and Sunday afternoon saw the kids on stage singing the Balão Magico's hits to capacity audiences of young fans.

After five action-packed years, the Magic Balloon Gang's gravy train started to slow down and finally came to an armchair stop. It had been a long and lucrative journey, now it was time for the kids to rest on their laurels and enjoy the sweet smell of their success as they planned what to do with the rest of their young lives. Not surprisingly, to me, the member of the Gang to go on and have the most success as an adult in the music industry is Jairzinho, both as a musician and a producer, and he and Mike remain close friends.

Another person who chose to move on was Tomas Munoz. He had made CBS the most successful and profitable record company in Brazil and now he got the call to the corporation's office in New York.

Twenty-five years on A Turma do Balão Mágico continue to sell well with a new greatest hits collection doing good business for Sony BMG as recently as 2009. Occasionally there is talk of a reunion concert, and who knows what the future holds and if Mike will ever take to the stage again with his former band mates. For now he has a cupboard full of gold and platinum disc to look at and show to his daughters and my grand children as a reminder of his time as a genuine star when he sold over 10 million albums and was part of the 20th most successful Brazilian acts of all time. For many Brazilians, Mike remains by far the most famous Biggs and I'm happy for it to stay that way.

AN ENGLISHMAN ABROAD:
OLD FRIENDS COME CALLING

You and the night and the music
Thrill me but will we be one
After the night and the music are done

You and the Night and the Music
(Howard Dietz & Arthur Schwartz)

We never took shit from no one; we just didn't give a fuck.
If you didn't like our music, that was just your bloody hard luck.

Die Toten Hosen / Ronnie Biggs , *Carnival in Rio (Punk Was)*

After five hectic years of travelling around Brazil with the Balão Magico, it felt good to return to a somewhat more 'normal' life. Mike had missed a lot of school and had fallen asleep over his homework once too often. He had a lot of catching up to do. Although we were sitting on a fairly healthy bank balance it wasn't going to last forever and with Brazil's high rate of inflation at the time, I thought I had better look at ways to protect our capital and make it grow.

Shortly before the Balão Magico folded, Raimunda had returned to Brazil pregnant and married to a Swiss bank clerk named Gerard. At first they went to live with Raimunda's parents in the north of Brazil then, when their child was born, a boy they named Andre, they came back to Rio. Gerard was supposedly a good cook and interested in opening a restaurant in Rio - all he needed was the cash. Not wishing to look a gift horse in the mouth, I put up the money and Mike and I became fifty-fifty partners with Gerard and Raimunda in a small restaurant in a popular resort town close to Rio called Buzios.

Buzios had been put on the map in the 1960s when the French actress Bridget Bardot chose the tiny fishing village for her honeymoon. Since that time the once remote fishing village had grown into a sophisticated weekend getaway for Rio's 'beautiful people' who arrived to take advantage of the peninsula's many beaches during the day and in the evening, the village's many bars, restaurants and nightclubs.

I hired a team of builders to give our place a face-lift and stocked the cellar with a good selection of wines. A barman and a waitress were engaged and 'Mr Big' opened to the public with great expectations.

But the customers were few and far between and Gerard, as chef, found himself with little to do except tipple our best wine and 'fall' asleep behind the bar. The competition was just too strong and like so many would be restaurateurs who have been lured to Buzios before and since, we went broke.

Fortunately, I was still considered good copy and was regularly sought out to give interviews for newspapers, magazines and television. Journalists came, it seemed at times, from all the corners of the globe but it was still mostly the boys and girls from London's Fleet Street that knew that 'Ronnie' could be relied upon for a good quote, whatever the topic.

I had also been invited over the years to take part in a number of advertising campaigns that have included coffee, locks, security systems and even the Australian Split-Cycle engine. The attention these campaigns received earned me a sharp reminder from the federal police that I was still not permitted to work in Brazil.

Ironically I never received a penny for one of the most successful advertising campaigns to use my name. It was a campaign for the British Leyland Mini that, according to the advert and billboards, *'Nips in and Out Like Ronald Biggs'*.

Tour operators, who had begun to discover that in certain countries I was as much a symbol of Rio as Corcovado or Sugar Loaf, began to approach me with a view to entertaining groups of tourists who were interested in meeting up with me. 'The Biggs Experience' was the way one journalist neatly described it. For fifty US dollars tourists could visit me in my bolthole and enjoy my hospitality, eat, drink and splash around in the pool or sit fascinated whilst I held forth about the train robbery. What else? Photos were taken and autographs given. I often think I enjoyed these meetings as much as my guests.

Many of my fans and admirers never got the chance or the opportunity to get to Rio and so wrote or sent gifts instead. As my family and friends will tell you, I have never been a great letter writer so I apologise to those who did not get a personal reply then, or since my return to Britain.

Not all the mail or emails are of a friendly nature and I have had my share of hate mail over the years, even on my deathbed, and still do!

One of my first 'experiences' with visitors to Rio was a chance encounter in Copacabana. I was sitting at a seafront bar sipping a cold beer. It was quite early and there were only a few people about. The sea air was bracing and there was not a cloud on the horizon.

Four people were walking slowly towards me along the pavement, looking directly at me as they drew near. There were two men and two women. The younger woman came up to my table smiling.

'Are you really 'im'?' she asked.

'Yes,' I said, 'I think so.' Assuming she thought I was who I was.

'Ooh! Can I call my mum and dad and me boyfriend over? - I can't believe this! - Mum! Dad! It is Ronnie!'

The four were from Fulham; Mum and Dad, Brenda and Ted all gor blimey Londoners. They were on a cruise, like, and their ship had docked in Rio giving the passengers a few hours ashore. As they had left the docks on their way to explore Copacabana, Brenda had said, 'Wouldn't it be funny if we was to meet Ronnie Biggs!'

'And we've bloody well done it!' said her boyfriend.

Dad called for a round of beer and Brenda, still smiling, opened up with a string of questions. Ted butted in.

'She's a right fan of yours,' he told me, 'I reckon she's got more time for you than she'd ever have for me - straight! She'd take your socks as a souvenir if you'd give 'em to her.'

We drank our beers and chatted away. 'You must get fed up with people like us,' observed Dad. 'Perfect strangers, just coming up to you and wasting your time.'

I assured Dad to the contrary, telling him that I was always ready to meet my own people.

'One fing's for certain,' said Ted. 'When we get back to Fulham, no one's ever going to believe us when we tell 'em that we met Ronnie Biggs!'

On my way home I saw a t-shirt in a shop window that had printed on the front the old tourist favourite: *'I know someone who went to Brazil and all I got was a lousy t-shirt.'* It got me thinking and a couple of weeks later I took delivery of a thousand t-shirts similarly printed, but I changed the lettering to: 'I know someone who went to Brazil and met Ronnie Biggs - Honest!' They started selling like hot cakes.

Since Jack Slipper's historic first trip to Brazil in 1974 to arrest me I have been fortunate to have met many more equally illustrious figures, including lots of musicians, actors and other celebrities who passed through Rio to give shows or promote something. One of these was Sting who, during our first encounter, was still with the appropriately named Police, another was Rod Stewart.

From the rockers to the punks, I have met them all and on many occasions have joined them on stage or in the studio. Don't expect *Ronnie Biggs' Greatest Hits* any time soon, but it is out there somewhere if you pulled all the tracks together. One visitor was reggae star Maxi Priest who - I discovered - I had a lot in common with. Not only were we both Brixton boys, but we were also both carpenters at one time!

Another visitor was the record producer Gus Dudgeon and his wife Sheila. Any fan of Elton John will recognise Gus' name as having been responsible for many of Elton's best and greatest albums as well as David Bowie's *Space Oddity*. Gus and Sheila first dropped by to meet me as they were sailing through Rio on the QE2. They promised to come back for the party to mark the 30th anniversary of the robbery and were as good as their word, falling in love with Rio in the process. Gus also got to meet up with Bruce Reynolds in London and got to learn more about the train robbery than most. Sadly Gus and Sheila were killed in a car crash in July 2002.

They were good, good people and Gus even came to visit me in Belmarsh. His fancy belt setting off all the alarms!

Lord Snowden dropped by to take my photo on one occasion, while I was also proud to host one of my sporting heroes, Sir Stanley Matthews, arguably the greatest English winger of all time. John Simpson, the famous BBC's World Affairs Editor, also came by to meet and interview me, while the now globally famous Piers Morgan spent an afternoon at the flat with the Happy Mondays. Happy days indeed.

A certain George Harrison also put a note under my door to say he had dropped by to visit, but sadly I was not at home. I can't believe I did not keep the note.

Another fascinating visitor was Albert Spaggiari, the brilliant thief who tunnelled under the main road to rob the Société Générale bank in Nice in 1976. Albert popped down to Rio for a chat in 1981. A very nice fellow, but looking quite ridiculous in an obviously false moustache and large Afro wig. Albert's crime, you may remember, was carried out "sans haine, sans violence et sans arme" ("without hatred, without violence and without weapons"), a message that he left written on the wall of the vault. He was caught, but soon managed to escape by jumping out the window of the court and made his way to South America, in the process becoming France's answer to 'Ronnie Biggs'.

When the initial cloak-and-dagger style approach was made, there was no mention of who it was who wanted to meet me. I had to meet a French lady named Alice in Colombos, then an old-fashioned tearoom in Copacabana.

Once more into the lion's den I went. Alice, who turned out to be a handsome lady in her mid-thirties, came straight to the point.

'How much do you want to be paid to meet Albert Spaggiari?'

The name sounded as if he might be some Mafioso so I was cautious, especially after what had gone on the previous year.

'Who's Albert Spaggiari?' I asked.

This was pre internet and Wikipedia days, so Alice gave me the facts. Paris Match was in Brazil and they decided it would be a major scoop to film Albert and me together. I did not ask how Paris Match came to know that France's most wanted man was in Rio, but I hoped he would have better luck with *Paris Match* than I had had with the *Daily Express*.

In less time than it had taken for me to decide to become one of the train robbers, I asked Alice for $5000 in cash to meet with Spaggiari who was to pretend to interview me for French TV. 1980 had been a fairly lean year and I had accumulated more nagging debts. Alice got back to me the following day with the news I had been waiting to hear. *Paris Match* had agreed to my terms.

Albert and I were introduced to each other in an apartment near Colombo. We got on famously, but for the fact that he couldn't speak a word of English and I only had the smattering of French guide-book phrases that I had picked up in Paris. Without the false moustache and large wig, Albert could probably have walked the streets of Copacabana quite unnoticed but when we did go out everyone stared. My old mate Eric Flower would have loved him!

Our meeting was recorded for television, but the director swore to me that the encounter was exclusively for screening in France. I can't say that I was altogether surprised, however, when our little get-together was shown by TV Globo on *Fantastico* the following Sunday evening.

For the recording I had to pretend that I did not know who it was who was interviewing me.

'What would you do, Mr Biggs, if you came face to face with Albert Spaggiari?' Spaggiari asked.

'Who is Albert Spaggiari?' I replied.

'He, Mr Biggs, is the most famous runaway in the world.'

'Sorry pal,' I said with a large grin. 'You're looking at the world's most famous runaway.' Spaggiari was in no position to argue.

There were some rather more pertinent questions awaiting me when I went to sign in at the federal police headquarters the following week. Interpol would have liked to sit in on our little chat, I was lead to believe, and I was warned that I was skating on very thin ice.

Interpol and the French authorities never did get their man. Albert, who had been sentenced to life in prison in absentia, sadly died of throat cancer in June 1989. His mother, in front of her house, found his body.

If you want to see my meeting with Albert, it often pops up on You Tube.

By 1986 I was hoping that my hustling days were well and truly over after Freddie Foreman introduced me to Polish film director Lech Majewski.

Majewski had read all about me and decided that he was the person who had to make the film of my life. He only had a couple of quite ordinary films to his credit, including one called *Flight of the Spruce Goose* which was about as commercially successful as the Howard Hughes' airliner of the same name.

Lech visualized *Prisoner of Rio* as a masterpiece in the making. A Swiss based sales-distribution company, Multi Media, had arranged finance for the making of the film but, like most of the deals I find myself involved in, the movie was to be made on a budget that was far too low for its pretensions.

Initially, Lech said that his intention was to make a true film of my life, a good film, a film that he and I would both be happy with and proud of. The problem was, said the director, it would take at least half a dozen full-length films to tell the whole 'Biggs story'.

As we were in Rio, Lech saw my kidnapping as a good base for the film he had in mind and I was invited to join him and his American girlfriend, Julia Frankel, in writing the screenplay. We began work immediately. Every day I would go to the hotel, where Lech and Julia were staying, to work on the project. We seemed to be making good progress when, after nearly two weeks of work on the 'true story', Lech changed his mind and announced that we were going to turn to fiction and write yet another kidnap plot, this time to be carried out by an outraged Scotland Yard Inspector, 'Jock' McFarland, who was obsessed with the idea of getting 'that bastard' out of Brazil. Up until that moment I had given the work my best shot, but all my interest died when I heard Lech's decision. The stuff Lech and Julia wrote was wishy-washy at best, and sometimes downright corny. A number of times I clashed with the hard headed Pole and in the end I let him get on with it although I still ended up with a screenwriting credit.

Paul Freeman was chosen to play 'Biggs', walking into a kidnap set-up for the third time, and Steven Berkoff was to play the role of the avenging

Glasgow-born Inspector McFarland. Other actors involved included Peter Firth and the Brazilians José Wilker, Florinda Bolkan and Zezé Motta.

Production proper finally got underway in July 1987 and I had a cameo role as a guest at my own party. During the following months of bickering and back-biting *Prisoner of Rio* struggled through to the end, going way over budget in the process.

Everybody hated Lech, especially Berkoff, but Lech took this in his stride; it was customary for everyone to dislike the director, he said. I discovered a certain affinity with Steven and it turned out that we shared a common experience; we had both been to Stamford House Remand Home and we both remembered the perverted old director of that disgraceful establishment, Johnny O'Hare. Steve lamented the fact that he had not thought of making a film with me. He said he would have written the screenplay, directed the film and played the leading role, instead of getting involved with 'this megalomaniac Majewski.'

'I myself fail to understand why people can change a perfectly good yarn for some hokum,' Steve told *Time Out* on his return to London. 'But that is the nature of people who film the people who live... If someone like Biggs expresses doubts about some elements of the script, then a producer who fails to listen does so at his own peril. After all, it comes from the horse's mouth. He was there.'

Prisoner of Rio was finally unveiled for the first time to its' expectant buyers at the Cannes Film Festival in May 1988. Now if ever there is an event that is fuelled by hype, it is the Cannes Film Festival. Hundreds of new films are launched at the event each year and if your film doesn't have a gimmick or a hook it can easily get lost in the crowd. The Cannes Film Festival also claims to be the world's largest annual media event with more than 3,000 journalists packing into the French Riviera town for the ten days of festivities.

A publicity scam was concocted for *Prisoner of Rio* for the benefit of the world's press. 'Mr Biggs would be putting in a personal appearance at the festival', the producers announced. Speculation and rumour suggested that they had me hidden away on one of the luxury yachts that were anchored off the beach. When the pressmen - and the cops - gathered to take advantage of what could be the biggest single media event of the

1988 festival they were not to be disappointed. Mr Biggs was in Cannes, only it was Mr Michael Biggs. Surprise, surprise!

While the press on the whole took the scam well, the same could not be said for the film that got a critical mauling from the critics. By coincidence or mis-management, the film was released in Britain at around the same time that a film about Buster Edwards. *Buster* starred everyone's favourite rock star of the time, Phil Collins, alongside the equally popular Julie Walters; predictably, *Prisoner of Rio* did not receive the kudos that Lech Majewski had forecast.

Neither *Buster* nor *Prisoner of Rio* is exactly a masterpiece, but you will probably find them at your local DVD store where hopefully they are both firmly catalogued under 'fiction'.

My share of the proceeds from *Prisoner of Rio* came to a paltry $13,000, falling far short of the vast sums that had been mentioned at the beginning of the negotiations. But it was enough to keep the wolf from the door for a year or so.

What Majewski may not have been aware of was just how much of a film buff I was. I was a familiar and regular face at film industry screenings in Rio, thanks largely to my good friend Fred Sill, a senior executive with Paramount who is one of the few people living in Brazil who has the right to vote for the Academy Awards.

Fred has a very dry sense of humour and is always great fun to be with, as well as being a very generous host and friend. Generosity that continued even after my return to Britain and where when a Fortnum & Mason hamper turns up on my doorstep or bedside, it was invariably from Fred. A great man and a true friend is Fred.

Over the years I lived in Rio I met hundreds of tourists. A lot of them became my friends who made return trips to Rio to maintain our friendship. Irish Americans, Dennis and Maura Clare, for instance, are a kind-hearted couple from New York, who had visited me since Mike was a year old. Richard Keaney, another Paddy, came to Rio for the first time in 1987. His friends 'back home' had told him that he couldn't return without some pictures of him and me together. So one Saturday morning Richard - a wacky Gene Wilder look-alike - found his way to our home in Santa Teresa.

He turned up carrying an airline bag which contained a bottle of whisky and a cheap camera. Drinks were poured and Richard shot off the roll of film that was in his camera. It was evening when he left. Early the next morning he telephoned with a tale of woe; he had been held up by a brace of street kids and they had taken off with his watch, his cash and his camera - with the 'precious' film inside it. He had bought another camera, he told me, and he wanted to know if I would let him return to take another set of photographs? I agreed and arranged a friend for life. Richard returned to Rio many time, always arriving with a ten-pound slab of cheddar cheese and other gifts. He was also one of the first to visit me when I got out of prison and a regular visitor to the nursing home, although sadly I can no longer enjoy the cheddar.

Richard was in Rio when I received a most illustrious guest; my friend and hero, bantam Paul Seabourne.

At the time, 1990, I was engaged in making a documentary film with an Australian bloke named, Bob Starkey. He was going to cover a party that I was giving to mark my twenty-five years on the run and he had asked me who I thought should 'star' in his production. Without hesitation I suggested Paul - I was having the celebration thanks entirely to him. Bob agreed and contact was made with Paul in London. Miraculously he wasn't inside.

Paul was quite ready for a trip to Rio and a first class flight was arranged. Bob wanted to get our first meeting in twenty-four years on film so set up his camera at the airport where the passengers disembark. First class travel had provided Paul with a fine selection of alcoholic beverages to choose from and my old pal arrived very obviously drink-lagged. But it was just fantastic to see the little bugger again.

Our re-encounter was shot by a drinks stand where we were to toast each other with double whiskies. This scene was repeated several times, as were the doubles. We laughed and joked and took the piss out of each other's old looks. Wet though he was, his wit was as dry as ever. I didn't tell him, but the long years that he had spent in the nick showed. A number of his front teeth were missing and he walked with a stoop. But it was the same old Paul and it was great to have him in Rio.

Back at the 'Biggs mansion', I introduced Paul to Richard who had crashed out on a settee the previous evening. A bottle of vodka was produced and my two guests were soon chatting away, both smoking like chimneys. Richard, who knew who Paul was and why he was in Rio, was 'honoured to meet the man who got Ronnie out of prison'. He was loving every minute in Paul's company. During the afternoon they both passed out.

Seeing that Paul was hors de combat, Bob proposed that we should forget filming for the day and get off to a seven o'clock start the next morning. With this in mind I went to bed early, leaving the guests to sleep it off.

No one seems to know what hour it was when Paul woke up and found that he and Richard had smoked all their fags, but it was certainly after midnight. Driven by the craving that only cigarette smokers will understand, Paul went off to look for a tobacconist or perhaps a slot machine, as he would have back home in London. It was late and dark: only a fool would be abroad on a night like this. Thinking that he only had to 'pop up the road', he had gone out wearing a pair of thin-soled airline slippers. Santa Teresa is not the easiest area to find your way around in, but Paul followed the tramlines that he presumed would lead him back to the house. He kept walking and finally came to an area where he found bars and nightclubs that were open. With £500 in his pocket and not a word of Portuguese, Paul had wandered into Lapa, a very tough neighbourhood at the time, where transvestites swung their handbags and muggings were commonplace.

We were on the point of organizing a search party when Paul turned up in a taxi just after seven o'clock. The taxi-driver, who claimed that he had been driving my houseguest around for the last four hours in the hope that he recognizes the road, was demanding $300 from the gringo louco (mad gringo). Needless to say, despite his age, Paul, who had followed the wrong tramlines back, wanted to sort the bloke out.

We got on 'location', Paradise Island, by two that afternoon and Paul promptly fell face down in the sand. Bob loved the footage that he was getting of the two old jailbirds 'havin' a fuckin' ball'. This was the stuff he wanted; 'warts an' all!'

By the evening Paul had made a remarkable recovery and looked quite reasonable. We were off to do some more filming. This time, the two old lags across a dinner table in a swanky waterfront restaurant, with the Sugar

Loaf looming in the background. The strains of *'You and the Night and the Music'* reached us. We were rolling!

Bob, who was playing the role of the interviewer, asked me if I was 'suffering' in Brazil. This was in reference to a remark that Jack Slipper had made on one of our various satellite encounters. Asked if he thought I deserved to be pardoned or not, Mr Slipper replied that he thought I should continue to 'suffer' in Brazil. Keeping a straight face, I was giving Bob a list of the ways I suffer. Not allowed to work. Not permitted to marry. Not allowed in bars or nightclubs. Have to sign in twice a week at the police station...

'Why don't you say something about your 'mansion' in Santa Teresa with the heated swimming-pool?' Paul said helpfully. 'And while you're about it you should mention Rosa, the maid, and the houseboy you've got working for you....'

Interfering old fool. I was glad to see the back of him!

Sadly that visit was the last time I was to see Paul. His passing in 1994 was a sad day and I miss him. Hopefully he will be standing waiting by the Pearly Gates, if and when I get there. Perhaps this time he can help me to break in.

While Paul was in Rio I was approached by the then cult BBC TV program, *Saturday Night Clive*, to see if I would be willing to do a satellite link up with the show's genial host, Aussie Clive James, to talk about crime on television and television in general. Much to their surprise, I think, I agreed to do the show and was ready to cross-humorous swords with Mr James but either he or the BBC got cold feet and I was told my services would not be required.

My dear friend, Bruce Reynolds was another very welcome and distinguished guest in our 'sumptuous' apartment overlooking Rio's industrial zone. Bruce came to Brazil for a short spell in 1991 with a tough-looking customer named Tony Thake, the boss of a transport business. The last time I had seen Bruce was on that fateful day way back in August 1963 when I had moved into the 'big time'. Although we had spoken on the phone before he came over, it was still an enormous pleasure to meet my friend again. Bruce, who had served ten years out of a twenty-five-year sentence for his part in planning and executing the train robbery, was also marked by the long period of incarceration, which had left him emaciated and looking much older than he should have. Nevertheless, we had a great get-together and a lot of laughs. Tony, a gentleman, if not a scholar, filmed our reunion and the fun and games, in the hope of finding someone interested in buying the unusual footage. Tony had financed the trip to Brazil for both of them as Bruce was living on the dole at that time.

A day or so after Bruce arrived in Rio, we were joined by his son, Nick, who is as every bit as likeable and irreverent as his old man. Their stay in Rio was all too short, but in my waters I was certain that we would all get together again in the not too distant future, only I had not foreseen that one of Bruce and Nick's future visits to Rio would be to accompany me back to Britain.

Nick was back in Rio in 1995 to make a plaster cast of my head that was eventually cast in bronze for his 'Heroes and Villains' exhibition. I had to sit still for him for well over an hour with a couple of straws stuck up my nose, but I told him after having been put in a bodybag for nearly 20 hours after being kidnapped, this was nothing.

Visitors came from far and wide and while I would expect to be known in Britain and Australia, I also found I had a stream of visitors from Scandinavia, South Africa, Canada, Japan, Poland and Germany. I even found that I had a growing following in the US from where a visitor, Steve Koschal, discovered that there was quite a market for 'Ronnie Biggs' autographs. Steve is an autograph expert and I think even he was surprised by the interest the collectors had in my scrawl. Appropriately Steve still has me classified under 'undesirables' on his web site.

At the time of his visit to Rio, Steve was a near neighbour of my nephew Terry in Florida. Terry was also a regular visitor to Rio and Chez Biggs and had taken after his 'Uncle Ron' and liked to dabble in the kitchen, only he does it on a professional scale with his own catering company. But when Terry came to town all hell broke loose in the kitchen as he, Rosa and I fought for space on the stove or the barbecue.

Besides Charmian and the boys, Terry and his brothers, Jack and Chris, plus Terry's own son, Steve, would be my closest relatives. Terry's father was my older brother, Jack, who died on the eve of the Great Train Robbery.

Shortly after the visit of Bruce Reynolds I received a visit from the German punk band Die Toten Hosen. Formed in Dusseldorf in 1982 they remain to this day one of Germany's biggest bands, with a huge following in South America, Australia and Eastern Europe.

I enjoyed the company of the band members and a strong and long friendship was forged. Typically the band were one the first people to be in contact when I was released from prison in 2009, sending me a magnificent box set of their CDs. Not sure it is to the taste of the other people in the nursing home, but I love it.

During the band's visit to Rio in 1991 I did a 'Sex Pistols' with them and wrote and recorded a couple of tracks and videos. They included the hit *Carnival in Rio (Punk Was)* and the appropriately titled *Police on My Back*.

Talking of the police, a visitor to Rio who I had never expected to see again was ex-sleuth Jack Slipper.

Hearing that I was about to stage a party in August 1993 to commemorate the 30th anniversary of the train robbery, the *Sunday Express* telephoned me to see if I would be willing to meet Slipper in Rio. There had been rumours in the press that I was planning to invite Slipper to the party. The BBC had also shown a lot of interest in the bash and were talking about turning up in Rio with as many of the train gang as wished to come along and talk about old times.

Anxious not to miss out on a story of an encounter between the ex-cop and myself, the *Sunday Express* was ready to 'do the dirty' on the rest of Fleet Street and the BBC.

I was not expecting to see Slipper turn up under any circumstances, so I was quite surprised when Oonagh Blackman, the *Sunday Express* reporter, phoned to say that Slipper had agreed to come to the mountain, although not to the party. Well, one thing was for certain; neither one of us were going to do it for love. My fee was £1000. I don't know what Jack's payment was, but I do know that his first class airfare would have shown very little change from five thousand quid.

Our meeting, in June 1993, was much ado about nothing and the *Sunday Express* had nothing specific in mind when they planned it. They were hoping that something 'newsworthy' might come from Slipper and I being brought face to face after all these years.

We met in a quiet corner of the pool area at the back of the Inter-Continental hotel in São Conrado. The same hotel where I had gone to meet Bobby Moore and Kenny Lynch in 1979.

'I'm not going to say the obvious,' said Slipper as we shook hands.

Seeing Oonagh Blackman standing close by waiting to hear our first gems of conversation I said: 'You don't have to say anything. But what you do say will be taken down and will result in the *Sunday Express* selling a lot of newspapers!'

We left the hotel and went for a stroll along the beach chitchatting while Stuart Mason, the newspaper's photographer, snapped away with a variety of cameras. I told Slipper that I was surprised that he had accepted the *Sunday Express'* invitation to meet me, knowing that his gesture was sure to meet with disapproval in certain quarters. But he was no longer a policeman and he was able to come and go as he saw fit. He was just anxious to keep his visit as secret as possible so that it didn't turn into a 'circus'. He had even made his flight reservations under an assumed name.

He asked after Mike and Ulla, whom he had met in Tokyo. I politely asked after his wife, who I knew had suffered for a number of years from arthritis. Nobody would have guessed – or believed – that the two white-haired old gents ambling along the beach in the winter sunshine were the ex-guv'nor of the Sweeney and Britain's most wanted man.

It had been thirsty work and Jack and I were in need of a drink. Jack suggested that we should go to a bar where we would be unrecognized, so I took them to a shopping mall a couple of hundred yards from their hotel where there was then a comfortable bar-restaurant called, Guimas. A female acquaintance, Beatriz, who I had not seen for several years, was working at the bar as a waitress and immediately came to our table to greet me. Moments later an American musician friend, Bill Horn, walked through the door: 'Hi, Ron, who are your friends?'

So far Slipper and I had not had a chance to exchange a word. As Bill moved away from our table Slipper commented, 'I'm glad that I didn't suggest going to a place where you're well-known!'

Over drinks, with Oonagh ever at the ready with her pen and note-pad poised, the two one-time adversaries opened up the conversation that the *Sunday Express* team were waiting for: 'The Last Secret of the Great Train Robbery'.

We found ourselves talking about 'the man who had coshed the train driver.' Slipper assured me that the 'Yard' knew the identity of this person, who was never taken into custody. 'It was the big fellow,' said Slipper with conviction.

'If I gave you the initial of his first name, would you give me the initial of his second name?'

'Not likely!' I replied. 'You can say whatever initials you like but I'm not about to say yea or nay to anything.' And that was 'the last secret' which must have set the *Sunday Express* back about £20,000 to find out!

The next morning, when I was due to meet Slipper in Copacabana, I took Johnny Pickston along. For some years John had been playing 'golf' on Copacabana beach, hitting a tennis-ball from one litterbin to the next. He had become quite a dab hand at it and, knowing of Jack Slipper's passion for golf, was anxious to challenge the ex-policeman. On 'holiday' in Rio, how could he refuse?

It was a fun day, with beers on the beach. Later the photographer suggested that Jack and I should stand with our arms around each other's shoulders in front of the Trocadero Hotel where he had 'nicked' me nearly twenty years earlier. But that, said Slipper, was going a bit too far.

For me, the highlight of his visit came when we all sat down to dinner in a Japanese restaurant in Ipanema called Madame Butterfly.

Besides Slipper, the *Sunday Express* couple and myself, Mike and Johnny Pickston were in the jolly company. We ordered drinks and a 'jumbo' sized dish of mixed sushi and sashimi. The food was beautifully served in a large flat boat and was placed in the centre of the table. We all fell to with our chopsticks.

Man of the world Jack Slipper had no difficulty manipulating the little sticks of wood, but the lights were low and Jack wasn't wearing his glasses so he couldn't see the little pieces of Japanese culinary art too well. He reached out with his chopsticks, deftly picked up a walnut sized piece of wasabi - the fiery green paste made from horseradish - and, as we watched in horror, popped it into his mouth. As the wasabi hit his sinuses, Slipper leapt up from the table looking for somewhere to spit and reaching for his glass of beer at the same time to put the fire out.

Thanks for the dinner Jack, it was a nice one!

John Pickston offered to take the group to the airport when it was time for them to return to England, and as I had nothing on I went along for the ride. Over a drink or two at the airport Jack and I talked about the 'flak' he was certain to receive when he got back to England. But Jack's was an old campaigner and well accustomed to the shit that's thrown in the press. When there's a few quid to be earned he'd have been a fool not to go for it. And the readers loved it, so why not?

As he was leaving we shook hands firmly.

'All the best, Ronnie.'

'You too, Jack. See you soon.'

It turned out to be sooner than we had expected as just over a month later, but this time over a satellite hook-up, we again came face-to-face. The travelling tec was in Hamburg to have a chinwag with his favourite fugitive. But this time I had to say the obvious: 'Jack, we're going to have to stop meeting like this...'

I was to do a number of other satellite links with Jack over the years. We both appreciated each other's points of view on crime and punishment and the Great Train Robbery. Jack was generous with his comments about my autobiography and on my return to England in 2001. He was a class act. I was genuinely very sorry to hear of his passing in August 2005. It would have been nice to meet him one last time, and on his patch.

Thankfully the family also came calling. Chris and a group of his school friends spent almost a year in Rio in 1986, giving Chris and Mike a chance to get to know one another. Chris returned to Rio in 1988 with Charmian and Farley. We all went to carnival together before Charmian went off to explore Peru and Bolivia before returning in time to celebrate Farley's 21st in Rio. Chris then managed to drop by in August 1992 with his then fiancée, and now his wife, to help Mike celebrate his 18th. Chris had been visiting the Galapagos Islands and Peru.

There were some people who, after all my years on the run, still asked me if I had any money left from the train robbery. Some laughed indulgently when I told them that my whack was gone after only three years. But it is true. Over a third of the money went in my escape from Wandsworth to

Australia; my minders ripped off other large sums, while I was also probably too generous for my own good in the early days by giving large cash handouts to family and friends. So don't go looking for buried treasure, because you won't find any. If I still had my pot of gold why, by the end of 1992, was I back hustling my t-shirts?

Despite a radio spot during the Rio Earth Summit, 1992 was a tough year financially. The tourists had thinned out and the pickings were meagre. Johnny Pickston and I were 'working' together. He was the funny man who would get the punters interested and so four nights a week John and I would sit in the bar of the Leme Palace Hotel playing countless games of cribbage, waiting for the horde of tourists that never came. Then our luck changed; one night the bar suddenly filled up with a crowd of people who were participating in the British Steel Global Challenge, a round-the-world yacht race organised by Sir Chay Blyth.

While I was signing autographs, accepting numerous drinks, posing for photographs and answering questions, John was exposing the merchandise. You lucky people!

Most of them were pleasant, friendly people looking for a little adventure in their lives. One was an ex-prison officer who spoke fondly of 'Gordon' (Goody) who he said he had got to know well over the years. Another fellow, a carpenter from Bath who was a crewmember on Heath Insured, introduced himself as Bill Vincent and lost no time in telling me that he had a murky past and had 'done a bit of porridge'. He was rather drunk when I met him and he stayed that way for the best part of the time that the crews were in Rio. He took to becoming a regular at the Leme Palace bar and we became quite pally. I got the impression that Bill was a deeply unhappy man and, subsequently, on the last leg of the 28,000 mile race he 'executed a perfect dive' from Heath Insured and swam away from the yacht, never to be seen again.

On 15 November 1992 I went to see the boats sail out of Rio on their nine thousand mile leg to Australia and noticed that a lot of the sailors were wearing their recently acquired 'Ronnie Biggs' t-shirts. A few people, writers and newsmen who had been covering the yacht race, were still in Rio and I received a phone call from one of them who was interested in taking some of my shirts back to the UK with him. I threw a dozen shirts in a bag and met my 'customer' in a bar close to his hotel in Copacabana. He was with several other people who turned out to be buyers as well, and within a few minutes I had autographed and sold my twelve shirts.

While I was 'working' I was answering their questions, the 'evergreens' as I call them. One of the group was an enthusiastic Scot, Jock, who listened in silence as I related the timeworn facts. Finally he asked: 'Have you ever thought of writing your story?'

'It's funny that you should say that,' I told him, 'because I'm working on it right at this moment!'

'If you need an agent or any help in London,' he said, handing me his business card, 'get in touch.'

I had become fond of writing as a kid. Something of a dreamer, my favourite subject at Santley Street School was 'Composition' and I was the only kid in the class who ever asked for extra paper to write my little stories, frequently being called a 'crawler' by the less literary minded.

Some years before the encounter at the British Steel Challenge, I had met and become friends with a fellow Englishman and almost equally long-time Rio resident, Christopher Pickard. Chris was a writer and journalist who was well known in Rio as being the author of the best-selling guide book to the city and as the opinionated columnist of *Rio Life*. Chris also made everyone very jealous by going off every year to write a gossip column at the Cannes Film Festival.

One year Chris got me to list my favourite films of all time for him to publish in his Cannes column. In alphabetical order in 1992 I listed them as *Angels With Dirty Faces* (1938), *Cape Fear* (1992), *Convict 99* (1938), *The Frog* (1937), *The Lavender Hill Mob* (1951), *Murder Incorporated* (1960), *Odds Against Tomorrow* (1959), *To Catch a Thief* (1955), *Two Way Stretch* (1960), and *We're No Angels* (1955).

Chris and I met socially from time to time over the years and we began kicking ideas around with a view to producing a light-hearted guide book, tentatively entitled, *'Ronnie's Rio'*. Chris made a number of enquiries regarding the feasibility of our project but always came back with the same answer; there was far more interest in my life story.

At the start Chris and I would meet over lunch with every intention of getting my life down on paper, but as the beer and caipirinhas flowed, we tended to get sidetracked on other topics as we put the world to rights on more than one occasion.

Chris decided it was time for me to become computer literate and brought an old Amstrad over to my house, a machine I managed to burn out in no time at all. Next up was an Apple Mac, one of the first in Brazil.

With a little help from the Mac we had a first chapter, the story of my escape from Wandsworth, knocked up in no time and a few weeks later, when Chris had business to take care of in London, he took the first chapter to present to the friendly Scot I had met during the Global Challenge. He was to take this to publishers he knew and worked with, but told us to get on with writing the book as these things took time and they may want to see more of my masterpiece. The results of my labours in 1992 and 1993, and my growing computer proficiency, are part of what you have before you!

Quentin Crisp once wrote that there are three reasons for becoming a writer. 'The first is that you need the money; the second, that you have something to say that you think the world should know; the third is that you can't think what to do with the long winter evenings.' I wholeheartedly agree with Mr Crisp on all three points.

Another very good reason to write *Odd Man Out* was that over the years there had been many misleading comments and gross exaggerations in the press with regard to my person and it was time to put the record straight. It's worth a laugh when I read that I'm supposed to have laid five hundred more chicks than Bill Wyman, but it's no laughing matter to see myself headlined as an assassin.

When members of the Royal Family visited Rio, certain newspapers would be sure to report that I was doing my best to get an audience with whoever it might be to plead for a pardon, or some similar crap. When Princess Diana was visiting Rio in April 1991, the pack of newsmen who follow the royals paid me a visit. They had organized a whip-round among themselves and offered me £500 to pose in a Princess Di t-shirt and to say a few words about the dear lady's visit. 'Smile, Ronnie!'

During the session, a couple of reporters drew me aside with an offer they thought I couldn't refuse. They knew the Princess' itinerary for the following day and at a certain hour she would be in downtown Rio, bestowing smiles upon the barefoot street urchins. For a further 500 quid, one of the conspirators said, all we want you to do is reach through the crowd and lay your hand on Lady Di's arm... And say, I suggested, 'We've got to stop meeting like this!' I declined the offer.

I suppose I shouldn't be too hard on the press, after all, it is the press that brought me the cock-eyed fame that I enjoyed over the years in Rio. The only thing that ever bothered me is when I tell a reporter the truth and they then chose to ignore it. Most of the media still can't even get the number of people at the train robbery right. It is 16 at the track, if you need to ask.

When Eric Flower and I went over the wall from Wandsworth, the papers warned that we were probably armed and ready to shoot. The public was advised not to 'have a go'. Gradually the image changed as it became obvious that I was not the vicious desperado I was first painted to be and eventually I found myself on first name terms with Fleet Street and the press in general. When a crime of any magnitude occurred in Britain or involved Brits, the press invariably telephoned me in Rio for my comments. When a driver of a security company drove off with a million pounds, the press got in touch immediately. 'What would you do, Ronnie,' asked one reporter, 'if this fellow was to turn up on your doorstep? What would be your advice to him?'

'To let me take care of his cash!' I said, and the reporter hung up delighted with my reply and the quote.

In the 1990s the newspapers often carried the stories to the effect that I longed to see the green, green grass of home, homesick for jellied eels and Bird's custard powder etc. Dreaming of the Pardon that would enable me to return to spend my last years in England. But at that time they could forget it! I didn't expect to be pardoned and to be perfectly honest I didn't want to be. Stop being Ronnie Biggs? You must be joking, I was having too much fun!

It was just after Jack Slipper's visit to Rio in 1993 that Chris got the call from Jock in London. We had a publishing deal for my autobiography and it was with Bloomsbury Publishing no less. At the time Bloomsbury was considered very highbrow, and known for publishing serious authors such as Margaret Attwood, Nadine Gordimer, Michael Ondaatje, Joanna Trollope and Jane Campion, to name just a few. At this point in time a certain *Mr Harry Potter* was not even a glint in the eye of Bloomsbury managing director, Nigel Newton, and he knew he needed some best sellers if he was to take the company public.

Happily my autobiography fitted the Bloomsbury bill alongside an account by Anna Pasternak of Princess Diana's alleged affair with James Hewitt, *Princess in Love*. We were too late for a Christmas launch, so Bloomsbury's MD set a 21 January 1994 release date. I declined the kind invitation from Nigel to the London launch, but agreed to send Mike to represent the family.

Clearly at some point I would have to finish the manuscript and my closing words written towards the end of 1993 were: 'The future is as uncertain as my past and my position is as precarious as ever. Technically I still may not work and I still face possible deportation. If I could have a wish granted it would be for the Brazilian authorities to finally grant me my permanent visa and accept that for nearly 25 years I have lived in their country as a law abiding citizen and a Carioca at heart! But tomorrow is another day and as I still can't work and have no old age pension as such to look forward to, I have another group of visitors arriving for a barbecue lunch and *'The Biggs Experience'*. It's a rare rainy day in Rio today, but tomorrow I expect it will be sunny again!

'There were times when I was writing this book that the two most important words in my life were, 'The End'. Yet now the time has come to say goodbye, I realise that this is not the end but only a new beginning.'

And a new beginning it was. The rest of 1993 was spent planning for the launch of *Odd Man Out*. Photos were taken and promotional videos were shot. If I could not physically be in London for the launch, it was decided that we would do a satellite link up between the press in London and me in Rio.

Mike, accompanied by Gus Dudgeon and his wife, made their way to the Groucho Club in London that January morning where they met up with Jack Slipper and a crowd of Fleet Street's finest.

Due to the time difference between London and Rio, Chris and I, plus his PA and girlfriend at the time, Ana Claudia, along with Johnny Pickston, were up at the crack of sparrow and made our way to a studio in downtown Rio where we met another old Rio friend, Bob Nadkarni, a filmmaker who was going to produce the Rio end of the show and make sure all the technical stuff worked. Bob was taking no chances, so if you see the footage you can see I am wired up with two microphones. More mics were out of shot. Fleet Street's finest would not miss a word.

The Brazilian press, many of whom I knew well, were also up early and invited to the studio for breakfast and to watch the trans-Atlantic press conference. I promised to talk to all the Brazilian media, including TV Globo, just as soon as the British press had got their pound of flesh via the costly satellite link.

Knowing that I was not always at my best in the early morning, Chris had thoughtfully supplied a bottle of brandy to loosen my tongue. The brandy, along with some strong black coffee, did the trick and despite not being able to see who was asking me the questions in London, and trying to remember to look straight into the camera, it all went as well as we could have hoped for and the resulting coverage was generally very positive. Even my critics, including Slipper, seemed to like the book. At times though I felt that some of the journalists asking the questions from the Groucho Club could not actually believe their luck and that they were talking to the real Ronnie Biggs.

Slipper, who was to assure them that I was the real Ronnie Biggs, had got hold of an early copy of *Odd Man Out* to review it for the Express.

'Though it pains me to say it, I enjoyed the book, and I think a lot of other people will too,' wrote Jack. 'So Ronnie, if you are reading this, there's only one thing left to say: it's nice to see you earning money legitimately at last!'

With our work done for the day, except for a couple of scheduled telephone interviews with British radio stations, we decided it was time to celebrate. It was still only mid morning, but it was a gloriously sunny day and we decided to head for the Rio Palace Hotel, now the Sofitel Rio, and sit by the pool area. We could relax and enjoy the view down the length of Copacabana as well as partaking of a few beers and caipirinhas.

As morning moved into afternoon a small crowd started to build up in front of the hotel. Modestly I thought this might be for me as news of the book launch spread, it was John Pickston who pointed out that from their shouts and banners it looked as if they were more interested in the stars of the Hollywood Rock festival, who were staying at the hotel, than in yours truly.

Now well and truly refreshed, thanks to the beer, caipirinhas and the earlier brandy, we decided to call it a day and that is when I spotted Whitney Houston sunning herself by the pool. In my state it seemed the most natural thing in the world to say hello and welcome her to Rio. I was a big fan of her music, and hoped to get to the show. I had not considered that being one of the biggest stars of the day she might have a bunch of minders looking out for her, so as I approached and Whitney looked up from her book, a number of large gentlemen hove into view.

'Ronnie Biggs! It is Ronnie Biggs isn't it?' I heard a voice say off to the side. 'Whitney it is Ronnie. You do know Ronnie Biggs?'

The voice belonged to Steven Tyler, lead singer of Aerosmith and now an American Idol judge, who were also headlining at Hollywood Rock. The heavies melted away as quickly as they had appeared and Steve was shaking my hand while trying to explain to a somewhat surprised and shaken Whitney, who the strange man was standing in front of her.

We headed back to my house in Chris' car. It seemed a good time to take a quick 40 winks and recharge the batteries. The next thing I know Chris was shaking me awake and thrusting a mobile phone in to my hand. It was the BBC and I was live on air, Radio 5, I think. I don't remember too much about the interview, but I think I got away with it!

Initial reports from Bloomsbury were very encouraging. There were good displays of the book in many stores and it was selling well. In fact I was told it would have been the number one best seller at the time but was kept off the top of the charts because of the bookshops that refused to report sales of *Odd Man Out*. The reason given was that some of the staff objected to a 'criminal' benefitting from his crime. I wonder if they still feel that way about certain politicians and their autobiographies?

Four years later Guy Ritchie's film, *Lock, Stock and Two Smoking Barrels*, would make gangsters 'chic' and fashionable, and the shelves and sales charts were full of criminal autobiographies, biographies and other tales. No complaint then from the shops or their staff as they counted their own ill gotten gains.

As I could not go to Britain to promote the book we had to come up with a few clever promotional ideas, one of which was to hold what I believe to be the first ever book signing by fax. If you don't know what a fax is, ask your grandparents!

The bookstore chosen was Murder One on the Charing Cross Road, a shop that had always taken crime writing seriously. We agreed a time and Murder One put the news out to its regulars. I addressed the gathering over a speakerphone and then one by one the people came on the line to talk to me. Once I had their name Johnny Pickston would take over the phone and have a natter while I wrote out a personal dedication that we then faxed through to the store. Once it was all over we packaged up the faxes and sent them to Murder One so each of the people could pick up their original. For many years people would tell me that behind the till you could see the fax I sent to the store. Sadly in 2009 Murder One shut up shop and was restricted to on line sales. Now that is a crime.

Odd Man Out continued to sell well and had put me back in the spotlight. I was pleased that it had been well received, and heard that even a Polish and a Japanese language version had been published. But not everyone was a fan. A certain lady in Australia had taken umbrage and was far from happy by what she had read.

The lady was Charmian, and for what seemed liked months she avoided my calls. When I did get to speak to her she let me have it with both barrels. 'Did I really need to list all of my conquests?' she asked. She was clearly hurt so I took the only course open to me and blamed Chris who had helped me to write the book. I told her he had been a typically cunning journalist who had got me to reveal all. Perhaps he had hacked my phone. Charmian was far too smart to fall for that one, and knew me too well. She knew there was the only one person to blame, and it certainly wasn't Chris.

In my defence, the reaction I got from people who had read the book was that they all wanted to meet Charm, and said she came across as a very special lady. A lot said they could not work out what a nice girl like Charm had ever seen in a man like me. I often wonder myself, and never took it for granted. She is a very special lady and remains so to this day. She will always be very, very special to me. Hopefully I have now corrected the errors she spotted in the first edition. I have a good memory, but Charmian's is better.

During April 1994 the British Foreign Secretary Douglas Hurd made a visit to Brazil. In Rio, Hurd was staying at the Copacabana Palace. I had received a call from a lady travelling with the Foreign Secretary's party who was the daughter of a Lord who had met me on a previous visit. He had asked his daughter to deliver a little present to me and I agreed to meet her in the new bar at the Copa. Little did she or I know that we were sitting exactly in the path of where Hurd was scheduled to pass on his way to dinner with the Governor of Rio. Hurd's handlers were convinced I was sitting there to confront and embarrass the Foreign Secretary. Nothing could have been further from my mind, as at the time I did not even know he was in Rio. It is how rumours about me start and take on a life of their own.

But as 1994 came to a close things overall were looking good. I was a best selling author and I was enjoying life in Rio where lots seemed to be going on. I even got a call from my Scottish agent to say that Bloomsbury were asking 'what's next?'

Sales of *Odd Man Out* were good enough for Bloomsbury to want a follow up and they were looking at ways to develop their budding author. I still had my plan for a Rio guide, but they didn't fancy that. I also liked the idea of doing a cookbook, *Ronnie Biggs' C(r)ook Book For the Single Man on the Run*. I was going to open with porridge, which can be deceptively difficult to make. Bloomsbury, on the other hand, thought I should try my hand at crime fiction, and if possible a crime that had a link with the Great Train Robbery, my 'calling card', as they politely put it.

I retired with Chris to one of our favourite Rio watering holes, the Casa da Suica in Gloria, for an extended lunch. Later over a glass or two of schnapps with the owner, Volkmar Wendlinger, we came up with the plan to tell the fictional story of the three robbers who got away. The three for whom the train robbery was the perfect crime.

Chris and I had a lot of fun coming up with the story line and the plot twists, and there were a few outrageous ones we had to bin. At times I also had to rein in Chris when some of his fiction came a little too close to the facts for comfort. I have always believed it was up to the three involved to tell their story if they ever wanted to. I was once offered one million dollars to name names, but despite what some people might like to think, I don't always have a price.

The new book had a working title of *Running Three*, but ended up being published as *Keep On Running* on 31 October 1995. Despite being billed clearly as a work of fiction, it did not stop some of the media going over the text with a fine-toothed comb looking for leads. Even the august *Sunday Times* ran with a sizeable story under the title of *'Did great train robber flee with fortune in diamonds?'*

Michael Argyle QC, who had defended me at the trial in 1964, and who went on to become an Old Bailey judge, told the paper that a prosecution witness had informed him about the diamonds. Well Michael, I have one thing to say: Bollocks! If there were any diamonds on the train I certainly did not see any of them, or get my hands on them, and neither did anyone I knew.

At the end of November 1994 I received a number of calls from the media in London. They called after Buster Edwards had been found hanged in his lock up. I did not have much to say, but promised to have a couple of beers for him and remember him as a jolly fella who was not too serious about life. In truth I had never spent that much time with Buster, other than at the farm. Many of the gang I only got to know when we were being held in Bedford and Aylesbury in the run up to the trial. Buster was on the run, and by the time he was caught I was long gone and had been living in Australia for nearly a year. But Buster's death, along with that of Paul Seabourne, was a stark reminder that we couldn't all live forever and that Old Father Time was catching up with us all, however fast or far we chose to run.

A LONG DARK TUNNEL:
DEATH AND FAILING HEALTH

Stick 'em up, put your hands in the air and samba on your feet.

Unidos do Porto da Pedra, Carnival 1998

'Never walk backwards into a madman's cage... especially if you are wearing a kilt.'

Charles Bronson, August 1999

At the beginning of 1995 you would have found me hunkered down in Santa Teresa in front of my computer putting the finishing touches to *Keep On Running*. Chris and I were giving the manuscript one final polish before getting our masterpiece off to Bloomsbury.

Anyone who has spent serious time in Rio will know that at the start of the year there is a certain amount of anticipation and excitement in the city as the locals turn their attention to carnival, which would take place at the end of February. But in 1995 the city seemed extra excited as it was going to get an early bonus in the shape of the Rolling Stones. The band was coming to Rio at the beginning of February to perform its full *Voodoo Lounge* tour for two nights at the Maracanã Stadium.

As a great believer that all work and no play can make Ron a dull boy, I was looking forward to taking a break from my literary endeavours and getting the chance to see the Stones.

This would be the first performance of the Rolling Stones in Brazil, although Charlie Watts had brought his quintet on a tour in 1992, and back in 1981 Mick Jagger had been expected to spend several months in the Amazon while filming *Fitzcarraldo* with Werner Herzog, but when the lead fell ill, the project was delayed and Jagger had to drop out. Jagger did return to Rio in 1984 to shoot a series of videos for his solo album *She's the Boss*. Among the cast were Dennis Hopper, Rae Dawn Chong and Jerry Hall, and a certain Julien Temple, the man who had been responsible for the Sex Pistols' documentary, *The Great Rock 'n' Roll Swindle*, directed them.

Now in these celebrity and media driven times the Stones' people should have contacted my people to set up a meeting. The only problem is I didn't have any 'people', so it was Rosa my cook and housekeeper, who answered the phone. The outcome was that the Stones were inviting me to the second show and that I should come to the Inter-Continental Hotel in São Conrado where the band were staying from where they would take Mike and I across to the stadium for the show. Keith Richards was Mike's idol, so there was no way he was going to miss out on this. Radio and TV in Rio were reporting that the Stones had been on fire for the Friday night show.

As so often seemed to happen, Mike and I were running a little late when we set out on the Saturday from Santa Teresa for the hotel in Mike's rather beaten up car. A car, I assured Mike, that nobody would want to beg, steal or borrow, not even in Rio.

Traffic was bad as people headed for the beach and when we got to the hotel the Stones' tour party had already set off for the stadium. There was only one thing to do, and that was to turn around and drive back across town to the Maracanã, although with a crowd of more than 150,000 expected, parking was never going to be easy. There was also the little problem of not having any tickets or passes in our hand.

Fame and notoriety can have its benefits, so we drove to the back gate of the stadium that Mike and I had often used when the Balão Magico had played shows at the Maracanã. Luckily the man on the gate recognised us and we were waved into the stadium and shown where to park. Word was passed through to the Stones' production team that 'Mr Biggs and party had arrived.'

We were collected and taken backstage, but I had never seen the Maracanã kitted out like this. It was a fantasy world. Mike and I were placed in the *Voodoo Lounge*, a room where we were plied with food and drink; by chance many of the serving staff were from one of my favourite barbecue houses so knew my tastes only too well. Not only was there food and drink, but also a full-size snooker table and video games. Mike and I were in seventh heaven.

We were then taken further into the inner sanctum where we found Keith slumped on a couch looking every inch the rock'n'roller he is. When he saw me he jumped up and we hugged.

'Keith, we're indestructible,' I joked as we continued our hug. Shortly after Ronnie Wood came and joined us along with Keith's dad, Bert, who turned out to be a fan.

'Right Ron, what do you and Mike want to drink?' Keith asked taking us back to the lounge. 'We've got everything.'

Forget the champagne, that I could get in Rio, I settled instead for a Guinness, which was to flow for the rest of the night, including during the show.

Charlie Watts was now introduced to us. The only one who kept his distance was Jagger who was more content to watch and video everything on a little camera he was holding. Mike was now talking music with Keith who was showing him his guitars. He asked Mike to play a few Brazilian numbers and joined in.

The band were incredibly relaxed considering they were about to step on stage and play to one of the biggest crowds in their long and illustrious career, and although it may sound like a cliché, it was as simple as one of the backroom boys coming into the lounge and announcing: 'Gentlemen, it's show time.' The band bid us a fond farewell, and exited out on to the stage.

Minders were sent to take us to the side of the stage from where we could watch the show. I stood with Bert Richards and we had a great time necking back the Guinness and cheering the boys on. It may only have been rock'n roll, but I loved it. Carnival was going to have to be really hot in 1995, if it was going to rival the Stones.

Sadly I wasn't in Rio when the band returned in February 2006 to give a free concert on Copacabana Beach for a crowd that I heard to be more than 1.5 million strong.

I also wasn't in great form to enjoy carnival in 1995 as I had managed to break the bottom of my left leg. I would love to tell you some dramatic story about how it happened, such as avoiding another kidnapping attempt or saving a runaway pram, but it wasn't quite like that. In truth I was looking up and admiring the carnival decorations going up around the Teatro Municipal in down town Rio and failed to notice the ornate chains they hung across the sidewalk to stop cars parking around the theatre. It caught me totally on the wrong spot and on the hop; as a result I went arse over tit and broke my left leg. I still bear the scars!

On 18 July 1995, during an official visit to London, the Brazilian Foreign Secretary, Luiz Felipe Lampreia, signed a new Extradition Treaty with his opposite number, Malcolm Rifkind. The press naturally put two and two together and came to five, and so assumed the treaty was all about getting Mr Biggs back to Blighty. But a treaty, as my lawyer pointed out, is not a law and so I put it to the back of my mind.

Despite the shadow of extradition, life in Rio was busy and fun, and on 31 October 1995 my fictional literary efforts were served up to an unsuspecting public. *Keep On Running* was in the British bookshops and selling well. Again I was called on to do a number of media interviews, most were trying to second guess what was true and what was fiction in the book, and I wasn't letting on. They all pushed for the names of the three that got away. They could dream. I am not a grass.

Whatever dreams I may have had, dark clouds were building on the horizon. Buster was not the only one to call it time. Tragically great friends Paul Seabourne and Armin Heim had passed on, two people without whom I would not have been enjoying my liberty. In August 1997 it was Roy James, the brilliant racing driver and London's best getaway driver, who died of heart disease aged just 62. He had been great company during the time we spent together in prison.

In late 1995 it had been the turn of my 'best friend', our pet Rottweiler, Blitz, who died suddenly and without warning. Blitz was a good companion and, despite being a softy if you knew him, he had a presence that made him an outstanding guard dog. I never doubted that he would fight to the death to protect me. If he had been with me when Miller and his gang jumped me, he would have made short work of them and it would not have been the dog's bollocks that Miller would have had to worry about.

We had other pets, including an aging Miniature Pinscher, Lua, who was going blind. Lua was lost without Blitz, so Mike persuaded me to go to the vet and pick out another baby Rottweiler, which we did. In honour of his noble predecessor he was also christened Blitz. He was a lovely dog, but not as passive as the original Blitz, and it took me a bit more time and effort to train him.

The death that hit me hardest was that of my long-time companion in Rio, Ulla Sopher. Ulla had been part of my life in Rio for over 20 years. She was a special lady who had helped keep me sane and on track on more than one occasion. She was gracious and generous. She was my best friend in Rio.

When I met her, Ulla was already the divorced mother of three young children, Carla, Felipe and Alex. Over the years we lived together off and on, but realised that the best formula for us was to have our own places; our own spaces apart – a form of 'marriage' I would recommend without hesitation. The arrangement certainly seemed to work for us, as we both liked to be free to follow our individual interests and hobbies. Ulla was into art and loved to paint, while I liked to spend hours pottering around the potting shed and my small garden.

Ulla always said she loved Ronnie Biggs the man, but she hated the circus that sometimes became part of my life by necessity. Ulla preferred to stay in the shadows and would be there to support me when I needed her. She was always there with a wise word, but stepped back into the shadows when I had to 'perform' or had to do a lot of entertaining.

It was from Ulla's apartment in Santa Teresa that I first set eyes and my heart on the apartment below, the flat that I eventually bought for Mike with his Balão Magico earnings. Ulla, meanwhile, had moved herself to an apartment in the back streets of Copacabana. She and I spent most weekends together. We played cards, Scrabble and snooker, went to the cinema. Everything that a normal couple of our vintage might do.

Ulla's death in January 1996 was not a death foretold. She had been having problems with her stomach, but nothing to raise any real concern other than she was having difficulty sleeping. Because of it, we had not seen each other for a couple of days and so I offered to go around to her flat and be with her, even fix some food if she felt like it. Being there I might even be able to take her mind off the pain.

When I got to Ulla's flat that afternoon I let myself in. I had keys to her flat and she had keys to mine. I saw Ulla sprawled out on her bed asleep. She was in a t-shirt with a towel wrapped around her waist. I decided to let her sleep on, as lack of it was what she had been missing and complaining about the most. I unpacked the food and wine, and the video I had picked out for us to watch. I put the television on at a low volume and settled down with the paper.

A couple of hours passed and I thought I should think of waking Ulla or she would not be able to sleep later in the evening. To start with I started to make a little more noise. I turned up the volume on the TV and when there was still no sign of Ulla, I decided to make her a cup of tea and wake her up. I took it into her and sat next to her on the bed. I noticed that she was bruised on her pale legs. I touched her leg to wake her and as soon as I did I knew something was wrong. I knew she was dead.

It was a terrible, terrible experience. In Brazil the repercussions of death move very quickly and most people are buried within 24 hours. I had to call Ulla's doctor to confirm my worst fears, as well as her family, including her children and brother. I also called my flat and left a message for Mike to call me.

I was in shock. At the funeral the following day all I could muster was 'Goodbye Ulla' as she was being lowered into the ground. I tried to force back the tears, but Mike could see my torment. He held me tight. 'Cry Dad,' he whispered in my ear. 'Do it. Do not hold back. Cry.'

I broke down in tears and wept and wept and wept. I had not felt like this since the day I got news of Nicky's death 25 years earlier. I knew for Mike's sake that I would have to gather up the pieces of my life and take this blow on the chin. Ulla's death left a big hole in my life. It left me broken. Normally in Rio I would have turned to Ulla at such a moment, but she was no longer around to help me.

My humour and state of mind was not improved when a few weeks later I put the food down for the dogs and Lua did not appear as usual. I called for her, but she did not come. I found her floating in the pool. She had been going blind and I still don't know if she simply lost her directions and walked into the pool or if the playful Rottweiler puppy gave her a push.

In the weeks that followed I moped around not discussing Ulla's death and how I felt with anyone. But a good friend was to come to my rescue. It was Wolkmar from the Casa Suiça who invited me for lunch in an attempt to shake me out of my lethargy. I drank far, far too much that day, even by my standards, but it is what I needed. Wolkmar knew I should not be left alone so took me back to his flat where I poured my heart out to him about Ulla and life in general.

Eventually I blacked out and Wolkmar put me to bed. I woke up around 4 am, but in my state I hadn't got a fucking clue where I was. I called Mike who had been worried sick by the fact I had gone missing, which was very unlike me. I told Mike I was in a dark room, but did not know exactly where. Eventually enough stuff started coming back to me and through my drunken haze I worked out where I had to be and asked Mike to come and get me. I snuck out of Wolkmar's house without waking him. Thanks for the shoulder to cry on Wolkmar. I needed it.

What I didn't need was the raging hangover, but I think it was the first warning that I need to start taking more care of my body. I decided I would drink less and eat healthier food. Which in Rio is often easier said than done. Prior to Ulla's death I had accepted an invitation to address the Young Presidents' Organization's annual summit that was going to take place in Manaus in May. They wanted me to talk to the young CEOs on the topic of crime and rehabilitation, something they could all probably put to good use later in their careers. I was not sure if I was in the right frame of mind to attend such a public event, but I knew that Mike and I could do with the money, as well as the break. Mike was also keen to visit Manaus so that he could pick up some new music equipment in the tax free zone.

I'll give credit to these young presidents and CEOs, they sure knew how to put on a good spread and enjoy themselves. Part of the millionaire event was an overnight trip on the Amazon on a couple of luxury yachts. As some of the cabins were better than others an American lady, who was one of the organisers, suggested we put all the cabin keys in a basket and picked them out at random. I sent Mike to pick out our key, but told him to try and get hold of number eight as that is my lucky number. Lucky, having been born on the eighth day of the eighth month. Mike managed to get hold of the key without letting anyone see he was peaking. Like father, like son, you could say, but there was nothing underhand, it was just a hunch I had, but a hunch that paid off as cabin eight turned out to be the presidential suite. I'm not sure Mike has ever believed me that I didn't know the number of that suite, but I really didn't Your Honour!

Back in Manaus Mike also made the discovery that his dad had been a porn star when he spotted a magazine in a shop with my name across the cover. When he picked it up he found it was a porn mag with lots of photos of me frolicking in a pool with scantily clad young ladies. He took great delight in bringing it back to the hotel to show me and I had to explain that Armin had taken the photos during a shoot for the *Electric Blue* video series. Sadly I no longer had a copy to show him, but if anyone comes across a copy, do let Mike know.

Most of the rest of 1996 and 1997 were something of a blur, but just as I was starting to pick myself up and get back to some form of normality came the hammer blow that the new extradition treaty between the British and Brazilian governments was about to become law. The details of how the new treaty might affect me were not at first clear, but on 14 August 1997 both governments ratified the treaty. Just two months later, on 29 October, the British Foreign Secretary, a certain Mr Jack Straw, officially asked Brazil to send me back to Britain.

I think it was the first time I had come across Jack Straw, but it certainly was not going to be the last. In many ways Straw seemed to pick up the mantle from Jack Slipper in pursuing Ronnie Biggs. What is it with people called Jack?

The newspapers, of course, were straight on the phone wanting to know my thoughts on the extradition treaty. I told them that I had no plans to fight extradition if that was what the Brazilian Government agreed to, but by choice I wanted to stay on in Brazil.

I have no idea if the British Government, which over the years I have learnt works in mysterious ways when it chooses to, already knew what the answer to its extradition request would be, or if they were just going through the motions to keep a certain section of British society happy. Happily for me, Brazil's

Supreme Court did not take long to rule, and on 12 November my lawyers, Luiz Fernando Gevaerd and Edson Abdalla, called me to say the court had rejected the request as it had ruled that the statute of limitations had run out on the robbery as the crime had been committed more than 20 years earlier.

For the second time in my life a court in Brasilia had granted me my freedom, and this time they had closed the book once and for all. I now knew if I was ever to return to Britain it would be on my terms and because of my decision and nobody else's, unless 'somebody' decided to be the new 'John Miller' and have me kidnapped.

While I had tried to remain calm on the outside, the ruling was a huge relief. There was now a very small chink of light at the end of what had been becoming a very long and dark tunnel.

I had also tried to remain calm when in 1996 the news reached me that Charmian had been diagnosed with two primary cancers. She was operated on and spent over a week in intensive care before undergoing over six months of chemotherapy. Always the fighter, Charmian thankfully fought the cancer and won, but as so had often been the case I could not be at her side to help and, in fact, it was Charm who came to see me. Dropping in on Rio on her way back to Australia after a visit to the UK.

Not long after the Supreme Court's decision that allowed me to stay in Brazil I was approached by one of Rio's major samba schools, Unidos do Porto da Pedra, who had decided they wanted to give me the ultimate accolade and make me the theme of the school's carnival presentation for 1998.

To a non-Brazilian audience it is difficult to explain just how big a deal it is to be honoured by a samba school in such a way. This was like a knighthood in Britain, but bigger. Very few foreigners have ever been honoured in such a manner, and even fewer have been alive to actually enjoy the honour. Given my love of samba and carnival I was hugely flattered. The samba was *Samba no pé e mãos ao alto, isto é um assalto*, which roughly translates as *Stick 'em up, put your hands in the air and samba on your feet*.

I am not sure exactly what happened, but I was suddenly struck down by an unusual and rare dose of common sense. Something was making me very uneasy and I realised that after the kind and considerate way the Brazilian government, its courts, and its people had treated me; I might just be over stepping the mark to become a focal point of carnival, an event that was so important to so many. I had no wish to offend or embarrass my hosts and when I heard the samba school planned for me to stand in front of a replica of the train from the robbery, I decided it was a step too far and declined the offer to appear with the school on the night of the parade.

My decision was not to deter Mauro Quintaes, the carnavalesco or director of Porto de Pedra, so he put the word out that he needed a Biggs look alike. 'I'm not going to change my plans just because he refuses,' he told the press. 'We must now search for a replacement Biggs.'

It was not very flattering to hear he was looking for a 'large old man with white skin and slicked back hair.' I think it is fair to say that the man who stood in for me, looked nothing like me. In fact he looked more like the bloke from the *Sopranos*.

Sadly for Mauro and Unidos do Porto da Pedra the presentation did not go down well with the judges that year and the school ended up coming 14th out of the 15 schools parading, and was relegated to a lower division. Happily they did bounce back to the top division the following year, but by then Mauro had been fired as its canavalesco.

Maruo, it turned out, had been working through a trilogy of themes that looked at groups 'marginalised by society'. In 1997 he had focussed on madness, my year was to be thieves and robbers, and if had continued with the theme, it would have been prostitutes in 1999.

Unidos do Porto da Pedra wasn't the first honour bestowed on me by Brazilian musicians. In the early 1990s I was approached by a local group calling themselves Os Intocáveis (The Untouchables), who asked me to appear in a video for their single *Ronald Biggs prá presidente*, or *Ronald Biggs For President*. The song was a catchy, light-hearted protest song about what had been going on with the Brazilian government and made the point that if you were going to have a bunch of crooks running the country, you might as well elect a professional crook, a crook such as 'Ronnie Biggs'. I'm not sure of the message, but I had fun making the video which can still be be found on YouTube.

Mike was also getting more heavily involved in the Rio music scene, although he was having to make the difficult adjustment of not being a major child star who could demand, and usually get exactly what he wanted from his record company, promoters, etc. Now he had to graft to make his mark

One of Mike's projects was to build and operate with his friends their own studio in Rio. As some of his friends had more 'live' money, as we say in Rio, to invest than Mike or I, I decided my investment would be my time in helping Mike to build the actual studio. I worked daily from 6.30 am to 4 pm and soon had the studio ship shape and ready for business. It did me good as it gave me a purpose and kept my mind off other sadder things.

In early March 1998, about a month after the carnival parade, I was sitting at home chatting with my friend Lou, the wife of Kevin Rawlings, and her son, Sol, as well as Ian, an Aussie pal up to visit from São Paulo. As per usual we were having a cold beer or two, and sitting around shooting the breeze. What happened next I can only describe as an out of body experience. I found myself observing the other people in the room, but it was as if I was looking at them from behind a window. There was no sound, just vision. I could see mouths moving and people looking at me, even touching me. Then nothing. I had had a stroke.

According to those in the room I even managed to keep a grip on my beer throughout, and they had to prise it out of my hand. What a way to go! When I did come around I apparently decided for no good reason that a bath would make me feel better. Luckily I did not pass out again in the bath, but I wasn't feeling any better so Lou drove me across to the São Silvestre Hospital.

The next thing I remember is coming around in hospital. I say remember, but it was all a bit of a blur and my speech, I am told, was a total slur. John Pickston and Lia were there by now, as was Mike's good friend Eric.

Mike had been away, but was tracked down by Eric and he rushed to the São Silvestre. He found me confused and in tears. Not only was I having problems speaking, but I could not remember the most basic facts such as the names of my mother and father, or even when I was born. But the doctors assured me that it was quite normal and that in a week or so I would be as right as rain, or as right as a 68-year old man living my life style in Rio could be.

I was released from hospital to recover at home. Mike took time off from the studio to look after me, along with Rosa who seemed to show me little or no sympathy, which was probably exactly what I needed.

The stroke was a warning and the doctors told me I would now have to watch what I ate and drank. The memory thankfully started to return and so did my speech, but much to Rosa's amusement I seemed to have far more trouble with my Portuguese than my English, and she enjoyed pretending she could not understand me.

Once I could look after myself, Mike went back to work in the studio as well as touring Brazil with his band. Mike's stock musically was rising and he got an invitation to play percussion at the Montreux Jazz Festival behind Roberta do Recife, the daughter of Robertinho do Recife. A visit to Switzerland would also allow him to catch up with his mother.

Mike was now more committed than ever to his girlfriend, Veronica, and had moved in with her, living in a small bedsit but still coming home for food and to get Rosa to wash his clothes. In early 1999 Veronica discovered that she was pregnant and Mike broke the news to me that I was going to be a doting grandfather, he also suggested that given the news he and Veronica should both move back into the house. I was delighted for them; it would be good to have them around.

I was now feeling well enough to receive paying visitors again, and to enjoy the odd glass of wine or two with them. My doctor, however, had other ideas and decided it was time to curtail one of life's little pleasures. He told me that it was not a good idea for a man of my age, and who had suffered a stroke, to still be smoking dope.

With my seventieth birthday looming in August 1999, I was coming under pressure from several quarters to throw one last big party. A last big bash until I retired to a quieter life. At the time I was seriously considering moving out of Rio to free up the house for Mike and his family, and go and live on a friend's farm and breed carp. Not rock'n roll, but I could cope. I also learnt that I had become a grandfather with the birth of a daughter to Chris and his wife, so I was stating to feel my age!

Word quickly spread about the party and I was pleased to hear that a few old mates and some new ones were going to cross the pond to celebrate.

Bruce and Nick Reynolds said they would be there. Roy "Pretty Boy" Shaw, who had shared mailbag-sowing duties with me in Wandsworth, and who had visited me for a lively Christmas in 1998, was another. As was Tony Hoare, one of the writers of Z Cars and Minder. Dave Courtney, who I had never met, also jumped on the bandwagon thanks to a media deal he had done to help get the others out to Rio.

Gus and Sheila Dudgeon confirmed they would be coming, as did Breiti from Die Toten Hosen, and Chris Pickard, who had been up in Los Angeles trying to get interest from the Hollywood studios for a film of my life. Filmmaker Max Carlish had also put a deal together to come down and film the gathering of the great, the good, and the not so good.

In total I was expecting about 150 friends to descend on the house in Santa Teresa, and not just to celebrate my 70th, but also the 36th anniversary of the train robbery and my improving health. The invitations to the party were printed on the back of a £5 Monopoly note and said 'Advance to GO collect £2,631,784 and scarper.'

The planning was something of a military campaign as Mike and I worked out the food, the drink, the entertainment, and where to house the overseas guests. I was also coming to the realisation that this was going to be more than a one-night stand, as I would have to entertain and wine and dine my British guests for at least a week. And these were people who liked to enjoy themselves and party hard, seriously hard.

Through a Scottish friend, Billy, who had a bar in Botafogo, thousands of bottles of beer and soft drinks were delivered to the house, along with crates of champagne and wine, and over 50 kilos of meat for the barbecue. I did not know at the time, as Mike was sworn to secrecy, but it was another good and very generous Scottish friend, Brian Running, who I had enjoyed many a long drinking session with over the years, who covered the cost of the beers. Thanks, Brian, that was one hell of a round to get in.

Brian, who lives in Miami, remains a very good and generous friend through good and bad times and he often finds time to come and see me at the nursing home and take me out to hear some live jazz, something that remains a passion. Brian also took me to see Brazil play Scotland at the Emirates.

The media in Britain was now speculating who might turn up for the 70th celebration. A full train robbery reunion was mooted in one paper, others suggested that Jack Slipper would attend, about the only one missing from the guest list was Lord Lucan.

The main group of overseas guests made quite a splash as they strode through Gatwick Airport to catch the flight to Rio. The Sunday Telegraph referred to them as 'a charabanc load of sixties villains.' It included Bruce, Nick, Roy, Tony and Dave, and thanks to a generous media benefactor they would all be flying in business class, as was a certain Prince of Darkness to be, Peter Mandelson, who was a little surprised and I am sure put out by the passenger manifest on his flight.

It was a great party, even by my standards, with guests from every walk of life. There were politicians, judges, lawyers, doctors, musicians, all rubbing shoulders with a good mix of what the Guardian classified as 'rogues'. Lovable rogues, I would like to think.

The media were out in force. Five TV crews mingled with the guests, as did photographers and journalists, many of whom had become close friends during my time in Rio. If they could make some money off me, I was happy for them. Brand 'Biggs' was alive and well.

The booze and the stories flowed as we all made up for lost time. To the bemusement of some of the Brazilian guests Roy demonstrated his knack of eating a series of beer and wine glasses, as well as some other party tricks involving a cigarette and a certain appendage that are not suitable for a family audience.

Dave Courtney presented me with a hand-made birthday card from Charles Bronson. It said 'Never walk backwards into a madman's cage… especially if you are wearing a kilt.' Perhaps that was the best way to describe my house that night, a madman's cage.

At one point I had to cut the cake and thank the guests. Somebody had put a plastic bobby's helmet on my head and I wore a special t-shirt that said 'Happy Birthday Ronald Biggs' and had a picture of my head on a £5 note. To give the press the picture that they really wanted, Bruce and Roy flanked me.

That picture nearly came back to haunt me as when I was waiting for my parole in 2009 the Ministry of Justice used it as an example that I been consorting with criminal elements, even if they were retired. It had to be pointed out to them that just off camera were a High Court Judge, a member of the House of Lords, several senior police officers, and I could go on.

In the early hours, as the party was in full flow, I was talking with my lawyer and good friend, Wellington Mousinho, when we saw that the people standing at the bottom of the stairs that lead down to the apartment from the street, were getting a little agitated. I looked up to see a full SWAT team from the Federal Police descending on the apartment and armed to the teeth. The leader of the team came in, opened his arms and gave me a big hug. He was an old, old friend from my time of having to sign on each week with the federal police, since when he had risen up through the ranks. He was on his way to raid a nearby favela for drugs, but was not going to miss the chance to drop in and wish me a happy birthday. And people ask me what I love about Brazil and the Brazilians?

As the night wore on I started to wilt, but tried to put on a brave face for my guests. Mike voiced his concern that I should sneak off to bed, as did Gus and Breiti, but I stayed put.

The next week passed in a blur of activity, and for all the wrong reasons. This was serious party time with the boys and girls as we burnt the candle at both ends and then some. When my band of merry men had to head back to dear old Blighty I was sorry to see them go, but glad of the chance to catch up on some much needed sleep and get back to my proper diet. There would be no wine, beer or red meat for a time.

It's all too easy to be wise after the event, but did my party contribute to my later health problems? I would be a fool to think otherwise.

With the expense of the party, I needed to think of ways to restock the coffers. Luckily a few months previously I had been contacted by an Australian outfit called Advanced Hair Studio, a hair loss treatment that was being touted by the likes of England cricketer Graham Gooch and Wimbledon striker John Hartson, and in more recent times by their poster boys Shane Warne and Austin Healey. I was to shoot a print and TV ad for them and the make-up people would be brought in to give me a before and after look, although I had been undergoing the hair graft treatment for a few weeks. One of my lines was to be: 'I have been involved in the greatest robbery of all time - the one off the top of my head!'

What I have always liked about the Aussies is that they have never been afraid to use controversial figures and humour in their ad campaigns, and the Advanced Hair Studio was certainly not making any excuses for using me. A date in September was set to do the photo and TV shoot.

'We used Ronnie Biggs in our advertising because he was the last person you would expect to be in an advertisement for the Advanced Hair Studio,' company chairman Carl Howell told the press. 'We are trying to make this treatment more acceptable, like visiting the dentist and that is why we use celebrities.'

I was slowly coming to the realisation that I had not fully recovered from the party. I was feeling tired and drawn. Mike was telling me to take it easy, and he could sense that the photo and TV shoot was troubling me, something I would normally do in my sleep and without thinking about it.

On the eve of the TV shoot I found myself having problems remembering my script. I wanted to call the treatment a 'wig' rather than an extension or graft. 'Wig' was strictly not in the Advanced Hair Studio vocabulary.

My mind was taken off the task by a call from Chris Pickard who was now in London. He had an update on our film project, although not the news I was exactly expecting.

Chris had been talking with a couple of the big Hollywood studios and somehow the book and the project had found its way over to the television division of one of the studios in New York. They called Chris and told him how much they loved the story of Ronnie Biggs, but they had a couple of questions to ask. The first was if it would be okay to relocate the train robbery from England to the U.S., as this would play better with their viewers. Chris was slightly bemused, but said we could think about it. There were other questions and clarifications until it reached the point of casting when the studio executive told Chris that they were thinking of approaching Wesley Snipes to 'play the part of Ronnie Biggs'. It was at this point that the penny dropped and Chris realised the studio thought my story was fiction and not fact. We did not hear from them again, although I still like the idea of Wesley Snipes playing me.

Chris wished me well with the TV recording and said if I was worried about my lines I should get Mike to stand beside the camera with a prompt board. In fact Chris joked it needed just one prompt: 'Not a wig!'

I never did get to shoot the ad or finish my hair treatment as that evening, 15 September 1999; I had another and much stronger stroke. Luckily Veronica spotted it and called Mike who was at the studio. He rushed back and decided he had to get me to a hospital. I thought I was making total sense and everything was okay, but he could not understand what I was saying as I was slurring my speech very, very badly. As I did not qualify for free treatment under the Brazilian health service, Mike had to scrape some cash together and get me down to a private clinic.

I had not been long at the clinic when my condition deteriorated and they had to stabilise me. Mike was not about to give up on me and kept talking, even though I appeared to be asleep. He asked me a number of questions and said if I could understand him to give the thumbs up. Which I apparently did. He even checked where I had stashed some money for a rainy day, as he would need it to pay for the hospital. He gave me various options until he hit on the lampshade, and I gave him the thumbs up. It just shows how ill I must have been to tell Mike where my secret stash was!

Fortunately I was still in hospital when a week later I was hit by a third and even stronger stroke. This was the stroke, I have been told, that did most of the damage as far as my speech is concerned.

I was in hospital, an expensive hospital, for over three and a half weeks before they said it was safe for me to return home. Even then I needed round the clock nursing, as although the stroke had not done too much damage to my movements and mobility, I still could not dress myself, or shave, or even feed myself. The nursing was costing £40 a day, which for Mike and I was a fuck of a lot of money. Money we did not have.

However bad I looked from the outside, at least my brain was still functioning and it was becoming clear to me that the damage done by the recent strokes was far, far greater than by my first stroke.

I knew I was facing another sentence; only I had no idea for how long. Was this a life sentence, a couple of years, or would I recover, including my voice, quickly.

For now the tunnel was darker than it had ever been and without the smallest chink of light. What made it worse was that I could scream; yet nobody could hear me.

Chapter Seventeen

TIME FOR HOME:
SAUDADES FOR RIO

The loss of his speech is a painful blow for a born gabber and a man who, as Hamlet says of Yorick, 'could set the table on a roar'.

Steven Berkoff

We are locked together by our past and it's only right that I bring Ron home. It's what the Americans would call closure.

Bruce Reynolds

Recuperation was turning in to a long, boring and frustrating period. Perhaps because I had recovered so quickly from my first stroke I was finding it difficult to accept my current state, especially not being able to talk. I was starting to feel like a prisoner in my own body.

One of the first people to drop by and visit was quite unexpected. It was Steven Berkoff who was back in Rio to perform his one-man show. He had heard of my stroke and made a point of coming around to see me.

The nurse did her best to make me look respectable for Steve and I shuffled through to the sitting room to meet him. Steve was on great form and did everything in his power to cheer me up. He talked and reminded me of little events from the past when he was filming *Prisoner of Rio*. He talked of the director and when I agreed with him I gave him the thumbs-up. He compared the director's obsession with having dozens of takes to having a wank, and I clapped my hands in glee. We clearly had similar views of Mr Majewski's artistic talents.

Steve was wonderfully patient with me as I scribbled down questions and answers on a pad. He reminded me that during the filming we decided to have a joint birthday party. His fiftieth and my fifty-seventh. I had suggested we split the costs, it was only later that he realised he had about four friends in Rio, while I had hundreds.

Steve later wrote an article in *The Times* about our meeting. He ended it: 'We leave and climb the stairs, accompanied by a friendly black cat that walks us to the corner as if it was standing in for its master. Yet one cannot help but feel that this is a hint to show us that Biggs still has one more life left.'

I did not know how many lives I did have left, but meeting Steve made me feel a bit more normal, yet it also made me realise how difficult it was going to be to communicate with people. I was also tiring easily. I had real concerns for the future. In my state there was little chance that I could or would be a breadwinner. Ironically, however, the print versions of the Advanced Hair Studio ads were starting to appear in Britain. Complaints to the Advertising Standards Authority followed, including one that suggested the campaign would encourage crime!

Thankfully just before I had the second stroke I had been contacted by Jane Cavanagh, the MD of a British computer games company called SCi Entertainment. SCi was famous for having developed the controversial hit, *Carmageddon*. Jane had the idea of developing a game based around the Great Train Robbery, but I told her that if the game was going to be more 'robbery' than 'Biggs', then Bruce Reynolds also needed to be involved. Even with my stroke Jane was happy to go ahead with the contract and Mike flew to London to pick up a much needed advance payment and to sign the contract alongside Bruce. If we were careful the money would just about keep us going through the year.

With the contracts signed and sealed, SCi could start planning how they would announce the game to the world. Jane realised they would need some promotional shots and as I could not go to them, they would have to come to me, and that included bringing Bruce out to Rio. It was a real tonic to see my old friend, but he could not hide the fact that he was concerned at my appearance and state of health. I think we both secretly thought this would be the last time we saw one another.

It was certainly the last time I saw SCi, as after all the talk and payments, nothing ever did become of the game, but it did generate a lot of positive coverage for the company in the business press and helped boost its stock price.

Charmian also took the trouble to come and see me in 1998. She tried to help me with my speech therapy and to cheer me up, but I know I was not a very good patient and not a lot of fun to be with. Before she left Charm bought me a new gas stove to replace the one that was on its last legs. I'm not sure I ever thanked her properly.

Towards the end of 1999 an ever-darkening cloud was settling over my head. I had no quality of life and I was only causing problems for Mike and Veronica. I could not see how it would get any better. At that point I decided it was time to put an end to it.

Early one morning I went into my bathroom with a sharp knife and slit both my wrists. I was sorry for how I might be found, but in my mental state I really did not care. I could not go on. It took a surprisingly short time until I blacked out.

Luckily, and I do say luckily, Mike woke early that day. He had come into my room to give me my medication. When he did not find me in bed he assumed at first that I was either in the lounge or the garden. When he could not find me he decided to check the bathroom. The sight that greeted him was not a pleasant one for any son. There was blood on the walls, blood on the ceiling, and on the floor. I was passed out face down in a growing pool of my own blood.

My timing, looking back, could have been better, as poor Veronica was nearly eight months pregnant and when you are in that state you really don't need to deal with what I had served up for her and Mike. The sight of her father-in-law on the floor started her contractions, so Mike had to try and calm Veronica while attempting to save my life. Multitasking to the nth degree.

Mike grabbed a couple of towels and tied them around my wrists to try and stop the immediate bleeding. I tried to kiss Mike goodbye, but fell back on the floor. I was passing out and coming to, occasionally trying to say how sorry I was. In my mind I could hear Mike singing. Mike lifted me up and got me to the bed, but I was still losing a lot of blood. He called a friend who was a doctor and he rushed straight round to see what could be done. He managed to stop the worst of the bleeding and then called for another doctor to come around and stitch me up. My right wrist was not too bad, but I had cut through the vein in my left. The doctor told Mike that in another twenty minutes I would have been a goner. A sobering thought, and I still bare the scars.

Despite all the excitement, Veronica had managed to stop her contractions by doing some deep, slow breathing. It was not an easy time for her because I was not the best of patients and often made things very difficult for her, even when she was getting up at three in the morning to give me one drug or another. Veronica was now running the day-to-day of the house, and trying to keep my often crazy demands under control. My mind and life was in turmoil.

Anyone who knows me well will tell you that attempting suicide was totally out of character, but that was the depths I had sunk to. Years later I discovered that to die you did not need to cut your wrists, as you can will your own body to shut down. That is exactly what I did when my parole was denied in 2009. Then, like in 1999, I decided to call it a day. On both occasions that was very nearly the end of my story.

A ray of light came into our lives on 22 January. Just before 6 am Veronica woke Mike to tell him the time had come. Her waters had broken. It was a Caesarean birth and Mike stayed in the room to watch. He felt sure that after dealing with all my blood he would be fine, but he admits to having wobbly legs.

At 8.52 am Ingrid arrived, weighing in at 3.33 kg about 7.3 pounds. Mike was a father and I was grandfather again. And son like father, just as had been the case when Mike was born, the father was not yet married to the mother. And just as when Mike was born, the media were lining up for a first photo of granddad and granddaughter. Mike sold the photos to the *News of the World*, which was very fitting as that had been his first UK cover story. Mike, however, did not want the photographer to see my bandaged wrists.

Mike now had a family to look after and to pay for, so he had to look at how we could make money. One suggestion was to set up a

'Ronnie Biggs' web site. The site did get launched, but Mike just missed out on a £100,000 investment as the dot.com bubble burst.

An opportunity that fell in our lap was the visit of Manchester United to Rio in early January 2000. The club was in town for the inaugural FIFA World Club Championship, but it is not a tournament they look back on with much affection. Their first game was a tepid one all draw with Necaxa of Mexico, which was followed by a 3-1 thumping from Rio's Vasco da Gama. The Red Devils did beat South Melbourne 2-0 in their last game, but by then it was too little too late and they were out of the tournament and on their way home.

Mike and I gambled that with Man U in town, so would a good number of their followers, some of which were likely to try and track down Ronnie Biggs. Mike had a new batch of t-shirts made up and we waited.

I was still not well enough either physically or mentally, so Mike launched a new 'Biggs Experience' where he had to entertain the visitors. He put videos on, told stories and did everything he could to keep the punters happy. At a suitable time I would then make my entry, shake a few hands and have my photo taken before retiring to bed.

It was depressing for everyone, and not what Mike and I would want to do, but we had no choice, as we desperately needed the money. Veronica gave us both a much-needed kick up the backside, pointing out that we were selling the t-shirts far too cheap. We had priced them at $10, but Veronica said that anyone who was coming to meet me would happily pay $20. She was right.

One of the other reasons I needed to raise money was to pay Rosa back. Rosa had scraped together all her life savings and given them to Mike to pay for the medical help and medication I needed to stay alive. I was very lucky with the people around me, but I knew I could not go on abusing or taking these friendships for granted.

One new friend I met in 2000, and whom I have been abusing ever since when he lets me, is Roy Pickard. I say met, but I had been corresponding with Roy since 1994. He had decided to read *Odd Man Out* while he was being held at Her Majesty's pleasure in HMP Wayland after a little misunderstanding over a robbery. Roy had enjoyed the book and sent me a cheeky letter to say so.

When I could, I did try and reply to fellow cons who had written to me from prison, so I dropped Roy a line and included a signed photo of me sipping champagne. I think Roy fancied the lifestyle as he eventually dropped by to see me in Rio and we hit it off from the start.

I kept in touch with Roy over the years and he was one of the few regular visitors to come and see me in both Belmarsh and Norwich, and was to become a rock that I could lean on once I was released.

In Rio it was now my turn to start to worry about Mike. Because of the strain I put him under he was drinking, putting on weight and even losing his hair. He admitted to his friends that he was a psychological wreck. I knew I was putting him under unimaginable pressure, but I did not know that our debts had ballooned to over £30,000 in the year since my first major stroke. Health care, if you are not insured, is not cheap in Brazil. Mike had had to put an album he was recording on hold, as he neither had the emotional strength or the money to pay the musicians to carry on.

Friends did still rally round. An American friend of ours, Diamond Dayne Henry, or Woody, not only offered financial support but offered Mike the opportunity to run an orphanage in Goiania in the north of Brazil, and take the family with him.

I did get another small payday in January 2001. I was contacted by DuLoren, Brazil's biggest lingerie company, who wanted to use me as part of a promotion for a new lingerie range. Would I object, they asked, to posing alongside a couple of underwear models and getting paid for it. Even in my weakened state I could not particularly see a downside to accepting the offer. That is how Milene Zaro and Francine Mello from the Elite Agency came to turn up on my doorstep.

They stripped for action and then wrapped in a Union Jack I was flanked by the two truncheon-wielding models for the shoot. I was never sure what exactly was in the advertising agency's mind, but I gather it was a clever play on the Portuguese word for lace (renda) and surrender (render-se), and so in their lacy finery the campaign slogan was 'Sr. Ronald Biggs, Renda-se.' Little did DuLoren, the agency, or the models know at the time of the shoot that the pictures from that day were going to go all round the world, and are still a favourite with the media and editors to this day.

In search of financial salvation, Mike headed off to London in late February to see what might be available for us back in the UK. Brian Running, who had paid for over 1,000 beers at my 70th birthday party, came to the rescue yet again and offered Mike $10,000 to help with the building and running of the web site.

During the trip Mike was introduced to Kevin Crace, an old friend of Bruce and Nick Reynolds. Nick thought Kevin might be able to help in a campaign to get me an 'amnesty' in the UK in case I ever needed it. It was Kevin who introduced Mike to people at *The Sun*. Not that *The Sun* had much interest in my amnesty, but they did like the idea of bringing me back to Blighty.

Kevin first made contact on 8 March with *The Sun's* Assistant News Editor, Graham Dudman who was to end up with the glamorous by-line in the paper of *'Head of Sun's Biggs Team'*.

'I've got a bloke here who wants to talk about Ronnie Biggs. Can you have a word with him?' the Editor's secretary asked Dudman. On the basis that it was always worth listening, if just for a minute, Dudman told the secretary to put the caller on.

'Ronnie Biggs wants to come home – and he wants *The Sun* to help him,' Kevin told a not unsurprisingly suspicious Dudman. However Dudman had heard enough and set up a meeting with Kevin and Mike for the following week.

Just after 2 pm on Friday, 16 March, Kevin took Mike and Nick Reynolds through the newsroom at *The Sun's* Wapping headquarters to meet with Dudman. Crime Editor Mike Sullivan, who was to be part of the meeting, looked up. 'Bloody hell,' he exclaimed, 'that is Michael Biggs!'

Negotiations started, and as always happens both parties were far apart on what we wanted and *The Sun* would offer. I'm not sure if I was the prostitute and *The Sun* was the john, or the other way around. But we knew we were simply haggling over the price to pay. Both parties were consenting adults and we weren't going to hurt anyone.

Mike was not at all happy with *The Sun's* offer or of my returning to the UK, and said as much on his return to Rio, but he still felt I should know the options open to us. I wrote on a piece of paper: 'I want to go'.

The next few weeks turned into a battle of wills. Mike simply did not want to entertain the thought or option of me returning to prison in the UK. Veronica even suggested selling the house if it would solve the financial issues.

When I first wrote *Odd Man Out* in 1993 I said that the thought that I might be returned to prison one day did not worry me unduly. It still did not. 'It's a bridge I'll cross if and when I have to,' I wrote. 'Pretty soon I'll be entering into the last scene of all and, if I'm to become a dribbling nuisance, one of Her Majesty's hostelries might be just the place to spend my twilight years.'

I had become that dribbling nuisance and felt that if I was to give Mike a real chance with his life, and new family, I had to unburden him and take my chances in Britain. I had not gone soft though, and my decision was based on Mike being able to negotiate a suitable payday from *The Sun* that would set him up and clear our debts. What was clear was that with my failing health and lack of any health insurance or pension plan, I would only drag the family down further if I were to stay on in Rio to die.

To be totally honest, I also quietly liked the idea of one last great adventure, even if they did end up slamming the prison door behind me and throwing away the keys. But if I was going to return to Britain, it was going to be on my terms. I would go there because I chose to, not because anyone else told me to go.

Back in London the group Mike had met at *The Sun* were like a dog with a bone, and they were just starting to appreciate how juicy this bone might be. They kept calling Kevin in London and Mike in Rio to put a series of proposals and counter offers for me to come back to the UK with them. Some of their initial ideas were a little far fetched. One had me flying back on a borrowed passport disguised as an elderly woman. I would then present myself at immigration and say 'Ronnie Biggs is back!'

If possible I had no wish to break any more laws to get myself back into Britain. Certainly none that could be used against me in the future. Unlike the team at *The Sun*, I had not got a single doubt about the massive egos at play in the British government and Scotland Yard. I knew if they had the chance to get me back behind bars they would jump at the chance. No questions asked.

To move the negotiations along *The Sun* sent Mike Sullivan and John Askill to Brazil on 6 April to try to persuade me to close the deal with them. After a week of talks *The Sun* camp came up with a plan and offer that was worth considering, and that included being flown back in a private jet. It did mean, however, that we would have to announce to the world that I was coming back so that we could apply for a British passport on which I could travel. For all my travelling it would be my first genuine British passport. I had never had one in my life as I had returned from Barbados to Brazil on temporary Brazilian papers.

Once everything was agreed, and Kevin and my UK lawyer, Jane Wearing, were happy with the arrangements in London, we set the time of my return for mid-May. Time enough, I hoped, to get my things in order in Rio and say a proper goodbye to the people that mattered most and who I loved. Mike was given the job of giving a heads up to a number of key insiders who should not be taken by surprise when the news did break. On 13 April Sullivan and Askill returned to London.

Sod's law came into play shortly after when on 1 May *The Sun* got wind that its exclusive had been compromised and a freelance journalist was shopping the story around in London that I was about to return to the UK. Sullivan rang Kevin with the news and Nick Reynolds called Mike. Shortly after Kevin rang Mike to say the proverbial was about to hit the fan, and we should be ready for all hell to break lose. The problem for Mike was that I was not at home but up at the Oscar Clarke Centre that helped people like me who had had strokes. They were giving me much needed speech and body therapy. Mike rushed around to pick me up and by the time we got back to the house *The Sun* had a simple message, and that was that it was now or never if we wanted the deal that was on the table.

The Sun's John Askill and photographer Harry Page rushed to Heathrow to catch the first flight to Rio. Mike Sullivan, not wanting to make the mistakes the *Express* had all those years earlier, went to Scotland Yard to brief the head of the Flying Squad, Detective Chief Superintendent John Coles, with what was about to go down.

To confirm what Sullivan was telling Coles, *The Sun* asked me to drop a note to Scotland Yard. The note addressed to Coles said:

'I would like to give myself up to you.
What I need is passport documentation to travel back to Britain.
I am prepared to be arrested at the gate when I arrive at Heathrow airport
and submit myself to the due process of the law.'

Ronald Arthur Biggs, Rio de Janeiro, May 2nd 2001.'

Just as I had done with my letter to the *Daily Express* back in 1974, I added my thumbprint for good measure. I thought Slipper would appreciate the gesture. Coles, who probably did not understand the significance of the print, was the officer in overall charge of the Met's Serious and Organised Crime group.

Despite appearances, the old adage of 'don't panic!' did not seem to be part of *The Sun* team's vocabulary or planning. Even I was calmer than they were. Graham Dudman and Mike Sullivan's first decision was that they would publish two spoof front pages on its early editions of Thursday, 3 May, giving Askill and Page one day in Rio to pull stuff together, then break the 'World Exclusive' of my return in the main edition that would circulate in London. Reporter Nick Parker and photographer Nigel Cairns had also jumped on a plane to Rio to join the fun.

As *The Sun* came to realise that the international correspondents based in Rio and the Brazilian press would be on the look out for me, and knew where I lived, it was clear that I had to be moved quickly from the apartment otherwise I would end up a prisoner in my own home. There was only the one way in to and out of the flat, and that was up the narrow stairs to the street. *The Sun* at first had the idea to take me to one of the main hotels in Rio and hide me away in a room. The hotel of choice was the Sofitel. With Mike's help, I got it across to them that I was actually quite well known in Rio and if I did enter a hotel they could kiss goodbye to any idea they had of keeping my location a secret.

Mike made a few calls, one to our good American friend, Diamond Dayne Henry, who was something of the American 'Ronnie Biggs' having escaped the clutches of the US tax authorities to escape what he called 'selective prosecution'. Dayne had a very big and secluded house at the end of Barra in a small-gated community that used to belong to one of the samba school bosses. The previous owner was also one of the bosses of the city's illegal numbers game, the Jogo do Bicho. When he was rounded up with the other bosses and put in prison, he sold the house on to Woody.

Everything moved very quickly and I had no real time to say goodbye to the house that had been mostly a very happy home to Mike and I for 17 years. There was no time for reflections or to feel sorry for myself. We had to move and very fast.

In a scene from a best spy thriller we made our way across Rio, double backing on ourselves and checking we had not been followed. We stopped en route to take a few photos with Corcovado and other Rio landmarks as a backdrop. When we got to Barra my American friend was pleased to see us, and from the open mouth of *The Sun* team I could see they were suitable impressed by the safe house we had organised for them.

As the news of my imminent return was broken by *The Sun* in their issue of 3 May, the world's media started to play 'Where's Ronnie?' Little did they know that I was sitting comfortably by the pool enjoying my last days of freedom and the Rio sun. Mike had put a message on the answer phone at home directing callers to contact Kevin Crace in London. He got his first call at 4.15 am on that Thursday morning. Welcome to the crazy world of Ronnie Biggs!

The Sun reporters were going to babysit its prize and world exclusive 24/7, but early on they got in to a dispute with Mike when they started trying to video everything. Mike pointed out that this was not part of the agreement. After a faceoff with Mike, they reluctantly backed down. Mike was doing me proud.

Behind the scenes *The Sun* had been exploring their options with the Foreign Office, the Home Office and Scotland Yard. Just because I said I wanted to come back to Britain did not mean they had to accept me. While *The Sun* fretted, I still had no doubts that the authorities would like to see my head served up for them on a silver platter, even if the platter belonged to Rupert Murdoch and a tabloid newspaper.

With my departure date brought forward *The Sun* now had to officially get me the passport on which to travel. The British Consul in Rio was put on stand-by to issue me with an Emergency Passport. But first, the then Foreign Secretary, Robin Cook, had to give his approval. Not wishing to take any chances with what had now become a sizeable investment for the paper, editor David Yelland put in a personal call to Cook.

The splash on the cover of *The Sun* of 3 May was 'Biggs On Way Back', which was accompanied by a rather glum photo of me signing the note to Scotland Yard. I was quoted as saying 'I'll face whatever punishment the authorities give me. I hope they will show me mercy.'

It was in this issue of *The Sun* that my famous wish to walk into a pub in Margate to buy a pint of bitter came out, as well as my apparent craving for a curry. As *The Sun* had a monopoly on the news and access to me, the story and quotes were printed verbatim in most of the other papers. It did not seem to matter that I had not touched booze or solid food for months.

That Thursday night saw another couple of The *Sun's* men, reporter Andrew Parker and photographer Marc Giddings, heading for Rio.

The Friday issue of *The Sun* milked the exclusive for all it was worth. The cover was me with my arms outstretched with the Christ statue behind in the distance, and the headline of 'CheeRio'.

A *Sun* poll had 57 per cent of its readers in favour of letting me go free, and 43 per cent saying I should rot behind bars. Sadly one of that latter group was the Home Secretary, Jack Straw, who told *The Sun*: 'The law is that any individual who is unlawfully at large from prison is liable to immediate re-arrest and return to prison as soon as it comes to the notice of the police.'

The Shadow Home Secretary, Anne Widdecombe was no fan either. Calling for a 'hard headed' attitude to me on my return, she told *The Sun*: 'It is not an advertisement for the rule of law that somebody can escape, live a playboy existence at a great distance, laugh at British law and come back saying. 'Now I'm here it's not worth pursuing me."

Miss Widdecombe, now a national treasure, never did become a fan or put me on her dance card, but she was strong enough as a politician to be quite outspoken as to why the refusal of my parole in 2009 was a farce. Even in the House she said it was time to let me go. Thank you Anne for that, I think. Now how about that dance?

Given I was not a very good interviewee, not being able to speak, and the journalists not having the patience or time to follow my spelling board, they decided it was easier to track down other people in my life to speak on my behalf.

Charmian, as always, was a class act and told *The Sun* when they called: 'I don't want to say anything yet, I just don't know enough.' Asked if she knew of my plans her reply was a sharp, 'not exactly, no.' She was telling the truth.

With my return I was happy to give Jack Slipper another payday. He was pictured with a copy of *The Sun* and gave them a suitably appropriate quote. 'I never thought I'd live to see the day when Biggs would be bought to justice. But I bear him no grudges.' Jack even admitted that when he met me in Rio I came across as 'a likable bloke'.

'I look back on the whole thing with fondness,' Jack told *The Sun*, 'because, in a way Ronnie made me famous and you do get philosophical in your old age. But it has been a lifelong saga. And when Ronnie does return and is brought to justice, it will mean my wife Anne and I can enjoy some peace of mind.'

The Sun was also quicker than Scotland Yard in tracking down members of the train robbery gang. Bob Welch and his wife Jean kindly said that if I had nowhere to go when I came back, their front door was always open. Roger Cordrey thought I was mad to come back, while Gordon Goody, who they tracked to Spain, said 'I just hope for Ron's sake they put him in a prison hospital. I don't envy Ron. I'd rather have been buried under that big mountain that overlooks Rio than end my days in a British nick.'

As I have come to expect in any story involving the Great Train Robbery, the Mills family was also tracked down for their thoughts which this time had me down as not only causing the death of Jack Mills but also his brother. Mills' nephew accused me of 'laughing' at his family. Nothing could have been further from the truth, either for myself or any other member of the gang.

Margate was enjoying its moment in the sun, despite some rather uncomplimentary photos comparing Copacabana today to Margate in the 1960s. Most of the people interviewed in Margate got in the spirit of the coverage and said they would be pleased to see me on my return. I'm sure the tourist board was happy, but naturally the local Tory MP, one Roger Gale, put out a statement that: 'He is a criminal – and criminals are not welcome in Margate. I would not be happy to see him here.' Considering Mr Gale is an ex-pirate disc jockey for Radio Caroline, you would think he would have been a little bit more sympathetic and hip to life. I wonder how many of his fellow MPs he barred from Margate after the expenses scandal?

Under the heading 'Daylight Robbery' *The Sun* pointed out to its readers that at the time of the Great Train Robbery a pint of beer would have cost 9p in Margate while in 2001 it was £1.90. Fish'n Chips had gone from 10p to £2.75.

Now nobody could ever accuse Rupert Murdoch, News Corporation or *The Sun* of being stupid or unprofessional, or at least they couldn't until the phone hacking scandal broke, but they wanted and were going to get their full pound of flesh from the Biggs circus.

Timing was now everything as there was no way *The Sun* was going to hand the initiative, and its 'Biggs exclusive' over to the other papers, even its' stable mate, the now late, great News of the World. It meant my return had to be stage managed not to benefit the Sunday papers. For that to happen I would have to fly out of Rio on Sunday afternoon, 6 May, in time to be the cover of the Monday paper, landing on Monday would give the paper further exclusive coverage of my return in Tuesday and Wednesday's editions. I would be *The Sun's* cover boy for an entire week, and not many people can say that, not even Jordan. Although for the tabloids you could say I had been the 'Jordan' of the 80s.

On the Saturday, in a neat twist and under the headline of 'We're Ron Our Way', The *Sun* ran a photo of its plane leaving Farnborough to pick me up and another photo of me looking seriously glum. The *Sun* also had the advantage of having a copy of the photo that would be on my temporary passport. Not one of my best, I got John Pickston to counter sign the passport application, as at least the consulate knew who he was and that he did know if he had Ronnie Biggs sitting in front of him or not.

The rest of *The Sun's* Saturday coverage was taken up with their "Flying Squad", or rather the group of people flying to Rio on the 14-seater Dassault Falcon 900EX. At the time is was rumoured to be Rupert Murdoch's own private plane, but I was later told it had been leased from TAG Aviation.

On board for the flight to Rio was *The Sun's* Crime Editor, Mike Sullivan, along with reporter Simon Hughes. Also on board in a gesture of solidarity to me were Bruce and Nick Reynolds. Bruce was resplendent in the same blue discharge blazer he wore when he left Maidstone Prison in 1978.

'I'm going to get my mate and bring him back before he dies, Bruce told Sullivan. 'I got him into it all those years ago when I persuaded him to join the gang and now I feel responsibility to be there for him now. Ronnie is a gambler and this is the final adventure for him. This is the final chapter in his life and it is the right way for it to end. We are locked together by our past and it's only right that I bring Ron home. It's what the Americans would call closure.'

The plane took to the sky at 3.07 pm that Friday, at the start of its 6,000 mile journey to Rio. It would stop to refuel at Ilha do Sal in the Cape Verde Islands. Before taking off Nick, always one to see the bigger picture, told *The Sun:* 'I know Ronnie is doing this partly because he feels he has become a millstone round his son's neck. The robbery has cast a huge shadow over Mike as well.'

On the plane's arrival in Rio early Saturday morning *The Sun* had to play another elaborate game of cat and mouse to avoid the attentions of the growing media pack that was building up in Rio as journalists were being flown in from all over the world. Bruce and Nick only had time for a quick wash and brush up at the Meridién Hotel before being brought to the house for an emotional reunion. We all knew it was going to be a very, very emotional few days.

Bruce and I both had a tear in our eyes as we hugged. 'I'm sorry I got you into this mess in the first place', he whispered in my ear. I tried to convey with my face, that I did not blame him in any way. It had been a great adventure, one I would not have wanted to miss for anything. I was a Great Train Robber and I was proud to be so.

As Bruce has noted there has always been warmth in our souls for each other that was hard to describe, going all the way back to when I had organised some hot chocolate for Bruce after he had been beaten up by some prison guards.

Also arriving that Saturday was Chris Pickard who had flown in from London. Chris had been tracked down by BBC Breakfast through Bloomsbury as they were looking for a talking-head for its Friday edition's coverage of my return. The BBC just assumed that Chris was an acquaintance and never thought to ask him if he was going to Rio or when he had last spoken to me. Even with the world and his friend looking for me, they forgot to ask if Chris knew where I was. Chris was bringing all the UK papers with him for me to see, *The Sun* team only having brought *The Sun*.

Having swapped taxis at various points in Rio, Chris met up with Mike and joined us at the house. The team was complete. We went through the papers seeing who was pro and who was against my return. Not surprisingly, being a *Sun* exclusive, the *Mirror* had myself, Murdoch and *The Sun* down as the devil incarnate. The editor at the time was a certain Piers Morgan who, I am certain, would now admit that he would have loved the story if he had had the opportunity. As it was, the entire *Mirror* coverage was going to be sour grapes from start to finish but I forgive you Piers.

Playing the tabloid games, as I have over the years, can be fun, but it can also be very hurtful to those around you that don't have the thick skin I have grown over the years.

Across the world in Australia the media were now door stepping Charmian in Melbourne, and *The Sun's* Jamie Pyatt got her to say a few words after he presented her with some photos of me in Rio. She thought I looked like a 'walking corpse'.

At the house Bruce, Nick and Chris all kept asking me if I was sure I wanted to return to Britain? Did I fully appreciate the likely outcome? From the coverage they had seen in the UK, and the way the government was reacting to the story, they had no doubts I would be locked up and the key thrown away. Clemency and forgiveness were not to be found on the government or Scotland Yard's dance card.

Under my agreement with *The Sun* I had the right to have a letter published on my return, so with the help of Bruce, Nick, Mike and Chris we started pulling something together. Because my contract with *The Sun* was torn up while I was on the flight back to Britain, the letter never got to be published, but much of its content is included in the opening chapter, 'Confessions, Apologies and Thanks'. At the time I did not think much about its non-publication, but it came back to haunt me years later as one of the reasons the Justice Department gave for not granting my parole was that I had never apologised or shown remorse. But what did they know?

Despite seeing the clock tick down on my time in Rio and as a free man, I tried to stay as upbeat as possible, although a lot of tears were spilt that day, especially when I cradled Ingrid in my arms. I realised this might be the last time I would see my granddaughter whose innocence shone through. Bizarrely I was going to have to spend my last night in Rio alone, except for the good company of Woody and his family. The reason was that the house and the neighbouring property had been hired out for a wedding reception. Now normally I might have been tempted to join in with the party, but it turned out the bride was the daughter of a senior Rio police chief and many of the guests would be law enforcement officers. Not that any of them were looking for me, I had done nothing wrong in Brazil, but it would certainly have blown the cover of the safe house and might have been an embarrassing distraction for them.

I woke up early on Sunday and enjoyed breakfast with Dayne who was supervising the clearing up after the party. Perhaps it was a case of the condemned man eating a hearty breakfast. As I had become accustomed to over the years, it was looking like it was going to be another glorious, hot and sunny day in Rio. But it was to be my last one.

As the morning ticked by we started to regroup at the house. One of *The Sun* team turned up with my Emergency Passport that I had to countersign. Bruce and Nick also arrived, and looked as if they had had a good night out on the town. Sadly I had been in no fit state to join them.

Mike checked and double-checked that all my most precious personal possessions, including my photos, favourite CDs and medications, were packed and ready to go.

I posed for a few last photos for *The Sun*, including one with the paper's entire "Biggs Team". I like to think that most of them in the few days they had been with me had started to realise that I was actually okay, and not the mythical figure, sometimes of hate, that had been painted in some sections of the media, including their own.

For hose who fancied it there was lunch and a few beers to be enjoyed, and I handed over my letter to Sullivan who duly dictated it over his mobile to the editorial desk in London.

As per my contract I swapped my Die Toten Hosen *'Carnival in Rio'* t-shirt for a bright red *Sun* t-shirt that I had to wear on the drive to the airport and while getting on to the plane. I was also wearing a baseball hat but the ever-generous Diamond Dayne insisted that I took and wore his prized cowboy hat. Some of the media made a lot out of the choice of the cowboy hat, but there was nothing more to it than wearing a present given to me by a good and kind friend.

Just after 1 pm I could tell *The Sun* team was starting to get itchy feet. It had become clear that they were still far from convinced that I would ever get on the plane. Probably not helped by the fact that Mike, Bruce, Nick and I had been winding them up whenever we could.

Word had also reached them from Rio Airport that the waiting press pack at Terminal 2 were growing in numbers and getting restless. Given the potential for things getting out of hand, *The Sun* suggested to Mike that it would be better if Veronica and Ingrid did not come out to the airport in the mini-van. I should have probably warned them about trying to take on Veronica and Mike. There was only ever going to be one winner.

Veronica told them that if she could not go to the airport to see her husband off, a partner she was not sure when she would see again, then Mike was not getting on the bus. No Mike also meant no Ron. Check-mate. Veronica and Ingrid were on the bus.

At 1.30 pm it was decided it was time to hit the road. I had one last bit of theatrics up my sleeve. As we were about to board the mini van I started to whisper something in Mike's ear. He turned to Mike Sullivan and said 'Dad's changed his mind. He's not going'. I'm just sorry I did not have a camera to catch the look on the faces of team *Sun*. I broke into a grin and gave them the thumbs up and a few nervous smiles filled their faces.

I gave Woody a big hug, and thanked him for all his hospitality. I would miss him, along with many other good friends I had come to know and love in Rio.

The actual ride across town to the airport was fairly uneventful. A bit of good natured bantering between Mike, Nick, Bruce and *The Sun* guys, but no sign that anyone had spotted us or was following us. Even Ingrid slept quietly in Veronica's arms as we crossed the city.

Close to the airport we pulled into a petrol station and again *The Sun* team suggested that Veronica should leave the van with Ingrid. Veronica made it very clear what she thought of that idea, and won her battle again.

The approach road to Rio's international airport is wide and open and required us to loop back on ourselves to get to the terminal building. But we would be able to see the terminal from a good distance. Sullivan explained that the British Consul would be there and that the airport had a wheelchair waiting to push me through immigration. I should not say anything to the media, he explained. Fat chance, given I could not speak. While they wanted to keep the photos exclusive, they were not too concerned given that any photo would have to feature me in *The Sun* t-shirt.

As we got closer we could see the assembled press pack that now numbered in the hundreds. From our viewpoint we could see that they were behind a barrier, but not penned in. It was still not clear if they realised this was the van they were waiting for, but they sure as hell would when we pulled up.

As we swung up to the terminal I was pretty certain this was not going to end happily ever after. We had not even come to a stop and the pack had broken out from behind the barrier and was now surrounding the minibus which, just as you've seen in the movies, was being rocked from side to side by the sheer weight of the people leaning on it and pushing it. All hell had broken loose and amongst the crowd I could see the tearful face of Rosa who had come to the airport to see me off. Snappers desperately stuck their cameras to the window to try and get a shot off, and when the door of the van was opened some even tried to get in. I stayed put but my hat got knocked sideways, so if you see the photos it often looks as if I had been on the piss.

You did not need to be a genius to know this was not going to work, and airport security told the van driver to drive on and come back around. They pulled people off and away from the van so we could make our escape.

Nobody was sure what to do or where to go, until Mike pointed out to *The Sun* guys that Chris, who was sitting at the back of the bus, knew the airport better than most people. Chris suggested to the driver that he took us around to the old terminal building on the other side of the airport, where I had first stepped foot in to Rio. There we could park under some trees that would hide us from the helicopters that were now circling overhead.

We seemed to have a number of options, none of which included going back to Terminal 2. The sensible option was to drive on to the airfield from the old terminal and then cross the airfield to the new terminal buildings. However, it became clear that certain parties wanted to have us walk through the airport, as it all made for a better story.

The eventual solution was boringly simple. We would go back to the airport but at the last moment break off the road and go to Terminal One. There was a good distance between the two terminals and given the athletic build of most journalists I have met, if we moved quickly there was little or no chance they could all get across to meet or intercept us.

We composed ourselves in the van and when the word came from the airport, we set off again. The helicopters spotted us as soon as we broke cover from under the trees and TV viewers in Rio could now follow our movements as we headed back to the airport. A few quick goodbyes were said in the van to those staying behind. There would be no time for proper goodbyes or other pleasantries once the van pulled to a halt at the airport. Security at Terminal Two had not been tipped off that we were going to Terminal One, so when they saw the van approaching they started trying to reorganise the press pack that was now baying for blood.

The driver of our minibus did well. As we came up the approach road to the airport he started to slow down, it looked to all appearances as if we were positioning ourselves to pull around into the terminal. At the last moment he floored it and we sped on around to Terminal One. Looking back we could see the penny had slowly started to drop and the press pack was splitting in every direction. Those that knew the airport would try and sprint down the indoor bridge that liked the two terminals. Those that didn't thought they could leg it around the road to catch us up. They had no chance.

We pulled up to an almost empty Terminal One where there were only a few bemused tourists to be taken by surprise. A wheelchair was waiting and everything went like clockwork. Bags were bundled on to the trolley and Mike quickly kissed Veronica and Ingrid goodbye as John Askill pushed me at double time through the airport. The authorities just wanted to get me airside, so they had more control of the situation.

Mike quickly caught up with me, as did a couple of quick thinking snappers. One was from *O Globo*, the main Rio paper that had the manpower to send a photographer to cover each terminal in case we tried a switch. The other, a freelance photographer, who simply took his chance and swapped terminals. Those photos went around the world as *The Sun* continued to sit on its exclusive. In fact as we were being pushed through the airport *The Sun* was already beaming photos back to London where they were hard at work on Monday's paper.

The chosen photo was of me being pushed through the terminal by Askill and Simon Hughes, the cowboy hat still knocked to one side. The headline was simple and to the point. 'GOT HIM'. Inside were more photos of me taken at the house over the weekend, and photos of me boarding the plane. For good measure there was a screen grab taken from Sky News showing the moment we were airborne.

On the day, we still had a way to go. We might have out smarted the press pack, but now *The Sun* had to deal with the Brazilian authorities. The point at which Slipper had become unstuck.

I have said it before, and I will say it again, I have the utmost respect and admiration for the Brazilian authorities and the way I was treated throughout my time in Brazil. I had my differences on occasions, but I was never treated as a number, always as a human being.

Mike unfortunately was by now fairly highly strung and was convinced that he had heard some junior police officers make some disparaging remarks behind my back. He squared up to them and a row broke out with

Mike nearly being arrested for abusive behaviour towards a federal agent. *The Sun* team were not best pleased, but they got Mike to apologise and some more senior officials managed to defuse the situation that could have derailed my return with Mike ending up behind bars rather than me.

Once we were safely airside, the senior federal police officers took Mike and I aside and put us in a separate room from *The Sun* team. The officers painstakingly made certain I was getting on the plane and going to London by choice. They questioned if I was under any form of intimidation, if any family member or friend has been kidnapped, and if this was being used to get me to Britain. One word from me, and *The Sun* team would have been sent packing empty handed.

Once I had convinced the federal police that I was genuinely happy to get on the plane and fly to London they shook me by the hand and wished me well. They even said they hoped to see me back in Rio in the future. I had been with them for 40 minutes.

There was now no turning back. We reassembled the team and were taken to the gate where a mini van was waiting to take us out to the plane. At the stairs to the plane I stopped for one last photo. Then we settled ourselves in to prepare for take off. At least it was slightly more comfortable than the last time I had flown out of Rio in a private plane. That time I was trussed up in a body bag.

On board were Mike, Bruce and Nick, as well as Mike Sullivan, John Askill, Simon Hughes, Harry Page, and Nigel Cairns from *The Sun*.

As a world television audience can attest from the images beamed live from Rio, I took to the sky at 5.18 pm Rio time, 9.18 pm in London.

The Sun had their man, but for Scotland Yard there was still a question of some 13 hours to wait and 6,000 miles to cover.

I do not deny that tears filled my eyes as I took one last look at Rio and Brazil, a city and country that had been so hospitable and generous to me since I had landed at the same airport from Caracas, 31 years and two months previously. I shed a few more tears as I thought about the city that had been my home for so many years, and had brought me so many more adventures than I could ever have dreamt of way back when I was a simple builder in Redhill.

Brazil and I had come along way together. We could both be proud.

As the plane started to climb I decided I was going to enjoy my last hours of freedom as much as I could. I was helped by Bruce and Nick who kept the atmosphere buoyant. I knew it was much harder on Mike to see the up side. Once the seat belt sign was off, I relieved myself of *The Sun* t-shirt and put on a yellow Lacoste sports shirt. There was time to relax on the flight as we were wined and dined. I posed for a toast with Bruce, but I didn't drink.

Following on a few hours behind us were Johnny Pickston and Gio who, along with the remaining members of *The Sun* team, were jumping on the first commercial flights to London.

At 2.55 am on Monday morning the Falcon 900EX landed on Ilha de Sal on the Cape Verde Islands to refuel. We had been flying for nearly six hours. Everyone on board was keen to stretch their legs with *The Sun* team making their way to the terminal building, leaving me alone with Nick. There was an empty Land Rover parked near by and Nick joked about him driving me into the night with it as I disappeared from the claws of justice one final time. But a joke was all it was.

While we were on the ground Mike Sullivan spoke with his office in London to help plan for my arrival. What he was hearing was that the other newspapers were putting pressure on the government to investigate exactly what the deal was that *The Sun* had with me. They were going to have to explain themselves to the Press Complaints Commission.

The Sun had already changed its posture over the week. From originally it all being about 'Ronnie Asks Sun to fly him home' it was now how the paper was flying me home to justice.

The paper's main editorial on the day of my return, was very much *The Sun* cosying up to the authorities, everyone from the Metropolitan police to the RAF were thanked. A *Sun* spokesperson also noted: 'The PCC code makes clear that payments to convicted criminals are only permissible where there is a public interest. We are happy to cooperate and will make it clear the massive public interest in returning a convicted criminal home to face justice at no cost to the taxpayer.'

Due to the state of my health, I had not paid much attention to the detail of the agreement with *The Sun*. All I now discovered was that having paid us, they were very happy to tear up the rest of the contract. This would have given them certain interview rights if and when I ever emerged from prison, as well as photo exclusives. Mike and Kevin thought it was beneficial in the long term to agree to tear up the contract, as it would also help *The Sun* with its discussions with the PCC and government. The downside was my letter of apology and regret to family and friends would never be published.

An hour after landing on Ilha de Sal, at 3.45 am on Monday, 7 May, we were airborne on the final stretch to London. Next stop was to be RAF Northholt, a secure RAF base in Hillingdon, in northwest London.

Given the stress and strains of the previous week and the day ahead, I decided to catch a bit of shuteye at the back of the plane while the others partied on through the night. I put on a thick new jumper to keep me warm. In the morning I returned to my seat by the window so I could watch Britain come into view across the English Channel, the same Channel I had escaped across 35 years earlier. I could recognise below the green fields of southern England. My 13,068 days on the run were about to come to an end.

Down below at RAF Northolt last minute preparations were being made for my arrival. Security was tight and only Kevin Crace and the legal team had been allowed in. Jane Wearing of Leftley Mallett Solicitors and my barrister, Guy Kearl, of St Paul's House Barrister's Chambers, Leeds would be allowed on the plane first on landing to explain the legal procedures to Mike and I.

I later learnt that there were some heated discussions as to exactly who would be the person to board the plane to arrest me. In the end Detective Chief Superintendent John Coles outranked the lot and got the job. The papers worked out he would have been 9 years old when I took flight.

We landed at 8.47 am. Again the images were beamed around the world as the plane touched down and taxied to a secure area. What the images did not show were the sharp shooters who were on stand by. They were part of a team of 90 police officers and 20 RAF police with dogs that had sealed off the base. Not sure if they thought I was going to do a runner or what, but the legal team were told that if I did not leave the plane when instructed, then the plane would be stormed.

Perhaps they thought I was going to rush across the tarmac and throw myself on the mercy of the Chancellor, Gordon Brown, who was boarding a Queen's flight minutes before I landed. Mr Brown would have been less than impressed that I was stealing the thunder from the government as he would have known that Tony Blair was going to Buckingham Palace that Tuesday to ask for the dissolution of Parliament and set the date for the General Election for 8 June. I would not be voting.

Having sorted ourselves out, and made myself as presentable as possible, Jane and Guy came on to the plane. Mike gave me a kiss on the cheek and then explained to Jane and Guy about my medication and how I needed my food to be cut up very small if I was to swallow it. Mike sat next to me as he could understand best what I was trying to say or write.

At precisely 9.05 am, 18 minutes after we landed, and what must have felt like an eternity for Scotland Yard and the other authorities, Cole was allowed to enter the cramped cabin with Detective Terry Wilson in tow. This was their big historic moment, but it was also mine. I extended the hand of friendship to greet the Flying Squad boss.

At first he ignored me. Pleasantries were clearly not in his script which was in a blue folder that he was nervously clutching.

'Are you Ronald Arthur Biggs?' he demanded. I nodded in reply. 'Were you born on 8 August 1929?'

I managed a barely audible: 'Yes'.

Cole then showed me his warrant card and announced: "I am Detective Chief Superintendent John Coles from New Scotland Yard.'

It was clear everything was going to be done by the book so that my legal team and I would have no come back later on for anything they might have overlooked. Perhaps they had learnt a lesson from Barbados.

I extend my hand again and managed to croak out 'Pleased to meet you.' Mike translated.

It took a while, but to give Coles his credit he firmly grasped my hand and looked me in the eyes. 'Pleased to meet you,' he replied. 'How do you do?

'I have here in my possession a warrant granted at Bow Street Magistrates Court on 27 July 1990 for your arrest for being unlawfully at large from Her Majesty's Prison Wandsworth,' he continued in the arcane language of a bygone time. 'The warrant issued at Bow Street Magistrates Court addressed to each and all the constables in the Metropolitan Police, accuses Ronald Arthur Biggs, address no fixed abode, of he being a prisoner of Her Majesty's Prison Wandsworth, serving sentences of 25 and 30 years imprisonment concurrent passed upon him at the assizes of the county of Buckingham on 16 April 1964 upon conviction of (a) conspiracy to stop mail with the intent to rob the said mail and (b) robbery with aggravation, and having escaped from the said prison in which he is required to be detained after being convicted of the said offences pursuant to section 72 of the Criminal Justice Act 1967.'

Then just as you have seen a million times in the movies I received my caution from Coles. 'You do not have to say anything but it may harm your defence if you do not mention when questioned something which you later rely on in court. Anything you do say may be given in evidence. Do you understand that?'

I nodded and at the same time was advised by Guy not to say anything else. I was back in England and well and truly nicked! The running had stopped. I was home, but not exactly free.

Pardon me, boy
Is that the Chattanooga choo choo?
Track twenty-nine
Boy, you can gimme a shine
I can afford
To board a Chattanooga choo choo
I've got my fare
And just a trifle to spare

Glen Miller, "Chattanooga Choo Choo", recorded 7 May 1941 exactly 60 years to the day before the Great Train Robber's return to the UK.

JUSTICE FOR SOME: THE PRISON YEARS

'Mr Biggs has returned to the United Kingdom voluntarily. He has been arrested upon the warrant outstanding against him and has been brought before a court this afternoon. He is aware of the immediate consequences of his return and will remain in custody.'

A Statement from Ronald Biggs' legal team on his return to the UK

He was quite a likable chap, a man's man, didn't talk about shopping or anything like that.

Jack Slipper on Biggs' return to UK

'Biggs added a rare and welcome touch of humour to the history of crime.'

Sir Robert Mark, Metropolitan Police Commissioner

As I sat on the private jet that had brought me back to Britain, Detective Chief Superintendent John Coles explained that I was to be taken from RAF Northolt to a local police station, and then on to the magistrates' court. At the station I would have access to my legal team, but not to Mike.

Scotland Yard having done its bit, it was time for the immigration and customs officers to have their moment in the spotlight. An immigration officer took my emergency passport from me. I had had a passport, but not for long. The officer then explained that I could leave the plane but the others would need to stay on board and would be taken to the main terminal building where they would go through their own immigration checks.

Mike was allowed to help me off the plane, as was *The Sun* Crime Editor, Mike Sullivan. I squinted in the sunlight and did a quick double take on the number of police vehicles surrounding the aircraft. Thirteen in total I counted. Somebody on high seemed to have missed the point that I was a sick and elderly man who had chosen to come back to the UK under my own steam. I was not about to make some mad dash for freedom.

I was put in a police transit van with blacked out windows and under heavy police escort driven to what turned out to be Chiswick Police Station. As I was being driven away Mike returned to the plane and dissolved into tears.

I knew that this was going to be much harder for Mike than for me. I had been through it all before. Mike never wanted me to come back to England, a foreign land for him, yet here we all were. C'est la vie, you might say.

Back on the plane an immigration officer kept asking Mike how long he expected to stay for in the UK. Mike had no British passport, just his Brazilian one. He tried to explain that he didn't know how long he would need to be in the country; in the end he was given temporary admission into Britain for just one month, but was told an extended visa was just a formality.

As I disappeared into the distance the plane taxied on up to the terminal where Mike cleared our luggage. I had not bothered to bring many clothes with me. I knew I would not have much use for them, and most of what I had would not be suitable for the weather conditions in the UK. One case, however, was packed full of photos, videos, newspaper cuttings and other precious memorabilia. Mike's prized possession was his guitar.

At Chiswick Police Station, not far from where Mary Manson had bought a black Austin Healey for Bruce on the day after the train robbery, they gave me a perfunctory medical once over and allowed me time to catch my breath. Jane Wearing and Guy Kearl from my legal team arrived, along with Guy's boss, Nigel Sangster QC of St Paul's House Barristers' Chambers in Leeds.

As one newspaper put it, they were a legal team that any self-respecting villain would kill for. There was also the publicist, Judy Totton, who Kevin

Crace had brought in to look after the media. With no voice of my own, I would need one.

I had met Jane Wearing in Rio on several occasions. Her husband was a British Airways pilot and she often travelled to Brazil with him. In 1997 I had called her and asked her to help with my extradition case, which she helped win. She was the obvious friend to call on for legal help.

Jane explained that Kevin was taking Mike to a hotel that had been organised by *The Sun*. Her husband, Steve, would be there and they were expecting John Pickston and Gio to turn up soon from Rio. Raimunda, Mike's mother, was also on her way over from Switzerland to offer our son some morale support. Team Biggs were also organising a press conference for Mike.

In a nice twist *The Sun* did not want Mike to check into the hotel under his own name, so he chose one of my old aliases and was registered as Terence King. *The Sun* had blocked off the rooms either side of Mike as well as the ones above and below. For a paper that now claimed not to care, they were being very caring.

After the long flight and excitement of recent days, I wanted to get the rest of the legal formalities out of the way and discover where I would be spending my first night back in Britain. It crossed my mind that somebody might have a sense of humour and send me back to Wandsworth. I certainly would have. I might have even lowered me back over the wall.

Before midday we were on the move again. This time to the West London Courthouse on Talgarth Road in Hammersmith. As I was leaving Chiswick Police Station some photographer and a TV crew managed to snap off a couple of photos and some footage of me in my blue sweater, yellow shirt, beige trousers, and walking with a stick. They were the images the media would turn to again-and-again for the next nine years and whenever they ran a story of my return. Just Google me and you will see what I mean.

I arrived at the Hammersmith courthouse at 11.55 am in a white police van and an escort of two police cars and an unmarked Flying Squad Vauxhall. I shuffled into a packed Court No 4 where there were a lot of people who wanted to get a first glimpse of the 'notorious Ronnie Biggs'.

I was starting to realise that stories of my fame in Britain had not been over stated.

I probably disappointed them that day in court, but I'm not sure what they expected from a frail old man who had suffered a couple of debilitating strokes and had been up most of the night on a transatlantic flight in a small jet. There was no spring in my step, and there was not or ever likely to be. The clerk of the court stood and addressed me: 'Mr Biggs, I'm going to ask you to identify yourself. Is your full name Ronald Arthur Biggs?'

I got to me feet and grunted in the affirmative as best I could. I was then asked to confirm my date of birth, which I did with another grunt and a thumbs-up.

'And were you the person sentenced at Buckingham Assizes on April 16, 1964 to 25 year's imprisonment for conspiracy to stop mail and to 30 years for robbery with aggravation?'

If I hadn't been so tired I might have been tempted to signal no with a thumbs down, just to see how they would have reacted. Instead I simply grunted again in the affirmative.

The district judge, Tim Workman, had heard enough: 'I am satisfied that you are the person named in the warrant and have been unlawfully at large. The law requires me to return you to prison which I will do now.'

My day in court that the authorities had craved for 13,000 days had lasted exactly 8 minutes and by 1.30 pm I was on the way to HMP Belmarsh in Thamesmead. Built in 1991, on the east site of the former Royal Arsenal in Woolwich, Belmarsh was home to about 900 prisoners and considered to be one of Europe's most modern and secure. As a Category A prison the inmates are those whose escape would be considered 'highly dangerous to the public or national security.' If I hadn't been so fuckin' tired, I should have felt flattered.

Jack Slipper told the press that he was astonished that I was being sent to Belmarsh. 'I saw him get off the plane at Northolt aerodrome and unless he's a John Gielgud, he looked as if he was finished. I hope they will give him the chance to be with his son for the last few months of his life. You know, I had a certain amount of respect for Biggs because he brought up Mike by himself. I had time to sit down with him, have a few beers with him.

He was quite a likable chap, a man's man, didn't talk about shopping or anything like that. He loved to say he'd done this and he'd done that, but take it from me, I had his file out for years and it surprised me because he'd hardly done anything. He was never a gangster, he was a cheap thief. I tell you what he was, he was a good tea boy because that's basically what he did - he cleaned up after them.'

As I was being taken across London, Jane Wearing read a brief statement to the media at the courthouse:

Mr Biggs has returned to the United Kingdom voluntarily. He has been arrested upon the warrant outstanding against him and has been brought before a court this afternoon. He is aware of the immediate consequences of his return and will remain in custody.

'In due course he will seek a hearing before the Court Of Appeal in respect of his outstanding sentence. All he seeks is a fair and balanced hearing at which all relevant issues can be addressed. He is confident that he will receive such a hearing. We are assured by the Police that he will not face any further charges and are proceeding upon that basis.

'Mr Biggs is not in good health. The authorities responsible for his welfare are aware of this and he will receive proper medical attention as soon as possible. Mr Biggs would like to thank the United Kingdom authorities for assisting in the expeditious processing of his passport application which has allowed him to return to England in order to resolve his future.

On arrival at Belmarsh I was subjected, just as any other prisoner, to a strip search for illegal substances. I was finger printed, and filmed. My prison number was just the same as when I went over the wall at Wandsworth. I was again a number. Number 002731.

I swapped my clothes for a prison tracksuit and was taken to the prison's three-story medical unit where I was allocated one of the unit's 38 beds. I would be under observation as they tried to assess my true physical and mental state. Good luck boys!

Many people thought I must have had a screw loose to come back to the UK, now the doctors would have the chance to find out. All I knew was that if I had stayed on in Rio I would not have lasted very much longer and would have dragged Mike down with me. Perhaps I wasn't so crazy after all.

What I was keen to find out, was how much time I might have to serve. It would be upsetting not to see Mike, but I expected that once the initial dust had settled and we knew how long I would have to serve, he could head back to Rio to his wife and child and try and pick up the pieces of his life. This was, after all, one of the main reasons I had come back to Britain. On Tuesday, 8 May my return was the lead story in most of the papers, the exception was some of the tabloids who in an attempt to down play the success of *The Sun*, lead with the marriage of a couple called Chris Evans and Billie Piper in Las Vegas. People who at the time I would have had to say 'who?' as they had not been on my radar in Rio.

Not only was the fact that I could not speak going to be a problem in Belmarsh, but I realised I was totally out of step with what Britain was like and the country's likes and dislikes. British musicians and films might have made there way to Rio, but little in terms of television. I had never seen an episode of *Eastenders* or *Countdown*. About the only shows I recognised from the 1960s were *Coronation Street* and *Blue Peter*.

That Tuesday *The Sun* lead with a photo of me stepping off the plane. The attention-grabbing headline was 'THE END: Moment justice caught up with Ronnie Biggs thanks to The Sun'. The paper now had a strip across all its spreads that read 'The Sun Puts Biggs Back in Jail'. One splash inside had a photo of Mike kissing me under the headline of 'Kiss Freedom Goodbye Dad', and the *Sun's* own story of the events surrounding my return had the headline 'How We Got Our Man'.

But any advantage *The Sun* had had over the rest of the media pack had now dissolved as since Northholt and the court appearance every paper had equal access to me, which wasn't much. Instead *The Sun* would have to make the best it could out of its access to Mike.

Back at the hotel, the Tower Thistle, Jane Wearing was shocked to discover that Mike did not have a suit. He never had. In Rio he lived in jeans and t-shirts. Gio took Mike off to Marks & Spencer to kit him out for his press conference. Gio and Johnny Pickston did their best to keep Mike's spirits up, much as the two of them had done for me in the dark times in Rio.

Considering the prisons I had been in over the years, Belmarsh wasn't that bad, but I knew it would still be a big shock for Mike. He got the okay to visit me on the Tuesday before his press conference. *The Sun* organised for a car to take him across from Tower Bridge to Belmarsh. A trip he was to make many, many times, although not always in the luxury of a chauffer driven car.

None of the waiting media spotted Mike on the way in to Belmarsh, which was just as well as he did not know the ropes and had stuff on him, like cash, that was not allowed inside the prison and should have been left in the lockers in the visitors' centre. But rather than tip off the press pack, they let him into see me.

Mike was brought in through multiple doors and security checks to a cell in the medical centre. He found me being poked and prodded by a doctor and a couple of nurses. The doctor was glad to see Mike as he was having a problem understanding the medication and dosages that were all in Portuguese. It helped distract Mike and I wanted him to stay strong in front of the screws. I had yet to establish myself in the nick, and did not want the screws to see Mike or our relationship as a weakness that they could target.

When the doctor left we were given some time to sit at the table and chat. Three screws remained to watch and I could see this was upsetting Mike and getting up his nose. It was the first time I had seen Mike in a suit so to break the ice I scribbled on my pad. 'You look like a doctor from the clap clinic!' We both laughed. It was good to have tears of laughter again. I then jotted down for Mike: 'Don't break down in front of the slags. Don't give them the satisfaction.'

Mike told me that since leaving Brazil my web site had received over 8,000 emails of support, another 3,000 were to come in over the next few days. It gave me a warm feeling that somebody still cared.

All too soon it was time for Mike to leave and it was explained to us that as I was a Category A prisoner he would only be allowed to visit me once every 15 days in Belmarsh. I tried to assure Mike not to worry. I could not see any reason why I would be kept for long either as a Category A prisoner or within Belmarsh. They must have had prisoners that offered a far greater risk to society than me, and I was certain they would just use Belmarsh as a staging post until I was allocated to another lower grade prison. As it turned out I was seriously wrong, very wrong. Belmarsh was to be my home for the next six years and two months.

Mike returned to the Tower Thistle where he was going to hold the press conference. The thinking behind the location was a double bluff with the media, in that they would never think that Mike would be so stupid as to be staying at the same hotel where the conference took place. A bluff that worked.

Mike admitted to being more nervous facing the British press that day, than performing before 200,000 people in Maracanã. He had also been told how much the legal fees would be to put up any sort of case for an early release. It was many times more than what he had been expecting.

To make things simpler for Mike, the legal team and Judy Totton had helped prepare a statement that he could read out. He tried, but after just a few words he started shaking and broke down. Judy took over.

Mike's statement explained that I had voluntarily returned to Britain, contrary to his wishes, to end my days in England, 'a country that he (Ron) still thinks of as home.'

'As far as the financial payments are concerned,' Mike's statement continued, 'any payments made by the press are not for my father's direct benefit. As he knows all too well, he has no need for money now. Any payments received will be used to contribute to his retrial and legal expenses. He does not wish to be a burden on the British taxpayer.'

Mike left the conference as soon as Judy finished reading the statement. It left the press somewhat frustrated that they could not grill him, but this was not a sympathetic press pack given the mauling they had received in the circulation war by The Sun's scoop.

Judy and Jane did their best to answer the hostile questions the press still wanted answers to. Jane cutting them short by saying that she would need to examine the legal options open to her before deciding what route to take. Having met me in Rio prior to my strokes, Jane was also in a position to sum up my physical state.

'He is not the man he was four years ago when I acted for him,' she told the press. 'He was an articulate, very intelligent man then. He is completely different now.'

Thanks Jane!

The more intelligent members of the press pack had picked up on the fact that *The Sun* logo, which had been so prominent on my return, was nowhere to be seen at Mike's press conference as the paper distanced itself further from me and my story. I could not blame them and two months later the paper learnt they would not face censure from the Press Complaints Commission.

The PCC's report said: 'it was impossible for the Commission to conclude that the result of the newspaper's payment was contrary to the public interest. To do so would - in effect - be to condone the continued presence of a wanted criminal abroad.'

The Sun told the PCC that it had paid Kevin Crace, who had acted as the broker in the deal. The payments to Kevin included payments to me, Mike and Bruce. The report, said *The Sun*, 'was keen to point out that these payments were considerably less than had been speculated upon elsewhere in the media.'

The PCC accepted *The Sun*'s defence that having been approached by the 'Biggs family', it was clear to them that I would only return to Britain if I was offered a 'financial incentive'. The Commission also accepted that the paper 'had worked at all times with the relevant authorities, including the Foreign Office, the RAF and the Metropolitan Police.' It had 'secured the return to justice of a notorious criminal'.

The Sun's editor, David Yelland, made a statement that the ruling 'is a complete vindication of *The Sun*'s decision to bring Ronnie Biggs to Britain to face justice after 35 years on the run.'

Ironically Mike's first major interview on my return was done with the *Sunday Times*, the sister paper of *The Sun* and also owned by Mr Murdoch. I'm not sure what he would have thought of his journalist, Margarette Driscoll, saying of my return: 'It was all in the worst possible taste, with Biggs, frail and disabled by two strokes, in a straw hat and Sun t-shirt.'

Margarette was surprised that Mike, who told her he was a 'psychological wreck' due to lack of sleep, was 'thoughtful' and 'articulate'. At least her piece was generally sympathetic to us both.

The same day as the piece in the *Sunday Times*, the *Sunday Mirror* ran a story with the headline 'Biggs Will Be Dead in Month.' It quoted a prison hospital source as saying that I was 'far more seriously ill' than they were led to believe when I was flown back from Brazil.

The source also told the *Mirror:* 'A specialist was called in from one of London's top hospitals and he says Biggs will die before the end of the summer. He is in a very bad way. The staff here are certain he has a degenerative condition, probably Parkinson's Disease. From initial tests they think it is at a very advanced stage. The specialist reckons Biggs has been terminally ill for some time.'

Just goes to show that you can't believe everything you read in the papers. I knew I was ill, but not that ill, and I have no idea where the *Mirror's* story came from. Next time I run into Mr Morgan, I must ask him.

I now had to adapt to life in Belmarsh as Mike adapted to life in London. Don't expect many exciting stories and tales from my time behind bars as they are few and far between. In truth the way I got through my time in Belmarsh and Norwich was to cocoon myself in sleep and sleep through as much of the day and night as I possible could. Watching TV when possible, or listening to my CDs. The general tedium only broken by the friends and strangers who dropped by to visit. If you were one of those people, thanks for taking the time and trouble. If you wrote to me in prison, many thanks, and sorry if I did not always write back, but as the day's ticked by my writing got weaker and weaker and now almost non existent.

A typical day in Belmarsh for a typical inmate – although I was far from typical –started at 8.40 am when the cells were unlocked for breakfast. At 9.30 prisoners were allowed to carry out work, go to the gym or receive visits from their legal team before returning to their cells at 11.30 am.

At 1.45 pm the cells were unlocked for lunch before prisoners fitter than I had another work or gym session. If you had any visitors you could see them between 2.15 and 4.00 pm. There was another lock down between 5.00 and 6.45 pm when we were allowed some social time before being locked up for the night at 8.30 pm. On average most prisoners at Belmarsh probably spent about 20 hours a day locked in their cells, my average was 23 hours.

After all the strain and uncertainty of my return, I did feel I was starting to get stronger in the first few weeks at Belmarsh. The doctors told me my heart and lungs were in good nick. I was even starting to put on weight and was able to give up the wheelchair and take short stumbling walks during the exercise periods.

The recuperation did not last for long. On the afternoon of 2 June I collapsed after complaining of severe head pains. I was rushed from Belmarsh to Queen Elizabeth Hospital in Woolwich, where I was diagnosed as having had another stroke.

Not being able to reach Mike, the governor of Belmarsh managed to get hold of Kevin Crace. He was not allowed to tell Kevin what the problem was, but told him it was urgent that Mike contacted the prison.

Tracked down to the Tardis, a cultural centre in Farringdon that Nick Reynolds used as a base, Mike got through to the duty governor who told him what had happened and where I was. It cost Mike £100 to find a taxi to take him 'south of the river' at that time of day. When he got to the hospital, the press were already camped outside and Kevin was waiting for him.

Mike found me in a hospital room with a drip attached to one hand while my other hand was cuffed to a prison officer. There were a total of six prison guards and four police officers in the small room.

'Why?' Mike inquired.

The only answer Mike got was that the orders had come from 'way above'. Mike could sense that even the hardened prison officers were uncomfortable with the scene.

Thankfully in a hospital the doctors tend to outrank all others. It was the doctors that decided that as I was drifting in and out of consciousness I would need a CAT scan and possibly an operation.

The hospital staff and Mike had to negotiate with the guards, as the CAT scan was not going to work if I was still chained to a screw. The doctors had no problem with a guard being in the room, but not with all his bells and whistles attached. A room that had no windows and just one door, where did they think I was going to go in my state? Finally they relented and the scan went ahead which confirmed I had had a stroke, although not as bad as first feared.

As the hospital was waiting for the results of the scan, Mike took it upon himself to go and brief the waiting press and tell them that I was being guarded by ten men and chained to the bed.

'I am deeply concerned about my dad's condition. He is a dying man, ' he told the media. 'This is yet another sign that says he should not be inside prison and should be released immediately. My dad should be afforded the dignity to die at home.'

By chance a live feed was going out on one of the news channels and surprise, surprise in a matter of minutes a call went through to the hospital telling the guards to remove the handcuffs.

I was in hospital for a week, but was still guarded around the clock by four guards which Mike worked out were costing the taxpayer £6,000 a day in overtime. During my time in Queen Elizabeth, I had surgery to install a feeding tube. The doctors feared my throat muscles were now so weak that food would enter my lungs instead of my stomach.

Because of the hospital's concern over my health, the governor did call Mike and said he could visit me twice a week on compassionate grounds. It was nice to see that at times common sense could prevail, although not for very long.

As I was recuperating in Belmarsh, Mike was called in by the Home Office to discuss his visa situation. At the time he thought little of it, and now had the support of Veronica who had arrived in London with little Ingrid. At his first interview the immigration officer said there could be problems as the paper work from Mike's arrival at RAF Northolt was wrong. Hardly Mike's problem, you would think, given the manner of my arrival.

The following day, Mike was planning to bring Veronica and Ingrid to see me for the first time since their arrival in London when he got a call to go back and see the immigration officer again. Still not overly concerned, he told Veronica he would call her when the meeting was over.

The authorities grilled Mike for several hours and told him that it was clear to them that his wife and child were coming to settle illegally in the UK. Whatever argument Mike put up, they swept it under the carpet. They declined his application for a visa and his only way to stay in the country was to appeal the decision and keep appealing.

In case you are confused as to why my son did not have the right to be in the UK, you would not be alone. While nobody was questioning I was British, or that my children had the right to a British passport and to live in

Britain, the problem was that I had never legally married Raimunda and therefore Mike was not considered by the law to be my son and had no rights to live in Britain.

Mike's visa problems would keep him occupied for many months. If you are a fan of conspiracy theories you might want to take note that many of Mike's appeals were heard and turned around in record time. A person or persons unknown wanted to get him out of the country and quickly.

Not surprisingly Mike, Veronica and Ingrid did not make it to Belmarsh on the day they had been set to visit, and I did not know why. I urgently wanted to talk to Mike about some health problems I had, as I had been shitting an alarming amount of blood.

After a few days Mike managed to reschedule the visit. It was a real boost to see my granddaughter and Veronica again. I spelt out my health problems to Mike and he went and spoke to one of the supervising guards who said they would investigate.

A week later the doctors discovered I did have a problem and had lost several pints of blood. I found myself back in an ambulance heading to Queen Elizabeth Hospital for a much needed blood transfusion.

During my six years in Belmarsh I became something of a regular visitor to Queen Elizabeth Hospital. The staff always did what they could to keep me alive, for which they have my thanks and admiration, but I often felt they wanted to do more and were not allowed to. In one instance the hospital had to overrule a Home Office doctor who wanted to return me to Belmarsh before the doctors at the hospital considered I was in a fit state.

In January 2004 I made two visits to Queen Elizabeth in just 48 hours. The first was after suffering what the prison thought was a heart attack, but which turned out to be pneumonia that may have caused my heart to beat erratically. After tests I was discharged, but I was back in hospital within 48 hours to be treated for dehydration and vomiting caused by a chest infection. Over time I even managed to pick up MRSA, but I don't know if Belmarsh or Queen Elizabeth was to blame for that.

One illustrious guest to arrive in Belmarsh while I was there was Jeffrey Archer. Following his conviction for perjury and perverting the course of justice, Archer arrived on 19 July 2001 and was gone by 9 August. He even managed to turn his twenty-two days and fourteen hours in Belmarsh into a best selling book, *A Prison Diary Volume 1: Belmarsh: Hell.* Little fuss was made of Archer benefitting from his prison time, somehow I doubt the same courtesy will be shown to me.

I imagine I was one of the few people in Belmarsh that his Lordship might have heard of, or recognised on sight. Because there were concerns as to how Archer might take to Belmarsh they put him in the hospital wing and on suicide watch. When he saw me he came over to shake my hand. At first I pretended not to recognise him, but then I wrote down: 'Nice to meet you, Lord Archer.'

'Please don't call me Lord,' he replied. 'Call me Jeffrey.'

Jeffrey became my neighbour and was put in the cell next to mine until somebody tried to torch it and he had to be moved.

I would love to be able tell you that it was Archer's friends in high places that helped him to move along so swiftly from Belmarsh, but I can't. While they certainly did him no harm, for the sort of threat that Archer represented to society the time he spent in Belmarsh was about par for the course. You have to ask yourself then, why the authorities thought six years in Belmarsh was the correct decision for a man in my condition? The stock answer was always that the medical wing at Belmarsh provided the best prison medical facilities in the land. If that is the case, then God help the other sick prisoners in the other prisons, is all I can say. Could I suggest that somebody in the media might like to have a look at this issue and help the poor sic bastards.

One footnote to Lord Archer's time in Belmarsh. At the end of July 2001, when I was still recovering from my stroke, Mike received a call from the *Daily Mail. The Mail* and its readers are traditionally not the most sympathetic or supportive of my plight. At times being hung, drawn and quartered was too lenient for many of them for the way I had put two fingers up to 'their' beloved establishment.

The reporter told Mike he had something of interest to show him and needed to meet up. What he had to show Mike was a picture of me in my bed in Belmarsh.

I looked terrible in the picture. My head was back and propped up against some towels. Also visible were the tubes that fed me and kept me alive. It all looked very tired and squalid. The reporter did not want to tell Mike how they got the photo, but because of privacy laws they felt they needed Mike's permission to publish the picture. Looking at the picture Mike decided that making the photo public could only help with the argument that I should not be in Belmarsh, and that I was not a threat to anyone.

Given where my cell was located in the hospital wing, and the security that surrounded it, I can tell you that a visitor or another prison inmate could not have taken the photo. It had to be taken by a guard or another member of the prison staff. My theory, given where and when it was taken, was that the big money shot for the *Mail* was of Archer in Belmarsh. I don't know if the photographer panicked and lost his nerve, or simply never got the chance to get a shot of my then neighbour, but what the *Mail* got for its money was Biggs in bed and not Archer in chokey.

The photo was published on 28 July 2001, about a week before my legal team formally submitted appeal papers to the Criminal Cases Review Committee. My QC, Nigel Sangster, was arguing that my original sentence was 'excessive'. He was also looking at a direct plea for clemency to the new Home Secretary, David Blunkett, who had taken over the position on 8 June from my best friend to be, Jack Straw.

8 June was the day after the 2001 General Election that took Tony Blair and Labour back into power for a second term. Blair had called the election on the day after I returned to Britain.

In the election shuffle Straw replaced Robin Cook at the Foreign Office. Cook, who had given the okay for my passport and return, was moved, people say against his wishes, to become Leader of the House of Commons. The 'curse of Biggs' had struck again!

I had noticed since my return to prison that the set up was not that different from when I was inside in the 1960s. Even in a maximum-security prison like Belmarsh if you wanted something brought in, it could be organised. And it is the staff and screws that bring the contraband in, not the visitors. In a place like Belmarsh the visitors are far too well screened.

Visiting Belmarsh was never easy for my friends, especially as I was classified as Category A. If you wanted to visit I had to have a Visiting Order – a VO – sent out to you in the post, and there was a strict limit of two VOs per month, although three adults could be on each one. You then had to call Belmarsh and book the visit 48-hours in advance. Visiting times were 2.15 to 4.00 pm, with no visits on Wednesday, while at the weekend there was also a morning slot.

Coming to visit me was a bit like taking a flight. You had to turn up early to check in at the visitors' centre, and as everyone wanted to maximise the visiting time most visitors turned up at the same time resulting in lengthy queues. You would then have to get in line and show some form of picture ID plus proof of address. Fingerprints would be scanned, photos taken, and ID cards issued. You then had to put everything you were carrying away in the lockers. The only items you could bring in were the VO, the locker key, and £10 in cash to buy something at the coffee bar. If you had brought anything for me, that had to be handed over at the visitors' centre and it would eventually, if suitable, make its way through to me.

You would then cross from the visitors' centre to the main prison and go through a series of security checks for your identity. Men had their hand stamped with a symbol that showed up under an ultra violet light. Sniffer dogs would check you for drugs, and then you would go through airport type scanners.

Any of us who were expecting visitors were rounded up and put in the visiting hall in set locations. Mine was normally 'A1'. We would wear our normal clothes, but had to put on a fluorescent strap like cyclists wear to be seen at night. We were not to move from our set locations. Visitors could go to the coffee bar, and there was an area with toys for the kids to play.

As I sat down I never knew how long it would take for my visitors to arrive or if they even would. It all depended how quick they had been in the queue and how fast they had got through security. Mike pretty much had it down pat, and was always one of the first through the door.

The visiting hall at Belmarsh was not what you probably imagine from the movies. There were no glass partitions, no phones, just tables and chairs.

Although they were all firmly nailed down so nobody could start chucking them about. One visitor described it as being like a run down regional airport departure lounge from 1980s. Never having been in a regional airport lounge in the 1980s I can't say, but I'll take their word for it.

During visits I was allowed my spelling board and a box of tissues, but the screws kept a beady eye out for any visitor passing anything to one of the prisoners. Mike occasionally slipped me the balance of his £10 or his watch, as I was always having mine nicked.

Mike would say: 'Dad, for Christ sake it's a prison. If you leave things unguarded they will get taken.'

I'm surprised most of my watches have not turned up on ebay.

Most of the inmates of Belmarsh were not thieves, rather a colourful mixture of murderers, terrorists, and general undesirables. If visitors realised who they were sharing the visiting hall with they would probably be surprised and alarmed. I was aware that I was often pointed out, and some visitors would break the rules and come across to shake my hand and say a few kind words. The other long-term celebrity prisoner was Ronnie O'Sullivan Senior, the father of the snooker player Ronnie O'Sullivan. Ronnie was serving 17 years for fatally stabbing Bruce Ryan, who is said to have been a one-time driver to Charlie Kray. O'Sullivan was finally released in February 2009.

Some of my visitors also attracted attention. Record producer Gus Dudgeon looked suitable rock'n'roll when he came to visit, his big buckled belt setting of all sorts of alarms. Setting of alarms for a very different reason was a visit from Uri Geller who I had met in Brazil. Mike got a right bollocking from the prison authorities for that, and was told he must warn them in advance of other high profile visitors.

In Brazil Uri had visited me in 1995, just after I had broken my leg. I had talked about him doing a trick that was going to involve the disappearance of a train. Hopefully one day he will pull it off. I think in Belmarsh the screws thought he was going to pull off the trick with a disappearing prisoner.

As my time passed in Belmarsh I noticed that there were fewer and fewer English speaking prisoners. Many were held under the anti- terrorism act.

Inmates included Abu Hamza, Dhiren Barot, Lotfi Raiss and Manfo Kwaku Asiedu. The prison became in effect Britain's Guantanamo Bay.

Charles Bronson passed through Belmarsh before my time, and Dave Courtney spent a spell inside after I had left. I just missed the nail bomber, David Copeland, but I did cross paths with the Soham killer, Ian Huntley.

I was not happy when Huntley was moved to a cell close to mine, and told the screws as much. They told me they were concerned for Huntley's safety and decided the hospital wing was the safest place to keep him and I was simply ignored.

Early in his stay Huntley approached me as I sat in my wheelchair. With nothing much else to hand, I threw my box of tissues at him, and he got the gist of my message and feelings.

A few months later a fellow prisoner, Freddie Asher, managed to get in a punch at Huntley. I sent him over a handwritten note: 'All power to Fred, a job well done. I'm glad to know you.'

There were the occasional happy days in Belmarsh, and one of the happiest would have been the day of my marriage to Raimunda in 2002. She had come to my rescue once, and now she was to come to the rescue of our son.

Immigration officials were still harassing Mike, and even Veronica found herself stopped at Heathrow while coming back into Britain from Brazil with baby Ingrid in her arms. She was held for four hours and not even offered a glass of water. On another visit, Veronica had per passport removed and Ingrid, at he age of one-and-a-half years of age, was given a red stamp in her passport to say she was persona non grata!

During an interview with the Home Office Veronica was even asked how she felt about Mike putting me before her and the family. It took Mike's solicitor, Angena Josi, to put an end to this line of questioning, pointing out to the Home Office that the questions had nothing to do with Veronica's immigration status. Whichever way you look at it, it seemed vindictive and Veronica never got an apology.

The Home Office were also refusing Mike's requests to stay indefinitely in the UK. That was followed by further bad news that the Criminal Cases Review Commission had rejected the application to send my case to the Court of Appeal. So we had to lodge a further appeal on those findings based on my sentence being 'inappropriate and unnecessary.'

It was during this time that one of the legal team decided to check a hypothetical case with the Home Office of what would happen to a child's status if the mother and father do legally wed. The answer was that the child's status would be the same as any child of a couple married at the time of the birth.

To help Mike and I, Raimunda offered to come over from Geneva and become my legal wife in the eyes of the British authorities, but first I had to show I was no longer legally married to Charmian. Mike searched high and low through my papers for the right documents. But none were to be found. Mike and the lawyers contacted Australia House, but the authorities were not inclined to help, and so in January 2002 Mike got on the phone to ask Charmian for her help. As much as it must have hurt, Charmian came up with the goods and sent over the necessary documents from Australia even knowing that the wedding would put her and the family back in the spotlight and open a number of old wounds.

I married Raimunda Rothen inside Belmarsh on 10 July 2002 and even got to wear a suit again. The nearest I got to consummating our marriage was a quick pinch of her bum as she stood next to me. Our courtship had lasted almost exactly 31 years from when we first met in Rio to getting her to the alter.

Sadly I could not attend my own wedding reception, but I'm told a lively time was had even without me. It was held at The Punch Bowl Pub in Mayfair, which was then owned by Freddie Foreman's son, George. He later sold it to Guy Ritchie, director of Lock, Stock and Two Smoking Barrels and Madonna's ex.

Less than two weeks after the wedding Mike was granted his British citizenship. Once Mike got around to making an honest woman out of Veronica, so were she and Ingrid. Even Raimunda can have a British passport if she wants one, and I think she could even have a British pension if she wanted one. It just goes to show how some of the people when trying to fuck me over just manage to shaft themselves and the country.

Being behind bars meant there was very little I could effectively do to improve my lot. That was left to Mike and the legal team who investigated every avenue open to us, and despite many knock backs kept on fighting. I was still very much in the public eye, and made headlines and news bulletins every time I was rushed off to Queen Elizabeth with another health scare.

At this stage I think I should apologise to the web site *Death List* and its followers. I have been high up on its list as the next one to pop his clogs since I came back to Britain. I first featured in the top 50 in 2000 in a very modest 40th. By 2002 I was at number one on the list and have been solidly in the top 10 ever since. I was back to number one in 2009, but slipped behind the Lockerbie bomber in 2010, but was back on top again for 2011. Their only consolation is that one-year they will get it right, but happily I won't be around to care!

A couple of documentaries in the UK also kept me in the news. Channel 5 did a two hour, two part doc in January 2002 called *The Legend of Ronnie Biggs*, while Sky aired *Ronnie Biggs: Last Escape?* in March 2005. Both were well received, but I never got to see them in Belmarsh. I finally got to enjoy them when I was released and I can say both did a good and fair job.

That is more than you can say for Channel 4's *Kidnap Ronnie Biggs*, which was a pure piece of fiction, pulled together by kidnapper John Miller and his sidekick Patrick King. We pointed out the many errors to Channel 4, but they did not seem to care or show any concern that Patrick King owned the 'unbiased' production company behind the show.

I tried to keep my sense of humour alive while I was in Belmarsh, and sometimes it would get me in to trouble. In Brazil, for example, it is quite common to give people nicknames and I continued to do so. A nurse who was particularly hard on me at the start of my time I nicknamed Whoopi, as to me she looked like Whoopi Goldberg. The name stuck and soon everyone was calling her that. Happily she finally thawed to my boyish charms and we got on well.

Due to his looks and his way of walking that reminded me of a little penguin, another guard I christened Pingu. He had a total sense of humour failure and reported me to the governor saying I was racist and God knows what else. It was probably the worst thing he could have done as it meant the entire prison population referred to him as Pingu. Eventually he transferred out to another prison.

On another day I discovered that at lock up somebody had forgotten to lock the door to my cell, so I found a post-it note and put it on the outside of the door. It just said: 'Cheers – Rio here I come!' I then went and hid in the toilet block and waited for a reaction. When I heard all the alarms go off I realised I might have overstepped the mark. Honestly, where did they think I was going in my state and how?

Saying that, when I first arrived at Belmarsh I received a lot of offers to get me out. There were certain groups of people who thought it would be the ultimate two fingers up to the establishment if 'Ronnie Biggs' was to disappear from Britain's most secure prison within weeks of getting there. In the end I had to get the word out that I had not come all the way back from Brazil to start running again. Or shuffling, more like.

During one visit Mike was shocked to hear that I had got an official warning and reprimand for having things in my cell that I shouldn't. Extra razor blades, to be exact.

Not unreasonable perhaps in a place like Belmarsh, where they wanted and needed to keep an eye on anything that might be used as a weapon. The restrictions on razor blades were quite tough. Somehow they seemed to forget about this when dealing with an old fool like me and often when I got a new blade they did not ask for the old one back, so I built up a nice stock of them which were eventually found during a search of my cell. Mike asked me why I had done it?

'Because I could,' was my reply. He understood.

I can't remember the exact date when Giovanni di Stefano came into my life. It must have been in the early part of 2005, although Giovanni says he once met me in Rio back in the 1970s. In 2005 it was at a point in time when any funds that Mike might have had had all but dried up. There was no way Mike could afford to go on paying for a top legal team like Mallets that seemed to have exhausted just about every option and avenue open to us.

Mr di Stefano, a colourful character to say the very least, did not see it like that and rarely, if ever, takes no for an answer. He also did not want any payment. A strong point for any lawyer.

Labelled the Devil's advocate, di Stefano is an Italian who was raised in the UK but who now operates out of Rome as the head of Studio Legale Internazionale. I could not tell you what makes Giovanni tick, but some people put it down to being motivated by a sense of injustice after he had been unfairly convicted of fraud back in the 1980s. Since that time he has fought tooth and nail for the underdogs, for the undesirables, or as he himself has put it, he will 'defend the indefensible.'

In 2011 Giovanni found himself defending his own name and reputation after being arrested in Majorca on a European Arrest warrant issued by Britain. It accused him of "fraud, theft and money laundering". The argument being that he had received money for representing people in the UK when he was not licensed to practice law in the country. He found himself on trial in Britain.

How many of his clients actually pay Giovanni, I have no way of telling, but his client list certainly makes interesting reading. It goes from Garry Glitter to Saddam Hussein, Jonathan King to the Butcher of the Balkans, from Charles Bronson to Ian Brady. He has tried to buy Norwich and Dundee football clubs, and found time to launch a political party and to record a couple of albums. In many ways he is bigger than life, and enjoys a scrap with the authorities, often embarrassing them in the process. Like a dog with a bone, he does not give up easily. I had no money to pay him, but he offered to come and fight in my corner.

In 2005 Giovanni petitioned the then Home Secretary, Charles Clarke, who had replaced Blunkett, to release me on compassionate grounds. It took until October to get an answer, and have it turned down, but Giovanni kept niggling away at the Home Office throughout 2006.

In early 2007, constitutional changes were being made which appeared to slightly move the legal goalposts. The post of Secretary of Justice was created and Tony Blair's mate Lord Falconer, then Lord Chancellor, was given the role. A role that gave greater power to the Ministry of Justice.

Falconer did not last long because on 27 June Gordon Brown took over from Blair as Prime Minister. In his first cabinet he appointed Jacqui Smith to take over as Home Secretary and a certain Jack Straw to fill the new role of Secretary of Justice as well as holding the post of Lord High Chancellor. Now Mike likes to credit a woman's touch, but a week after Jacqui Smith took over at the Home Office I was on the move.

Without warning, and without even informing Mike, I was shipped bag and baggage out of Belmarsh and moved to the 'nursing home' wing of HMP Norwich, which had been specially kitted out to look after elderly patients, serving life terms. The date was 4 July 2007. My independence day from Belmarsh after six long, long years.

The media was told that I had been switched to the Category C prison on compassionate grounds. Mike said it was a victory for common sense, even if he did question the common sense of not telling him or I about the move.

Yet again the stench of government paranoia hung in the air, suggesting that they felt there were still groups out there ready to spring me to freedom at a moment's notice if they had a tip off I was being moved.

Norwich, which I had last called home back in 1959, was a big improvement on Belmarsh, even if it did mean a lot longer round trip for Mike and friends to visit me.

It had first opened as a prison way back in 1887. The Inspector of Prisons had blasted Norwich in a report in 2003 for its poor hygiene and the lack of work and education opportunities. It was also criticised for overcrowding, and in 2005 the Victorian era A-Wing was said to be unfit for 'human habitation' and closed down.

In theory the brand new L wing offered 24-hour nursing care for just 15 elderly lifers. The prison held 450 prisoners over nine wings, although it is now up to 760 with the opening of the renovated A Wing.

My unit had been designed, decorated and installed with facilities with the elderly in mind. The living room was furnished with matching upholstered chairs and round tables, so that if one of us elderly prisoners were to fall, we would not be injured by a sharp edge. The walls were painted magnolia and extra-wide doors and corridors allowed wheelchair access to the rooms and cells when we needed it.

The barred windows even had blinds, and my personal joy, a small garden area, had been provided to allow us a place to sit outside, weather permitting. I even had an electric bed that could be lowered to make it easier to get in and out of if required.

Even the prison regime was in theory tailored to meet the needs of the elderly and frail. What you have to take into account, and no offence is meant to the fine people that looked after me while I was in Norwich, but if you are at the top of your game as a doctor or nurse, why choose to work in the prison system? The care, as it turned out, was not what it was cracked up to be in the brochure and I now started to wonder if I was being used as a poster boy for the 'new' Norwich Prison.

But the entire prison and atmosphere was more relaxed and a lot more pleasant than at Belmarsh and I was both pleased and proud to see that the prison roof that I had helped to build back in 1958, was still there and still water and weather proof.

I quickly discovered that the new generation of inmates were unlikely to have to get off their backsides and build a new roof. Health and safety would not allow it, they explained to me. As a result I saw that the kids, many of whom couldn't even read or write, spend their waking hours playing with their game stations. You don't have to be a genius to know that they are probably going to be in and out of the prison system for the rest of their lives.

My guardian angel in Norwich was a man called Bob Sharpe. Bob helped me with just about everything, including communicating with fans and friends that wrote to me in Norwich. A good man is our Bob. Tim was also a great help.

Although visiting me became easier in Norwich than Belmarsh, Norwich is not the easiest place to get to, so visits were fewer and further between. Regulars, besides Mike, included Roy Pickard, Maria del Medico, Mike Gray, and a number of others. If you did make the trip, I appreciated it.

With most of the legal avenues now blocked or tried, Mike and I were reduced to making the occasional appeal for my release from Norwich on compassionate grounds. But there was simply no sign of life or compassion coming from the government of the day. They had a war to fight and I was not part of it.

Chapter Nineteen

CLUTCHING AT STRAWS: IN SICKNESS AND WEALTH

'The problem with Mr Biggs is that no-one has formally asked me for his release.'

Jack Straw, Secretary of State for Justice, February 2009

'For the reasons given, I have declined the Panel's recommendation and so refuse Mr Biggs parole.'

Jack Straw, Secretary of State for Justice, 1 July 2009

Biggs: 79, Dying, but "Still a Risk"

Evening Standard, 1 July 2009

'I am granting Mr Biggs compassionate release on medical grounds.'

Jack Straw, Secretary of State for Justice, 6 August 2009

The clock seemed to tick ever slower in Norwich. The days dragged. Sleep was my only release. In my dreams I was free and I could still talk.

My lawyer, Giovanni di Stefano, now focussed his attention on making sure I got the best possible shot at parole, if and when I was considered eligible.

Giovanni opened discussions with the Justice Department. He wanted to make sure that we were all doing the same maths. His argument was that when the authorities calculated time served, it should not only consider the time I spent in Wandsworth before my escape, but also the time I was held in prison in Brazil and Barbados at the request of the British Government. As a certain supermarket likes to say, every little helps.

As the Justice Department should have learnt from its previous dealings with Giovanni, you argue with him at your peril. It was amazing how Giovanni's threat to go to the European Courts or some other body would get the Justice Department and the stuffed suits of Westminster to rethink and refocus. What had been a definite 'no' suddenly became a 'maybe'.

In September and December 2007 further appeals to get me released on compassionate grounds were made by Giovanni and Mike to Jack Straw, the new Secretary of State for Justice.

A statement put out in my name said: 'I am an old man and often wonder if I truly deserve the extent of my punishment. I have accepted it and only want freedom to die with my family and not in jail. I hope Mr Straw decides to allow me to do that. I have been in jail for a long time and I want to die a free man. I am sorry for what happened. It has not been an easy ride over the years. Even in Brazil I was a prisoner of my own making.'

At first it was the governor of Norwich, James Shanley, who vetoed my request, and this despite the clearance from his prison doctors, who said I was 'physically incapable of committing further crimes'. Even the probation services were making the right noises and said they were satisfied with Mike's plan to put me in a private nursing home in Barnet, close to his house.

But in the governor's view, when asked if I should be released, he wrote: 'No. There is little evidence that Mr Biggs is likely to die imminently and I do not think that he is incapacitated enough to not cope with the prison environment. HMP Norwich is able to adequately care for Mr Biggs.'

It would seem the governor wanted to hang on to his poster boy. With the governor blocking my release, Giovanni turned his attention again to Jack Straw.

'It is not the role of the Prison Service to provide nursing care,' he wrote to Straw, 'but a role that should be for the National Health Service or, as it is conceded that Mr Biggs is clearly of no risk to anyone including himself, he should be released on compassionate grounds.'

Answer came there none.

Speculation began to mount in the press as to when I might be eligible for parole. 2010 was talked about as the worst-case scenario, but Giovanni was pushing for 2009, even Christmas 2008, and kept the issue bubbling nicely in the papers and along the corridors of power.

By 4 April 2008 Giovanni had shown the Ministry of Justice that I had been in custody for a total of 3,385 days. By any calculation I should be eligible for parole after 3,652 days in custody, one third of my 30-year or 10,957 day sentence. It was Giovanni's submission that I should be eligible for release on 25 December 2008.

In July 2008 Giovanni got agreement from the Parole Board that in principle 130 of the days I had served in Brazil and Barbados would now be counted.

'I am cautiously optimistic that Mr Biggs will be released from HMP Norwich, God willing, on February 14,' Giovanni told the press. 'The Parole Board still have to agree to it, but I can't see why they won't grant this to a man of nearly 80 years old who is no danger to anyone.'

It appeared that almost since the first time I got back to Britain, things were finally moving in the right direction. My direction. It was not going to be a Christmas Day release, but Valentine's Day also seemed appropriate. A probation officer met with Mike and visited his home in Barnet. Talks started between Norwich and Barnet Primary Care Trusts as to which authority would fund my care. The view was that I needed 24 hour care as I would be unable to look after myself. It would have to be a care home and not Mike's house.

During this period the only excitement in Norwich was the case of the 'missing key'. And for once, I was not to blame! Somehow a screw mislaid a crucial key and as a result a whole series of locks in the prison had to be changed at a cost of some £250,000.

At the start of 2009 my health took a serious turn for the worst. In February, when I had hoped to be released, I made my first visit to Norfolk & Norwich University Hospital where I spent three days being treated for pneumonia, something that became increasingly difficult to shake off. Mike was blocked from seeing me in the hospital, the governor telling him that he should wait until my return to prison and normal visiting times.

The media again speculated as to why, given my health, I was still locked up. There was a wall of silence from the Ministry of Justice but Mark Leech, editor of the Prisons Handbook, told the press that the answer was really quite simple. Jack Straw had told him: 'The problem with Mr Biggs is that no-one has formally asked me for his release.'

Behind the scenes a lot was going on that not even I was aware of. In February 2009 various bodies and agencies met to discuss the case and tried to tick all the appropriate boxes, of which there were many.

In March Giovanni filed the official request to the Parole Board for my release under the Discretionary Release Scheme. The paper work ran into hundreds of pages of documents and forms.

A slight SNAFU occurred in early April when Barnet Primary Care Trust decided without warning, put possibly spotting a PR disaster with local voters, to question if it was really its responsibility to look after me. The concern was linked to the 'resident test' that is based on where a person 'currently or most recently lived', or even where they last received treatment. The problem was that other than Belmarsh and Norwich prisons, I had not lived in Britain since 1963 when I was resident at Alpine Road in Redhill. The link to Barnet was because Mike lived there, and for all intents and purposes his house was now the family home.

In time for the full meeting of the Parole Board on 23 April the Probation Officer in charge of my case filed her report. Her recommendation was straightforward and to the point.

'Based on the information available to me and following interview I have assessed Mr Biggs as being suitable for early release on parole licence to a suitable provision with a full care package in place to manage his health needs. The risk of reoffending and harm he poses is assessed as low.'

As nobody at the prison or Parole Board had the time or the patience to sit with me to go through everything point-by-point, it was left to Giovanni to help fill in the details on the interminable forms, most of which had not been designed for a crime such as the Great Train Robbery. Sweeping generalisations were taken, so it was put down that I was carrying an offensive weapon at the robbery, an iron bar. I did not, but I was told these were minor bureaucratic details, and not to worry.

Throughout the report it was noted: 'Due to his (Biggs) current state I am not able to access him properly, he cannot speak or write.'

The Probation Officer herself wrote: 'Due to his lack of communication and his reliance on a very basic tool as a substitute, it has not been possible to establish in any depth his current or past attitude to the offence. Mr Biggs fully admits taking part in the robbery as a member of the group. He denies being the person who struck the train driver on the head. When asked if he had any regrets Mr Biggs said 'positive', however, it was difficult to ascertain whether he was referring to his life in general, or specifically the commission of the offence, although I gained the impression that this was meant in the context of having no regrets in general.'

It was also clear that the timescale for many of the questions on the form were intended to cover recent happenings, not events that had taken place nearly 50 years earlier. It meant the appeal Judge's view that my crime, the Great Train Robbery, was 'an act of warfare against the state,' still stood. At the time of the Great Train Robbery in 1963 I was considered by the probation service to be a risk to 'members of the public and the Post Office and its employees', but now, in 2009, I was thought not to be a personal threat to anybody, in fact the form noted that the press and media was seen as a possible threat to my good self and anybody close to me. Especially in the first 72 hours of my release, or if I should 'pass away.'

Despite my ill health, my hopes were raised and the light at the end of that long, long, tunnel was starting to shine a little brighter.

The meeting of 23 April turned out to be major anti-climax. Without an agreement between Barnet and Norwich Primary Care Trusts, nothing could move forward. The only positive factor was that for the first time I saw in writing that it was agreed that my Parole Eligibility date would be early July. Even the press reported that I had been judged as being 'suitable for parole'.

It took until 3 June for an acceptable deal to be struck, but a solution was found with the London borough of Barnet agreeing to fund my care at a new nursing home that was to open later in the month and which was located next to the town's main hospital. Hopes were again raised for a July release.

On the 15 June the Parole Board finally came up with its report. Its version of the events surrounding the Great Train Robbery was an interesting read to anyone who knew the facts. It had me saying that what happened to Jack Mills was a 'light tap', not language that I ever used or would use. There were a number of other major errors, but I was told to ignore them, as the bottom line was that the Parole Board had recommended my release. It was, I was told, a bit like quibbling over the small print in an insurance policy. It was the stuff that nobody was ever meant to read.

The Parole Board sent its recommendation through to Jack Straw and the Ministry of Justice that I should be released. It was nearly time to celebrate and 3 July was now being talked about as the date for my probable release, almost two years to the day that I had been moved from Belmarsh to Norwich, and eight years and two months since I had landed back in Britain from Brazil.

As my release was certain to be a media circus, Mike started to look at my options. One suggestion was to do a joint deal with a newspaper and TV company that would set up a safe house in which I could enjoy my first days of freedom.

This was based on a real concern that in the narrow roads out of Norwich I would be chased all over the country by the press pack. If I could slip out the back way, I could go to a safe house where I would have a full medical check up and tell my story in a less stressful setting. I would then hold a press conference or photo opportunity where I would ask the media to respect my privacy and that of the other patients in the care home.

The last thing I wanted was somebody's granny being bowled over into the rhododendrons by some over keen paparazzi hiding in the bushes.

Mike, along with Chris Pickard, started to talk to a number of interested media parties. Chris already knew that he would be helping me to update my autobiography. The original *Odd Man Out* only went as far as 1994. We had 17 years and a lot of troubled water flowing under the bridge to catch up on.

Having learnt never to count my chickens, I remained calm on the exterior and told Mike I would only believe I was a free man on the day it actually happened. We were still waiting for Jack Straw to sign off on the Parole Board's decision, but Giovanni assured me it was just a formality.

On 28 June, just a week before my release, I had a stupid fall in Norwich Prison that resulted in me being rushed to Norfolk & Norwich University with a suspected broken hip and, for good measure, a serious chest infection.

It was immediately clear that I was unlikely to be fit to go anywhere by 3 July and so the idea of a safe house went straight out of the window. I would gain my freedom lying in a hospital bed. I could cope with that.

Wednesday, 1 July 2009 is a day I will never forgot. Nor will anybody close to me.

Giovanni had received a devastating fax from Jack Straw. In a covering note of just two paragraphs Straw told Giovanni: 'I have considered very carefully the recommendation of the Parole Board Panel of 15 June that Ronald Biggs, currently detained in HMP Norwich, be released early, when he becomes eligible for early release on 3 July. For the reasons given in the attached statement, I have declined the Panel's recommendation and so refuse Mr Biggs parole.'

It was a hammer blow, and nobody knew how to tell me, or Mike. There seemed no logical reason for Straw's decision and even the Parole Board were stunned, as never before had its recommendations been ignored. And why wait until just two days before my expected release date? Even my bed was made up in the care home. We were that close.

Among the reasons Straw listed for not releasing me was that I had undertaken no formal risk reduction work. Yet the Parole Board had addressed the fact that my medical condition did not allow me to undergo such work.

Straw's main beef, however, was that I remained 'wholly unrepentant' for my crime or my life on the run. This all based on the Parole Board report, rather than anything that had gone on in my life before or might have appeared in the press. Even comments on film or in my autobiography that I had made about my regrets were ignored. The fact that the Parole Board had never asked me directly if I was repentant was not apparently relevant. According to Straw's office I should have second-guessed them and recorded that I was.

To add insult to injury, in his note to me Straw wrote: 'Whilst the medical evidence indicates that your ability to commit further acts of violence has reduced to a very low level, I am concerned that you might incite and be involved in such acts of violence, through association with criminal peers. I am supported in that concern by your lack of repentance for and attempt to minimise a crime, in which the train driver was knocked out with an iron bar, as a result of which he could never return to work and from which he never fully recovered.'

As I have said many, many times before. I never committed an act of violence at the train robbery. I did not hit Jack Mills. I was not even on the train when Mr Mills was coshed.

If Mr Straw really subscribed to the belief of collective responsibility, then the government would have to charge and arrest all the police officers on duty at the G20 Summit in London in April 2009, as the violence used by the police on the protestors, which resulted in injury and a death, was far more extreme than anything that happened or was used at the Great Train Robbery.

I have always worked on the assumption that Mr Straw was not a stupid man and was at heart a decent man, so I had to believe that he was either being very badly and inaccurately briefed by people in his department, or by other outside forces that had other interests.

Nothing made sense anymore, although the following day, and slightly lost by the media interest in my story, Jack Straw also turned down the opportunity to grant a pardon to one Michael Shields, the Liverpool supporter who had been accused of murdering a Bulgarian football supporter in 2005.

I was being told to reapply for parole in a year or two's time. Mr Straw had affectively passed the death sentence on me and the state of my health immediately caused concern at the hospital who called Mike and said he should get over to the hospital immediately as they had concerns if I would make it through the night.

Even in my weakened state I was stunned. Mike, who called Straw's decision 'vindictive', was in shock. Even the media, which were preparing themselves for my release, were left speechless and – trust me – that doesn't happen very often.

Giovanni may also have been stunned, but he was also outraged and demanded an immediate judicial review, pointing out to the Justice Secretary the factual errors in the judgement, and that he appeared to have made that judgement based on 'speculation, gossip and opinions', rather than the facts.

'You have stated,' Giovanni wrote to Straw, 'that Mr Biggs poses thus a risk of re-offending. I think it is safe to presume both de facto and/or de jure that the said ration is simply unsustainable and beggars belief from an eminent political figure and lawyer as yourself.'

To the press Giovanni said the decision was a 'cruel and unusual punishment'.

Mentally I was spent. I had no interest in staying alive and spending another year in Norwich, and my body started to shut down. It had been a good run, but now it was over.

Photos reached Giovanni in Italy that showed the state I was in and these went out to the press to show what a 'dangerous man' I clearly was. Giovanni also discovered that it was not actually clear in law if the new position of Secretary of State for Justice had any power to block the Parole Board's recommendations. The issue was even raised in the House of Commons by Kate Hoey, but her concerns were dismissed by the argument that the government could treat me under old laws relevant to the time of my crime, rather than current legislation. I'm surprised that they had not decided to burn me as a witch, as a witch-hunt was what it was turning out to be.

After a few terse letters between Giovanni and Straw's office, it was suggested by the Ministry of Justice that 'this correspondence is now at an end'.

The correspondence, as you can well imagine, did not end there. Bollocks to that, and Giovanni continued to explore each and every legal avenue still open to us, including the legality of Straw's decision. Other people close to me opened a more informal dialogue with Straw's office to try and work out how Straw and his team could get it so wrong.

One example is that Straw's office mentioned photos taken at my 70th birthday party in Rio as proof that I would 'associate with criminal peers' as it showed me flanked by Bruce Reynolds and Roy Shaw. The fact that Bruce and Roy had not been involved in any criminal activity in years, did not seem to cross their mind, so it had to be pointed out that if the camera had panned around it would have also caught lawyers, politicians, rock stars and senior police officials, all of whom were at my party and enjoying themselves and the company of Bruce and Roy.

The penny, it would seem, had still not dropped with the Ministry of Justice that I had not committed a crime since the Great Train Robbery in 1963, unless you count jumping over the wall at Wandsworth, entering a few countries without the proper papers, and enjoying a few joints and driving without a licence. I was a risk to nobody, but myself.

Mike kept the case in the press and made it quite clear he was not going to take it lying down, even if I would have to. Mike had to say some harsh thing about Mr Straw and his office, but he really wasn't left with much option.

As my health deteriorated I do think it finally crossed the minds of a few people in the government that I might die on their watch. Certainly the hospital did not want me to die in their care, especially as they could not treat me in the way they wished. But Norwich Prison also did not want to be held responsible.

Legal opinion, and this has subsequently been backed up, is that Giovanni had a very strong case and a judicial review would throw out Jack Straw's ruling. But did I have time?

In November 2009 the Chairman of the Parole Board, Sir David Latham, would admit that there was no 'rational reason' for Jack Straw not to have released me earlier. He accused Straw of allowing public opinion to cloud his judgement as well as there being a 'political element' involved. He added that had my lawyers challenged the ruling by judicial review, we would probably have been successful.

The judicial review was filed on 17 July, the same day that I was recalled to Norwich Prison against the wishes of some of the doctors looking after me. I slipped in to deep depression. I was not well physically or mentally, and the will to live was ebbing away.

Ten days later I was rushed back to Norfolk and Norwich University Hospital suffering with severe pneumonia. Mike was called and told to get to the hospital as they felt it was now simply a question of time. They were talking hours to Mike, days at best.

Doctors looking after me told the press that I had 'little hope of recovery'. They also came to an agreement with Mike that I would not be resuscitated if my heart stopped. Mike stayed by my side telling me to keep fighting and not to give up on him.

Mike, Veronica and Ingrid were the only people allowed in to see me. My hospital room was being treated as an extension of the prison, with even a metal detector at the door and three guards on constant watch. MPs who wanted to come and see for themselves how ill I was, were turned away. Glibly being told they could visit me once I was back in Norwich.

Just as the MPs were split on if or not I should be released, so were the media with many inaccurate and misleading pieces about why I should be kept behind bars and the key thrown away. Even the Religion Editor of The Daily Telegraph, George Pitcher, decided to put the boot in on a dying man. Clearly no forgiveness or turning the other cheek in his church. This Anglican priest went as far as to call me a 'monumental shyster, who used and abused those closest to him.'

The easy course of action for any journalist writing about me is to back the ill-informed lynch mob, and so my admiration, respect, and thanks, go out to the journalists who took the trouble to look at my case and had the guts to go on record that I should be released. Fiona Phillips in The Mirror was one of these who backed the case for my release, as did Robert Chesshyre in *The Independent*, Simon Hattenstone in *The Guardian*, and Nick Cohen in *The Observer*. Judy Totton kept my story in front of the key journalists and Steven Berkoff also took the trouble to write a stinging letter to *The Sunday Times* that said: 'Jack Straw's dismissal of the recommendation by the parole board for the release of an ageing and sick Ronnie Biggs can only appease the puritan and the self-righteous, and those with a lust for punishment.'

By now so many calls for my release on compassionate grounds had been made that it was felt to be a futile gesture that would yet again fall on deaf ears and fallow ground, but one that should be made all the same.

There was a difference, however. In talking to the doctors Mike had been told that I would never recover from my chest infection as the saliva would always be running down my windpipe, as I could no longer control my throat muscles. Mike asked them if they would put this in writing, and they said yes. After nine years an emotional Mike finally had the piece of paper that said I would never recover. He quickly scanned it and sent it over to Giovanni to add to the growing paper work.

On the Thursday a spokesman for the Prison Service told the press: 'We can confirm that an application for the early release on compassionate grounds of a prisoner at HMP Norwich has been received by the Public Protection Casework Section in the National Offender Management Service.'

Two days later, on 30 July, the High Court granted the legal review of the decision surrounding the blocking of my parole. It would take time, and time was not what I thought I had on my side if I wanted to die a free man.

A week later Mike received a number of calls from friendly journalists. They had been called to the Ministry of Justice where Jack Straw would issue a statement in regard to my condition, and they wanted to know if Mike knew why? There had been no warning and the feeling was that the Ministry would not call the press together unless they had something of importance to impart. It certainly wasn't going to be for an updated medical bulletin or to tell them what I had eaten for breakfast.

On Thursday, 6 August Justice Secretary Jack Straw issued a short statement on the 'release of Great Train Robber Ronnie Biggs':

'Mr Ronald Biggs has been informed today of my decision regarding his application for compassionate release on medical grounds.

'On 1 July I refused Mr Biggs' release on parole. These two decisions however involved different considerations. I made the decision to refuse parole principally because Mr Biggs had shown no remorse for his crimes nor respect for the punishments given to him and because the Parole Board found his propensity to breach trust a very significant factor.

'In this case, I have had to consider the medical evidence against well-established criteria – specifically whether death was likely to occur soon and whether the prisoner was bedridden or severely incapacitated. The medical evidence clearly shows that Mr Biggs is very ill and that his condition has deteriorated recently, culminating in his re-admission to hospital. His condition is not expected to improve.

'It is for that reason that I am granting Mr Biggs compassionate release on medical grounds. I have therefore been satisfied that the relevant conditions have been met, which I was not in respect of the recommendation for parole.

'Mr Biggs will be subject to the same strict licence conditions as other prisoners on release. He must live at an approved address, behave well, and cannot travel abroad without approval. If he were to breach those conditions or commit any further offence, he would be liable to immediate recall to prison.'

As I've said before, I am a great believer in fate. Although the date of the train robbery had taken place on 8 August, it had been a Thursday. So news of my release from Mr Straw came exactly 46 years after that fateful day in 1963 when the 16 of us ambushed the Glasgow-to-London mail train.

Exactly a year later, on 6 August 2010, Jack Straw was to announce that he was stepping down from frontbench politics. The 'luck' of Biggs had struck again.

The actual date for my release was set for the following day, Friday 7 August. The weight of the world was being lifted from my shrivelled shoulders, but I was far too ill to fully appreciate what was going on.

I can confirm that neither Mike or I had any prior warning of the decision to release me on compassionate grounds. Nothing had come out of the Ministry to suggest this decision was even on the table. Why common sense suddenly prevailed, I do not know, but fuck it, I will be forever thankful.

One suggestion is that by losing the judicial review, irreparable damage would have been done to the new office of Secretary of State for Justice. As it was the law would be changed or clarified so that in future cases the Secretary of State for Justice would have no or only limited say over the Parole Board's recommendations.

Lovers of a good conspiracy believe that my release was a simple smoke screen for the more politically and internationally sensitive release of the Lockerbie bomber, Abdelbaset al-Megrahi, on similar compassionate grounds just two weeks later.

You can't argue that the press had thoroughly debated the issue of a 'compassionate release' when I was freed, and so there was a whole lot less to discuss or say in editorials in the case of al-Megrahi.

If you really like a good conspiracy, consider that a month later Jack Straw's office announced that due to 'new evidence' he was going to pardon Michael Shields, the Liverpool supporter. Not a word of complaint was heard from Bulgaria, a country I might suggest that had good ties to Libya.

To be honest I did not and do not give a bollocks as to what was true and what was fiction, or who was running with what conspiracy. I was just grateful that I was a free man and could die a free man. I had never given up, and neither had my family and close friends. I had served a total of 3,875 days for my part in the Great Train Robbery out of the original sentence of 10,957 days. I had also spent 13,068 days on the run. It had been a long, challenging and tiring 46 years.

Despite slipping in and out of consciousness, I felt I was almost home and free. For once I might no longer be the odd man out, and for once I slept well and had pleasant dreams.

As news of my impending release broke, the press started to gather outside the hospital, as well as at Mike's house in Barnet. For some of the press and media, especially the TV reporters such as Keir Simmons of ITV and Martin Brunt of Sky, they were getting rather more familiar with the delights of Norwich than they might have cared to. Please accept my apologies gentlemen.

Giovanni explained to Mike that despite Straw's announcement there was still paper work to take care of, including the licence for my release, and that is why my 'official' release would take place on the Friday.

As far as Giovanni knew, somebody from Norwich Prison would turn up at the hospital with the papers I needed to sign for my release. After I had signed them I would officially be a free man and the guards could leave my bedside.

I would no longer be a guarded man, but equally I might be exposed to any nut job that might decide that the only good Ronnie Biggs was a dead one. With that in mind Mike got on the phone to Roy Pickard, a good and trusted friend who had come to visit me in Rio in 2000 and who had been a regular visitor at Belmarsh and Norwich. Roy knew how to look after himself and others. He has the presence that would stop people taking any liberties and he agreed to come and babysit me around the clock by sleeping on the floor of my room for ten days until I was well enough to move to the care home.

The hospital itself had done a great job of keeping unwanted guests at arms length. Even the most tenacious of the paps had not got in to see me. The hospital reassured me that they would keep me safe, even once the guards had left.

Mike drove across to the hospital early that Friday and we waited. It was early afternoon when the deputy governor of Norwich Prison turned up with the paper work. He explained to me the rules by which I was being released, and I put my weak scribble on the licence at about 1.50pm. With that the guards packed up their stuff and bade me a fond farewell. I shook each of them by the hand and then gave them a little wave as they left the room. A room that was no longer a prison cell, but a hospital room. You can't even start to imagine how good that feels after 46 years.

The Ministry of Justice formally told the press at 2 pm that I was a free man. Mike said he felt he owed it to the waiting press pack to go and say a few words and give them a photo opportunity. As he went to leave the room he turned back and thanked me for 'sticking around'.

Mike went out to meet the press and took a copy of my licence with him. He waved it for the cameras; he kissed it, and told the press it 'smelt like freedom'. 'As a family, we are absolutely thrilled,' he told the press. 'My father is now a free man and that's all there is to say. It was very emotional when the guards left. The media made Ronnie Biggs into what he is, and the media is here when Ronnie Biggs is about to close this last chapter. He will now be retreating fully from public life. This is not going to turn into a media circus. There is absolutely no chance of my father being seen in the West End with a couple of girls around him. This is not going to turn into some sort of freak show and my father is not going to turn into some sort of Z-list celebrity. It is going to be very private from now on.'

Speak for yourself, Mike!

At the time I thought the Great Train Robbery was a very special birthday present, but this was even better. Even in my frail state I was looking forward to celebrating my 80th birthday, and the 46th anniversary of the robbery, as a free man.

Well-wishers inundated Mike's phone and the hospital switchboard, but given my health we decided that I should have a quiet family birthday on the Saturday with just Mike, Veronica, Ingrid and Roy in the room. But some friends could just not stay away and made the trek down to Norwich, they included Frank Werner, who had popped over from Germany, Tony Hasting, Gio, Dickie Finch, and even the chaplain from Norwich Prison.

Given the media interest, Mike allowed *The People*, which had been supportive to my cause, to come in and get some exclusive photos of the birthday boy for the Sunday paper. I was still in a daze.

We owed one other journalist a favour, and that was Marcos Losekann, a good friend and neighbour of Mike's in Barnet who was also the TV Globo anchor in Britain. It was nice to be able to do something that would be seen by my many friends that I had left behind in Rio and not had the chance to say my proper goodbyes to.

In a nice twist the material aired that Sunday on *Fantastico!* The prime time show that had often followed my exploits in Brazil from Raimundo's tearful thoughts at the time of my arrest, that first press conference with Charmian in Brasilia in February 1974, to Mike's first TV appearance pleading for my release from the kidnappers in 1981, and my interview with Albert Spaggiari that same year.

The doctors and nurses at the hospital seemed genuinely pleased for me, and said as much. A doctor also explained that they wanted to submit me to a small operation and change all the tubing that was feeding me and keeping me alive. He felt it could have been one of the causes of all the infections I was picking up, and which were slowly killing me.

I appreciate my health is always going to be an issue, one that won't be settled until I do die. I think I am going to have to follow Spike Milligan and put on my tombstone, 'I told you I was ill.' Or perhaps I should allow Jack Straw to pay for it and it can read: 'I told you he was ill.'

Even Prime Minister David Cameron got in on the act during a Commons debate in February 2011 about the release of the Lockerbie bomber when he was asked if it was a coincidence that I was freed just weeks before al-Megrahi. Cameron told the Commons: 'It does seem to me to be a pretty good medical record that people released from prison, normally on the brink of keeling over, then last for a very, very long time.'
I am dying. It is simple as that. I may even be dead by the time you read this. If the pneumonia doesn't get me, then another stroke surely will. The doctors have not been lying to anyone when they say I have been at death's door. They did not call Mike and tell him to rush to the hospital because they were having a laugh.

What has kept me going all these years when I should have been dead and buried, is my sheer bloody mindedness not to give in. Fuck 'em I thought. Once I was a free man I decided the least I could do was to fight for my health and try and keep myself alive. I did this by setting myself little targets and steps.

On the news of my release I promised Mike that I would stick around for his birthday. I promised him I would get myself well enough to make it to the care home and visit his house.

Using Mike's mobile we put in a few calls to people that mattered to let them know I was a free man.

The first was to Charmian in Australia and there was not a dry eye in the room I am told. I wept and wept as I heard her voice over the speakerphone. I could not talk, but I could make a noise to let her know I was there and that I still cared, and always would. Through the tears she promised to come and see me, which set me another target to aim for.

We also caught Johnny Pickston in Rio. He helped raise my spirits, as did the fantastic staff at the hospital that started giving me the treatment they felt I needed. Starting with the replacement of all the rotten tubing.

At 2.40pm on Monday, 17 August, the day after Mike's birthday, I was covered from head to toe in a blanket and wheeled out from my room under the watchful eye of Mike and Roy and into an ambulance for the transfer to the care home in Barnet.

Barnet has had a few famous residents over the years. It was about to get one more.

A man went on *"Who Want's To Be a Millionaire"*. He had made it all the way to the million pound question and still had all his lifelines intact. A hush fell over the audience as the host, Chris Tarrant, asked him: Which of the following Ronnies was the Great Train Robber?

a) Ronnie Corbett
b) Ronnie O'Sullivan
c) Ronnie Barker
d) Ronnie Biggs

Quick as a flash he says: 'I am going to take the money and I don't want to use my lifelines, final answer.'

He takes the money and after his friend asks him: 'How come you didn't know the answer, everyone knows who the Great Train Robber was?

'Of course, I know it was Ronnie Biggs,' he replied, 'but like Ron I ain't no grass!'

FIFTY YEARS ON: END OF THE LINE

This is like putting Ronnie Biggs in charge of the Royal Mail. You despair for the British electorate.

Having me look after the wine is rather like putting Ronnie Biggs in charge of the trains.

Ronnie Biggs would be envious of Tony Blair's escape record.

Putting Gordon Brown in charge of the country's finances is like putting Ronnie Biggs in charge of train security.

As for the Speaker being put in charge of a review of Parliamentary expenses, that's like putting Ronnie Biggs in charge of the Crown Jewels.

Various commentators take Ronnie's name in vain.

If you had told me when I returned to Britain in May 2001 that I would survive for eight years in prison and still be alive a decade later, I would have said you were taking the piss and would not have believed you. And neither would anyone who had seen me in Rio in the days before I left for the UK. But here I am. I hope.

My story stands as it began - hard up. Hard up, but happy, contented and thankful; although in truth I might be dead and buried, and long forgotten, by the time you do get to read these words.

For the want of a few quid fifty years ago, I had plunged headlong into an enterprise that was to lead me into almost forty years of a life 'on the run' and ten years locked up behind bars. Had I heeded the advice of the old fortune-teller in Hastings back in 1963 things might have turned out to be very different. I might have spent the rest of my life freezing my nuts off on some bleak building site somewhere in Britain. So, if you want to ask me if I have any regrets about being one of the train robbers, I will answer, 'NO!' and without hesitation. I will go further: I am proud to have been one of them. I am equally happy to be described as the 'tea-boy' or 'The Brain'. I was neither, but I was there that August night in 1963 and that is what counts. I am one of the few witnesses to what was 'The Crime of the Century'. I am also proud of the fact that my 'track record', such as it was, enabled me to be considered to work alongside such eminent fellow thieves and good company. But a 'thief' in 1963, was a very different animal to a 'thief' today.

In 1964 controversy did rage over the sentences the train gang were given. Some thought the punishment was too harsh and there were those who thought the thirty-year sentences fitted the crime. I was one of them. Armed with coshes, we had attacked the Royal Mail, injured a defenceless man and made off with more than two million quid belonging to the banks. Don't believe the story that the money was on its way to be destroyed. Much of it was in mint condition. It was obvious that we were going to go down for a long time.

In retrospect, I don't think the coshing of the train driver had a major bearing on the sentences that were handed down at the time. Had he not been injured, I believe that we would have still been fitted up with thirty year terms as that is what the government of the day wanted. It wanted to send a message that it would not tolerate organised crime. Robbing the Royal Mail was also a crime against the Crown and came close to being an act of treason. We all well knew what we were getting into and we all knew we'd get 'big bird' if we were nicked.

For my part, I was prepared to do my time, keep my nose clean and try not to break the rules. Although parole did not exist in the British penal system in 1964, it was evident that a parole scheme would be introduced and I believed that it would be possible to get out after ten years or so. Not a pleasant prospect to think of 'treading out' that length of time, but I was ready to get on with it, for the time being anyway. Had the then governor of Wandsworth prison given more serious thought to my plea to be treated like any other con, when I was being harassed into a probable nervous breakdown, I might well have served out my time as a model prisoner and been released along with the other members of the gang in 1975.

But I didn't. I ran away, and I'm glad I did! And I would do it all again without the slightest hesitation!

'But, Ronnie you must regret the fact that you can't go back to England!' the British tourists and the press always insisted when they met me in Rio.

'You're wrong!' I told them. 'I could go back tomorrow if I wanted to!' And, of course, I didn't want to! At least, not at that time if it meant going to jail. To hell with that, I still had a life to live!

But the strokes and other health and emotional difficulties made me have a rethink. I don't think I was looking for closure, but we can call it that if you want. I prefer to think that I made the decision because I did not want to become an even bigger burden to my family and friends than I already was. During my life I have disrupted far too many lives, and on both sides of the law, and it was simply time to stop running. Something that is easier said than done when you are still one of the world's "most wanted", but I knew deep down that the time had come to return to Britain under my own steam and face the consequences of my actions.

Although I have said that I have no regrets with regard to my involvement in the train robbery, that isn't strictly true. It is regrettable, as I have said many times before, that Mr Mills was injured and terrified out of his wits. During Jack Slipper's visit to Brazil we spoke about the train driver and his injuries and Mr Slipper voiced the opinion that the coshing of Jack Mills amounted to 'unnecessary violence'. I agreed with him, but I pointed out that the driver was only struck once, and by mistake, and not 'beaten repeatedly, with blows from an iron bar and left broken and bleeding beside the railway track', as I had read in a copy of the *Daily Express* at the time of my capture in 1974. Even in 1993, the *Sunday Express* still saw fit to describe how Jack Mills was 'cut down by a blinding whirl of iron bars.' A lot of people still think Jack Mills died at the robbery and I was the one who hit him. One of my nurses had even been told that I had shot him!

For the crime it was, remarkably little violence or force was used on the night of the Great Train Robbery compared with other crimes of the day, and it pales into insignificance compared with what goes on today. You will see far more violence and risk to life and limb in an average episode of Road Wars than occurred that night back in 1963, but most of the people using violence today are let off with a warning or a light slap on the wrist, and nobody says anything or raises so much as an eyebrow.

And not taking anything away from the injuries that Jack Mills suffered on the night, but he did not die of those injuries. He died seven years after the robbery and of leukaemia. So can we at least get the facts right.

And let us not forget about Billy Boal, the truly forgotten victim of the Great Train Robbery as far as an injustice is concerned.

It goes without saying that I will always regret that I lost my wife and children when I left them in Australia and went on to Brazil. Perhaps that is when I should have given myself up. Perhaps not. Of course I love them today as much as ever, despite the time and the distance.

Charmian and the boys came back to Brazil several times after our tearful parting in 1974. Sadly at the time of writing they have not yet made it to the UK for a reunion. Farley and Chris are now both grown men with their own families. Charmian did a magnificent job of bringing them up. She also found time to study and won herself a BA degree with honours in history and English literature.

She still lives in Melbourne and has held some responsible positions over the years, including with the Australian Wheat Board. Charmian has never remarried, but I believe had a number of 'flings' that never worked out; she once declared that she had 'an unhappy knack of picking wrong uns'.

She may not believe it after all I have put her through, but she remains the love of my life and always will. I hope that when I am gone, history and people will be kind to her. Charmian and the boys deserve it for what I put them and their families through.

Mike is still Mike. What more can I say? He has developed into a handsome young man, or perhaps middle-aged man is now nearer the mark. A fine mixture of Brazilian Indian and South London, who speaks English with a distinct Cockney and Carioca twang. He blames his receding hairline on the pressure I heap upon him. He is his own man, a family man, who for his sins and for the part he plays in my story, will always have to walk in the shadow of the 'legend' that is Ronnie Biggs.

My illness and return to the UK certainly disrupted Mike's life and that of his family. For the moment they are settled in Barnet, but who knows what the future will bring for them and where the wind will take them. Hopefully good, happy and more settled times lie ahead. And if it is a question of the weather, the food and the booze I think, if I was them, I would be on the next plane back to Rio. From what I see and read these are exciting times for Brazil, and I know Mike still has big plans. One day he will hit the bullseye. Of that, I have no doubt.

Raimunda is settled in Geneva, Switzerland, where she lives happily. I'm glad to say that we are still close and she showed what a true mum she was in coming to Mike's aid and marrying me in Belmarsh. I am still waiting for her to drop by the Nursing Home so that I can consummate the marriage, but I think she may have other ideas. *Obrigado por todo Xuxu.*

From the sublime to the ridiculous. As you have read, John Miller - or, McKillup - is a very dangerous man. As a result of his confessed mischief, I came close to suffocating in a canvas bag and drowning in shark-infested waters. He was also guilty of traumatizing my six-year-old son. Kidnapping is a very grave crime; a despicable crime, punishable by death in some enlightened parts of the world. Tragically, kidnapping has been rife in Brazil in the past and for a time almost every day the television news showed a heartbroken parent pleading for the return of their loved-ones, just as Mike pleaded for me.

Many people have asked why charges were never brought against Miller and his gang. I ask the same question but nobody ever seems to want to give me a straight answer. Describing his adventures in Barbados in a book that was supposedly written by him, Miller tells how 'Our Man' from the High Commission arrived at his hotel and told him, quote: 'Mr. Miller, Her Majesty's Government would strenuously advise you to leave Barbados.' Unquote.

Representatives of the Brazilian government were on their way to the island, he was informed, and wanted to return with me to Brazil. They were also arriving with a request to the Barbadian government for Mr Miller's extradition to Brazil on a charge of kidnapping. He and the rest of the rabble should have been detained but they were allowed to flee from the island unhindered. Perhaps the late Sir Hugh Fraser had a hand in it - or one of

Sergeant Miller's old officers, or someone even higher in British government circles. I have even been told of the involvement of the Masons.

I am not sure we will ever know the truth as Miller still throws up the occasional smoke screen, like the Kidnapping Ronnie book and TV programme that he dreamt up with Patrick King to squeeze yet more money out of his crime.

There is a postscript to the Miller conspiracies. Soon after I arrived back in Brazil from Barbados, an official enquiry was held with regard to my kidnapping. I had to make a statement which was taken down by a Federal Policeman on a typewriter. Dr Bizzo, the delegado, was conducting the enquiry. Describing my arrival on the Nowcani II, I remembered the piece of paper that Miller had held up, the piece of paper with the circular emblem at the top, that Miller had said had 'made doors open like magic'. The delegado stopped me. It was not necessary, he said, to enter into details, and the reference to the document did not appear in my statement that I signed. Later, together with Armin and John Pickston and the pilot of the Lear jet that had taken me to Belem, I appeared before a court where charges of kidnap were read out against Miller and his accomplices.

Back to happier thoughts. Frederick Smith Q.C., or Sir Frederick Smith as he became in 1987, Ezra "Sunshine" Alleyne, and Alan Shepherd. I cannot thank you three learned gentlemen enough for your magnificent work in getting me back to Brazil from Barbados. Without doubt, the three finest lawyers I ever met - and I've met a few! I remember them with true affection and admiration. I believe that these fine gentlemen continue to apply their legal skill to the benefit of many in the Caribbean. It would be interesting to know if 'Perry Mason' ever did lose a case.

Perhaps this would be a good point to convey my thanks to all the other good and 'bad' people in Barbados who gave me their support and friendship when I was there, especially the gang on Death Row. I love you all! And please let me hear from someone, telling me that hanging has been abolished in Barbados. Except for kidnappers, of course.

My admiration also goes out to my lawyers in the UK. They include Jane Wearing, Guy Kearl and Nigel Sangster Q.C. who all went the extra yard for me when I returned from Brazil. These are decent people who were willing to stand alongside me when I needed them.

And what can I say about Giovanni di Stefano, the thorn in the side of the British authorities, who stuck at it until they basically shouted ENOUGH! Who loves you Giovanni? If I still had my voice I would be there to duet with you on your next album. Well it helped the Sex Pistols!

Giovanni's client list is, to say the very least, eclectic. It says something when I am one of the more normal people and cases on the list of those he has represented. You may not agree with what he does, but you should, because the legal system is a complicated mine field and us mere mortals, whatever our shortcomings, do need a good guide to help us pick our way through it if there is to be any semblance of justice in the world.

I also need to thank the people who not only helped me when I got back to Britain, but also stood by Mike in his hour of need. Take a bow Judy Trotton and John Taylor, Daniel Manzi, Michael Beckford, Mel Griffin, Joe Pyle, Breiti, the Crockers, Barnet Rob, Carlos Alberto (yes, that Carlos Alberto) and Tranters Solicitors.

So all that is left to do for now, is to tidy up a few loose ends of my story.

I am often asked about 'the four who got away' at the robbery, but as I've never had any contact from any one of them there's little I can or will say about them. The novel I wrote with Chris, *Keep On Running*, was pure fiction.

Old Peter, who was in his 60s at the time of the robbery, has almost certainly passed on. It's quite amazing that the police never discovered his identity. I heard from Slipper that the police had 'made enquiries' among railwaymen at Redhill but the old man was never suspected so I hope he got to enjoy his whack. What happened to the other three members of the gang proper is anyone's guess; I just hope their good luck continues! As for the rest of the gang, I lost contact with most of them during my years on the run and living in Rio, only keeping up with Bruce Reynolds who, of course, I knew long before the robbery. Sadly I did not get to see Angela, Bruce's wife who I knew as Frances or Franny, before her death at the end of 2010.

Of the old gang, Jimmy Hussey has been kind enough to drop by and see me at the nursing home. It has been great to see him and catch up on too much lost time. It reminded me that Jimmy was a great one for the rhyming slang, so I was "Syrup of Figs – Biggs', while despite not being the 'Weasel', Jimmy used to pull Roy James' leg and refer to him as the 'Board and Easel'.

All of the robbers are now old men and living on borrowed time. We have already lost Buster, Charlie Wilson, Roy James, and old Peter, of the 16 people known to be at the track, and at least one of the lucky three. We also lost Billy Boal, who died of cancer in prison in 1970 and was never one of the train robbers. Brian Field died in a car crash in 1979 after being released, while his wife at the time of the robbery, Karin, died more recently having returned to Germany with her and Brian's secrets.

And I am not sure what it says for our respective life styles, but Old Bill has fared even worse than the robbers. Slipper died in 2005, as did Malcolm Fewtrell. Gerald McArthur died in 1996 and the Grey Fox, Tommy Butler, back in 1970. The judge, and our high chief executioner, Lord Chief Justice Edmund Davies, died in December 1992 at the age of 86.

Roy "Pretty Boy" Shaw, who I shared mailbag duties with in Wandsworth, and who very nearly joined my escape plan, has been another very welcome visitor to the nursing home. Roy, who came to Rio for Christmas 1998 and my 70th in 1999, has his own health problems, but regularly dropped by to see me.

Dave Courtney tried to organise a tribute evening for Roy and I, but by the time the media had got hold of the story the tribute had become a lifetime achievement award for my "life of crime", not something that would have sat very comfortably with the Home Office or Justice Department, so I made my excuses to Dave and stayed at home in front of the TV.

Mike Haynes and Jessie split up and found themselves new mates. I've lost contact with them but I would dearly love to hear from them or anyone who knows their whereabouts. Likewise Eric Flower and his wife, Carol, and all my other friends and acquaintances that I have mentioned throughout the book and who are still with us.

I can understand if you want to remember me as I was, but if you can put up with my spelling board then I would love to see you. The nursing home does make a mean cup of coffee and the staff will make you laugh.

I do hope to see my old friend from Rio, Tim O'Toole, when the Spanish authorities have finally finished with him. Despite what the Spanish may think, Tim was a great laugh in Rio and always a pleasure to be in the company of.

I also had the pleasure of removing $200 from his wallet when I bet him that Buster Douglas would beat Mike Tyson. Just my luck Tim!

I also hope that Johnny Pickston and Fred Sill will make it over to London from Rio before I call time.

Friends new and old do come calling. And I appreciate it. Roy Pickard, has been a rock and good friend. I kept him fit by getting him to push me around Barnet in a wheelchair when the weather allowed. The home is on a hill, so you have to be as strong and as fit as Roy to get me moving, but some of the nurse of shown they are up to the challenge.

Chris (Pickard), no relation to Roy, has also been a regular caller as we painstakingly updated the autobiography you are now reading on my spelling board. At times it was like pulling teeth. Not sure if they were Chris' or mine, but we made it. Chris still can't spell, and is still a fan of all things Mac and has taken great delight in showing me my photos and videos on his iPad. Hopefully I will have one soon. Chris has often been the quiet voice of reason behind the scenes and tries to keep me out of trouble when he can.

The ever-generous Brian Running drops by to cheer me up on a regular basis when he is in town from Miami, and he even managed to take me to the Scotland x Brazil game at the Emirates, as well as a number of jazz lunches. Terry Dunne, who lives locally, has been another good source of company. One-Arm Kev Rawlings and Kerry have also been in, as has Richard Keaney, Nick Reynolds, Frank Werner, Alan from Bristol, Tony Last, Aaron Smith, Jack Cook, Rene Moserman, Mike Wade, Dee Morris, Andy Jones from Littledean Jail, Tony Hastings, Steve Stephens, Alan Wilson from Western Star, Gio, and, of course, Dickie Finch. Dickie being Mike's neighbour and the reason we all now call Barnet home.

I would also like to thank Dickie's good friend, Lee Thompson, a man better known for his sartorial line in headgear and as the saxophonist of Madness, who generously donated a mobile scooter to me. Sadly the scooter got vandalised by some local youths, but the up side was I did get a letter from the Metropolitan Police that began: 'Dear Mr Biggs, We are very sorry that you have become a victim of crime...'

Many may argue I have been a victim of crime ever since 1963. The crime of the mobile scooter remains unsolved.

And while I am talking about bikes, but rather more powerful motors, I would like to send my thanks and best wishes to Lea Valley Hells Angels. You know what for. Very much appreciated and very enjoyable is all I will say. Otherwise my lips are sealed.

My release has allowed me to meet and make new friends. One colourful character is David Worrow, a man who can happily lay claim to owning the best selection of train robbery memorabilia. You'll have to ask him how he got hold of much of it, because I'm no grass. A collection, he says he will eventually pass on to Nick Reynolds to curate. I would very much like that.

One item David tracked down was my old prison file from Wandsworth. These were the files that registered my every movement around the prison. The last page is of my movements on 8 July 1965 and that at 2.30pm I left the shop and went to the exercise yard, never to return. According to the file, I must still be there!

David did cause me a little spot of bother on one of his visits by taking me back to Bridego Bridge. This was something that was to remain a secret, or at least a secret until I was no longer around to worry about it.

Unfortunately for all the wrong reasons one of David's photos taken that day ended up in *The Sun* newspaper. On this occasion I can honestly hold my hands up and say 'not guilty your honour', as there was an offer on the table of £20,000 from another paper for the first photos of me at the bridge. An offer I had refused. Put it down to a lapse of judgement on my part, which is exactly what the Parole Board did when it read me the riot act and threatened to put me back behind bars.

It should not be surprising to anyone that I did feel the need and urge to visit the bridge, a location that was to totally change my life, but which I had only visited once before, and then in the dark. One day there will be a plaque on bridge 127 to mark it as the site of the Great Train Robbery, but somehow I doubt it will happen while I am still around. Pathetic, but true.

Yes, I am still on licence, and unless I have got the card from the Queen, will probably be so until my dying day. There are still restrictions as to what I can do, where I can go and whom I can meet, but I make do. I did get the thumbs up from the Parole Board to go and see my beloved Arsenal thump Fulham and Brazil beat Scotland at the Emirates Stadium. I think it helped that a couple of my nurses and parole officers are Gooners, and I even managed to pull off the visits by going unnoticed. The tabloids are clearly losing their touch, or perhaps its because I don't have a phone!

While the Royal pardon remains firmly stuck in the post (perhaps she sent it to Rio), I still have a few things to tick off on my wish list before the great publican in the sky calls time. Before then I hope to see Charmian and the boys again. I also hope to go and see our old house in Alpine Road, and other places from the past that I feel are special to me. I also feel I owe it to Margate to get there for that pint that I promised myself. It is the least I can do for the town.

Sadly I can't drink that pint of bitter any longer, but if I could I would raise my pint and drink a toast to absent family and friends, and to you, dear reader.

I want to thank you all for being a part of my life and my journey. It does not matter if you love me, or hate me, the journey would have been nothing without you. So for now it is time for me to clutch that last straw, and time to stop running. From the odd man out, it is over and out for now. And as you ask, yes it was a life worth living, even with the regrets.

Say goodbye, my own true lover,
As we sing a lover's song.
How it breaks my heart to leave you;
Now the carnival is gone.
High above, the dawn is waking,
And my tears are falling rain,
For the carnival is over;
We may never meet again.

Now the harbour light is calling;
This will be our last goodbye.
Though the carnival is over,
I will love you till I die.

The Carnival is Over, The Seekers, November 1965

Keep On Running, my first novel.

Ready to launch Odd Man Out to the world on 21 January 1994.

A couple of old posers celebrate. Me and my 'ghost' and good friend, Christopher Pickard, celebrate the launch of Odd Man Out in 1994.

Best mates. John Stanley Pickston, Brian Running and I.

Mr. Pickston at play.

John, Fred Sill and I in happy 'Rio' times.

My great friend and housekeeper, Rosa.

Not sure the hair treatment did much for me. Taken days before my major stroke.

A very tired birthday boy.

New family. Veronica with Ingrid, Mike and I. The effect of the strokes starting to show.

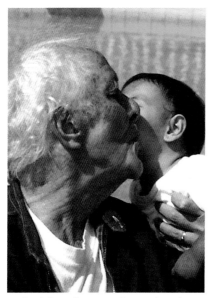

A final kiss for Ingrid, on the day I headed back to England.

Being pushed the last few yards by Mike through Rio Airport on 6 May 2001.

Mike and the blushing bride, his mother. 10 July 2002.

Chiswick Police Station. First day back in the UK. 7 May 2001.

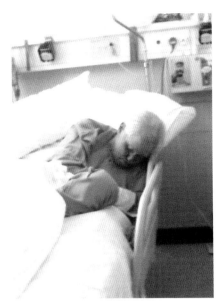

At death's door. July 2009.

The Right Hon. Jack Straw MP.

Who is the man! Giovanni di Stefano.

'Still At Risk'. You could not make it up.

The sweet smell of freedom. Mike celebrates with the media the news of my release on 7 August 2009.

Arriving 'home' on 17 August 2009.

Protecting me for once!

The reason my freedom is so precious to me. Mike, Veronica and Ingrid.

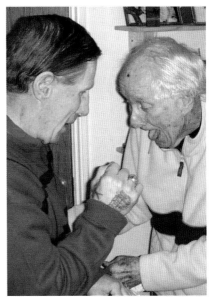

I still think I could take Roy (Shaw).

My special girls. Ingrid and Lilly.

Once a Gooner, always a Gooner. Unless Brazil is playing.

One day a commemorative plaque will tell you that this is the site of the Great Train Robbery. But I don't expect to be around to see it.

Bah! Humbug! Off with you! But thanks for coming along for the ride. My life would have been very dull without you. Merry Christmas.

THE LIFE & TIMES OF RONALD ARTHUR BIGGS

1929 - 8 August
Ronald Arthur Biggs is born in Lambeth, south London.

Son to Henry Jack and Lillian Edna (née Clayton) Biggs. Brother to Jack, Victor, Terry and Iris.

Lived in Dalyell Road, SW9, close to what is now the O2 Brixton Academy.

1931 - 7 September
Bruce Richard Reynolds born in the Charing Cross Hospital in the Strand.

1936
Biggs family moves around the corner from Dalyell Road to 30 Kimberley Road, SW9.

Biggs goes to school in Lingham Street.

1939 - 17 May
Charmian Powell, the future Mrs Biggs, is born.

1940-42
Due to World War II and the Blitz, Biggs is evacuated from London to Coombe-in-Teignhead in Devon and Delabole in Cornwall.

He returns to London in 1942. Biggs goes to Stanley Street School and Brixton School of Building.

1943 May
Biggs' mother, Lillian, dies at the age of 53 from a duodenal ulcer. Biggs is 13.

1945 - 9 February
Biggs' first court appearance at Lambeth Juvenile Court at the age of 15.

The charge is stealing a pen refill and eraser of 1/2d value from a shop display.

8 June
Second appearance at Lambeth Juvenile Court for stealing four radio valves and an eggcup.

Bound over for 12 months and find £1. Discharged.

October
Mrs Elis moves in with the family. Biggs' father had met her while on holiday in Ramsgate.

16 November
Third appearance at Lambeth Juvenile Court for stealing his brother's watch. Bound over for a further 12 months and find £1.

Prior to case Biggs is held at Stamford House. After the case moved to McGregor House, a home for working boys in Tulse Hill.

1947 May
Biggs enlists in the Royal Air Force. Signs on for eight years as a regular and four years in the reserves.

Posted to Cardington and then Melksham in Wiltshire. Finally to RAF Halton close to Aylesbury. At Halton does a cookery course.

1949 - 8 February
First court appearance as an adult at County of London Sessions.

17 February
First prison sentence – sentenced to six months for shop breaking, housebreaking, stealing and using a false ID card.

Items stolen included an electric iron, a brooch and musical instruments.

Dishonourable discharge from the RAF.

26 June
Released from Wormwood Scrubs.

28 July
Sentenced to three months in Wormwood Scrubs at the North London Magistrates Court for 'taking and driving away a motor vehicle'.

Meets Bruce Reynolds in Wormwood Scrubs.

26 September
Released from Wormwood Scrubs.

30 November
Sentenced to Borstal training after being found guilty at Essex Quarter Sessions for shop breaking and stealing.

1950 - 21 March
On trial at the Old Bailey for the first time for robbery of jewellery and money, and being armed with an offensive weapon.

28 March
Sentenced to three years and six months on "special watch" as an A list prisoner.

April
Meets Eric Flower in Wormwood Scrubs.

Second spell in HMP Lewes for Young Prisoners. Reacquainted with Bruce Reynolds.

1952 - 19 August
Released from HMP Lewes.

Meets up with Bruce Reynolds.

1953 - 24 March
Found guilty at Country of London Sessions for garage breaking and stealing a motorcar.

30 March
Found guilty at Buckinghamshire Quarter Sessions for house breaking and stealing a bottle of sherry valued at 18 shillings.

Concurrent sentences of three years from Country of London Sessions and four years from Buckinghamshire Quarter Sessions.

Sent to HMP Wandsworth, where he meets Bruce Reynolds again.

1954
Transferred to HMP Dartmoor.

1955 - 13 December
Released from HMP Dartmoor.

Goes to live in Merstham, close to Redhill in Surrey.

Meets Michael Haynes.

1956 - 15 June
Two-year probation order at Surrey Appeals after being charged for stealing paint and a bike.

Starts work as a carpenter on building sites in Redhill.

1957
Biggs changes jobs to erecting partitions in offices in central London.

October
Meets the 17-year-old Charmian Powell, the future Mrs Biggs, on the train between Redhill and London.

20 December
Elopes with Charmian to Swanage, Dorset.

1958 Early
Arrested in Swanage with Charmian and Michael Haynes

1 April
Sentenced to 12 months at Dorset Quarter Sessions for 'taking and driving away a motor vehicle'.

Charmian and Michael Haynes receive suspended sentences and probation.

25 April
18 months added to sentence by Surrey Appeals under probation order for stealing paint and a bike in 1956.

Biggs transferred from HMP Dorchester to HMP Norwich after one month.

Builds a new roof for HMP Norwich extension.

1959 July
Transferred from HMP Norwich to HMP Wandsworth.

2 December
Released from HMP Wandsworth. Moves to Elm Road, Redhill with Charmian.

1960 - 20 February
Marries Charmian Powell at Reigate Register Office.

17 May
Charmian Biggs' 21st birthday.

23 July
Nicholas Grant Biggs born at Redhill County Hospital.

Moves to 37 Alpine Road, Redhill.

1961 July
Visits Hastings with the Searles and sees a fortune teller.

1962
Biggs sets up a building business with Ray Stripp in Redhill.

Bruce Reynolds' gang pull off a minor train robbery close to West Drayton in West London.

27 November
Nucleus of Bruce Reynolds' train robbery gang pull off the London Airport Robbery at Comet House. Biggs not involved.

26 December
While hauling the up Midday Scot,

diesel loco D326 runs into the back of the Liverpool – Birmingham Express between Winsford and Crewe.

18 passengers are killed and 34 injured.

D326 (40126) is the engine that will be involved in the Great Train Robbery.

After the robbery a secondman was electrocuted in 1964 when working on the engine.

In 1965 the engine had total break failure when entering Birmingham New Street and hit a freight train injuring the guard.

1963
THE YEAR OF THE GREAT TRAIN ROBBERY

February
Brian Field contacts Gordon Goody with information about a very large regular transfer of money by train.

24 March
Christopher Dean Biggs born at Redhill County Hospital.

Biggs plans to buy Alpine Road.

March onward
Planning and preparation for the Great Train Robbery.

Introduction by Field of Gordon Goody and Buster Edwards to the "Ulsterman" in Finsbury Park.

Meeting at Waterloo Station to introduce Roger Cordrey, head of South Coast Raiders, to Buster and Goody.

Subsequent meeting at Buster's flat in Twickenham for Bruce Reynolds to talk details with Cordrey and Tommy Wisbey.

1 May
Legal start of "conspiracy" that becomes the Great Train Robbery.

Full meeting of train robbery gangs.

Countryside outside of Leighton Buzzard chosen by Reynolds and Cordrey as the best location for the robbery.

June
Biggs asks Bruce Reynolds for the loan of £500. First time Biggs hears of the robbery.

Bruce Reynolds along with his wife and son visit Biggs at home and he is invited to be part of what will become the Great Train Robbery.

Biggs to supply a train driver for the job.

Gang meeting held as a football kick-around on Wimbledon Common.

Biggs introduced to Gang at Roy James' flat in Nell Gwynn House, Chelsea. Voted on to job. James votes against.

Biggs takes Peter, the train driver, to Euston to check on the trains.

Establish that pressure is needed for the breaks to be released and for the train to move.

24 June
Bruce Reynolds visits Midland Marts Estate Agents in Bicester to look for "hideout".

Visits Leatherslade Farm.

Offer made on Leatherslade Farm.

July
Drivers test the route between Bridego Bridge, south of Leighton Buzzard, and Leatherslade Farm.

Low-key rehearsal at Stewarts Lane, Nine Elms, Battersea.

Final roles decided for robbery, but all the roles are interchangeable in case someone is missing or incapacitated.

Everyone told to make their own arrangements for after the robbery.

21 July
Land Rover stolen from Oxenden Street, London WC1 to be used in the robbery

26 July
Ex-War department Land Rover purchased from London motor dealer. Number plate is BMG 757A that is also used on stolen Land Rover.

29 July
Leatherslade Farm purchased by gang via Leonard Field for £5,550 (about £95,000 in 2011 values).

30 July
Austin goods platform truck purchased from government surplus contractor in Edgware.

31 July
Goody and Edwards hold last meeting with the "Ulsterman".

Date of robbery set for the morning of Wednesday, 7 August.

2 August
Gordon Goody flies to Northern Ireland to establish an alibi.

5 August
Bank Holiday Monday. Biggs takes his family to Brighton.

A £10 bet on the horses wins him over £600, but bookie has £500 limit (£8,500 in 2011 values).

6 August
Biggs and Peter travel by train from Redhill to meet Reynolds at a café in Wilton Road, next to Victoria Station for breakfast.

Also at Victoria Station are John Daly, Jimmy White and Mr Three.

Group from Victoria arrive at Leatherslade Farm mid-morning in one Land Rover.

Leatherslade Farm is located 300 yards off the B4001, the Thame Road, close to the villages of Brill and Oakley, between Bicester and Thame.

Part of the Gang turn up in the afternoon in the Austin truck.

Charlie Wilson and Roy James arrive in the second Land Rover.

Roger Cordrey turns up at the farm under his own steam.

Goody goes to the house of Brian and Karin Field in Pangbourne to wait for the go-ahead from the "Ulsterman".

Robbery postponed for 24 hours.

7 August
Biggs' brother Jack has died overnight.

Charmian calls Redhill Police Station and asks the police to look for Biggs who is "tree felling in Wiltshire." The call is logged.

Mr Wyatt, a neighbouring farmer, calls at Leatherslade Farm to meet the "new" owner. Reynolds tells him they are just the decorators.

Night Flyer, Up Postal, consisting of an engine and five coaches leaves Glasgow for London at 6.50 pm.

Night Flyer arrives at Carstairs at 7.32 pm where four coaches that had left Aberdeen at 3.30 pm are added to the train. Departs at 7.45 pm.

The engine and nine coaches arrive at Carlisle at 8.54 pm where three further coaches are added. Departs at 9.04 pm.

Gordon Goody slips out of Leatherslade Farm to find a local phone box and call Brian Field (10 pm). The job is on.

Train stops at Preston from 10.53 to 11.03 pm; and at Warrington from 11.36 to 11.43 pm.

8 August
GREAT TRAIN ROBBERY – RONALD BIGGS' BIRTHDAY

Night Flyer, Up Postal arrives at Crewe Station at 12.12 am and leaves at 12.30 am with Jack Mills and David Whitby now in charge.

Just before 1.00 am the Gang leaves Leatherslade Farm dressed as an army detail on night manoeuvres.

Sorters Joseph Ware and John O'Connor join the train at Tamworth at 1.23 am and settle into the High Value Package (HVP) carriage.

2 am
Gang arrive at Bridego Bridge (Bridge 127).

Bridge 127 takes the rail track over a quiet county road west of the B488, two miles north of Cheddington Station.

At Bridego Bridge the Gang swap their army uniforms for overalls to appear as track workers if spotted by passing trains.

Markers placed at Bridego Bridge to show Peter where to stop.

Roy James, John Daly and Bruce Reynolds cut local telephone wires.

At the track: Bruce Reynolds is look out for the train just south of Leighton Buzzard. John Daly at the Dwarf signal.

Buster Edwards, Roger Cordrey, Jimmy White, Roy James, Bob Welch, Mr One, Mr Three to east of track at Sears Crossing.

Gordon Goody, Charlie Wilson, Tommy Wisbey, Jimmy Hussey, Mr Two, Peter and Biggs to west of track at Sears Crossing.

Train arrives at Rugby at 2.12 am and departs at 2.17 am, passing Bletchley at 2.53 am.

At 3.00 am Reynolds warns the Gang that the train is arriving having passed through Leighton Buzzard.

Night Flyer, Up Postal stopped at Sears Crossing at 3.03 am, 38 miles north of London's Euston Station.

Fireman David Whitby leaves the cab to look for a trackside phone to check why the train has been stopped.

Cab is stormed. Buster Edwards and Gordon Goody first of the Gang on train.

Jack Mills is coshed by Mr Three and in falling strikes the back of his head against the cab wall.

Biggs enters cab with Peter. Peter fails to move the train so Jack Mills does.

Engine and HVP carriage detached from the rest of the train and moved south to Bridego Bridge (3.14 am).

Five sorters in the HVP carriage, a further 70 sorters spread through the rest of the train.

Roy James, riding on the outside of the engine, sees the marker at Bridego Bridge and tells Goody to stop.

As the train stops at Bridego Bridge the assault starts on the HVP coach.

Biggs takes Peter to sit in Land Rover and watch the rest of the robbery unfold.

The assault team on the HVP coach is lead by Charlie Wilson and includes Hussey, Goody, Welch, Buster, Wisbey, Mr One and Mr Three.

Chain of men moves 120 bags containing 636 packages from the HVP carriage to the lorry. 8 bags left behind.

40 minutes after stopping the train at Sear's Crossing, and 24 minutes since stopping at Bridego Bridge, Reynolds calls a halt (3.40 am).

New Scotland Yard receives a call at 4.24 am from Euston that Cheddington Signal Box is requesting the attendance of police and an ambulance.

First police arrive at the scene of what will be known as the Great Train Robbery at 4.35 am.

Gang arrive back at Leatherslade Farm at around 4.40 am.

Malcolm Fewtrell, Head of Bucks C.I.D. arrives at the train at 5.00 am.

It takes Reynolds, Biggs and Mr Two three hours to unpack the money. Cordrey and Wilson act as the accountants.

Final tally from the robbery is £2,631,784 of which only £343,448 was ever recovered. (First official figure was £2,595,997.10s)

The take of the Great Train Robbery at 2011 sterling rates is over £44 million.

Money split into 16 equal "whacks" of £147,000 (approximately £2.5million in 2011 rates).

15 "whacks" for the 15 robbers at the track and one "whack" for the Ulsterman.

£40,000 for Peter. £100,000 to be split by Brian Field, John Wheater and Leonard Field.

Reynolds remembers that it is Biggs' birthday and wishes him all the best.

By noon police say on the radio that they believe the hideout is "30-miles or a 30 minute drive" from Bridego Bridge.

At Bridego Bridge the police collect evidence – a bloody cloth, the coupling. But clues are few and far between. No finger prints, no tyre marks.

First newspaper reports say £100,000 stolen.

From Mills, Whitbey and the HVP sorters' statements, the police estimate that there were around 15 hooded men involved.

Jimmy White starts to paint the Austin truck yellow.

Roger Cordrey cycles 20 miles into Oxford to get the newspapers and check the lay of the land.

Reynolds encourages everyone to wipe the place down. "No dabs are to be left".

9 August
The Gang awake early on Friday morning. "Cleaners" get to work again after breakfast.

Morning BBC Radio news report quotes the police as saying that they are certain the train robbers are still in the area.

Bruce Reynolds and John Daly leave the farm to organise transportation.

Mary Manson buys an Austin Healey in Chiswick.

Roger Cordrey returns with the newspapers and a car.

Gang members start to leave the farm.

Biggs leaves Leatherslade Farm with Reynolds in an Austin Healey.

They stop close to Heathrow airport so that Biggs can call Charmian to say he is on his way home,

Farewell between Reynolds and Biggs at Biggs' house in Redhill.

They would next meet 29-years later in Rio de Janeiro.

Leatherslade Farm has been abandoned.

10 August
Gang members start to hide and "bank" their cash. Some head to London's West End to celebrate.

The Great Train Robbery is the dominant story on the TV and radio and in the newspapers.

11 August
'Ulsterman' visits Brian Field's house to pick up his 'whack' from Gordon Goody.

Police records show they were given the name of Bobbie Welch as one of the possible robbers.

13 key locations searched by police.

12 August
Farm worker calls the police about a lorry at Leatherslade Farm. The call is one of over 400 calls logged in Aylesbury that Monday.

13 August
Concerned about no news of the farm being burnt down, Reynolds, Buster, Wilson and James meet at a transport café on the North Circular.

Farm worker persists and calls again. Leatherslade Farm is discovered by PC John Woolley at 10.50 am.

"We found the farm pretty much as they had left it," Woolley recalled.

"Their vehicles were still in the yard, their foodstuffs in the kitchen, and the cellar was full of empty mailbags, overalls and masks."

Head of Bucks CID, Fewtrell, tells the media: "The whole place is one big clue."

Evening papers report that the "hideout" has been found.

Papers also mention that Det Chief Inspector Tommy Butler, the Grey Fox, has been brought in to head up the investigation.

14 August
First arrest at 9.00 pm in Bournemouth. Roger Cordrey and Bill Boal. Cordrey will plead guilty at the trial.

Mary Manson ("Cockney Mary") arrested while shopping and charged with receiving.

Police start three-day examination of Leatherslade Farm. 243 photographs are taken of 311 fingerprints and 56 palm prints.

Fewtrell visits Brian Field.

16 August
At 9.00 am a suitcase with £100,900 is found in Dorking Woods. It belongs to Brian Field.

A dress shop in Reigate is suspicious of a lady customer paying with dirty £1 notes. Customer traced to Clovelly Caravan Site at Boxhill.

Caravan belonging to Jimmy White found with £30,440 cash from the train robbery hidden in it.

19 August
Lorry and Land Rovers moved from farm to Aylesbury police station.

22 August
Charlie Wilson arrested at his home. The first major player in Reynolds' firm to be charged.

Wilson's fingerprints found on the kitchen windowsill, Saxa salt drum, and the cellophane wrapping of a Johnson's First Aid Travel Kit.

Mug shots circulated for Reynolds, White, James, Buster, and Wilson.

23 August
Gordon Goody arrested at the Grand Hotel in Leicester after being mistaken for Reynolds.

24 August
Inspector Basil Morris and Sergeant Church visit Biggs at Alpine Road in Redhill at 6.45 pm looking for Reynolds.

25 August
Police guard on Leatherslade Farm dropped.

Goody is taken to Aylesbury and interviewed by Butler, but released.

4 September
Biggs arrested at Alpine Road by Detective Inspector Frank Williams. Taken to Scotland Yard where Butler questions him.

Transferred to Aylesbury.

Police find Biggs' fingerprints on a blue-edged Pyrex plate and a bottle of ketchup.

5 September
Biggs is formally charged at Linslade Magistrates Court.

Sent to HMP Bedford.

7 September
Jimmy Hussey arrested. Evidence is a palm print on the Austin lorry.

11 September
Tommy Wisbey arrested.

Evidence is fingerprints on an attachment to the bath.

14 September
Leonard Field arrested as the purchaser of Leatherslade Farm.

15 September
Brian Field arrested. Fingerprints and a German receipt link him to the bag left in the Surrey woods with £100,000 of train robbery money.

3 October
Goody is re-arrested and his shoes are used as the evidence to charge him.

10 October
A man called Walter Smith is arrested and charged with receiving £2000 of train robbery money.

17 October
John Wheater arrested.

26 October
Bob Welch arrested. Palm print found on Pipkin of ale left in a cupboard in the farm.

November
Police by chance visit the house where Bruce and Frances Reynolds are hiding. They are not recognised.

3 December
John Daly arrested in Eaton Square. Fingerprints on a Monopoly board.

10 December
Roy James is tracked to his mews flat in St Johns Wood and arrested.

Prints on plate and Johnson's First Aid Travel Kit.

December
Butler tells the media he has 19 people in custody and is ready to start the Court case.

George Stanley, Biggs' solicitor, confirms to Wilson and Biggs that the main evidence against the Gang is fingerprints left at the farm.

Buster leaves England for Antwerp. Moves on to Cologne.

Jimmy White flees to Tangier.

9 of the 16 members of the Gang at the track are now in custody. [Wilson, Goody, James, Daly, Biggs, Cordrey, Wisbey, Welch, Hussey]

Gang transferred from HMP Bedford to the hospital wing of HMP Aylesbury for the trial to begin.

Goody, Wilson and Biggs work on an escape plan. Escape nearly comes off.

All the privileges are withdrawn from the prisoners and items smuggled in are confiscated.

1964 - 20 January
Opening of Great Train Robbery trial at the District Council Chamber in Aylesbury.

Charge is 'conspiracy to stop a mail with intent to rob said mail'.

Biggs represented by Wilfred Fordham and Michael Argyle QC.

Caught "bang to rights", Cordrey pleads guilty.

Fingerprint evidence presented.

Jack Mills gives evidence.

6 February
Retrial of Biggs ordered after Inspector Basil Morris lets slip that Biggs has served time in prison.

11 February
Prosecution rests. The defence starts.

14 February
John Daly acquitted.

10-14 March
Summing up.

23 March
Jury retires after 49-day trial.

26 March
Trial ends. Guilty verdict on the entire Gang.

8 April
Opening of Biggs' retrial.

14 April
End of second trial.

Guilty verdict on Biggs.

16 April
Lord Chief Justice Edmund Davies passes sentence on the Great Train Robbery Gang at Assizes.

BIGGS SENTENCED TO CONCURRENT SENTENCES OF 30-YEARS (10,957 DAYS) AND 25-YEARS

Most of gang get 30-year sentences.

The crime was 'robbery – being armed with an offensive weapon' (30 years) and 'conspire / robbery with violence' (25 years).

The trial lasted for 51 workings days over a period of 10 weeks.

Evidence had been heard from 264 witnesses and an estimated 2.5 million words had been spoken.

The words filled over 30,000 foolscap pages.

The 12 jurors, who were paid 50 shillings a day, had examined 613 exhibits and listened to 21 barristers.

Gang split up amongst some of Britain's most secure prisons.

Biggs transferred to HMP Lincoln.

May
Biggs transferred from HMP Lincoln to HMP Chelmsford.

4 June
Bruce Reynolds slips out of the UK. By private plane to Ostend and then on by car to Brussels.

5 June
Reynolds departs on a Sabena flight from Brussels to Mexico.

He travels as "K.C. Miller".

6 June
Reynolds arrives in Mexico.

Malcolm Fewtrell publishes *The Train Robbers.*

July
Frances Reynolds goes to Scotland Yard and asks to see Tommy Butler. Questioned for five hours.

Frances reunited with her son, Nick, who has been looked after by Mary Manson for over 10 months.

Frances takes Nick to the South of France for two weeks.

Gang reunited at HMP Brixton for appeal.

10-14 July
Appeals heard at the Old Bailey in London.

Wilson refuses to attend appeal so that he can stay at HMP Winson Green.

Cordrey and Boal get their sentences reduced to 14 years.

Brian Field has his sentence cut to 5 years.

Biggs transferred to HMP Wandsworth to serve his sentence. He meets Paul Seabourne.

July Late
Frances Reynolds and her son Nick join Bruce in Mexico. They travel as Angela and Kevin Green.

Frances would become known as Angela for the rest of her life.

12 August
Charlie Wilson escapes from HMP Winson Green, Birmingham, one year and four days after the robbery.

17 August
Gordon Goody's escape attempt from HMP Strangeways, Manchester, is uncovered.

Eric Flower sent to HMP Wandsworth. Roy 'Pretty Boy' Shaw also an inmate.

1965
Peta Fordham publishes *The Robbers' Tale.*

April
Charlie Wilson, who has been living in a safe house in Knightsbridge, leaves the UK for the South of France. Travels in the name of "Alloway".

Buster Edwards and family fly from Dusseldorf to Mexico City to visit Reynolds.

May
Paul Seabourne released from HMP Wandsworth.

7 July
Original E(scape) Day. Delayed due to rain.

8 July
For an alibi Charmian takes the children to Whipsnade Zoo.

Biggs arrives in the Prison workshop at 2.20 pm having missed the first exercise period.

2.30 pm
Biggs and Flower are moved from the workshop to the exercise yard.

BIGGS ESCAPES FROM WANDSWORTH AT 3.05 PM

Eric Flower escapes with Biggs from E Yard along with Robert Anderson and Patrick Doyle.

Seabourne is helped by Ronnie Leslie, as the getaway driver, and Ronnie Black.

Leslie and Black dropped at Tooting tube station. Anderson and Doyle given second getaway car.

Biggs and Flower taken to Seabourne's house in Dulwich.

Transferred by Freddie Foreman and Alfie Gerrard to a safe house in Bermondsey.

9 July
The house of Prince Carol of Rumania is raided by 150 police officers looking for Biggs.

16 August
Seabourne arrested and sentenced to four and a half years for helping Biggs to escape.

Ronnie Leslie gets three years for helping Seabourne.

Prime Minister Harold Wilson suggests to the Treasury that they secretly replace all banknotes in the hope of flushing out the train robbers and the money from the robbery.

July – Oct
Biggs and Flower are hidden in Bermondsey, Camberwell, Putney/Richmond and Bognor Regis.

Hideaways and travel is organised by Freddie Foreman, a friend of Eric Flower.

August
Charmian visits Biggs in Bognor Regis.

September
Biggs and Flower moved back to London, to the flat in Camberwell.

October
Biggs taken to Tilbury Docks with Flower and is put on a boat to Antwerp by Foreman.

BIGGS LEAVES THE UK

Travels as sports master "Ronald King".

Met in Antwerp and driven to Paris.

Oct – Dec
Paris. Biggs and Flower based in Rue Vivienne.

Biggs and Flower undergo plastic surgery.

Waxwork of Biggs and Charlie Wilson on display in the entrance to Madame Tussauds in London.

Charlie Wilson, now based in Rigaud, 20 miles from Montreal, visits Bruce Reynolds and Buster Edwards in Mexico.

22 December
Flower travels from Paris to Sydney as "Robert Burley".

Charmian and children visit Biggs in Paris for Christmas.

Biggs family spend Christmas at the Hotel Cécilia at 11 Avenue mac Mahon in the centre of Paris.

29 December
Biggs flies from Paris to Sydney via Zurich as "Terence Furminger", a writer born on 13 June 1928.

31 December
"Terence Furminger" (Biggs) arrives in Sydney.

1966 January
Biggs and Flower set up home in Botany Bay, Sydney.

Key train robbers transferred to HMP Parkhurst, Isle of White (Goody, James, Wisbey, Hussey, Welch, Cordrey).

8 February
Die Gentlemen bitten zur Kasse (The Gentlemen Require Payment) is first broadcast in Germany. Horst Tappert plays the part of Reynolds.

11 February
John Wheater released from prison.

FebruaryBruce Reynolds visits Charlie Wilson in Canada.

March
After their mail is intercepted, Biggs and Flower move from Sydney to Adelaide.

Biggs and Flower based at Surfside guesthouse in Grange.

"Terence Forminger" becomes "Terence King".

April
Carol Flower arrives in Australia with daughter Kim.

4 April
The Great St Trinian's Train Robbery has its premiere in London.

8 April
Life magazine runs a major feature Greatest Train Robbery Legend.

10 April
Sunday Express publishes photos of the "wanted" men.

12 April
Jimmy White arrested in Littlestone-on-Sea.

10 June
Charmian, Nick and Chris leave UK en route to Australia. Ferry to Ostend. Car to Brussels. Flight to Zurich to connect to Darwin flight.

14 June
Charmian, Nick and Chris land in Australia (Darwin) having flown BOAC from Zurich. Charmian travels as "Mrs Margaret Furminger".

15 June
Tommy Wisbey protests on the roof of HMP Leicester.

20 June
Jimmy White sentenced to 18 years.

July
Biggs family arrives in Adelaide after touring Northern Territory, Queensland, New South Wales and Victoria.

16 September
Buster Edwards and family leave Mexico.

19 September
Buster Edwards gives himself up.

8 December
Buster sentenced to 15 years at Nottingham Assizes. Half of what the other robbers received as a sentence just two years previously.

Judge decides that while Buster was 'in the hierarchy' he was 'not one of the leading planners.'

December
Bruce Reynolds and family leave Mexico and drive to visit Charlie Wilson for Christmas in Canada.

1967
Bruce Reynolds moves to the South of France.

21 April
Farley Paul born in Glenelg Community Hospital in Adelaide.

May
After receiving a warning the Biggs family move from Adelaide to Hibiscus Road in Melbourne.

Farley is just three weeks old.

"Terence King" becomes "Terence Cook". Charmian becomes "Sharon".

Brian Field released.

8 August
Robbery, starring Stanley Baker and directed by Peter Yates, opens in London.

December
Biggs family spends Christmas in Adelaide with the Flowers.

1968 25 January
Charlie Wilson arrested in Canada.

By chance Biggs meets up with Mike Haynes in Melbourne.

8 November
Bruce Reynolds arrested in Torquay, England.

December
Biggs family spends New Year in Adelaide with the Flowers.

1969 14 January
Reynolds sentenced to 25 years.

19/26 January
Frances Reynolds' story published in the UK in the *Sunday Mirror.*

4 February
Auction held in Measham, Staffs of personal effects of the Great Train Robbers as well as Reynolds' household furniture.

26 February
Chief Constable of Durham, Alec Muir, suggests in a speech that the Great Train Robbers should be shot.

March
Frances Reynolds' story published in Australia in *Women's Weekly.*

April
Anne Pitcher's son-in-law, Max Phillips, tells the police that Terry King has a strong likeness to Ronnie Biggs.

Flowers move from Adelaide to Melbourne after being questioned about 'Terry King'.

8 July
Biggs and Flowers celebrate fourth anniversary of the escape from Wandsworth.

July
Biggs has a bad car crash in Melbourne that results in a broken jaw and teeth.

16 October
Biggs' photo broadcast on Australian television.

17 October
FOURTEEN ARMED POLICE RAID THE BIGGS' HOUSE IN MELBOURNE

Charmian arrested and held at Fairlea Women's Prison before being transferred to Melbourne Police Watchhouse

Biggs checks into the Alexander Motel in Easden as Arthur Carson.

He leaves an unpaid bill of $3 when he leaves.

20 October
Charmian released from custody. Magistrates reject the Australian Immigration Department request to hold her for 7 days.

She sells her story to the Packer newspaper and television group for $A65,000 but only gets to keep A$25,000.

The Australian Tax Authorities take the rest.

24 October
Biggs and Charmian are the cover of Private Eye.

Eric Flower arrested in Sydney.

November
Alfie Gerrard arrested in Sydney.

Biggs moves in with Mike and Jess Haynes. Mike offers Biggs his passport.

Biggs uses his time with the Haynes to write down his story. Jess Haynes types it up. It is 77 pages long.

14 December
Eric Flower returns to UK and Wandsworth prison.

1970 January
Biggs gets to meet up with Charmian for the first time since being discovered in Australia. The meeting lasts for just one hour.

Biggs decides to try and travel to Rio de Janeiro, Brazil.

9 January
Australian police claim they have found two reels of 8mm film showing Biggs on holiday with the family in Spain.

Biggs has never been to Spain.

30 January
Pix magazine in Australia publishes a story about "Jack Mills: The Man Biggs Hurt".

4 February
Train driver, Jack Mills, dies of lymphatic leukaemia.

5 February
Biggs boards RHMS Ellinis in Melbourne as "Michael Haynes".

7 February
BIGGS LEAVES AUSTRALIA AS RHMS ELLINIS SAILS FROM SYDNEY

23 February
RHMS Ellinis docks in Panama.

26 February
Biggs flies from Panama to Caracas.

10 March
Biggs flies from Caracas to Rio de Janeiro.

11 March
BIGGS LANDS IN RIO DE
JANEIRO.

20 April
Det. Chief Superintendent Tommy
Butler, the Grey Fox, dies.

'Ronald Biggs Talks'. *The Sun*
publishes Biggs' story which he
had written while in hiding in
Australia.

Charmian had the manuscript
delivered once Biggs was safely
out of Australia.

26 June
The innocent William Boal dies in
prison.

September
Biggs takes a side trip to Buenos
Aires to renew his visa.

1971 5 January
Biggs' eldest son, Nicholas, dies in
a car crash in Melbourne, Australia.

February
News of Nicky's' death reaches Rio.

Biggs' first Carnival in Rio.

March
Biggs takes a side trip to Bolivia to
renew his visa.

April
Biggs rents his first apartment in
Rio de Janeiro.

Roger Cordrey is the first of the
main train robbery gang to be
released from prison.

July
Biggs meets Raimunda de Castro
for the first time at the Bola Preta.

September
Visa in Biggs' passport is no longer
valid for Brazil.

1972 6 January
Fireman David Whitby collapses
and dies, aged 34.

Charmian suggests Biggs returns
to Australia as he tells her he is
terribly unhappy in Brazil.

Mike Haynes asks Biggs for his
passport back.

1973 February
Biggs manages to send the
passport back to Mike Haynes
in Australia.

July
Haynes family plan to return to UK
from Australia.

Det Superintendent Frank Williams
publishes *No Fixed Address: The
Great Train Robbers on the Run.*

8 August
10th anniversary of the Great Train
Robbery.

November
Biggs talks with his friend
Constantine Benckendorff about
giving himself up.

December
Benckendorff travels to London
and meets with Colin Mackenzie.

1974 January
First contact with the *Daily
Express'* Colin Mackenzie.

24 January
Mackenzie and *Express* News
editor, Brian Hitchen, speak to
Biggs by phone.

30 January
Mackenzie arrives in Rio.

Biggs meets Mackenzie,
Benckendorff and photographer
Bill Lovelace in room 909 of the
Trocadero Hotel.

Trocadero (Av Atlantica, 2064) is
now the Arena Copacabana Hotel.

1 February
BIGGS IS ARRESTED IN RIO BY
JACK SLIPPER

Biggs taken to the Federal Police
Headquarters in the Catete Palace
in Rio de Janeiro.

Interviewed by Inspector Carlos
Alberto Garcia who decides Biggs
must be held over night while he
consults with Brasilia.

Biggs learns for the first time that
the father of a Brazilian child
cannot be extradited.

4 February
Det Chief Inspector Jack Slipper
and Det Inspector Peter Jones
return to London without Biggs.

Papers from the archives released
in 2005 reveal that the Foreign
Office demanded that Scotland
Yard apologise to Brazil's Federal
Police.

7 February
Biggs is transferred from Rio to a
prison in Brasilia.

Neighbouring cellmate is French
forger Fernand Legros

10 February
Charmian arrives in Brasilia.

16 February
Biggs and Charmian forced to
"hold" a press conference after
the press are allowed into their
private meeting.

Biggs tells Charmian that he needs
to divorce her so that he can marry
Raimunda.

Mackenzie offered a £65,000
advance by Grenada Publishing
for a book about Biggs.

March
Fernand Legros deported back
to France.

Michael Haynes prosecuted in Australia for helping Biggs. Serves time at Beechworth Prison, Victoria.

April
Family Court confirms paternity of Raimunda's expectant child.

6 May
Biggs is transferred from Brasilia to Rio and 'released from custody'.

Biggs stays overnight at the Catete Palace, leaving on 7 May.

The court orders that Biggs should be 'deported' not 'extradited'. This means finding another country without an extradition treaty with the UK.

Biggs moves into a rented apartment in Copacabana.

Colin Mackenzie organises tickets for Charmian and the boys to visit Rio.

16 May
Charmian, Chris and Farley arrive in Brazil.

5 June
Charmian, Chris and Farley return to Australia.

16 August
Michael Fernand Nascimento de Castro Biggs born in Rio de Janeiro.

25 November
Michael Haynes arrested in Leigh-on-Sea by Jack Slipper. Never prosecuted in the UK.

Slipper also talks to Mollie Evans who was on the RHMS Ellinis with Biggs.

1975
Colin Mackenzie publishes *The Most Wanted Man*.

January
Raimunda and Mike travel to England.

26 January
Raimunda and Mike are the cover story of *The News of the World*.

January
Biggs moves family to Sepetiba.

February
Mike christened in France. Legros acts as godfather.

April
Buster Edwards and Jimmy White released from prison.

August
Roy James, first of the "30 year" prisoners to be released.

September
Raimunda returns to Europe for a second visit but without Mike.

10 October
Buster Edwards sent back to prison for six months for shop lifting £65.76 worth of goods from Harrods.

November
Jim Hussey released.

International press discover Biggs in Sepetiba. He starts doing interviews for money.

December
Gordon Goody released.

1976 February
Tommy Wisbey released.

June
Bobby Welch released.

Roy James breaks a leg in a car crash during a race at Silverstone.

July
Albert Spaggiari robs the Société Générale bank in Nice.

Gary van Dyk visits Rio to explain the "German" hoax to Biggs.

Train robbers to jointly write a book about the robbery for W.H.Allen.

1977 February
Piers Paul Read visits Rio to talk with Biggs about the book and the German connection.

15-17 April
HMS Danae incident.

1978 February
Steve Jones and Paul Cook of the Sex Pistols, along with manager Malcolm McLaren, visit Brazil and Biggs.

Moonraker, the 11th film in the James Bond series, starts filming in Rio.

Biggs records and films with the Sex Pistols.

March
Raimunda returns from Europe after two and a half years.

Piers Paul Read's *The Train Robbers* is published in the UK.

6 June
Bruce Reynolds is released after serving ten years.

8 June
Piers Paul Read and five of the train robbers address the Cambridge Union.

30 June
Sex Pistols' *No One Is Innocent (A Punk Prayer)* is released with Biggs singing lead vocal.

The song, the Sex Pistols' 5th single, goes to number six in the UK charts.

Death of Mary Manson.

18 December
Charlie Wilson is the last of the imprisoned robbers to be released.

1979
Brian Field, the link to the "Ulsterman", dies in a car crash with his new wife, Sian. He had changed his name to Brian Charbren on release.

February
British Leyland poster campaign
for the Mini bears the legend:
"Nips In & Out Like Ronald Biggs"

April
First failed kidnap attempt on
Biggs by John Miller, Fred Prime
and Norman ("Norrie") Boyle.

Biggs is warned of the kidnap plot
by a number of UK journalists.

Biggs meets Bobby Moore and
Kenny Lynch.

For safety Biggs moves from
Sepetiba back to Santa Teresa
in Rio.

26 June
World premiere of *Moonraker*
at the Odeon Leicester Square
in London.

8 August
Biggs' 50th birthday.

1980 15 May
Release of the Sex Pistols'
The Great Rock & Roll Swindle,
directed by Julien Temple.

Alfie Gerrard dies in Brighton from
an internal haemorrhage while on
the run.

1981
Det Chief Superintendent Jack
Slipper publishes *Slipper of the
Yard.*

February
Biggs moves from Santa Teresa to
an apartment in Botafogo.

Albert Spaggiari visits Biggs in Rio
and interviews him for French TV.

9 March
Biggs agrees to be interviewed
by Patrick King of *National
Geographic*

16 March
BIGGS KIDNAPPED IN RIO

Biggs kidnapped at Roda Viva
restaurant and flown by a private
plane from Rio to Belem and put
on the yacht Nowcani II.

Kidnapped by John Miller, Fred
Prime, Mark Algate, Anthony
Marriage, Thorfinn Maciver and
Patrick King.

John & Lia Pickston apply to court
for custody of Mike Biggs. Order
is granted.

24 March
Biggs is landed in Barbados, where
he is arrested.

25 March
Biggs visited by Ezra Alleyne
'Sunshine', who would be his
lawyer along with Frederick Smith.

Author David Levy speaks to
Charmian about organising an
international lawyer for Biggs.

Levy hires David Neufeld and wires $6,000 to him in New York to take the case.

A further $6,000 is wired to the lawyers in Barbados.

April
David Levy's *Ronnie Biggs: His Own Story* published in London.

5 April
Biggs' first hearing before a magistrates' court in Barbados.

Charmian raises $10,000 for Biggs' appeal by selling her story to the Murdoch organisation.

23 April
Appeal hearing in front of two judges from the Barbados High Court.

Barbados Chief Justice Sir William Douglas and Deputy Chief Justice Denys Williams.

24 April
Case dismissed. Biggs is a free man and returns to Rio from Barbados forty days after being kidnapped.

Biggs flies by private jet from Barbados to Belem, leased by ITN and Globo, and then by commercial jet to Rio.

Desmond Hamill on the plane for ITN

May
As part of the deal with Murdoch, Charmian with Farley visit Biggs in Rio. They stay just four days.

Birth of *A Turma do Balão Magico* (Magic Balloon Gang) with Mike, Simony and Toby.

1982
Release of first Turma do Balão Magico album. Features Mike's solo track *"Oh! Suzana."*

On tour with Turma do Balão Magico.

December
Turma do Balão Magico Christmas show at Maracanã Stadium.

1983 17 February
Biggs' meets The Police back stage at the group's Rio concert in Maracanãzinho, part of the *'Ghost in the Machine'* world tour.

Turma do Balão Magico given its own morning show by TV Globo.

7 April
Death of Fernand Legros in France from throat cancer.

8 August
20th anniversary of the Great Train Robbery.

October
Release of second Turma do Balão Magico album, includes the hit *Superfantastico* recorded with Djavan.

Touring with Turma do Balão Magico.

December
Second Turma do Balão Magico Christmas show at Maracanã Stadium.

1984 February
Biggs buys an apartment for Mike at 470 Rua Monte Alegre in Santa Teresa.

Filming of Long Time No See Ronnie for Japanese TV.

April
Diesel engine D326, the engine involved in the Great Train Robbery, is withdrawn from service and cut up for scrap.

Opening of Crepúsculo de Cubatão nightclub.

Biggs invests in a restaurant, Mr Big, in Buzios.

September
Release of third Turma do Balão Magico album, first with Jairzinho.

Guest artists on the record include Roberto Carlos, Fabio Junior, Pepeu Gomes and Baby Consuelo.

October
Bruce Reynolds sent back to prison for three years for handling amphetamine sulphate.

December
Third Turma do Balão Magico Christmas show at Maracanã Stadium.

1985 January
Biggs and Mike move into their own Santa Teresa apartment.

March
Bruce Reynolds released from prison for handling amphetamine sulphate.

July
Biggs holds a party to celebrate 20 years on the run. Charmian, Raimunda and Ulla are all present.

October
Release of fourth Turma do Balão Magico album.

Guest artists on the record include Erasmo Carlos, Baby Consuelo, Moraes Moreira, Metro and Domino.

December
Fourth and final Turma do Balão Magico Christmas show at Maracanã Stadium.

1986
Biggs' son Chris comes to visit along with some school friends. They spend nearly a year in Rio with Biggs.

June
TV Globo cancels Balão Magico TV show and replaces it with *Xou de Xuxa*.

Release of fifth and final Turma do Balão Magico album.

Original Turma do Balão Magico disbands after five hit albums.

In total the group sold over 10 million albums making it the 20th biggest selling Brazilian act of all time.

Biggs meets Polish film director Lech Majewski. Introduced by Freddie Foreman.

Biggs and Majewski start work on the screenplay for *Prisoner of Rio*.

1987 2 May
Sir Hugh Fraser, who John Miller says financed the kidnapping of Biggs, dies of cancer.

July
Cameras role on *Prisoner of Rio*. Cast includes Steven Berkoff, Paul Freeman, Peter Firth and Desmond Llewelyn.

1988 February
Charmian visits Biggs in Rio along with Chris and Farley. Biggs shows them carnival before Charmian goes off to visit Peru and Bolivia.

21 April
Farley celebrates his 21st birthday in Rio with Biggs, Charmian and Chris.

12 May
Prisoner of Rio is screened at the Cannes Film Festival.

Mike Biggs attends the Cannes Film Festival.

August
Virgin Books publish *Biggsy's Bible: The World's Most Wanted Book.*

15 September
World premiere of *Buster* at Odeon Leicester Square.

1989
BBC screen's *The Great Paper Chase*, based on Anthony Delano's book *Slip-Up*. In 1990 Jack Slipper is awarded £50,000 in damages for libel.

26 July
Tommy Wisbey and Jimmy Hussey convicted for trafficking cocaine. Sentenced to 10 and 7 years respectively.

8 August
Biggs' 60th birthday.

1990 24 April
Charlie Wilson found murdered in Spain

10 May
Charlie Wilson's funeral in the UK.

July
Paul Seabourne visits Biggs in Rio.

27 July
Arrest Warrant issued for Biggs at Bow Street Magistrates Court. The same document would be used when he returned to the UK in 2001.

1991 January
In Rio to perform at Rock in Rio 2, Happy Mondays visit Biggs accompanied by Piers Morgan who is covering the festival for *The Sun*.

March
Steven Berkoff publishes *A Prisoner in Rio*, his account of making the film.

April
Princess Diana visits Rio with Prince Charles. British press want Biggs to meet Diana, but he declines.

Bruce and Nick Reynolds visit Biggs in Rio.

Die Toten Hosen visit Rio and record *Carnival in Rio (Punk Was)* and *Police on My Back* with Biggs.

1992
Record producer Gus Dudgeon and his wife Sheila visit Biggs. They become firm friends.

May
During the Cannes Film Festival Biggs lists his top ten films of all time in *Moving Pictures*.

3-14 June
Biggs has a radio spot during the Rio Earth Summit.

August
Chris and his fiancée visit Biggs after touring the Galapagos Islands and Peru.

16 August
Mike Biggs' 18th birthday. Stepbrother Chris is present.

October
Biggs decides to write his autobiography. Christopher Pickard, a friend, writer and journalist based in Rio, agrees to help.

November
British Steel Global Challenge, round-the-world yacht race, in Rio. Brisk T-shirt sales for Biggs.

26 December
Lord Edmund Davies, the judge at the Great Train Robbery trial, dies.

1993 March
Biggs starts work proper on his autobiography, *Odd Man Out*.

June
Jack Slipper visits Biggs in Rio for the *Sunday Express*.

Biggs sings vocals on three tracks for the album *Bajo otra bandera* by Argentinean punk band Pilsen

8 August
30th anniversary of the Great Train Robbery

"When I'm 64" - Biggs' 64th Birthday.

October
Biggs completes the manuscript to *Odd Man Out*.

1994 21 January
Biggs publishes his autobiography, *Odd Man Out*. A best seller for Bloomsbury publishing.

Live satellite link between Biggs in Rio and UK media at a press conference in the Groucho Club for the launch of the book.

Jack Slipper and Mike Biggs attend the press conference in London.

Biggs bumps into Whitney Huston and Steve Tyler (Aerosmith) at the pool of the Rio Palace.

23 March
Biggs holds a book signing by fax with Murder One bookstore in Charing Cross Road.

Roy James sentenced to six year for attacking his ex-wife and shooting his father-in-law.

April
Visit to Rio de Janeiro of British Foreign Secretary, Douglas Hurd.

Death of Paul Seabourne

29 November
Buster Edwards found hanged.

1995 4 February
Biggs and Mike visit the Rolling Stones backstage at Maracanã Stadium during the *Voodoo Lounge* tour.

Biggs breaks his leg.

Uri Geller visits Biggs in Rio. Biggs asks him to heal his leg.

April
Bruce Reynolds publishes *Autobiography of a Thief.*

18 July
UK and Brazilian Foreign Secretaries, Malcolm Rifkind and Luiz Felipe Lamprea, sign a new extradition treaty between the UK and Brazil.

August
Nick Reynolds flies to Rio to do a cast of Biggs for his *'Heroes & Villains'* and *'Cons to Icons'* collections.

31 October
After the success of *Odd Man Out*, Biggs writes a novel with his 'ghost', Chris Pickard.

Keep On Running, published by Bloomsbury, is based on the three train robbers who got away and were never charged.

December
Death of Blitz, Biggs' pet Rottweiler.

1996 12 January
Ursula 'Ulla' Margarita Sopher, Biggs' long time girlfriend, dies in her sleep.

February
Death of Lua, Biggs' pet Miniature Pinscher

May
Biggs addresses the Young President Organisation in Manaus

Charmian is operated on for two primary cancers (uterus and fallopian tubes) and is in intensive care for over a week after a radical hysterectomy.

Six months of chemotherapy follows, from which she slowly recovers.

21 July
Assistant Chief Constable Gerard McArthur dies.

1997
Charmian visits Biggs in Rio en route back to Australia from a trip to the UK.

14 August
New extradition treaty between Brazil and UK becomes law.

20 August
Roy James dies of a heart attack.

29 October
Foreign Secretary Jack Straw officially asks Brazil to extradite Biggs.

12 November
Brazil's Supreme Court rejects a request by the British Government to extradite Biggs.

Court rules that the statute of limitations has run out on the robbery, as the crime was committed more than 20 years ago.

1998 January
David Levy, author of *Ronnie Biggs: His Own Story* visits Biggs in Rio. Their first meeting in 17 years.

February
Unidos do Porto da Pedra samba school honours Biggs at Rio 's carnival with Samba no pé e mãos ao alto, isto é um assalto.

16 March
Biggs suffers a stroke.

Treated at the São Silvestre Hospital.

Following the stroke Biggs is temporarily unable to speak.

Charmian visits Rio to help Biggs with his recovery.

December
Roy 'Pretty Boy' Shaw visits for Christmas.

1999 4 January
Michael Argylle, Biggs' QC at the Great Train Robbery trial, dies.

May
Bruce Reynolds addresses the pupils at Eton.

Biggs becomes a grandfather after Chris' wife gives birth to a daughter.

8 August
70th Birthday Celebrations

Bruce Reynolds and his son Nick join Biggs in Rio.

Others attending include Roy Shaw, Tony Hoare, and Dave Courtney.

Brian Running buys Biggs 1,000 beers for the party as his birthday present.

15 September
Biggs suffers second stroke.

Biggs to appear in TV ad for hair grafts for Advanced Hair Studio.

22 September
Biggs suffers third, far more serious stroke, which leaves him without speech.

October
SCi announce plans for a computer game based on the Great Train Robbery.

November
Biggs attempts suicide.

2000 5-14 January
FIFA World Club Championship in Rio. Biggs greets Manchester United fans, but is not well.

22 January
Birth in Rio de Janeiro of Ingrid, daughter of Mike and Veronica.

Roy Pickard visits Biggs in Rio for the first time.

2 May
Julien Temple releases a new Sex Pistol documentary, *The Filth and the Fury*, featuring Biggs.

July
Mike launches *RonnieBiggs.com* and *RonnieBiggs.co.uk*, backed by Brian Running.

2001 25 January
Biggs poses with two lingerie models wearing plastic police hats.

A promotion for Brazil's biggest lingerie company, Du Loren.

8 March
Kevin Crace makes first contact with *The Sun* about Biggs' possible return to the UK.

16 March
Mike Biggs visits *The Sun* with Kevin Crace and Nick Reynolds.

Mike meets with Graham Dudman, *The Sun's* Assistant News editor, and Crime Editor Mike Sullivan

6 April
Mike Sullivan and John Askill of *The Sun* fly to Rio to meet Biggs.

6-13 April
Initial deal struck and negotiated with *The Sun* for Biggs return. A mid-May date considered.

13 April
Mike Sullivan and John Askill of *The Sun* return to London.

1 May
The Sun moves the date of Biggs return forward in fear that other papers have got hold of the story.

Mike Sullivan calls Kevin Crace, who in turn calls Nick Reynolds, who calls Mike Biggs.

John Askill and photographer Harry Page catch the British Airways flight to Rio.

Mike Sullivan briefs John Coles, head of the Flying Squad.

2 May
Askill and Page arrive in Rio and meet with Biggs.

Email to John Coles at Scotland Yard that Biggs wants to return.

Biggs moved to safe house in Barra owned by Diamond Dayne Henry.

3 May
News of Biggs imminent return breaks in the global media in a *Sun* world exclusive.

Sun editor, David Yelland, calls Foreign Secretary Robin Cook about Biggs' need for a passport.

4 May
The *Sun's* private plane, leased from TAG Aviation, departs from Farnborough at 3.07 pm to Rio with Bruce and Nick Reynolds on board.

5 May
Biggs reunited with Bruce and Nick Reynolds in Rio.

6 May
Biggs receives his Emergency British Passport: E.P.196182.

Biggs leaves Brazil on *The Sun's* private plane that takes off from Rio International Airport at 5.18 pm local time (9.18 pm in London).

7 May
BIGGS RETURNS TO THE UK
(Landing at RAF Northolt at 8.47 am)

Biggs had been on the run for 13,068 days.

Taken to Chiswick Police Station and then on to the West London Court House in Talgrath Road in Hammersmith.

Transferred to the hospital wing of HMP Belmarsh, Britain's highest security prison.

28 years of sentence still to serve. Biggs is given his old prison number from Wandsworth: 002731.

8 May
Mike Biggs holds a press conference in London.

2 June
Biggs collapses in Belmarsh and is rushed to Queen Elizabeth Hospital following a fourth stroke. He is handcuffed to his bed.

8 June
David Blunkett takes over from Jack Straw as Home Secretary. Straw takes over from Robin Cook as Foreign Secretary.

3 July
The Sun will not face censure by the Press Complaints Commission for its role in bringing Biggs back to Britain.

19 July
Sir Jeffrey Archer joins Biggs in Belmarsh. By 9 August he is transferred to the category-C Wayland Prison.

28 July
First picture of Biggs in Belmarsh published in the *Daily Mail*.

August
Lawyers file appeal papers with the Criminal Cases Review Committee.

Mike Biggs threatened with deportation after his visa request is denied.

Veronica and Ingrid, who have joined Mike in London, visit Biggs for the first time.

12 August
Biggs returned to Queen Elizabeth Hospital after losinga considerable amount of blood.

16 August
Veronica and Ingrid return to Brazil.

21 September
Biggs taken to Queen Elizabeth Hospital for more tests.

24 September
Mike Biggs temporary visa for the UK expires.

14 November
Biggs petitions the Belmarsh governor for early release on compassionate grounds.

2 November
Biggs rushed to Queen Elizabeth Hospital after vomiting and passing blood.

29 November
Mike Biggs' makes Immigration appeal.

3 December
Home Office refuse Mike Biggs leave to stay indefinitely in the UK.

2002 January
Mike calls Charmian in Australia and asks for her help in supplying the documentation to prove that she is no longer married to Biggs.

Australia House in London refuses to give Mike the documentation, so Charmian comes to his rescue.

30 January
Criminal Cases Review Commission rejects an application to send Biggs' case to the Court of Appeal.

31 January
A two-hour, two-part documentary, *The Legend of Ronnie Biggs*, airs on Channel Five in the UK.

Biggs argues his sentence was inappropriate and unnecessary.

28 March
Biggs' lawyers lodge papers at the High Court.

They argue it is an "exceptional case" that should be sent back to the Court of Appeal.

10 July
Biggs marries Mike's mother, Raimunda Rothen (54) at Belmarsh Prison in front of 11 guests.

Reception (without Biggs) held in the Punch Bowl pub in Mayfair.

21 July
Gus Dudgeon and his wife, Sheila, killed in a car crash.

24 July
Mike Biggs granted British citizenship following the marriage of Biggs and Raimunda.

Mike and Veronica wed.

26 September
Mike Biggs publishes *The Biggs Time*, his autobiography.

5 December
Mike says Biggs is effectively being kept in solitary confinement at Belmarsh despite his worsening health.

2003 April
Express photographer Bill Lovelace dies.

25 June
Biggs back in hospital.

8 August
40th anniversary of the Great Train Robbery.

2 October
Appeal against sentence is thrown out by a High Court judge. Appeal called "hopeless" and "misconceived".

Mike announces plans to go to the European Court of Human Rights.

2004 January
Biggs throws a box of tissues from his wheelchair at Soham killer Ian Huntley when he tries to shake Biggs' hand.

6 January
Suspected heart attack sees Biggs return to Queen Elizabeth Hospital.

9 January
Back at Queen Elizabeth following dehydration and vomiting caused by a chest infection.

15 March
Biggs sends hand written note to fellow prisoner Freddie Asher for punching Huntley.

"All power to Fred, a job well done. I'm glad to know you."

9 August
High Court bid to secure Biggs' release on compassionate grounds.

30 August
Biggs rushed to Queen Elizabeth Hospital for the fifth time.

15 December
Charles Clarke takes over from David Blunkett as Home Secretary.

2005 14 March
The 60-minute documentary *Ronnie Biggs: Last Escape?* airs on Sky One in the UK

Giovanni di Stefano becomes Biggs' lawyer.

14 June
Biggs' solicitors write to Home Secretary Charles Clarke to ask for his release on compassionate grounds.

10 August
Home Office admits that a Belmarsh prisoner (Biggs) has developed a local infection after treatment.

"Subsequent tests showed this to be MRSA".

24 August
After a long illness, Jack Slipper dies at the age of 81.

11 October
Channel 4 airs *Kidnap Ronnie Biggs* in the UK despite Biggs' protest to the channel that it is factually inaccurate.

The documentary claims that Patrick King, rather than John Miller, master-minded Biggs' kidnapping in 1981.

26 October
Biggs' appeal turned down by Home Secretary (Charles Clarke).

28 November
Det Superintendent Malcolm Fewtrell dies.

2006 March
Photo of Biggs in orange prison visitors vest published in press.

5 May
John Reid takes over from Charles Clarke as Home Secretary.

2007 19 January
Bloomsbury allow the rights to *Odd Man Out* and *Keep On Running* to revert to Biggs and Christopher Pickard.

9 May
Position of Secretary of State for Justice established. Lord Falconer appointed.

28 June
Jacqui Smith takes over from John Reid as Home Secretary. Jack Straw replaces Lord Falconer as Secretary of State for Justice.

4 July
Biggs is transferred from HMP Belmarsh to HMP Norwich on "compassionate grounds".

Biggs has been held in Belmarsh for nearly 74 months.

10 September
Giovanni di Stefano issues an appeal asking for Biggs to be released.

28 December
Giovanni di Stefano issues a further appeal asking for Biggs to be released.

2008 February
Giovanni di Stefano issues yet a further appeal asking for Biggs to be released.

June
Biggs case submitted to the Parole Board.

8 July
Media speculates that Biggs will be released on Valentines Day 2009 (14 February)

21 July
Robbery, starring Stanley Baker and directed by Peter Yates, finally released on DVD in the UK.

August
HMP Norwich has to change its locks at a cost of £250,000 when a key goes missing.

8 August
45th anniversary of Great Train Robbery

2009 13 February
Biggs taken to Norfolk & Norwich University Hospital for three days with pneumonia.

Mike Biggs barred from seeing Biggs for 48 hours.

17 February
Mark Leech, *Prisons Handbook* editor, says Justice Secretary Jack Straw tells him:

"The problem with Mr Biggs is no-one has formally asked me for his release."

March
Papers submitted by Giovanni di Stefano for Biggs' parole under the discretionary Release Scheme.

23 April
Parole Hearing. Biggs applies for parole.

Eligible for release on 3 July after he will have served one-third of his sentence.

Decision is delayed while arrangements are made as to who will pay for the 24-hour care Biggs will require.

5 June
Alan Johnson takes over from Jacqui Smith as Home Secretary.

15 June
Parole Board recommends to Justice Secretary Jack Straw that Biggs be released, saying the risk of him reoffending is "manageable".

28 June
Biggs is taken to Norfolk & Norwich University Hospital with a suspected broken hip and a chest infection.

1 July
Biggs is refused parole by the Justice Secretary Jack Straw who says Biggs is "wholly unrepentant".

Biggs' health deteriorates. Mike Biggs told to rush to hospital.

2 July
Giovanni di Stefano demands a Judicial Review of Jack Straw's decision.

3 July
Biggs eligible for parole.

Giovanni di Stefano questions the power of Jack Straw to block the Parole Board's recommendations.

17 July
Biggs transferred from hospital back to HMP Norwich.

Judicial Review submitted.

28 July
Biggs rushed back to Norfolk & Norwich University Hospital with severe pneumonia.

Mike Biggs told to go urgently to the hospital.

Request for clemency.

30 July
Judicial Review granted by the High Court.

6 August
Justice Secretary Jack Straw announces he will free Biggs on compassionate grounds.

7 August
BIGGS IS A FREE MAN

Biggs has served 3,875 days for his part in the Great Train Robbery out of a sentence of 10,957 days.

He had spent 13,068 days on the run.

8 August
Biggs 80th birthday.

46th Anniversary of the Great Train Robbery.

17 August
Transfer from Norfolk & Norwich University Hospital to a nursing home in Barnet.

Starts life at Carlton Court Care Home.

20 August
Release of Lockerbie bomber, Abdelbaset al-Megrahi, on "compassionate grounds".

September
Biggs starts work on updating his autobiography with his 'ghost' Christopher Pickard.

November
Head of Parole Board says Justice Ministry should have no say over Parole Board decisions.

2010 April
Biggs' mobile scooter, given to him by Madness saxophonist Lee Thompson, is vandalised.

8 May
Birth of granddaughter Lilly in London to Mike and Veronica.

1 August
Sunday Mirror runs a story about Biggs receiving an award for his "lifetime of crime".

6 August
Jack Straw announces he will quit frontbench politics exactly a year after he says he will free Biggs on compassionate grounds.

Biggs visits Bridego Bridge. Photo is leaked to *The Sun*.

4 December
Biggs visits the Emirates Stadium to see Arsenal beat Fulham 2-1, thanks to two goals from Samir Nasri.

30 December
Death of Frances 'Angela' Reynolds.

2011 9 January
Peter Yates, director of *Robbery*, dies.

14 February
Giovanni di Stefano arrested in Majorca on a European Arrest Warrant.

Warrant issued 'on matters relating to fraud, theft and money laundering.'

March
Biggs has a potential cancerous growth removed from the top of his head.

27 March
Biggs visits the Emirates Stadium to see Brazil beat Scotland 2-0, with two goals from Neymar.

12 April
Biggs goes to see the film *Rio* in the cinema.

7 May
10th anniversary of Biggs' return to the UK from Brazil.

25 May
Biggs finally gets to visit the seaside, although not Margate. It is a day out to Southend for the residents of Carlton Court.

10 July
Biggs outlives the *News of the World* as the paper that covered so many of his exploits is published for the last time.

July
Papers released by the National Archives show that *The Sun* newspaper sought advice regarding about the authenticity of a Biggs manuscript.

The 77-page manuscript was offered to the paper in Australia by a lawyer representing Charmian.

August
Biggs completes the update of his autobiography with the help of Christopher Pickard.

November
Biggs publishes his new autobiography, *Ronnie Biggs - Odd Man Out: The Last Straw.* Also relaunches his website www.ronniebiggs.com.

17 November
Biggs launches autobiography to media at Shoreditch House in East London.

2013 8 August
50th Anniversary of the Great Train Robbery / 84th birthday.

RON'S FREQUENT FLYER MILES
13,068 DAYS ON THE RUN

London - Paris	210 miles
Paris - Sydney	10,540 miles
Sydney – Adelaide - Sydney	1,720 miles
Sydney - Adelaide	860 miles
Adelaide - Darwin	1,970 miles
Darwin - Cairns	1,620 miles
Cairns – Sydney	1,325 miles
Sydney - Adelaide	860 miles
Adelaide – Melbourne - Adelaide	840 miles
Adelaide – Melbourne - Adelaide	840 miles
Adelaide – Melbourne - Adelaide	840 miles
Adelaide - Melbourne	420 miles
Melbourne - Panama	9,040 miles
Panama - Caracas (Venezuela)	860 miles
Caracas - Rio de Janeiro	2,810 miles
Rio de Janeiro - Buenos Aires - Rio de Janeiro	3,200 miles
Rio de Janeiro - Puerto Suarez (Bolivia) - Rio de Janeiro	2,500 miles
Rio de Janeiro – Brasilia - Rio de Janeiro	1,426 miles
Rio de Janeiro – Bridgetown - Rio de Janeiro	5,800 miles
Rio de Janeiro - London	5,750 miles

Approximate Total: 53,431 miles (86,000 kms)

For 13,068 days Ronald Biggs averaged over 4 miles a day on the run.

The above does not include the many tens of thousands of miles that Ronald Biggs covered in Brazil when he accompanied his son, Mike, on the nationwide tours of *Turma de Balão Magico*.